The Legal Limits of Direct Democracy

A Comparative Analysis of Referendums and Initiatives across Europe

Edited by

Daniel Moeckli

Professor of Public Law with a focus on International and Comparative Law, Institute for International Law and Comparative Constitutional Law, University of Zurich, Switzerland

Anna Forgács

PhD Researcher, Institute for International Law and Comparative Constitutional Law, University of Zurich, Switzerland

Henri Ibi

PhD Researcher, Institute for International Law and Comparative Constitutional Law, University of Zurich, Switzerland

Edward Elgar
PUBLISHING

Cheltenham, UK • Northampton, MA, USA

Published by
Edward Elgar Publishing Limited
The Lypiatts
15 Lansdown Road
Cheltenham
Glos GL50 2JA
UK

Edward Elgar Publishing, Inc.
William Pratt House
9 Dewey Court
Northampton
Massachusetts 01060
USA

A catalogue record for this book
is available from the British Library

Library of Congress Control Number: 2021938673

This book is available electronically in the **Elgar**online
Law subject collection
http://dx.doi.org/10.4337/9781800372801

ISBN 978 1 80037 279 5 (cased)
ISBN 978 1 80037 280 1 (eBook)

Printed and bound in Great Britain by TJ Books Limited, Padstow, Cornwall

Contents

Contributors

Nicos C. Alivizatos is emeritus Professor of Constitutional Law at the University of Athens and a member of the Venice Commission.

Kamil Baraník is Associate Professor of Constitutional Law with a focus on Comparative Constitutional Law and EU Law at the University of Matej Bel, Faculty of Law.

Julian Ivan Beriger is a Postdoctoral Researcher with a focus on Constitutional, Administrative and Comparative Law at the Centre for Democracy Studies Aarau and the University of Zurich.

Mārtiņš Birģelis is a Human Rights expert and a PhD student at the University of Latvia.

Marthe Fatin-Rouge Stefanini is Director of the Laboratory DICE and Research Director of the CNRS with a focus on Comparative Constitutional Law at the Aix-Marseille University, France.

Anna Forgács is a PhD Researcher at the Institute for International Law and Comparative Constitutional Law of the University of Zurich.

Pierre Garrone is Head of the Division of Elections and Political Parties, Venice Commission, Council of Europe.

Henri Ibi is a PhD Researcher at the Institute for International Law and Comparative Constitutional Law of the University of Zurich.

Igor Kaučič is a Professor of Constitutional Law at the University of Ljubljana, Faculty of Law.

Wilfried Marxer is Head of Research Politics at the Liechtenstein Institute in Bendern, Liechtenstein.

Daniel Moeckli is Professor of Public Law with a focus on International and Comparative Law at the University of Zurich.

Robert Podolnjak is Professor of Constitutional Law at the University of Zagreb, Faculty of Law.

Daniel Simancas is a PhD Researcher in Constitutional Law at the Complutense University of Madrid.

Bruna Žuber is an Assistant Professor of Administrative Law at the University of Ljubljana, Faculty of Law.

Acknowledgements

This book is the outcome of a meeting that was held at the University of Zurich on 28 February 2020. The meeting, as well as the book resulting from it, would not have been possible without the support of many people to whom we would like to express our gratitude.

First and foremost, we would like to thank the contributors for agreeing to draft their respective papers, presenting them in Zurich and then turning them into the book chapters that you now hold in your hands. Fernando Mendez, Lorenz Langer and Andreas Glaser generously agreed to chair the panels of the meeting and asked perceptive questions. We also would like to express our gratitude to Bruno Kaufmann, Regina Kiener, László Komáromi, Laurence Morel, Mathias Revon and Nenad Stojanović for attending the meeting and sharing their valuable insights. Alessandra Chies, Nils Reimann and Jacqueline Weiss were instrumental in organising the meeting. At Edward Elgar Publishing, Harry Fabian expertly steered us through the various editorial stages.

The meeting as well as the resulting book grew out of the research project 'Popular Sovereignty vs. the Rule of Law? Defining the Limits of Direct Democracy' (LIDD). We would like to thank the European Research Council (ERC) for funding the project (grant agreement 772160), including the research activities organised as part of it.

DM/AF/HI
Zurich, November 2020

1. Introduction to *The Legal Limits of Direct Democracy*

Daniel Moeckli

1. CONTEXT

Direct democracy is on the rise. Recent years have seen a mushrooming of direct-democratic mechanisms such as citizens' initiatives and referendums all over the world.[1] Beyond Switzerland and some US states, where direct democracy already has a long tradition, more and more states, especially in Europe, have started to introduce various forms of direct-democratic participation. Out of the 47 member states of the Council of Europe, 27 know, at the national level, the law-initiated referendum (here defined as a referendum that is triggered if certain conditions specified by law are met), 30 the legislature-initiated referendum (defined as a referendum that can be initiated by parliament (or parts of it)), 20 the executive-initiated referendum (defined as a referendum that can be initiated by government (or parts of it)) and five the subnational entity-initiated referendum (defined as a referendum that can be initiated by (a certain number of) subnational entities such as regions or provinces). Twenty-one Council of Europe member states provide for a proactive citizens' initiative (defined as an instrument that allows a certain number of citizens to initiate a referendum and formulate the topic of the referendum), a further eight for a rejective citizens' initiative (defined as an instrument that allows a certain number of citizens to initiate a referendum that is aimed at preventing new laws (or parts of them) from being passed or at repealing existing laws (or parts of them)) and 28 for an agenda initiative (defined as an instrument that allows a certain number of citizens to put an issue on the agenda of state organs but that does not lead to a referendum).[2]

---

[1] See for example Matt Qvortrup (ed.), *Referendums Around the World: The Continued Growth of Direct Democracy* (Palgrave Macmillan 2014).

[2] See the database of the project 'Popular Sovereignty vs. the Rule of Law? Defining the Limits of Direct Democracy' (LIDD), lidd-project.org/data, accessed 30 November 2020.

Use of these instruments is increasing: in 2006, 18 referendums were held in European countries; by 2016, this number had risen to 58.[3] Even states with hardly any direct-democratic experience, such as the Netherlands and the United Kingdom, have recently started to hold referendums.[4] In addition, in numerous countries direct-democratic instruments exist at the regional or municipal level. With the introduction of the European Citizens' Initiative (ECI) in 2012, direct democracy now even applies at the supranational level. Importantly, as for example the Brexit vote illustrates, not only are referendums typically reserved for deciding the most fundamental issues, but also are their results, even when not legally binding, assigned a special legitimacy and finality.[5]

One consequence of the increase in direct-democratic participation is that, more and more often, citizens propose measures, or are called to vote on measures, which are problematic from the perspective of the rule of law – be it because the proposed measure clashes with international legal obligations or human rights guarantees, be it because the process leading up to the vote does not conform to rule-of-law requirements.[6] In Switzerland, popular votes were

---

[3]   See the 'Datenbank und Suchmaschine für direkte Demokratie', www.sudd .ch , accessed 14 August 2020. See also Laurence Morel, 'Referendum', in Michel Rosenfeld and Andras Sajó (eds), *The Oxford Handbook of Comparative Constitutional Law* (OUP 2012) 501, 513–514.

[4]   On 6 April 2016, the Netherlands held its first referendum under the Advisory Referendum Act of 2015 on the Association Agreement between the EU and Ukraine. See Kiesraad (Electoral Council), 'Results of the referendum on the Association Agreement with Ukraine', 12 April 2016, https://english.kiesraad.nl/latest- news/ news/2016/04/12/results-of-the-referendum-on-the-association-agreement-with-th e-ukraine accessed 14 August 2020. On 23 June 2016, the United Kingdom held a referendum on the United Kingdom's membership of the European Union. See Electoral Commission, 'EU Referendum Results', available at http://www.electoralcommission .org.uk/find-information-by-subject/elections-and-referendums/past-elections-and -referendums/eu-referendum/electorate-and-count-information   accessed 14 August 2020.

[5]   Although the United Kingdom European Union membership referendum is not legally binding, there was never a real prospect of government or parliament ignoring it, as is exemplified by then Prime Minister Theresa May's famous mantra 'Brexit means Brexit'. See, e.g., Michael Wilkinson, 'No Brexit until 2022? Philip Hammond Warns EU Exit Could Take at Least Four Years', *The Telegraph*, 12 July 2016.

[6]   While the rule of law has been given different meanings at different moments in time and in different legal traditions, there is broad consensus today with regard to its most fundamental elements. According to the Venice Commission of the Council of Europe, these core elements include legality, legal certainty, prohibition of arbitrariness, access to justice before independent and impartial courts, respect for human rights and equality before the law. See Rule of Law Checklist, adopted by the Venice Commission at its 106th Plenary Session (Venice, 11–12 March 2016),

held on a ban on the construction of minarets[7] and immigration restrictions that violate international treaties,[8] to name just two examples. In Croatia, a citizens' initiative suggested restricting the use of minority languages.[9] In Ireland and Liechtenstein, voters decided that abortion should constitute a criminal offence.[10] In Hungary, a citizens' initiative demanded the reintroduction of the death penalty,[11] while in a government-initiated referendum the electorate decided that any refugee quotas imposed by the European Union (EU) should be rejected.[12] In Croatia, Slovakia and Slovenia, majorities of voters decided to deny same-sex couples the right to marry.[13] In the United Kingdom, the electorate was asked to decide on Brexit without knowing the exact legal consequence of the referendum, violating, it has been argued, the requirement of transparency inherent in the rule of law.[14] At the level of the EU, in December 2015, the ECI 'Mum, Dad & Kids' was registered, demanding 'marriage' to be

---

CDL-AD(2016)007, 7. Importantly for our purposes, the principle of legality requires any state action to be in accordance with the law, including international law, and establishes certain requirements with regard to the law-making procedure, such as the principle of transparency. *Ibid.*, 11–13.

[7]   *Bundesratsbeschluss über das Ergebnis der Volksabstimmung vom 29. November 2009*, Bundesblatt 2010, 3437.

[8]   *Bundesratsbeschluss über das Ergebnis der Volksabstimmung vom 9. Februar 2014*, Bundesblatt 2014, 4117.

[9]   'Croatia's Constitutional Court Says No to Cyrillic Referendum', *Croatia Week*, 12 August 2014, http://www.croatiaweek.com/croatias-constitutional-court-says-no-to -cyrillic-referendum/ accessed 14 August 2020.

[10]   Department of the Environment, Community and Local Government, *Referendum Results 1937–2015* (2015), 70–71; Regierungskanzlei, Ergebnis der Volksabstimmung vom 16./18. September 2011 über das Initiativbegehren zur Abänderung des Strafgesetzbuches (Hilfe statt Strafe), http://www.llv.li/#/1156/abstimmungsergebnisse accessed 14 August 2020.

[11]   National Election Commission, Decision 99/2015 of 27 May 2015, http:// valasztas.hu/hu/nvb/ hatarozatok/2015/2015-5673.html accessed 14 August 2020.

[12]   Since the required turnout quorum was not reached, the referendum result is not legally binding. National Election Commission, 'National Referendum of 2 October 2016: Data Relating to the Result of the National Referendum', http://www.nvi.hu/en/ ref2016/481/481_0_index.html accessed 14 August 2020.

[13]   State Election Commission of the Republic of Croatia, Results of the National Referendum of 1 January 2013, http://www.izbori.hr/2013Referendum/rezult/rezultati .html accessed 14 August 2020; Statistical Office of the Slovak Republic, Final Results of the Referendum of 7 February 2015, http://volby.statistics.sk/ref/ref2015/en/tab01 .html accessed 14 August 2020; 'Slovenians vote against same-sex marriage in referendum', *The Guardian*, 21 December 2015.

[14]   The argument that the Brexit referendum violated the rule of law has been advanced most prominently by Philip Allott, 'Forget the politics – Brexit may be unlawful', *The Guardian*, 30 June 2016.

defined as a union between a man and a woman and 'family' as being based on marriage and/or descent.[15]

These and similar referendums and initiatives have triggered vigorous political debates in the respective countries: should there be any limits as to what the people are allowed to propose or vote on? Who should decide what is permissible and what is not? The question of the relationship between popular sovereignty and rule-of-law principles is set to gain heightened importance throughout Europe: on the one hand, the body of international law that restricts the scope of decision-making at the national level continues to grow. On the other hand, especially 'populist' movements make increasing use of direct-democratic instruments to promote divisive measures that clash with the rule of law.[16]

Despite their great relevance for the future of democracy in Europe, these issues have remained almost completely unexplored. While there are a number of very useful books dealing with direct democracy and referendums in general,[17] none of these books, which have all been written by political scientists, addresses the question as to the legal limits of direct democracy in a meaningful way. Some authors have dealt with the relationship between direct democracy and the rule of law from a rather general or theoretical perspective,[18] others have explored conflicts between specific direct-democratic instruments and international (or national) law in the context of particular jurisdictions (notably the United States,[19] France[20] and Switzerland[21]). However, a comprehensive legal assessment of the limits of direct democracy or of systems of reviewing

---

[15] European Commission, Official Register of ECIs, http://ec.europa.eu/citizens -initiative/public/ initiatives/open/details/2015/000006 accessed 14 August 2020.

[16] On populism, see, e.g., Jan-Werner Müller, *What is Populism?* (University of Pennsylvania Press 2016).

[17] Laurence Morel, *La question du référendum* (Presses de Sciences Po 2019); Laurence Morel and Matt Qvortrup (eds), *The Routledge Handbook to Referendums and Direct Democracy* (Routledge 2018); Matt Qvortrup (ed.), *Referendums Around the World: The Continued Growth of Direct Democracy* (Palgrave Macmillan 2014).

[18] E.g. Wilfried Marxer (ed.), *Direct Democracy and Minorities* (Springer 2012); Anna Christmann, *Die Grenzen direkter Demokratie: Volksentscheide im Spannungsverhältnis von Demokratie und Rechtsstaat* (Nomos 2012).

[19] Shaun Bowler, 'When Is It OK to Limit Direct Democracy?' (2013) 97 Minnesota Law Review 1780; Kenneth P. Miller, *Direct Democracy and the Courts* (CUP 2009); Eric Lane, 'Men Are Not Angels: The Realpolitik of Direct Democracy and What We Can Do about It' (1998) 34 Willamette Law Review 579.

[20] Marthe Fatin-Rouge Stéfanini, *Le contrôle du référendum par la justice constitutionelle* (Economica 2004).

[21] Guillaume Lammers, *La démocratie directe et le droit international* (Stämpfli 2015); Roger Nobs, *Volksinitiative und Völkerrecht* (Dike 2006).

these limits does not exist. This book aims at providing the foundations for addressing these gaps.

2. QUESTIONS EXPLORED

All members of the Council of Europe have committed themselves to the fundamental values enshrined in its Statute, namely democracy, the rule of law and human rights.[22] These values are also codified in Article 2 of the Treaty on European Union (TEU).[23] Thus, the normative premise for all European states is that they must strive to realise all of these values at the same time, that none of them can take absolute priority over the others. If popular sovereignty, on the one hand, and the rule of law and human rights, on the other, come into conflict, an appropriate balance must be struck between them.

Yet how exactly should this be done? And how is it, in fact, done in practice? There is only one document that sets forth international standards for the use of direct-democratic instruments: the Code of Good Practice on Referendums (since October 2020 called Revised Guidelines on the Holding of Referendums) of the Venice Commission of the Council of Europe.[24] Part I of the book deals with this unique document. Chapter 2 gives an overview of the Code's relevance, contents and use. The Venice Commission was, at the time of writing of this book, in the process of revising the Code. Therefore, Chapter 3 explains the general thinking behind this process of revision, which was completed in October 2020.

The Code is a soft-law instrument, meaning that it is, as such, not legally binding. This raises the crucial question of whether its standards are grounded in state practice. To what extent do they reflect the laws and the practice of European states?

To answer this question, it is necessary to zoom in on the national level. Parts II and III therefore offer an in-depth analysis of the limits imposed on direct-democratic instruments and of systems of reviewing compliance with these limits in selected European states. Experts from 11 European countries were invited to draft reports that address a uniform list of approximately 20

---

[22] See Statute of the Council of Europe, ETS No. 001, Preamble, para. 3.

[23] Treaty on European Union (TEU), OJ 2016/C 202/01.

[24] Code of Good Practice on Referendums, adopted by the Council for Democratic Elections at its 19th meeting (Venice, 16 December 2006) and the Venice Commission at its 70th plenary session (Venice, 16-17 March 2007), CDL–AD (2007) 008rev; Revised Guidelines on the Holding of Referendums, approved by the Council of Democratic Elections at its 69th online meeting (7 October 2020) and adopted by the Venice Commission at its 124th online Plenary Session (8-9 October 2020), CDL-AD(2020)031.

questions for 'their' country. The questions revolved around the following basic issues:

1. What type of direct-democratic instruments exist in the country concerned? For the purposes of this study, we distinguish between the following types of instruments:

- *law-initiated referendum (often also called 'mandatory referendum')*: a referendum that is triggered if certain conditions specified by law are met;
- *institution-initiated referendum*: a referendum that can be triggered by the legislature (or parts of it), the executive (or parts of it) or (a certain number of) subnational entities;
- *citizen-initiated referendum (citizens' or popular initiative)*: an instrument that allows a certain number of citizens to initiate a referendum and formulate its topic (proactive initiative) or to initiate a referendum that is aimed at preventing a constitutional or legislative amendment from being passed or at abolishing it (rejective initiative);
- *citizens' agenda initiative*: an instrument that allows a certain number of citizens to put an issue on the agenda of state organs but that does not lead to a referendum.

2. What are the legal limits that apply with regard to these instruments?

- *Substantive limits* preclude referendums and citizens' initiatives on certain subject matters. Prohibited subject matters may, for example, include constitutional amendments, proposals that violate international law or fundamental rights, state finances, emergency powers, pardons and amnesties, etc.
- *Formal limits* are designed to ensure that the will of the people is formed in a way that conforms to the rule of law by imposing certain requirements regarding the formulation of the referendum question. These requirements may include, for example, that the referendum question (or the initiative proposal) must be clear and precise, must only address one subject matter (unity of substance requirement) or may not mix different normative levels or different direct-democratic instruments (unity of form requirement).

3. What type of institution is in charge of reviewing compliance with these limits and how is the review procedure designed?

- Is it the constitutional court, some other court, the parliament, a governmental authority, an election commission or some local authority that decides whether a referendum or an initiative complies with the limits? What exactly is the institutional position of this body, especially in terms of its independence?
- How is the review procedure designed? For example, when does the review take place (in the case of initiatives, for instance, before or after the collection of signatures)? Who can participate in the proceedings? Which due process guarantees apply? Is there a legal remedy against the decision on the admissibility of a referendum or an initiative? Who decides on the claim for remedy? What are the legal consequences in case of inadmissibility?

Most of the resulting country reports were presented and discussed, together with the contributions on the Venice Commission's Code, at a workshop that was held at the University of Zurich on 28 February 2020 and attended by leading experts on direct democracy. The feedback received at this workshop helped the authors further refine and improve their contributions and ensured that the key issues are addressed consistently throughout them. The resulting country analyses form the bulk of the book.

The conclusion provides a comparative analysis of the situation in the selected states, drawing out key commonalities and differences, as well as an assessment of the law and the practice at the national level when judged against the international standards contained in the Venice Commission's Guidelines on the Holding of Referendums.

3. COUNTRY SELECTION

The 11 European states that are covered in Parts II and III were selected because their legal frameworks of direct-democratic instruments and their direct-democratic practice are particularly interesting and relevant with regard to the research questions explored in this book. First, all of these states have a rather elaborate system of direct-democratic instruments and/or a rich practice of using such instruments. Liechtenstein and Slovakia, for example, are the states with the largest arsenal of direct-democratic instruments in Europe: they both have six out of the seven types of instruments that exist. Even the states with the lowest number of instruments, France and Hungary, still have three – and, moreover, an interesting and relevant direct-democratic practice. Second, all selected states constitute paradigmatic cases in that they impose specific types of legal limits on their direct-democratic instruments and/or use particular institutional and procedural systems of reviewing compliance with these limits.

Furthermore, we tried to achieve an even geographical distribution between, on the one hand, Western European countries or 'old' democracies (Switzerland, Liechtenstein, Italy, Spain, France) and, on the other, Eastern European countries or 'new' democracies (Slovenia, Croatia, Slovakia, Hungary, Latvia, Russia). Finally, a conscious effort was made to include states that, at least in the English-speaking literature, are hardly ever covered in this context (for example Russia, Slovakia, Latvia, Liechtenstein). As a result, the book also offers insights into the functioning of direct-democratic systems that are largely unknown in wide parts of the world.

With regard to 'old' democracies, Switzerland (Chapter 4) is an obvious choice because it is the state with the longest history of direct democracy and one that values popular sovereignty particularly highly. Liechtenstein (Chapter 5) may be a small state, but it has, as mentioned above, a sophisticated system of direct-democratic instruments and has conducted more than 100 referendums at the national level. Italy (Chapter 6) is a prototypical case of a parliamentary democracy that is complemented with a well-established system of specific direct-democratic instruments. The case law of the Italian Constitutional Court dealing with the abrogative referendum provides a particularly fruitful source of information for the purposes of the present inquiry. In Spain (Chapter 7), the representative system has undergone a crisis in recent years, causing direct-democratic instruments to take on an unprecedented role. Although in France (Chapter 8) referendum practice is scarce, it makes for an interesting case as the President can trigger referendums and is subject to hardly any legal requirements when doing so.

As far as 'new' democracies are concerned, Slovenia (Chapter 9) has a well-developed system of direct-democratic instruments as well as a quite rich practice of holding referendums. In addition, Slovene case law regarding the legal review of direct-democratic instruments offers some interesting insights. Croatia (Chapter 10) equally provides for a range of instruments of direct democracy, including the proactive citizens' initiative. However, the Constitutional Court applies a very stringent test to review the constitutionality of popular initiatives. Slovakia (Chapter 11) has no fewer than six direct-democratic instruments. Nevertheless, the promise to involve the people directly in decision-making has been largely unfulfilled as the signature threshold for initiatives and the turnout quorum for referendums are extremely high and referendum results need to be implemented by parliament. In Hungary (Chapter 12), an elaborate system of substantive and formal limits is imposed on direct-democratic instruments, coupled with a rigorous authorisation procedure. As a result, less than 10 per cent of the over 2,000 initiatives for a referendum launched by Hungarian citizens or institutions have been able to survive the admissibility procedures of the election commission and the supreme court. Latvia (Chapter 13) also has a sophisticated system of direct-democratic instruments, of which the agenda initiative and the proactive citizens' initiative are those used most often. While only few limits are imposed on the former, the latter is restricted by a range of open-ended substantive and formal legal limits. In Russia (Chapter 14), finally, the constitution grants the referendum an important status, but its practical relevance is, at least at the national level, very limited. This contrast can be explained by the strong legal limits imposed on the referendum by the legislator and the restrictive practice of Russian courts in the remedy procedures.

PART I

The Venice Commission's Code of Good
Practice on Referendums

2. The Code of Good Practice on Referendums

Pierre Garrone

1. INTRODUCTION

The Venice Commission, the Council of Europe's body specialized in constitutional matters, is now 30 years old, and one of its main fields of activities has, nearly since the beginning, been electoral law – including legislation on referendums and political parties.

The Venice Commission has been made known by its opinions on constitutional and other major legislative reforms, but it may also count amongst its main successes the drafting of texts developing the major international standards deriving from the three main pillars of the Council of Europe: democracy, human rights and the rule of law.

A number of these texts have become reference texts of the Council of Europe, supported by its main bodies: the Committee of Ministers, the Parliamentary Assembly and the Congress of Local and Regional Authorities. This was the case in recent years with the Rule of Law Checklist.[1] However, this had already been much the case previously with international standards in the field of elections and referendums, a field in which the Venice Commission is a pioneer in codification – after the United Nations Human Rights Committee, with its General Comment No. 25 of 1996.[2]

At the impulse of the Parliamentary Assembly, the Venice Commission thus adopted, in 2002, the Code of Good Practice in Electoral Matters.[3] This document defines not only the fundamental standards of the European electoral heritage, which are universal, equal, free, secret and direct suffrage as well as frequency of elections, but also the framework conditions necessary for organ-

---

[1]   Study No. 711/2013, CDL-AD(2016)007.
[2]   General Comment No. 25: The right to participate in public affairs, voting rights and the right of equal access to public service (Art. 25), 12 July 1996, UN Doc. CCPR/C/21/Rev.1/Add.7.
[3]   Opinion No. 190/2002, CDL-AD(2002)023rev2-cor.

izing proper elections, such as respect for human rights, particularly in the political field, organization of elections by an impartial body and an effective system of appeal and observation.

Due to the increased interest of the Assembly in the issue of referendums, the Venice Commission took the initiative to complement the Code of Good Practice in Electoral Matters by a counterpart specifically dedicated to referendums. This does not mean that there should not be common rules for both elections and referendums. On the contrary, the new document, the Code of Good Practice on Referendums ('Code'),[4] begins by listing the principles of Europe's electoral heritage applicable to both elections and referendums (universal, equal, free and secret suffrage) and the conditions for implementing those principles (including respect for fundamental rights, stability of the law, organization of the ballot by an impartial body, existence of an effective system of appeal), while adapting them to the peculiarities of a referendum. It includes, however, a third part, which focuses on the specific rules applicable to the referendum only.

2.   CONTENTS OF THE CODE

According to the Code's third part, entitled 'Specific Rules', the three main principles to be followed are:

- Respect for *the rules of procedure* in the *call for referendums*;
- Respect of *procedural standards* by *the text submitted to a referendum*;
- Respect of *superior law* by *the text submitted to a referendum*.

Respect for the rules of procedure in the *call for referendums* is dealt with first under the title 'the rule of law', which states:

> The use of referendums must comply with the legal system as a whole, and especially the procedural rules. In particular, referendums cannot be held if the Constitution or a statute in conformity with the Constitution does not provide for them, for example where the text submitted to a referendum is a matter for Parliament's exclusive jurisdiction.[5]

In other words, the call for a referendum must, first of all, comply with the law, including procedural rules which may – misleadingly – look technical and secondary. What ensures that the vote is the expression of the free will of the people is respect for these procedural rules – if they are themselves in conformity with the principle of free suffrage.

---

[4]   Study No. 371/2006, CDL-AD(2007)008rev-cor.
[5]   Code, III.1.

It is not rare that national rules of procedure are violated – such as through the use of referendums outside of the field in which they are authorized by law. This can lead to referendums on secession in contravention of the national constitution,[6] but also to less visible violations, such as a referendum intended to revise directly a constitution which does not provide for such a mode of revision[7] or a referendum on an issue, or on the initiative of an authority, not mentioned by the constitution.[8]

It is not only the call for a referendum, but also its *context*, which must respect superior law, including constitutional and international standards. Respect for fundamental rights, in particular freedom of expression and of the press, freedom of movement inside the country, freedom of assembly and freedom of association for political purposes, including freedom to set up political parties, is also essential to ensure democratic referendums.[9]

The second main principle to be followed is *respect of procedural standards by the text submitted to a referendum*, which is meant to guarantee free suffrage.

Some of these procedural standards are elements of the general freedom of voters to form an opinion that are applied, *mutatis mutandis*, to referendums. They include, first, the requirement that administrative authorities must be neutral. While this requirement is not as stringent as in the case of elections, administrative authorities must not influence the outcome of the vote by excessive, one-sided campaigning, and the use of public funds by the authorities for campaigning purposes must be prohibited.[10] Second, authorities are required to provide objective information.[11]

Other standards address issues which are marginal in the electoral field but central for referendums. Thus, the Code states, first, that '[t]he question put to the vote must be clear; it must not be misleading; it must not suggest an answer; voters must be informed of the effects of the referendum; they must be able to answer the questions asked solely by yes, no or a blank vote.'[12] In

---

[6]   Opinion on 'Whether the Decision Taken by the Supreme Council of the Autonomous Republic of Crimea in Ukraine to Organise a Referendum on Becoming a Constituent Territory of the Russian Federation or Restoring Crimea's 1992 Constitution Is Compatible With Constitutional Principles', Opinion No. 762/2014, CDL-AD(2014)002; Letter by the President of the Venice Commission to the President of Catalonia, Spain, 2 June 2017.

[7]   Opinion on the Constitutional Referendum in Ukraine, 31 March 2000, CDL-INF(2000)011.

[8]   Press release of 15 March 2010 (Republic of Moldova).

[9]   Code, II.1.

[10]   Code, I.3.1 a–b.

[11]   Code, I.3.1 d.

[12]   Code, I.3.1 c.

elections, on the other hand, it is sufficient to know who the candidates are and for which party they run. Second, the effects of the referendum must be clearly specified in the constitution or by law.[13] Although also electoral systems might not always be easily understandable, this question is even more crucial for referendums, especially given that some of them are not legally binding, but consultative.

Finally, some principles have no equivalent in the field of elections, namely those relating to the 'procedural validity of texts submitted to a referendum'.[14] According to the Code, questions submitted to a referendum must respect the requirements of unity of content, unity of form and unity of hierarchical level. Unity of content means that, except in the case of a total revision of a text, there must be an intrinsic connection between the various parts of each question put to the vote. Voters should not be compelled to accept or reject proposals as a bloc which are not interrelated. Unity of form means that the same question must not combine a specifically worded draft amendment with a generally worded proposal or a question of principle. The reasons for this requirement are set out in the explanatory memorandum to the Code as follows:

> A 'yes' vote on a specifically-worded draft – at least in the case of a legally binding referendum – means a statute is enacted and the procedure comes to an end, subject to procedural aspects such as publication and promulgation. On the other hand, a 'yes' vote on a question of principle or a generally-worded proposal is simply a stage, which will be followed by the drafting and subsequent enactment of a statute. Combining a specifically-worded draft with a generally-worded proposal or a question of principle would create confusion, preventing electors from being informed of the impact of their votes and thereby prejudicing their free suffrage.[15]

In other words, the purpose of the requirement is to prevent confusion and thus guarantee free suffrage. The requirement of unity of hierarchical level, finally, is equally intended to protect the voter's free expression of his or her will, although it might be less central. It implies that the same question should not simultaneously apply to legislation of different hierarchical levels, for example the constitution and ordinary legislation.

The third main principle concerns the *substantive validity of the text submitted to a referendum*. The Code provides that '[t]exts submitted to a referendum must comply with all superior law (principle of the hierarchy of norms). They must not be contrary to international law or to the Council of Europe's statutory principles (democracy, human rights and the rule of law).'[16]

---

[13]   Code, III.8.
[14]   Code, III.2.
[15]   Explanatory memorandum, para. 29.
[16]   Code, III.3.

These are general principles which apply whatever the internal mechanisms of control of conformity with superior law are, and irrespective of what national law has to say about the relationship between international law and domestic law. Like the requirement of conformity of the call for referendums with superior law, they are the expression of the more general principle of legality, which includes the requirement of conformity of legislation with the constitution,[17] but also the principle *pacta sunt servanda*, which is the way in which international law expresses the principle of legality.[18] The reference to the Council of Europe's statutory principles evokes more general international commitments of European states. These core values are interrelated; referendums – like elections – would be meaningless in their absence[19] and should not destroy the principles they are based on.[20]

The *sanction* in case of violation of the principles detailed above (call for the referendum in conformity with the law, procedural and substantive validity of the texts submitted to a referendum) should be that the text is not submitted to the popular vote.[21] In order to avoid declaring total invalidity, however, 'an authority must have the power ... when rules on procedural or substantive validity have been violated ... [to declare] partial invalidity ... if the remaining text is coherent'.[22] If the referendum nevertheless went ahead, this would be a serious irregularity implying its annulment.[23]

Direct democracy is not a substitute to representative democracy. It should not be a way to exclude *parliament* from the process, in particular when the referendum is initiated by the executive, but also in case of a popular initiative. Therefore,

> [w]hen a text is put to the vote at the request of a section of the electorate or an authority other than Parliament, Parliament must be able to give a non-binding opinion on the text put to the vote. In the case of the popular initiatives, it may be entitled to put forward a counter-proposal to the proposed text, which will be put to the popular vote at the same time.[24]

On the other hand, parliamentary procedures should not be used to circumvent decisions taken by a binding referendum.[25]

---

[17] Rule of Law Checklist (n 1) II.1.ii.
[18] Rule of Law Checklist (n 1) II.3, para. 47.
[19] Code, II.1.
[20] See Art. 17 European Convention on Human Rights.
[21] Code, III.3 last paragraph.
[22] Code, III.4.g.
[23] See Code, II.3.3.e.
[24] Code, III.6.
[25] Code, III.5.

Finally, the Code makes it clear that it disfavours *quorums*. A turnout quorum should be avoided, according to the Code, 'because it assimilates voters who abstain to those who vote no'. An approval quorum (requiring approval by a minimum percentage of registered voters), in turn, 'risks involving a difficult political situation if the draft is adopted by a simple majority lower than the necessary threshold'.[26]

3.   USE OF THE CODE

It must be noted that the Code is a reference text of the Council of Europe as it was not only adopted by the Venice Commission after approval by the Council for Democratic Elections – a tripartite body including members of the Venice Commission, the Parliamentary Assembly and the Congress of Local and Regional Authorities of the Council of Europe – but also endorsed by the plenary sessions of the Assembly and the Congress. The Committee of Ministers, for its part, adopted a Declaration on the Code of Good Practice on Referendums for the purpose of inviting public authorities in the member states to be guided by it.

What is, then, the use of the Code in practice? The Venice Commission quotes it regularly in its opinions and reports in the field, and this leads states to discuss the conformity of their legislation with its standards in the framework of the preparation of the Venice Commission's opinions. This has been true since the Code's adoption in 2007, both for joint opinions with the OSCE/ODIHR as well as for those drafted by the Venice Commission alone.[27] The formula, which by now has become traditional, is as follows:

> The ensuing recommendations are based on relevant Council of Europe and other international human rights standards and obligations, OSCE commitments, and good international practices. In particular, *they are based on the reference document of the Council of Europe in the field, the Code of Good Practice on Referendums drafted by the Venice Commission.*[28]

---

[26]   Code, III.7.

[27]   See, as a first example, the Joint Opinion on the Electoral Code of Moldova as of 27 March, 2007, Opinion No. 455/2007, CDL-AD(2007)040, fn 20; and, more recently, Armenia – Joint Opinion on the Draft Law on Referendum, Opinion No. 844/2016, CDL-AD(2017)029, *passim.*

[28]   Joint Opinion on the Electoral Code of Moldova (n 27), para. 13 (emphasis added); see also Turkey – Opinion on the amendments to the Constitution adopted by the Grand National Assembly on 21 January 2017 and to be submitted to a National Referendum on 16 April 2017, Opinion No. 875/2017, CDL-AD(2017)005, para. 32; Opinion on the Citizens' bill on the regulation of public participation, citizens' bills, referendums and popular initiatives and amendments to the Provincial

While opinions relating to specific legislation on referendums regularly refer to the Code, the Commission has other opportunities to quote it when dealing with referendum issues in the assessment of a broader piece of legislation or when drafting general reports.

A number of these quotations refer to the issue of quorums. As mentioned above, the Code is not in favour of quorums. However, the formulation it uses ('it is advisable not to provide for …') is not too strict.[29] This has led the Commission to take account of specific circumstances. It recommended to the Republic of Moldova[30] and to Serbia[31] not to provide for quorums. However, the Commission has specified that the Code is intended as applying to texts submitted to a referendum, defined as a specifically worded draft, repeal of an existing provision, a question of principle or a generally worded proposal, 'and not to the institution of the recall, which puts into question the elected body itself rather than an act it adopted'.[32]

Other references concern respect for the rule of law in the call for a referendum. The Commission has made it clear that referendums may not be held if they contravene the constitution[33] or 'to undermine a constitutionally mandated division of powers'.[34] Furthermore, a referendum should not be used as a means of settling a dispute between state institutions; accordingly, it would be more appropriate to submit to a referendum, rather than the question

---

Electoral Law of the Autonomous Province of Trento (Italy), Opinion No. 797/2014, CDL-AD(2015)009, para. 5.

[29] Code, III.7.

[30] Joint Opinion on the Electoral Code of Moldova (n 27), fn 20; Joint Opinion on the Election Code of Moldova as of 10 April 2008, Opinion No. 484/2008, CDL-AD(2008)022, para. 86; in the Joint Opinion on the Draft Working Text amending the Election Code of Moldova, Opinion No. 576/2010, CDL-AD(2010)014, para. 58, it stated, however, that 'turnout requirements may be acceptable in specific circumstances'.

[31] Opinion on the Draft Law on Referendum and Civil Initiative of Serbia, Opinion No. 551/2009, CDL-AD(2010)006, para. 38.

[32] Report on the recall of mayors and local elected representatives, Opinion No. 910/2017, CDL-AD(2019)011rev, para. 110; see also Opinion on a Draft Constitutional Law on the Amendments to the Constitution of Georgia, Opinion No. 519/2009, CDL-AD(2009)030, para. 16.

[33] Opinion on 'Whether the decision taken by the Supreme Council of the Autonomous Republic of Crimea in Ukraine to organise a referendum on becoming a constituent territory of the Russian Federation or restoring Crimea's 1992 Constitution is compatible with constitutional principles' (n 6) para. 24.

[34] Opinion on the law on national referendum of Ukraine, Opinion No. 705/2012, CDL-AD(2013)017), para. 18.

of the dissolution of parliament, the respective legal text whose non-adoption by parliament gave rise to a conflict with the president.[35]

The issue of freedom of voters to form an opinion[36] has also been addressed in several opinions of the Venice Commission. This freedom implies, for example, that 'the referendum should not be used as a tool to bypass the legislators or force parliaments to adopt constitutional amendments quickly. Referendums gain legitimacy when carried out within a reasonable time frame.'[37] The Commission has also insisted on the clarity of the referendum question[38] and balanced coverage by the media of referendum campaigns.[39]

4.   CONCLUSION

In short, the Code of Good Practice on Referendums, as the reference document of the Council of Europe in the field, details the standards which make possible the organization of democratic referendums in states based on the rule of law and respect for human rights. These standards are, *mutatis mutandis*, those applying to elections, but include also specific aspects proper to referendums. The Venice Commission and OSCE/ODIHR recall regularly their importance when addressing legislation on referendums in their opinions and reports, which has, in turn, led states to refer to them when preparing such legislation.

---

[35] Opinion on a Draft Constitutional Law on the Amendments to the Constitution of Georgia (n 32), para. 16–17.

[36] Code, II.3.1.

[37] Peru – Opinion on linking constitutional amendments to the question of confidence, Opinion No. 964/2019, CDL-AD(2019)022, para. 38; see also already Azerbaijan – Opinion on the draft modifications to the Constitution submitted to the Referendum of 26 September 2016, Opinion No. 864/2016, CDL-AD(2016)029, para. 8.

[38] Opinion on 'Whether the decision taken by the Supreme Council of the Autonomous Republic of Crimea in Ukraine to organise a referendum on becoming a constituent territory of the Russian Federation or restoring Crimea's 1992 Constitution is compatible with constitutional principles' (n 6) para. 23.

[39] Opinion on the law on national referendum of Ukraine (n 34), para. 32, 48.

3. Revision of the Code of Good Practice on Referendums

Nicos C. Alivizatos

In October 2016, under the impact of the Brexit referendum, the Venice Commission took the initiative to update its Code of Good Practice on Referendums from 2007 (Code).[1] For that purpose, it first adopted a questionnaire asking for information on the latest developments in the member states. On the basis of the answers, a first exchange occurred.

In parallel, the Parliamentary Assembly of the Council of Europe adopted a report titled 'Updating guidelines to ensure fair referendums in Council of Europe member states',[2] which led to a Resolution with the same title, adopted on 22 January 2019.[3]

In her opening speech, the rapporteur, Dame Cheryl Gillan, MP, insisted that the updated Code should reflect changes that had occurred since 2007 'so it can continue to provide modernized guidelines for all our members'.[4] In his address during the same debate, Gianni Buquicchio, the president of the Venice Commission, referred to two eminent Swiss personalities originating from the same city, Geneva, Rousseau and Fazy. He claimed that the former's unreserved support for the people's direct involvement in political decision-making through referendums should not obscure the historical fact that whenever representative government was weakened, democracy was sooner or later abolished. Should one recall the latter's poisonous aphorism that referendums are, in reality, 'l'appel de l'intelligence à l'ignorance'?[5]

---

[1]   Study No. 371/2006, CDL-AD(2007)008rev-cor.
[2]   7 January 2019, Doc. 14791.
[3]   Resolution 2251 (2019).
[4]   PACE, Winter Session 2019, Tuesday, 22 January 2019, Sitting No 3.
[5]   Ibid. James Fazy's famous phrase is mentioned in PACE, Référendums: vers de bonnes pratiques en Europe, *Documents de séance,* Doc 10498, Session ordinaire de 2005, 25–29 avril 2005, Vol. III, 397.

More concretely, in that Resolution, the Parliamentary Assembly invited the Venice Commission to take into account the following fundamental principles:

1. that referendums should be embedded in the process of representative democracy, that is, complement rather than substitute it;
2. that proposals put to a referendum should be as clear as possible and subject to detailed prior scrutiny; and
3. that campaign rules should ensure a balance between the different sides and guarantee that voters have access to balanced and quality information.

Both in America and in Europe, the period preceding the adoption of that Resolution was marked by systematic attacks, originating from both extremes of the political spectrum, against the so-called 'elites', including 'bankers', 'the rich' and the 'Brussels bureaucrats', members of parliament, ministers and party leaders. A very evocative example of an attack of such a type is the following extract from President Trump's inaugural address, in January 2017:

> Politicians prospered, but the jobs left and the factories closed. The establishment protected itself, but not the citizens of our country. Their victories have not been your victories; their triumphs have not been your triumphs; and while they celebrated in our nation's capital, there was little to celebrate for struggling families all across our land.[6]

In other words, until President Trump was elected, laws were allegedly voted in Washington, and decisions were taken, not to the benefit of the people but in the interest of the few. 'Today's ceremony', the newly elected president went on,

> has very special meaning. Because today we are not merely transferring power from one administration to another, or from one party to another – but we are transferring power from Washington, D.C. and giving it back to you, the American people.[7]

This crude flattery of the people is also behind the glorification of referendums as the only proper means to ensure the direct and, hence, genuine expression of the people's will. In an interview before the 2017 French presidential election, Marine Le Pen announced that, if she was elected, she would call two referendums immediately after her advent to power.[8] On the left, Alexis Tsipras,

---

6   Remarks of President Donald J Trump, inaugural address, 20 January 2017, https://www.whitehouse.gov/briefings-statements/the-inaugural-address/, accessed 22 June 2020.

7   Ibid.

8   The first on France's withdrawal from the EU, the so-called 'Frexit' (see Ingrid Melander, 'Far right FN party calls for French "Frexit" referendum on EU', Reuters, 24

the former Greek prime minister, before his shift to pragmatism, in 2018–19, promised to provide for no less than five different types of referendums in the country's amended constitution he was at the time contemplating. Because, as he explained, in democracies, decisions must be taken by the people and not by technocrats.[9]

The other dramatic developments that the rapporteurs of the amended Code could not ignore were technological innovations, which had profoundly changed the democratic landscape, such as the new reality of social media, in parallel with the increased access to information by the voters.

Finally, globalization has had a very significant impact on voting behaviour, through facilitating direct and indirect involvement of 'third' parties in voting procedures, including referendum campaigns. For instance, Russia has been accused of involvement not only in the 2016 US presidential campaign, but also in the 2018 referendum in North Macedonia, which concerned that Balkan country's name. Not surprisingly, even in countries with longstanding traditions of fair and impartial elections, there have been very serious complaints of violation of the relevant rules, in particular financial regulations. In the United Kingdom, for instance, more than two years after the 2016 referendum, the Electoral Commission imposed fines amounting to no less than £61,000 and £70,000 on pro-Brexiteers in respect of serious offences in breach of the rules on campaign spending.[10]

Therefore, in drafting the revised Code, the Venice Commission has focused primarily on procedural guarantees aiming to ensure the fairness of referendums. The need for an *independent and impartial body*, which would be in charge of organizing the referendum from national level to polling station level, was stressed, in particular for countries without a longstanding tradition of administrative authorities' impartiality in electoral matters. Starting from checking the validity and appropriateness of the questions proposed for referendum, that body's powers should include supervision of the referendum

---

June 2016, www.reuters.com.article/US-france-lepen-referendum-idUSKCN1190UW, accessed 30 July 2020), and the second on the amendment of the French Constitution for the purpose of introducing the principle of 'national preference', that is, the precedence of French nationals in hiring, dispensing of housing and other benefits (see Nicholas Vinocur, 'President Marine Le Pen's first 100 days', Politico, 20 April 2017, www.politico.eu/article/president-marine-lepens-first-100-days-hypothetical-french -election, accessed 30 July 2020).

9   Statement by Prime Minister Alexis Tsipras of 25 July 2016 (in Greek), http://primeminister.gr/2016/07/25/15039, accessed 30 July 2020.

10   Electoral Commission, 'Vote Leave fined and referred to the police for breaking electoral law', 17 July 2018, www.electoralcommission.org.uk/media-centre/vote -leave-fined-and-referred-police-breaking-electoral-law, accessed 30 July 2020.

campaign, enforcing the rules and timely sanctioning of possible breaches as the only efficient means of avoiding *faits accompli*.

Moreover, whenever a text is put to the vote at the request of a part of the electorate, parliament must be able to give a non-binding opinion on the text put to the vote.

As far as substantive limits are concerned, in the opinion of the Commission, the text submitted to a referendum should comply with superior law and must not be contrary to international law, including the Council of Europe's statutory principles, as interpreted by the European Court of Human Rights. For the complexity of the questions that may arise in that context, one may take a look at the important debates that occurred in Switzerland in 2009 on the occasion of the referendum on the ban of minarets and in Greece in 2015 on the occasion of the referendum on the bailout conditions proposed to Greece by the International Monetary Fund, the European Central Bank and the European Commission.

To conclude, a reference should be made to the statistics on national referendums of the LIDD project, grouped by country, since 1990.[11] As expected, with 274 referendums, Switzerland is far ahead at the top. First among all other countries comes Azerbaijan, with 69 referendums, and last come Monaco, Germany and Belgium, with no referendums at all. Whatever one's preferences are in relation to referendums, one cannot easily assert that, in terms of democracy, the first is more advanced than the latter are.

---

[11]   See http://lidd-project.org/data/, (tab 'referendum practice') accessed 22 June 2020.

PART II

'Old' European democracies

4. Switzerland

Daniel Moeckli

---

1. INTRODUCTION

Switzerland has a very extensive system of direct democracy, with various direct-democratic instruments existing at the federal, cantonal as well as municipal levels. The legal limits imposed on these instruments are, especially at the federal level, rather weak. At the federal level, it is parliament that is in charge of reviewing compliance with these limits. The result is a very low rate of popular initiatives and referendums that are declared invalid. A somewhat different picture emerges at the cantonal level, where the legal limits are more stringent and compliance with these limits can be reviewed in a judicial procedure.

2. DIRECT-DEMOCRATIC INSTRUMENTS

The direct-democratic instruments existing at the *federal level* include the mandatory referendum (a law-initiated referendum), the optional referendum (a rejective referendum that can be initiated either by a certain number of citizens or a number of cantons) and the popular initiative (a proactive citizen-initiated referendum). Apart from the optional referendum, which can also be initiated by a number of cantons, there is no institution-initiated referendum. Nor does the citizens' agenda initiative exist at the federal level.

The cantons are free to introduce further instruments of direct democracy. Therefore, at the *cantonal level* there are a number of additional instruments. For example, some cantons allow the rejective referendum to be combined with a proactive proposal;[1] certain cantons allow parliament to initiate a ref-

---

[1]   See for example Art. 63(3) Constitution of the Canton of Bern (*Verfassung des Kantons Bern vom 6. Juni 1993* (*Systematische Rechtssammlung* (SR) (Classified compilation of legislation) 131.212)).

erendum;[2] four cantons provide for the citizens' agenda initiative;[3] and the scope of the popular initiative, which at the federal level is restricted to constitutional amendments, extends to legislative acts in all cantons and, in four cantons, even to ordinances.[4]

Finally, there typically also exist a range of direct-democratic instruments at the *municipal level*.[5]

This chapter focuses on the three main instruments that exist at both the federal and the cantonal levels. Due to the significant variances between the direct-democratic systems of the 26 cantons, only the federal instruments can be covered in detail.

2.1 Mandatory Referendum

Article 140(1) of the Federal Constitution of Switzerland[6] provides that:

1. amendments to the Federal Constitution,
2. accession to organisations for collective security or to supranational organisations, and
3. emergency federal acts that are not based on a provision of the Constitution and whose term of validity exceeds one year

are subject to a mandatory referendum. The mandatory referendum can be classified as a law-initiated referendum as it is automatically triggered if one of the conditions specified by the Constitution is met. The measures listed

---

[2]   See for example § 51(2) Constitution of the Canton of Basel-Stadt (*Verfassung des Kantons Basel-Stadt vom 23. März 2005* (SR 131.222.1)); § 23(d) Constitution of the Canton of Lucerne (*Verfassung des Kantons Luzern vom 17. Juni 2007* (SR 131.213)).

[3]   Art. 47 Constitution of the Canton of Fribourg (*Constitution du canton de Fribourg du 16 mai 2004* (SR 131.219)); Art. 41 Constitution of the Canton of Neuchâtel (*Constitution de la République et Canton de Neuchâtel du 24 septembre 2000* (SR 131.233)); Art. 31 Constitution of the Canton of Schaffhausen (*Verfassung des Kantons Schaffhausen vom 17. Juni 2002* (SR 131.223)); Art. 34 Constitution of the Canton of Solothurn (*Verfassung des Kantons Solothurn vom 8. Juni 1986* (SR 131.221)).

[4]   See Andreas Auer, *Staatsrecht der Schweizerischen Kantone* (Stämpfli 2016) 427.

[5]   For the example of the City of Berne, see Art. 70 ff Regulation on Political Rights of the City of Berne (*Reglement über die politischen Rechte vom 16. Mai 2004* (SSSB 141.1)).

[6]   *Bundesverfassung der Schweizerischen Eidgenossenschaft vom 18. April 1999* (SR 101). An English version of the Federal Constitution is available on the website of the Swiss Confederation http://www.admin.ch/ch/e/rs/c101.html, accessed 15 May 2020.

above need to be approved by a double majority: the majority of citizens who participate in the vote and the majority of cantons,[7] the vote of the latter being determined by the result of the popular vote in the respective canton.[8]

At the federal level, 224 mandatory referendums have been held in total by summer 2020, resulting in 168 approvals and 56 rejections. Counting from 1991, there have been 63 mandatory referendums, with 49 approvals and 14 rejections.[9] In the 26 cantons, more than 1,000 mandatory referendums have been held since 1991, with a success rate that comes close to 90 per cent.[10]

2.2   Optional Referendum

According to Article 141(1) of the Federal Constitution,

1.   federal acts passed by the Federal Assembly (the federal parliament),
2.   emergency federal acts whose term of validity exceeds one year,
3.   federal decrees, provided the Constitution or an act so requires, and
4.   international treaties that
     (i) are of unlimited duration and may not be terminated,
     (ii) provide for accession to an international organisation, or
     (iii) contain important legislative provisions or provisions whose imple-
           mentation requires the enactment of federal legislation

are subject to an optional referendum. This means that, if within 100 days of the official publication of their enactment either 50,000 persons eligible to vote or eight cantons request it, these measures must be put to a popular vote. In the former case, the optional referendum can be classified as a citizen-initiated rejective referendum, in the latter case as a subnational entity-initiated rejective referendum. If it comes to a vote, a simple majority of voters is sufficient for these kinds of measures to be approved.[11]

At the federal level, 189 optional referendums have been held in total so far, resulting in 109 approvals and 80 rejections. In the last three decades there has been a significant rise in the number of optional referendums: counting from 1991, there have been 86 optional referendums, with 64 approvals and 22

---

[7]   Art. 140(1) and 142(2) Federal Constitution.
[8]   Art. 142(3) Federal Constitution.
[9]   The statistics are available on the website of the Federal Statistical Office https://www.bfs.admin.ch/bfs/de/home/statistiken/politik/abstimmungen.assetdetail.8126482.html, accessed 15 May 2020.
[10]   Auer (n 4) 448–449.
[11]   Art. 141(1) and 142(1) Federal Constitution.

rejections.[12] At the cantonal level, around 400 optional referendums have been held since 1991, with a success rate of around 50 per cent.[13]

2.3   Popular Initiative

The popular initiative foreseen by Articles 138 and 139 of the Federal Constitution gives 100,000 persons eligible to vote the right to propose a total or partial revision of the Federal Constitution. It is thus a typical case of a citizen-initiated proactive referendum. Since its introduction in 1891, the number of signatories required to launch a popular initiative has been only raised once, from 50,000 to 100,000 in 1977, not least as a reaction to the introduction of women's suffrage in 1971.[14] Today, that number equals 1.85 per cent of the 5.4 million citizens who are eligible to vote (out of a total population of 8.4 million).

The proposal for a partial revision can take the form of either a general proposal or a draft of the constitutional provisions proposed.[15] Any measure that can be formulated as a general proposal or a constitutional norm may be proposed by way of a popular initiative. This may include proposals that would entail radical changes to the political system of Switzerland, such as abolition of the armed forces[16] or accession to the European Union.[17] Thus, 'the popular initiative enlarges the realm of the politically thinkable and feasible.'[18] Apart from the very limited reasons for declaring popular initiatives invalid discussed in Section 3 below, they must be put to the vote in their original wording. The Federal Assembly must issue a recommendation to voters on how to vote.[19] Apart from that, the only way in which it can react to a popular

---

[12]   The statistics are available on the website of the Federal Statistical Office https://www.bfs.admin.ch/bfs/de/home/statistiken/politik/abstimmungen.assetdetail.8126482.html, accessed 15 May 2020.

[13]   Auer (n 4) 451–452.

[14]   *Botschaft des Bundesrates an die Bundesversammlung über eine Erhöhung der Unterschriftenzahlen für Initiative und Referendum vom 9. Juni 1975, Bundesblatt* (Federal Gazette) 1975 II, 129, 131 and 138.

[15]   Art. 139(2) Federal Constitution.

[16]   In 1989 and 2001 initiatives to abolish the Swiss army were rejected.

[17]   In 2001 a proposal to enter into negotiations on acceding to the European Union was rejected.

[18]   Wolf Linder, 'Direct Democracy' in Ulrich Klöti et al. (eds), *Handbook of Swiss Politics* (2nd edn, NZZ Libro 2007) 101, 117.

[19]   Art. 139(5) sentence 2 Federal Constitution.

initiative is to draft a counterproposal.[20] Popular initiatives need to be approved by the double majority of voters and cantons.[21]

Only 22 out of the 216 federal popular initiatives voted on so far have managed to overcome this hurdle.[22] In addition, six counterproposals to initiatives have also been approved.[23] The reason for this low success rate of popular initiatives as compared with optional and, especially, mandatory referendums is that the latter often concern rather uncontentious constitutional amendments, whereas the popular initiative is typically used by those in the political minority to propose changes that may be regarded as radical. However, the number of successful initiatives, as well as the number of initiatives in general, has risen considerably. In the years between 2001 and 2010 alone, six initiatives were approved. Furthermore, even if not approved, a popular initiative may have a significant indirect impact, putting issues on the political agenda or triggering legislative changes.

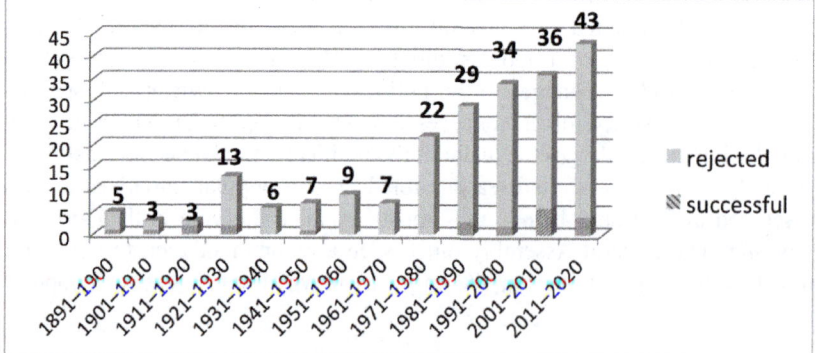

Source: The diagram is based on the statistics provided by the Federal Statistical Office accessed 15 May 2020.

Figure 4.1   Number of popular initiatives voted on

---

[20]   Art. 139(5) sentence 3 Federal Constitution.
[21]   Art. 139(5) sentence 1 and 142(2) Federal Constitution.
[22]   The statistics are available on the website of the Federal Chancellery https://www.admin.ch/ch/d/pore/vi/vis_2_2_5_9.html, accessed 15 May 2020.
[23]   See the statistics provided by the Federal Statistical Office https://www.bfs.admin.ch/bfs/de/home/statistiken/politik/abstimmungen.assetdetail.1866592.html, accessed 15 May 2020.

At the cantonal level, more than 500 popular initiatives have been voted on since 1991, around a third of which have been approved.[24]

3.   LEGAL LIMITS

The only substantive limits imposed on the popular initiative and, to some extent, the mandatory referendum are the requirements that proposals put to a vote must not violate higher-ranking norms and that it must be practically feasible to implement them. The optional referendum, as a rejective instrument, is not subject to any substantive limits: it can be used against any measure falling within its scope. In addition, there are a number of formal limits that apply to all types of direct-democratic instruments. They follow from the freedom to vote guaranteed by Article 34(2) of the Federal Constitution: referendum questions and initiative proposals must be clear and they must observe the requirements of consistency of the subject matter and consistency of form.

3.1   Substantive Limits

3.1.1   Compliance with higher-ranking law
Cantonal popular initiatives are declared invalid if they violate *any* higher-ranking norm, be it found in international law, federal law, inter-cantonal law or higher-ranking cantonal law.[25] Almost all cantons have explicitly established this substantive limit in their constitution or in an act. Lack of compliance with higher-ranking law, especially federal law, is the most frequent reason for the invalidity of cantonal initiatives.[26] For example, a cantonal initiative demanding the prohibition of certain schoolbooks on religion as well as an initiative directed against a centre for 'Islam and society' were declared invalid for violating the prohibition of religious discrimination of Article 8(2) of the Federal Constitution; these invalidity decisions have been confirmed by the Federal Court.[27]

In contrast, *federal* popular initiatives (which are aimed at changing the Federal Constitution) must, as a general rule, not comply with any pre-existing law, including international law. According to Article 139(3) of the Federal Constitution, the Federal Assembly can only declare a federal popular initia-

---

[24]   Auer (n 4) 454–455.

[25]   Auer (n 4) 432–433.

[26]   See Bénédicte Tornay, *La démocratie directe saisie par le juge – L'empreinte de la jurisprudence sur les droits populaires en Suisse* (Schulthess 2008) 90.

[27]   BGE (*Entscheidungen des Schweizerischen Bundesgerichts* (decisions of the Swiss Federal Supreme Court)) 139 I 292 (28 August 2013); BGE 143 I 129 (14 December 2016).

tive invalid if it violates '*peremptory norms* of international law'.[28] While some authors argue that this is a reference to the corpus of law that is internationally recognised as constituting *ius cogens*,[29] others think that it is an autonomous term of Swiss constitutional law that can be interpreted more broadly to also include fundamental norms of international law that have not (yet) attained *ius cogens* status.[30] The Federal Council and the Federal Assembly today seem to side with the latter group of authors and thus to understand 'peremptory norms of international law' as an autonomous constitutional term.[31] In any event, they interpret the term narrowly, limiting it to those rules that are of such fundamental importance to the international community that they must be regarded as binding upon any state that respects the rule of law and that can thus never be derogated from.[32] These rules are said to include the prohibitions of genocide, slavery and torture, the principle of *non-refoulement*, the core guarantees of international humanitarian law and the non-derogable guarantees of the European Convention on Human Rights (ECHR)[33] and the International Covenant on Civil and Political Rights (ICCPR).[34] [35] Since international responsibility for violation of this body of international law simply cannot be evaded, it makes good sense that norms of domestic law that are incompatible with it should never come into force, regardless of their democratic legitimacy.

Given its narrow definition, however, this validity requirement does not present a major obstacle; only two popular initiatives have been declared invalid on this basis. In 1996, the Federal Assembly adjudged an initiative

---

[28]　Emphasis added.

[29]　For example Yvo Hangartner/Andreas Kley, *Die demokratischen Rechte in Bund und Kantonen der Schweizerischen Eidgenossenschaft* (Schulthess 2000) 227–228.

[30]　For example Daniel Thürer, 'Verfassungsrecht und Völkerrecht' in Daniel Thürer, Jean-François Aubert and Jörg Paul Müller (eds), *Verfassungsrecht der Schweiz* (Schulthess 2001) 179, 184–185.

[31]　See, for example, *Botschaft zur Volksinitiative 'Zur Durchsetzung der Ausschaffung krimineller Ausländer (Durchsetzungsinitiative)'*, Bundesblatt 2013, 9459, 9467–70.

[32]　For an overview see Robert Baumann, 'Völkerrechtliche Schranken der Verfassungsrevision', (2007) 108 Schweizerisches Zentralblatt für Staats- und Verwaltungsrecht 181, 190–206.

[33]　Convention for the Protection of Human Rights and Fundamental Freedoms of 4 November 1950, 213 UNTS 222.

[34]　International Covenant on Civil and Political Rights of 16 December 1966, 999 UNTS 171.

[35]　For example *Botschaft zur Volksinitiative 'Zur Durchsetzung der Ausschaffung krimineller Ausländer (Durchsetzungsinitiative)'*, Bundesblatt 2013, 9459, 9467–70; *Botschaft zur Eidgenössischen Volksinitiative 'für demokratische Einbürgerungen'*, Bundesblatt 2006, 8953, 8962; *Botschaft über eine neue Bundesverfassung*, Bundesblatt 1997 I, 1, 362.

demanding the immediate expulsion of all asylum-seekers who have entered the country illegally to be incompatible with the principle of *non-refoulement*.[36] In 2015, an initiative designed to enforce the expulsion of foreign criminals was declared partially invalid. The Federal Assembly held that the part of the initiative that wanted to provide, for the purposes of the initiative, an exhaustive list of peremptory norms of international law that were to be respected in the case of expulsions was not compatible with the principle of *non-refoulement* as it defined this principle more narrowly than international law did.[37]

In contrast, numerous popular initiatives that are incompatible with norms of international law that do not amount to *peremptory* norms have been declared valid and thus put to a popular vote. Some of them have been accepted by a majority of voters and cantons; these include, for example, initiatives for a ban on the construction of minarets[38] and for the automatic expulsion of foreign nationals convicted of certain criminal offences,[39] both of which violate a number of human rights guarantees, as well as an initiative 'against mass immigration',[40] which conflicts with the Agreement on the Free Movement of Persons concluded between Switzerland and the European Union.[41]

---

[36] *Botschaft über die Volksinitiativen 'für eine vernünftige Asylpolitik' und 'gegen die illegale Einwanderung'*, Bundesblatt 1994 III, 1486, 1499; *Bundesbeschluss über die Volksinitiative 'für eine vernünftige Asylpolitik'*, Bundesblatt 1996 I, 1355.

[37] *Botschaft zur Volksinitiative 'Zur Durchsetzung der Ausschaffung krimineller Ausländer (Durchsetzungsinitiative)'*, Bundesblatt 2013, 9459, 9467–72; *Bundesbeschluss über die Volksinitiative 'Zur Durchsetzung der Ausschaffung krimineller Ausländer (Durchsetzungsinitiative)' vom 20. März 2015*, Bundesblatt 2015, 2701.

[38] *Bundesratsbeschluss über das Ergebnis der Volksabstimmung vom 29. November 2009*, Bundesblatt 2010, 3437, 3440. For an explanation of why this initiative was regarded as violating international law but not any peremptory norms of international law, see *Botschaft zur Volksinitiative 'Gegen den Bau von Minaretten'*, Bundesblatt 2008, 7603, 7609–7612 and 7630–7645.

[39] *Bundesratsbeschluss über das Ergebnis der Volksabstimmung vom 28. November 2010*, Bundesblatt 2011, 2771, 2773. For an explanation of why this initiative was regarded as violating international law but not any peremptory norms of international law, see *Botschaft zur Volksinitiative 'für die Ausschaffung krimineller Ausländer (Ausschaffungsinitiative)' und zur Änderung des Bundesgesetzes über die Ausländerinnen und Ausländer*, Bundesblatt 2009, 5097, 5102–5103 and 5106–5113.

[40] *Bundesratsbeschluss über das Ergebnis der Volksabstimmung vom 9. Februar 2014*, Bundesblatt 2014, 4117, 4120. For an explanation of why this initiative was regarded as violating international law but not any peremptory norms of international law, see *Botschaft zur Volksinitiative 'Gegen Masseneinwanderung'*, Bundesblatt 2013, 291, 298–300 and 334–342.

[41] *Abkommen zwischen der Schweizerischen Eidgenossenschaft einerseits und der Europäischen Gemeinschaft und ihren Mitgliedstaaten andererseits über die Freizügigkeit vom 21. Juni 1999* (SR 0.142.112.681).

According to Article 194(2) of the Federal Constitution, the requirement of compliance with peremptory norms of international law also applies to amendments of the Federal Constitution made by the Federal Assembly that, according to Article 140(1) of the Federal Constitution, are subject to the mandatory referendum. Since compliance with this limit can only be ensured by the Federal Assembly itself (see Section 4.1.2 below), it is not of any practical relevance.

3.1.2   Feasibility

A further substantive limit, although one that is of less relevance in practice, is that it must be practically feasible for a popular initiative to be implemented. Most cantonal constitutions explicitly list this validity requirement.[42] However, there have only been two cases so far where a decision to declare a cantonal popular initiative invalid on this basis was confirmed by the Federal Court.[43]

Although it is not mentioned in the Federal Constitution, it is commonly accepted that the requirement of practical feasibility also applies to federal popular initiatives.[44] In 1955, a federal popular initiative that demanded a reduction of the military budget within a certain time period was held to be in breach of this requirement as it was impossible to hold the popular vote on the initiative early enough to allow for its implementation.[45]

3.2   Formal Limits

3.2.1   Clarity of the referendum question/initiative proposal

Article 34(2) of the Federal Constitution guarantees 'the freedom of the citizen to form an opinion and to give genuine expression to his or her will'. It follows from this guarantee that any question put to the people must be clear. The

---

[42]   See for example Art. 59(2)(b) Constitution of the Canton of Berne; Art. 31 Constitution of the Canton of Solothurn; Art. 28(1)(c) Constitution of the Canton of Zurich (*Verfassung des Kantons Zürich vom 27. Februar 2005* (SR 131.211)).

[43]   BGE 128 I 190 (17 April 2002) para 5, 201 ff.; Judgment of the Federal Court 1P.454/2006 of 22 May 2007, para 3.

[44]   See Giovanni Biaggini, *BV Kommentar: Bundesverfassung der Schweizerischen Eidgenossenschaft* (2nd ed, Orell Füssli 2017) Art. 139, n 14; Astrid Epiney/Stefan Diezig, 'Art. 139' in Bernhard Waldmann, Eva Maria Belser and Astrid Epiney (eds), *Bundesverfassung: Basler Kommentar* (Helbing & Lichtenhahn 2015) n 45–46.

[45]   *Zweiter Bericht des Bundesrates an die Bundesversammlung über das Volksbegehren für eine vorübergehende Herabsetzung der Militärausgaben (Volksinitiative für eine Rüstungspause)*, Bundesblatt 1955 II, 325; *Bundesbeschluss über das Volksbegehren für eine vorübergehende Herabsetzung der Militärausgaben (Volksinitiative für eine Rüstungspause) vom 15. Dezember 1955*, Bundesblatt 1955 II, 1463.

Federal Court has held that referendum questions must be drafted in a clear and impartial manner and may not be misleading or suggestive.[46] It has, on occasion, annulled cantonal referendums because it adjudged the question to be suggestive.[47] With regard to referendums at the federal level, the issue of the clarity of the question has sometimes been raised,[48] but, to my knowledge, never has a referendum been called off for this reason.

The requirement of clarity equally applies to popular initiatives. With regard to the federal popular initiative, Article 69(2) of the Federal Act on Political Rights[49] provides that the Federal Chancellery will amend the title of an initiative if it is misleading. Although this rarely happens, there have been a few cases. For example, the Federal Chancellery amended the title of an initiative aiming at abolishing a law against racial hate speech that was originally entitled 'Das freie Wort' ('The free word').[50] At the cantonal level, a few cantonal constitutions explicitly state that popular initiatives must be sufficiently precise.[51] Yet the requirement is also applicable to the other cantons since, as has been confirmed by the Federal Court, it follows from Article 34(2) of the Federal Constitution.[52]

3.2.2 Consistency of the subject matter

According to the requirement of consistency of the subject matter (called 'unity of content' in the Venice Commission's Code of Good Practice on Referendums[53] and 'single-subject rule' in the United States), a referendum

---

[46] BGE 137 I 200 (24 March 2011) para 2.1, 203; BGE 121 I 1 (6 March 1995) para 5b/aa, 12.

[47] BGE 106 Ia 20 (28 March 1980) para 3, 27 (in this case, concerning a vote on the construction of a nuclear power plant, the authorities had suggested in the referendum question that the construction of the power plant was desirable).

[48] See for example Biaggini (n 44) Art. 34, n 24.

[49] *Bundesgesetz über die politischen Rechte vom 17. Dezember 1976* (SR 161.1). An English translation is available at www.admin.ch/opc/en/classified-compilation/ 19760323/index.html, accessed 15 May 2020.

[50] See Judgment of the Swiss Federal Court 1A.314/1997 of 30 March 1998, (1999) 100 Schweizerisches Zentralblatt für Staats- und Verwaltungsrecht 527. See also decision of the Federal Chancellery of 28 April 1998 regarding the popular initiative *'Die persönliche Souveränität der Bürger'*, Bundesblatt 1998 III, 2546.

[51] See for example Art. 28(2) Constitution of the Canton of Uri (*Verfassung des Kantons Uri vom 28. Oktober 1984* (SR 131.214)).

[52] BGE 139 I 292 (28 August 2013) paras 5.8 and 5.9, 296–297; BGE 129 I 392 (21 November 2003) para 2.2, 395.

[53] Code of Good Practice on Referendums, adopted by the Council for Democratic Elections at its 19th meeting (Venice, 16 December 2006) and the Venice Commission at its 70th plenary session (Venice, 16–17 March 2007), CDL-AD (2007) 008rev, para. III.2.

question or initiative proposal may not combine two or more issues or subject matters that lack an inherent connection. This requirement equally follows from the freedom to vote guaranteed by Article 34(2) of the Federal Constitution. If the requirement is not met, voters cannot genuinely express their will: either they have to approve the whole proposal, although they disagree with certain parts of it, or they have to vote 'no', although they agree with the other parts of it.[54]

At the federal level, the requirement is explicitly mentioned in Article 139(3) of the Federal Constitution for the popular initiative and in Article 194(2) of the Federal Constitution for the mandatory referendum. Whether it also applies when the Federal Assembly passes federal acts that are then subject to the optional referendum is contentious. The majority of legal scholars argue, correctly in my view, that it does, as it follows from Article 34(2) of the Federal Constitution.[55] This has, however, not prevented the Federal Assembly from, for example, joining together in one federal act, on the one hand, a corporate tax reform and, on the other hand, a scheme providing additional funding for the public pensions scheme, with a view to attract as many 'yes' votes as possible. Unsurprisingly, this 'package deal' was approved by a large majority of voters in 2019.[56] Also as far as popular initiatives are concerned, the Federal Assembly's practice of applying the requirement of consistency of the subject matter has been very generous: it has only declared two initiatives invalid on this basis. In 1977, it found an initiative against inflation that combined a number of various demands (including state control of prices and capital investments, progressive taxation and the introduction of guarantees of economic and social rights) to be incompatible with this requirement.[57] In 1995, it declared invalid an initiative that demanded that the military budget be reduced by half, while at the same time requiring that this money be used for purposes of peace-keeping and the provision of social security.[58] In

---

[54]   BGE 129 I 366 (27 August 2003) para 2.2, 370.

[55]   See for example René Rhinow, 'Die Einheit der Materie – ein Kompromisskiller?', (2019) 120 Schweizerisches Zentralblatt für Staats- und Verwaltungsrecht 113–114; Gerold Steinmann, 'Art. 34', in: Bernhard Ehrenzeller, Benjamin Schindler, Rainer J Schweizer and Klaus A Vallender (eds), *Die schweizerische Bundesverfassung – St. Galler Kommentar* (3rd ed, Dike 2014) n 23. For an opposing view, see Andreas Kley, 'Die Einheit der Materie bei Bundesgesetzen und der Stein der Weisen', (2019) 120 Schweizerisches Zentralblatt für Staats- und Verwaltungsrecht 3.

[56]   *Bundesratsbeschluss über das Ergebnis der Volksabstimmung vom 19. Mai 2019 vom 8. Juli 2019*, Bundesblatt 2019, 4985.

[57]   *Bundesbeschluss über die Volksinitiative 'gegen Teuerung und Inflation' vom 16. Dezember 1977*, Bundesblatt 1977 III, 919.

[58]   *Bundesbeschluss über die Volksinitiative 'Für weniger Militärausgaben und mehr Friedenspolitik' vom 20. Juni 1995*, Bundesblatt 1995 III, 570.

contrast, for example, the so-called 'Ecopop' initiative was declared valid in 2013, despite the fact that it demanded, on the one hand, enhanced immigration restrictions and, on the other, the promotion of birth control measures in developing countries.[59]

At the cantonal level, many cantonal constitutions explicitly refer to the requirement of consistency of the subject matter.[60] As with the clarity requirement, the Federal Court has confirmed that, in any event, this formal limit already follows from Article 34(2) of the Federal Constitution.[61] Therefore, the requirement of consistency of the subject matter applies to all cantonal direct-democratic instruments, be it popular initiatives, mandatory referendums, optional referendums or other instruments.[62] The Federal Court has elaborated the different aspects of this requirement in a rich jurisprudence, repeatedly coming to the conclusion that it had been violated.[63]

3.2.3 Consistency of form

The requirement of consistency of form only applies to popular initiatives. According to this requirement, an initiative must take the form of either a general proposal or a specific draft of the proposed provisions, but not a hybrid between the two. Also this requirement has been deduced by the Federal Court from the freedom to vote: if the requirement is not complied with, the Court has held, voters cannot foresee the exact consequences of approving the initiative.[64] Article 139(3) of the Federal Constitution explicitly lists the consistency of form requirement as one of the admissibility criteria for federal popular initiatives, and also some cantonal constitutions explicitly refer to it.[65] However, the requirement is of little practical relevance. Not a single federal popular initiative has been found to be in breach of this limit until

---

[59] *Bundesbeschluss über die Volksinitiative 'Stopp der Überbevölkerung – zur Sicherung der natürlichen Lebensgrundlagen' vom 20. Juni 2014*, Bundesblatt 2014, 5073.

[60] See for example Art. 59(2)(c) Constitution of the Canton of Bern; § 22(3)(b) Constitution of the Canton of Lucerne; Art. 28(1)(a) and 133 Constitution of the Canton of Zurich.

[61] BGE 129 I 366 (27 August 2003) para 2.1, 369–370.

[62] BGE 129 I 366 (27 August 2003) para 2.2, 370.

[63] See, for example, BGE 137 I 200 (24 March 2011); BGE 130 I 185 (26 May 2004) 195 ff; BGE 129 I 381 (25 September 2003) para 2, 383 ff; BGE 123 I 63 (12 March 1997) paras 4–5, 70 ff. For an overview of the relevant case-law, see Patrizia Attinger, *Die Rechtsprechung des Bundesgerichts zu kantonalen Volksinitiativen* (Schulthess 2016) 81 ff; Tornay (n 26), 76 ff.

[64] BGE 114 Ia 413 (14 December 1988) para 3c, 416–417.

[65] See for example Art. 59(2)(c) Constitution of the Canton of Berne; § 22(3)(b) Constitution of the Canton of Lucerne.

today, and also at the cantonal level initiatives are only very rarely declared inadmissible on this basis.[66]

4. INSTITUTIONAL AND PROCEDURAL FRAMEWORK

4.1 Federal Level

4.1.1 Popular initiative

In order to launch a popular initiative, its authors (the initiative committee) must, first of all, submit the signature sheet to the Federal Chancellery (the general administrative office of the Federal Council (the federal government)). The Federal Chancellery carries out a preliminary, purely formal examination of the initiative: it reviews whether the signature sheet contains the information required by law (names of the authors of the initiative, title of the initiative, a withdrawal clause etc.)[67] and whether the title of the initiative is not mis-leading.[68] Members of the initiative committee may challenge a decision of the Federal Chancellery on the validity of the signature sheet or its decision to amend a misleading initiative title before the Federal Court (Switzerland's highest court).[69] If these formal requirements are met, the initiative is pub-lished in the Federal Gazette.[70] From the moment of official publication, the authors have 18 months to collect and submit the required 100,000 signa-tures.[71] After the collection of the signatures, but before the popular vote is held, both chambers of the Federal Assembly, based on a report of the Federal Council,[72] review the initiative for its compliance with the limits set out above in Section 3. If one of the limits is violated, the Federal Assembly declares the initiative invalid.[73] It can also declare only parts of it invalid, but it cannot split an initiative up into different parts or amend its wording.[74] If the initiative is

---

[66] See Tornay (n 26) 72 ff.
[67] Art. 68 and 69(1) Federal Act on Political Rights.
[68] Art. 69(2) Federal Act on Political Rights.
[69] Art. 80(3) Federal Act on Political Rights
[70] Art. 69(4) Federal Act on Political Rights.
[71] Art. 139(1) Federal Constitution.
[72] See Art. 97(1)(a) Federal Act on the Federal Assembly (*Bundesgesetz über die Bundesversammlung (Parlamentsgesetz) vom 13. Dezember 2002* (SR 171.10)). An English translation of the Act can be found at www.admin.ch/opc/en/classified -compilation/20010664/index.html, accessed 15 May 2020.
[73] Art. 139(3) Federal Constitution.
[74] Art. 99 Federal Act on the Federal Assembly; see Daniel Moeckli, 'Die Teilungültigerklärung und Aufspaltung von Volksinitiativen', (2014) 115 Schweizerisches Zentralblatt für Staats- und Verwaltungsrecht 579, 597.

found to comply with the limits, it is put to the vote. Since the review is carried out by the Federal Assembly, the usual parliamentary procedure applies. As a consequence, there are no specific due process guarantees (such as a right of members of the initiative committee to be heard by parliament before the decision is made) that would apply. The reasons for the Federal Assembly's decision can only be gleaned from the minutes of the parliamentary debate.

The decision of the Federal Assembly on the validity of an initiative is final; it cannot be challenged before the Federal Court (or any other body). This follows from Article 189(4) of the Federal Constitution, which states in its first sentence that acts of the Federal Assembly (as well as those of the Federal Council) may not be challenged before the Federal Court. Although, according to the second sentence of this provision, exceptions to this general rule can be provided for by law, no such exception has been created with regard to initiatives or referendums.[75]

The fact that it is the federal parliament that decides on the validity of popular initiatives is highly problematic from the perspective of the rule of law: whether an initiative meets or does not meet the requirements listed in the Federal Constitution is a purely legal decision. Therefore, the final word on this question should not belong to parliament, a body that acts according to political considerations.[76] A look at the respective debates in the Federal Assembly (especially its first chamber, the National Council) confirms that it is often the case that political instead of legal arguments are advanced in favour of the validity, or lack of validity, of a given initiative.[77] Unfortunately, however, there is little prospect that the existing procedure could be reformed as a majority of parliamentarians are simply not willing to give up (or share) the power to decide on the validity of initiatives.

4.1.2 Mandatory and optional referendum

As in the case of popular initiatives, Article 189(4) of the Federal Constitution prevents federal mandatory and optional referendums from being challenged before the Federal Court (or any other body) for failing to meet the limits set out in Section 3 above. Thus, for example, a complaint brought against the vote on the corporate tax reform proposal mentioned in Section 3.2.2 above,

---

[75]   See Walter Haller, 'Art. 189' in Ehrenzeller, Schindler, Schweizer and Vallender (eds) (n 55) n 62 ff.

[76]   Biaggini (n 44) Art. 139 n 10; Yvo Hangartner/Bernhard Ehrenzeller, 'Art. 173' in Ehrenzeller, Schindler, Schweizer and Vallender (eds) (n 55) n 10–110; Pierre Tschannen, *Stimmrecht und politische Verständigung: Beiträge zu einem erneuerten Verständnis von direkter Demokratie* (Helbing & Lichtenhahn 1995) n 726.

[77]   See for the example of the *'Durchsetzungsinitiative'*: *Amtliches Bulletin* (Official Bulletin) 2014, N 490 ff.

which was triggered by an optional referendum, was declared inadmissible by the Federal Court: the decision of the Federal Assembly to link together in one federal act a tax reform and measures to increase the funding for the public pensions scheme, the court held, was covered by Article 189(4) of the Federal Constitution and could, therefore, not be challenged for violating the requirement of consistency of the subject matter.[78] Similarly, at the federal level, the formulation of a referendum question cannot be reviewed for its compliance with the requirement of clarity. There is only one exception where the Federal Court allows a challenge against a federal referendum, namely when it becomes clear after the popular vote that the Federal Council has provided, during the referendum campaign, incomplete or misleading information on the proposal voted on. This type of situation is, according to the court, not covered by Article 189(4) of the Federal Constitution.[79]

4.2 Cantonal Level

4.2.1 Popular initiative

The procedure for reviewing cantonal popular initiatives is largely similar to the one at the federal level, although there are some interesting deviations.[80] In virtually all cantons there is, before the collection of signatures is allowed to start, a preliminary formal examination of the initiative by some administrative authority, which is meant to ensure that the signature sheet contains the information required by law and that the information provided is not misleading. In two cantons, however, the review carried out before the collection of signatures also includes a substantive admissibility test: in St Gallen and Vaud, the cantonal government reviews the initiative proposal for its compliance with all the formal and substantive limits; it may declare an initiative inadmissible already at this stage.[81]

After the collection of the required number of signatures it is in most cantons, as at the federal level, parliament that decides on the validity of a popular initiative. In the canton of Zurich, a decision to declare an initiative

---

[78] Judgment of the Federal Court 1C_323/2019, 1C_324/2019 of 24 June 2019, para 3.

[79] Judgment of the Federal Court 1C_315/2018, 1C_316/2018, 1C_329/2018, 1C_331/2018, 1C_335/2018, 1C_337/2018, 1C_339/2018, 1C_347/2018 of 10 April 2019, paras 2.1, 2.5; BGE 138 I 61 (20 December 2011) para 4.5, 75 ff, para 7, 84 ff.

[80] For an overview, see Auer (n 4) 438–440.

[81] Art. 36 Act on Referendum and Initiative of the Canton of St. Gallen (*Gesetz über Referendum und Initiative vom 27. November 1967* (sGS 125.1)); Art. 80 Constitution of the Canton of Vaud (*Constitution du Canton de Vaud du 14 avril 2003* (SR 131.231)).

invalid requires a two-thirds majority in parliament,[82] in Basel-Landschaft and Graubünden such a decision can only be taken if the illegality of the initiative proposal is *obvious*.[83] In three cantons, the decision on validity is made by the government rather than parliament – in St Gallen and Vaud, as mentioned above, before the collection of signatures, in Geneva afterwards.[84] In the canton of Jura, the relevant legislation provides that parliament must provide the initiative committee the opportunity to be heard before it takes its decision on validity.[85] In other cantons, it is general practice to consult the initiative committee before the decision, without there being an explicit guarantee to be heard.[86] Nevertheless, the Federal Court has held that the Federal Constitution does not provide voters or members of an initiative committee a right to be heard when a parliament decides on the validity of an initiative; given the transparent procedure of parliament and the possibility for individuals to approach parliamentarians, there was no justification for such a right.[87] The Federal Court has recognised a right to be heard, albeit one that is rather limited in scope, only for those cases where the validity decision is taken by a government before the collection of signatures.[88]

In a number of cantons, the decision on the (in)validity of an initiative can be challenged before a cantonal court: in Nidwalden, Jura, Vaud and Geneva before the constitutional court,[89] in Graubünden and St Gallen before the administrative court.[90] In the canton of Basel-Stadt, parliament can, instead of

---

[82]   Art. 28(3) Constitution of the Canton of Zurich.

[83]   § 29(1) Constitution of the Canton of Basel-Landschaft (*Verfassung des Kantons Basel-Landschaft vom 17. Mai 1984* (SR 131.222.2)); Art. 14(1) Constitution of the Canton of Graubünden.

[84]   Art. 60(1) Constitution of the Republic and the Canton of Geneva (*Constitution de la République et canton de Genève du 14 octobre 2012* (SR 131.234)).

[85]   Art. 89(2) and 90(3) of the Act on Political Rights of the Canton of Jura (*Loi sur les droits politiques du 26 octobre 1978* (RSJU 161.1)).

[86]   Camilla Jacquemoud, 'Le droit d'être entendu lors du contrôle de validité des initiatives', Jusletter, 27 May 2019, n 1, https://jusletter.weblaw.ch/juslissues/2019/981/le -droit-d-etre-ente_2547d39135.html, accessed 15 May 2020.

[87]   BGE 145 I 167 (26 November 2018) para 4.2, 172; BGE 123 I 63 (12 March 1997) para 2, 66 ff.

[88]   BGE 145 I 167 (26 November 2018) para 4.3, 172 ff.

[89]   Art. 69(2)(5.) Constitution of the Canton of Nidwalden (*Verfassung des Kantons Nidwalden vom 10. Oktober 1965* (SR 131.216.2)); Art. 104(2)(c) Constitution of the Republic and the Canton of Jura (*Constitution de la République et Canton du Jura du 20 mars 1977* (SR 131.235)); Art. 19 Act on the Constitutional Jurisdiction of the Canton of Vaud (*Loi sur la juridiction constitutionelle du 5 octobre 2004*; RSV 173.32); Art. 130B(1)(c) of the Act on the Judicial Organisation of the Canton of Geneva (*Loi sur l'organisation judicaire du 26 septembre 2010* (SG E 2 05)).

[90]   Art. 14(3) Constitution of the Canton of Graubünden; Art. 59bis(1) Act on the Administrative Procedure of the Canton of St Gallen (*Gesetz über die Verwaltungsrechtspflege vom 16. Mai 1965* (sGS 951.1)).

deciding itself, refer the question of the validity of an initiative to the court of appeal.[91] If parliament decides itself, that decision can be challenged before the constitutional court.[92] Regardless of which organ has decided on the validity of an initiative at the cantonal level, the final cantonal decision can, according to Article 82(c) of the Federal Act on the Federal Court,[93] be challenged before the Federal Court.

4.2.2   Mandatory and optional referendum

The procedural system of the canton in question will determine the organ that is in charge of ensuring compliance of a referendum question with the limits set out in Section 3 and whether it is possible to challenge a referendum proposal before a cantonal court. As in the case of popular initiatives, however, based on Article 82(c) of the Federal Act on the Federal Court, it is in any case possible to challenge cantonal referendums before the Federal Court as final instance. For example, a voter can bring a complaint that a revision of the cantonal constitution by the cantonal parliament, triggering the mandatory referendum, violates the requirement of consistency of the subject matter[94] or that the wording of a referendum question adopted by the cantonal government or the cantonal parliament is misleading.[95]

5.   PRACTICAL RELEVANCE OF THE LEGAL LIMITS

At the federal level, out of the 342 popular initiatives that have attracted the required 100,000 signatures since the existence of this instrument, only four have been declared invalid: one for not being compatible with peremptory norms of international law, one for not being practically feasible and two for failing to meet the requirement of consistency of the subject matter. In addition, one initiative has been declared partially invalid. These cases have been described above. With regard to mandatory and optional referendums, I am not aware of a federal referendum that would have been annulled for failing to meet one of the limits described above.

For the cantonal level, there are no reliable figures for the total of initiatives or referendums declared invalid in all 26 cantons. What can be safely stated, however, is that the share of cantonal initiatives declared invalid is

---

[91]   § 91(1)(g) Constitution of the Canton of Basel-Stadt.

[92]   § 16 Act on Initiative and Referendum of the Canton of Basel-Stadt (*Gesetz betreffend Initiative und Referendum vom 16. Januar 1991* (SG 131.100)).

[93]   *Bundesgesetz über das Bundesgericht vom 17. Juni 2005* (SR 173.110).

[94]   BGE 129 I 366 (27 August 2003).

[95]   BGE 121 I 1 (6 March 1995); BGE 106 Ia 20 (28 March 1980).

considerably higher than that of federal initiatives. According to one author, 170 cantonal initiatives have been declared invalid since 1970, amounting to roughly 15 per cent of initiatives.[96] Similarly, it is not uncommon for a cantonal mandatory or optional referendum to be annulled because it fails to meet one of the formal limits. Interestingly, decisions regarding the (in)validity of cantonal initiatives that have been made by a judicial body are statistically more likely to be upheld by the Federal Court than those that have been made by parliament.[97]

6. CONCLUSION

The low legal hurdles that are imposed on direct-democratic instruments at the federal level, combined with the lenient standard of review employed by the Federal Assembly, have resulted in an increasing number of votes on popular initiatives that are, in all likelihood, contrary to international law.[98] Similarly, in recent years, the people have been repeatedly asked to vote on initiative and referendum proposals that arguably violate the requirement of consistency of the subject matter.[99] Thus, Switzerland's practice at the federal level cannot be said to be in line with the Venice Commission's Code of Good Practice on Referendums, which states that texts submitted to a referendum 'must not be contrary to international law' and that 'there must be an intrinsic connection between the various parts of each question put to the vote'.[100]

In order to address this problematic state of affairs, a number of reform proposals have been put forward by a range of actors, including the Federal Council, members of parliament and legal scholars. According to a first set of proposals, the review of popular initiatives prior to the start of the collection of signatures should be extended to include a non-binding assessment, carried out by a governmental department, of the conformity of popular initiatives with international law. Second, it has been suggested that the competence to review popular initiatives for their validity after submission of the required number of signatures should be transferred to the Federal Court or some newly created

---

[96] Maximilian Schubiger, '"In dubio pro populo": The Invalidation Process of Popular Initiatives at the Subnational Level in Switzerland', Poster Presentation (Geneva, 2019), on file with author.

[97] Tornay (n 26) 57–58.

[98] For some examples see Daniel Moeckli, 'Of Minarets and Foreign Criminals: Swiss Direct Democracy and Human Rights', (2011) 11 Human Rights Law Review 774.

[99] The votes on the 'Ecopop' initiative in 2014 and the tax reform proposal in 2019, both described in Section 3.2.2 above, are the most glaring cases.

[100] Code of Good Practice on Referendums (n 53), paras III.3, III.2.

expert body; or that it should be possible to bring a legal challenge against the Federal Assembly's decision; or, at the very least, that the Federal Assembly should be able to request a legal opinion from the Federal Court. Third, there have been proposals to change the legal limits themselves so that, for example, also popular initiatives that violate other norms of international law than those that are of a peremptory nature could be declared invalid or that the requirement of consistency of the subject matter would be applied more stringently.[101]

However, virtually all efforts to reform the legal regime of the federal direct-democratic instruments have failed so far. Now that these instruments have been in use for considerably more than a century, it has become politically nearly impossible to impose any new restrictions on them. In addition, as far as the institutional framework is concerned, parliament is apparently not willing to give up (or share) its power to decide on the validity of initiatives and referendums.

---

[101] For an overview of the most important reform proposals, see Ulrich Häfelin, Walter Haller, Helen Keller and Daniela Thurnherr, *Schweizerisches Bundesstaatsrecht* (9th ed, Schulthess, 2016) 551–555; Pascal Mahon, 'Les droits politiques' in Oliver Diggelmann, Maya Hertig Randall and Benjamin Schindler (eds), *Verfassungsrecht der Schweiz*, Vol. 2 (Schulthess 2020) V.14, n 41–51.

5. Liechtenstein

Wilfried Marxer

1. INTRODUCTION

There are two political levels in Liechtenstein: the national and the municipal. At the national level, the Government, the Reigning Prince and Parliament are the governing bodies of the executive and legislative powers. The judiciary consists, in public law matters, of the Administrative Court and the Constitutional Court as the highest instance. At the local level, consisting of 11 municipalities, the mayor as head of the municipality's administration presides over the municipality, accompanied by an elected, non-professional municipal council.

At both the national and the local levels, Liechtenstein has a broad repertoire of direct-democratic rights. These are clearly regulated by law,[1] the basis being the Constitution,[2] with further elaboration in the Political Rights Act[3] and the Municipality Act.[4] These laws lay down the formal and substantial requirements of the direct-democratic instruments as well as the control procedures and the relevant responsibilities. This applies in particular to the proactive initiative, which demands more guidelines than the rejective initiative.

The use of direct-democratic rights is limited to those entitled to vote, that is Liechtenstein citizens with residence in Liechtenstein, starting with the age of 18 years.[5] Foreigners and Liechtenstein citizens living abroad do not have the right to vote or to sign direct-democratic requests.

---

[1] Published in the Liechtenstein Legal Gazette (*Liechtensteinisches Landesgesetzblatt* (LGBl.)) <www.gesetze.li> accessed 29 March 2021.

[2] Constitution of the Principality of Liechtenstein (*Verfassung des Fürstentums Liechtenstein* vom 5. Oktober 1921; LGBl. 1921.015) https://www.regierung.li/media/medienarchiv/101_28_08_2019_en.pdf?t=3, accessed 29 March 2021.

[3] *Gesetz vom 17. Juli 1973 über die Ausübung der politischen Volksrechte in Landesangelegenheiten*; LGBl. 1973.050.

[4] *Gemeindegesetz* vom 20. März 1996; LGBl. 1996.076.

[5] Art. 29(2) Constitution.

2.   DIRECT-DEMOCRATIC INSTRUMENTS

The introduction of instruments of direct democracy in Liechtenstein was inspired and influenced by the adoption of corresponding regulations in Switzerland, with cantonal models playing a greater role than the federal one.[6] In practice, three procedures that lead to a popular vote are paramount: the proactive initiative, which can be triggered by the people or municipalities, the rejective initiative, also triggered by the people or municipalities, and the legislature-initiated referendum. Since the introduction of these instruments with the adoption of the new Constitution in 1921, more than 100 national ballots have been held. The scope of the rejective initiative was initially restricted to legal acts and financial decisions. In 1992 it was extended to international treaties. In 2003, a comprehensive revision of the Constitution based on a proactive citizens' initiative launched by the Princely House established several new direct-democratic instruments, but they have not yet been used in practice.[7]

Popular votes can be triggered by Parliament, by the people through the collection of signatures and by municipalities through concurring resolutions of a certain number of municipal assemblies with the goal to initiate a national ballot.[8] However, referendums initiated by municipalities have never achieved great practical relevance compared with citizens' initiatives.

There are no restrictions regarding the place where signatures can be collected. Signatures must be given personally on a sheet of paper as the electronic signature collection has not yet been implemented.

The regulations of direct-democratic rights and procedures at local, that is municipal, level differ from those at national level. In addition to municipal

---

[6]   See generally Wilfried Marxer, *Direkte Demokratie in Liechtenstein: Entwicklung, Regelungen, Praxis*, Verlag der Liechtensteinischen Akademischen Gesellschaft 2018; Christian Geisselmann, *Direkte Demokratie in der liechtensteinischen Landesverfassung und im österreichischen Bundes-Verfassungsgesetz*, GMG 2017; Martin Batliner, *Die politischen Volksrechte im Fürstentum Liechtenstein*, Institut du Fédéralisme Fribourg 1993; Herbert Wille, *Die liechtensteinische Staatsordnung*, Verlag der Liechtensteinischen Akademischen Gesellschaft 2015; Liechtenstein-Institut (ed.), *Kommentar zur liechtensteinischen Verfassung* www.verfassung.li, accessed 29 March 2021.

[7]   See Marxer (n 6) 316–29; the Venice Commission criticised several parts of the amendment: Council of Europe, European Commission for Democracy through Law, Opinion on the Amendments to the Constitution of Liechtenstein proposed by the Princely House of Liechtenstein, adopted by the Venice Commission at its 53rd plenary session (Venice, 13–14 December 2002).

[8]   Peter Bussjäger, Art. 64, 65, 66 and 66bis, in: Liechtenstein-Institut (n 6).

votes on regulations, financial expenditure and other matters,[9] naturalisation votes can also be held at the municipal level; only those municipal citizens[10] who are resident in the municipality concerned are entitled to vote in naturalisation matters.[11]

2.1   Proactive Initiative

The right to trigger a proactive initiative is laid down in the Constitution, which states that the right to table legislative proposals is vested in the Reigning Prince, Parliament and citizens entitled to vote.[12] In contrast to Switzerland, the right of initiative is not limited to constitutional amendments, but extends to ordinary legislation. In contrast, ordinances issued by the Government or administrative acts[13] cannot be targeted by means of a proactive initiative.

According to Article 80(2) of the Political Rights Act, proactive initiatives can be submitted in the form of a prepared draft (formulated initiative) or as a simple suggestion (non-formulated initiative). In practice, the non-formulated initiative has gained hardly any significance – only in 1925, 2008 and 2016 were non-formulated initiatives submitted.[14] The primary reason for this is that in the case of a non-formulated initiative, Parliament only has to debate it. If Parliament rejects the initiative, no popular vote is held. Thus, the non-formulated initiative amounts to a mere agenda initiative. In contrast, the rejection of a formulated initiative necessarily leads to a popular vote, the result of which is binding on Parliament. Thus, the initiators can pursue their objectives more effectively with a formulated initiative, while the effort required to collect signatures is the same for both variants.

The Constitution stipulates that initiatives can be brought about either by a nationwide collection of signatures from voters[15] or, alternatively, by res-

---

[9]   Art. 41 and 42 Municipality Act.

[10]   Liechtenstein citizenship is combined with citizenship of one of the eleven municipalities.

[11]   Art. 21(3) Municipality Act.

[12]   Art. 64 Constitution.

[13]   In 1938, an initiative concerning the authorisation of a wine tavern was rejected by Parliament as this was not a matter for the legislature but an administrative matter; see Marxer (n 6) 140.

[14]   In 1925, three non-formulated initiatives to amend the Tax Act were submitted simultaneously, in 2008 the issue was a pension insurance for state employees, in 2016 it was work-related health insurance premiums. All these initiatives had no immediate effect. See Marxer (n 6) 169–74.

[15]   Art. 64(2) and Art. 64(4) Constitution; Art. 67(b) and Art. 69 Political Rights Act.

olutions of municipal assemblies.[16] 'Municipal assembly' means the people entitled to vote in the respective municipality, thus not the municipal council or the mayor.

For a proactive legislative initiative, either 1,000 signatures from voters nationwide or the unanimous decision of three municipal assemblies are required.[17] If a proactive initiative targets the Constitution, either 1,500 signatures or resolutions from four municipal assemblies are required.[18] At present, the signature requirements correspond to approximately 5 and 7.5 per cent of those entitled to vote, respectively.[19]

In practice, municipal requests have not become important. The few municipal initiatives that were launched in the 1930s proved to be inadmissible, became invalid or did not come about.[20] The number of signatures which is required to achieve three or four municipal votes may be, depending on the number of inhabitants in the respective municipalities, even higher than the nationwide required 1,000 or 1,500 signatures, respectively. Thus, this instrument has become even less attractive over time, compared with the 1920s and 1930s when the nationwide quorum of signatures was relatively higher.[21] Although the necessary number of signatures at national level, laid down in the Constitution, has been raised several times since 1921, it has not grown to the same extent as the number of voters.[22] At the municipal level, on the other hand, one-sixth of registered voters in a municipality must sign a request, so the number of required signatures has increased steadily since 1921.[23]

---

[16]   Art. 64(2) and Art. 64(4) Constitution; Art. 67(a) and Art. 68 Political Rights Act.

[17]   Art. 64(2) Constitution.

[18]   Art. 64(4) Constitution.

[19]   At the latest national popular vote on 24 November 2019, 20,243 persons were entitled to vote.

[20]   Marxer (n 6) 263–68. One initiative was declared inadmissible as it targeted an administrative matter, one initiative failed to achieve a quorum of three municipal resolutions, another initiative became obsolete due to ongoing developments.

[21]   Moreover, until the 1970s decisions of the municipal assemblies were not taken in ballots but in real assemblies where citizens could submit a request spontaneously, including requests concerning a municipal initiative. Therefore, there was no need to collect signatures.

[22]   In 1921, either 400 or 600 signatures were required, which corresponded to circa 22 or 33 per cent of voters, respectively (women's suffrage was not yet introduced); see Marxer (n 6) 252.

[23]   See Marxer (n 6) 251–52 and 268–73.

A majority approval of a proactive initiative at the ballot box is binding on Parliament and the Government.[24] However, for a new law to enter into force, the Reigning Prince must also give the sanction, that is, sign the bill.[25]

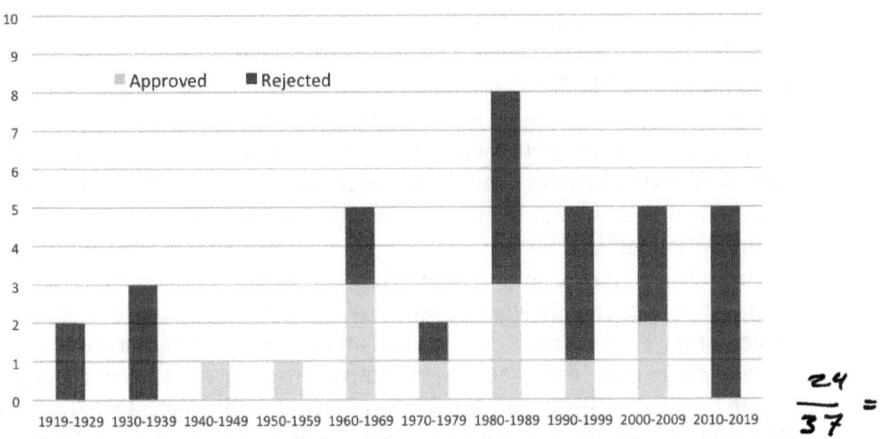

Sources: Official announcements after ballots; see Marxer (n 6) 551–56 (updated); (since 2002); Liechtenstein statistics (section 9: *Rechtspflege und Politik*).

Figure 5.1   *Number of proactive initiatives voted on (1919–2019)*

2.2   Rejective Initiative

The rejective initiative is directed against a resolution of Parliament. This may be a constitutional amendment, a law, a financial resolution or an assent to an international treaty.[26] Just as with the proactive initiative, ordinances issued by the Government[27] or administrative acts cannot be targeted by means of a rejective initiative.

---

[24]   Art. 66(4) and Art. 66(6) Constitution; Art. 83(6) Political Rights Act.

[25]   Art. 65(1) Constitution. The Prince has refused to sign a bill only once: in 1961, after a popular vote on a proactive citizens' initiative on the hunting law.

[26]   Art. 66 and 66bis Constitution.

[27]   In 1991, the Government decided to quit school education on Saturdays. This was regulated in an ordinance (*Verordnung*). A rejective initiative against the ordinance was declared invalid as it was directed against a law passed by Parliament. As a consequence, a committee launched a proactive initiative to amend the school law by

Parliament may declare resolutions as urgent, so that they are prevented from being subject to the rejective initiative.[28] In practice, this concerns only a few justified cases. For example, the resolution on the state budget for the coming year is regularly declared urgent.[29] Moreover, financial resolutions of Parliament are only subject to the rejective initiative if they exceed a certain threshold value. In the current version, this is a one-off expenditure of 500,000 Swiss francs (ca. 460,000 euros) or a recurrent annual expenditure of 250,000 Swiss francs (ca. 230,000 euros).[30]

Rejective initiatives against legislative or financial resolutions require either 1,000 signatures nationwide or the resolution of three municipal assemblies. Rejective initiatives against constitutional resolutions or resolutions on international treaties require either 1,500 signatures or the resolutions of four municipal assemblies.[31]

A rejective initiative may only be launched against parliamentary resolutions that have been published by means of an official promulgation after the session of the Parliament.[32] This includes all resolutions of Parliament that are in principle eligible for a rejective initiative, which are not declared urgent and, in the case of financial resolutions, exceed the above-mentioned threshold value. A rejective initiative may only be held against the resolution of Parliament as it is published. A rejective initiative against parts of a resolution is not permitted.[33]

The first rejective initiative was launched in 1926, the last one to date in 2018.[34] Twenty-eight ballots have been held during this period following rejective initiatives. Twelve parliamentary resolutions have been accepted, while 16 resolutions have been rejected. Of these 28 resolutions, 17 were bills, ten were financial resolutions and one rejective initiative targeted an international treaty. No rejective initiative has been triggered against a parliamentary resolu-

---

introducing the obligation to have school education regularly also on Saturdays. The initiative was rejected in the ballot and the Government was allowed to reduce schooling to five days. See Marxer (n 6) 162, 370, 427 and 436.

[28]   Art. 66(1) Constitution; Art. 75(4) Political Rights Act.

[29]   See for example Finance Act for 2020 (*Finanzgesetz vom 7. November 2019 für das Jahr 2020*, LGBl. 2019.314). The act ends with the wording: 'Parliament has declared this legislative resolution to be urgent.'

[30]   Art. 66(1) Constitution.

[31]   Art. 70(1a) and 70a(1a) Political Rights Act.

[32]   Art. 70(1)a, Art. 70a(1), Art. 75(1)b and Art. 76(1) Political Rights Act; Art. 66(1), 66(2) and 66bis(1) Constitution.

[33]   Marxer (n 6) 185–91.

[34]   See Marxer (n 6) 551–56.

tion on an amendment of the Constitution so far. Only one popular vote, in the 1930s, has been held as a result of a municipal rejective initiative.[35]

A majority approval at the ballot box supports the resolution taken by Parliament. However, for a new law to enter into force, the Reigning Prince must also give the sanction, that is, sign the bill. He has, so far, always done so when bills had been approved in a ballot after a rejective initiative. If a parliamentary resolution does not find a majority in the ballot, the draft is definitely rejected[36] and no further action of the Prince is required.

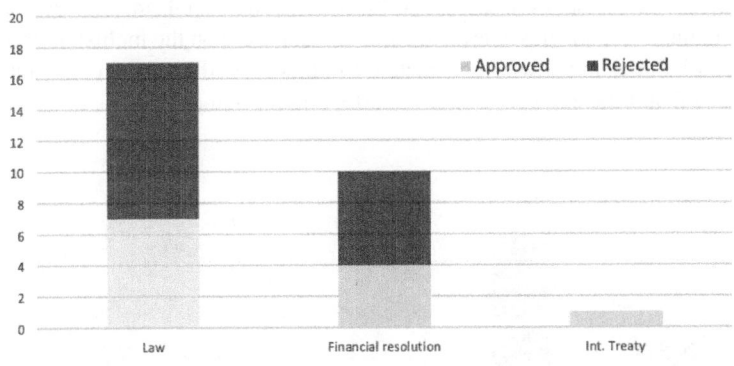

Source: See Figure 5.1.

Figure 5.2   Number of rejective initiatives voted on (1919–2019)

2.3   Legislature-initiated Referendum

Parliament may, on its own initiative, submit a resolution which has been approved by the required majority[37] to the people for a decision.[38] As in the

---

[35]   Marxer (n 6) 136–37, 140, 262–73. In 1937, Parliament passed a law banning warehouses against which decisions were taken in five municipalities to hold a referendum. In the vote, the parliamentary draft was adopted with 59.1 per cent of the votes; see Marxer (n 6) 266.

[36]   Art. 66(4) and Art. 66bis(2) Constitution.

[37]   As a rule, a resolution of Parliament requires the presence of two-thirds of the members of Parliament and a simple majority of those present (Art. 58(1) Constitution). For constitutional amendments, either unanimity at a meeting or a majority of three-quarters of those present at two consecutive meetings is required (Art. 112(2) Constitution).

[38]   Art. 67(c) Political Rights Act.

case of the rejective initiative, this may concern legal acts (constitutional amendments or laws), financial resolutions with the same expenditure thresholds as with the rejective initiative and assent to international treaties – and again only holds for resolutions that are not declared urgent by Parliament.[39]

While a partial rejective initiative requested by the people is not permitted, Parliament is free to split its resolution into different parts and submit them separately to the vote of the people.[40] However, this has not happened so far.

As with the rejective initiative, a majority approval at the ballot box will support the parliamentary resolution, but in addition the princely sanction is also required. On the other hand, a resolution is definitely rejected if there is no majority in the ballot, and then no further action of the Prince is necessary.

Parliament is also empowered to call a popular vote on the inclusion of individual principles in a law to be enacted.[41] In this case, the vote is consultative, meaning that it has no legally binding effect on Parliament.[42]

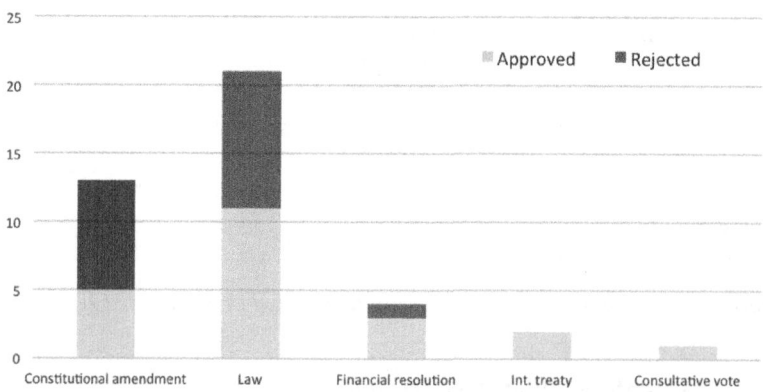

Source: See Figure 5.1.

Figure 5.3   *Number of legislature-initiated referendums voted on (1919–2019)*

---

[39] Art. 66(1) and (2) and 66bis(1) Constitution.
[40] Art. 77(3) Political Rights Act; see also Marxer (n 6) 185–91.
[41] Art. 66(3) Constitution.
[42] A consultative vote was only held once, in 1968. It concerned the question of whether women's voting rights should be introduced in Liechtenstein. Not only men were asked, but separately also women. The result was that women welcomed this by a narrow majority of 50.5 per cent, while only 39.8 per cent of men were in favour. Voter turnout was less than 60 per cent, whereas in other votes at that time it was usually above 80 per cent. Women's suffrage was finally introduced in 1984 by popular

2.4 Other Instruments of Direct Democracy

The Constitution of 1921 also introduced the possibility for the people to make a request to convene[43] or dissolve[44] Parliament, which results in a popular vote on this issue. At present, 1,000 signatures from Liechtenstein citizens eligible to vote or three resolutions adopted by municipal assemblies are required for the convocation; while for the dissolution of Parliament, 1,500 signatures or four municipal resolutions are required. Only once in 1928 did a request for the dissolution of Parliament come about, but it did not entail a popular vote as Parliament meanwhile had already been dissolved by the Prince and new elections had been called.[45]

In 2003, a comprehensive revision of the Constitution was carried out on the basis of a proactive citizens' initiative launched by the Prince and the Hereditary Prince.[46] The revision was approved in the referendum with 64.3 per cent. In addition to other constitutional amendments, various new direct-democratic instruments were introduced: a motion of no-confidence against the Reigning Prince, an initiative for the abolition of the monarchy, a referendum on the appointment of judges and a secession right for the municipalities. None of these instruments had been made use of at the time of writing. The instruments are briefly described below.

A motion of no-confidence against the Reigning Prince may be tabled by 1,500 voters, on which Parliament must make a recommendation and the people then vote.[47] If the motion is adopted in the popular vote, further deliberations are held within the Princely House in accordance with the Law on the Princely House[48] and measures may be taken by the princely family, such as a warning, disciplinary action or even dismissal of the Prince.

---

vote – only men being entitled to vote – after it had been rejected in popular votes in 1971 and 1973. All these popular votes were initiated by Parliament.

[43] Art. 48(2) Constitution.

[44] Art. 48(3) Constitution.

[45] See Marxer (n 6), 211–15.

[46] See Frank Marcinkowski and Wilfried Marxer, *Politische Kommunikation und Volksentscheid: Eine Fallstudie zur Verfassungsreform in Liechtenstein* (Nomos 2011). In fact, an appeal was made to the Constitutional Court as to whether the Prince could make use of the citizens' right of initiative. The court ruled that at least the Hereditary Prince was allowed to do so and thus the initiative was permitted: StGH 2002/73 of 3 February 2003; see also Marxer (n 6) 246.

[47] Art. 13ter Constitution.

[48] *Hausgesetz des Fürstlichen Hauses Liechtenstein* vom 26. Oktober 1993; LGBl. 1993.100.

A proactive initiative by 1,500 voters may also be submitted to abolish the monarchy.[49] If the initiative is adopted in the referendum, Parliament is charged with drawing up a constitution on a republican basis and submitting it to another popular vote. The Reigning Prince may also submit a proposal for a new constitution. The second popular vote is required by the Constitution and thus is to be qualified as a law-initiated referendum. If monarchy is abolished in this way by majority vote, the Reigning Prince cannot veto the decision of the people.[50]

Referendums initiated by the Government or the Reigning Prince (executive-initiated referendums) do not exist in Liechtenstein.

2.5   Instruments at the Municipal Level

Direct-democratic rights at the municipal level are regulated in the Municipality Act, while procedural regulations sometimes refer to provisions of the Political Rights Act.[51] Direct-democratic rights at the municipal level are exercised in the municipal assembly, that is, an assembly of the people entitled to vote in the specific municipality, as opposed to the competences of the mayor and the municipal council, which are elected by the voters for a term of office of four years.[52] The municipal council can also order a decision to be taken at the ballot box instead of at an assembly.[53]

The municipal assembly has, among other competences, the power to enact the municipal ordinance and certain regulations and to take decisions that involve high expenditures, that is, expenditures exceeding 35 per cent of municipal revenues in the case of one-time expenditures and exceeding 20 per cent of municipal revenues in the case of recurring expenditures. In other words, these municipal resolutions are subject to a law-initiated referendum.[54] The municipal ordinance can determine whether further powers fall within the competence of the municipal assembly.[55]

In addition to this law-initiated referendum, certain resolutions of the municipal council are subject to the rejective initiative. A rejective initiative may be launched against decisions involving expenditures exceeding a threshold value that the municipal ordinance may set between 100,000 and 300,000

---

[49]   Art. 113 Constitution.

[50]   Art. 113(2) Constitution.

[51]   Art. 88(2) Municipality Act.

[52]   See Marxer (n 6) 335–58.

[53]   Art. 26 Municipality Act.

[54]   Art. 25 (2)–(5) Municipality Act.

[55]   Art. 25(3) Municipality Act mentions certain other regulations, the establishment of municipal institutions and membership in special purpose associations.

Swiss francs.[56] In addition, a rejective initiative may be launched against certain other resolutions of the municipal council, regardless of the expenditure involved, including the approval of the municipal accounts, the setting of the tax surcharge, the enactment of the zoning plan and building regulations and the imposition of levies.[57]

Proactive initiatives may be launched with regard to the same subject matters as those that are subject to the rejective initiative.[58]

Both the rejective and the proactive initiative at municipal level can be triggered by a sixth of the respective municipal electorate, thus the number of required signatures has increased by time.[59] If a rejective or a proactive initiative is launched, the proposal concerned must be tabled at a municipal assembly or, which is more common today, put to a ballot vote.[60]

Since the revision of 2003, individual municipalities are allowed to secede from the union. The majority of the resident voters of the municipality concerned decides on the initiation of the procedure. Secession is eventually effected by law or a state treaty; in the case of a state treaty a second vote must be held in the municipality after the treaty negotiations have been concluded.[61]

3. LEGAL LIMITS

The relevance of legal limits, both at the national and the municipal level, is mainly limited to the instrument of the proactive initiative. In the case of the rejective initiative and the legislature-initiated referendum, the proposal in question has undergone a parliamentary approval process, so that no further substantive examination of the subject matter of the vote is required.

3.1 Substantive Limit: Compliance with the Constitution and International Treaties

The Political Rights Act provides for a preliminary examination of proactive initiatives at the national level by Parliament. Upon registration, initiatives are examined by the Government to determine whether they comply with the Constitution and international treaties. The report of the Government on this

---

[56] Art. 41(1) Municipality Act.
[57] Art. 41(2) Municipality Act.
[58] Art. 42(1) Municipality Act.
[59] Art. 41(1) and 42(1) Municipality Act.
[60] Art. 26 Municipality Act; Art. 41(1) and 42(1) Municipality Act; see Marxer (n 6) 355–56.
[61] Art. 4(2) Constitution; see Marxer (n 6) 227–29; Peter Bussjäger, Art. 4, in: Liechtenstein-Institut (ed.) (n 6).

question is sent to Parliament for further action.[62] Parliament considers the initiative request at its next session. If it finds that the initiative is not in conformity with the Constitution or international treaties in force, it declares it null and void, that is, inadmissible.[63] The initiators may appeal to the Constitutional Court against a declaration of nullity of Parliament.[64] The preliminary examination procedure was introduced in 1992 in the course of Liechtenstein's accession to the European Economic Area in order to avoid signature collections and popular votes on issues that contradict the Constitution or international law.[65]

Two proactive initiatives have been declared inadmissible by Parliament since 1992. One initiative on climate protection was declared inadmissible in 2004.[66] The initiative wanted all future laws and ordinances in Liechtenstein to be in conformity with climate protection goals. The Government had concerns about the compatibility with existing international treaties and also criticised that the tiered structure of the legal system was not taken into account, as any one law would have an effect on numerous other laws.[67] Parliament followed this argumentation.[68] The initiators substantiated their submission with two legal opinions,[69] but the Constitutional Court supported the inadmissibility decision of Parliament.[70]

In 2013, a parliamentary proposal on pension insurance for state employees was announced, aiming at significant pension cuts with the goal of restructuring the state pension fund.[71] As opposition to the solution chosen by Parliament, a citizen registered a proactive initiative with his own proposal.

---

[62]   Art. 70b(1) Political Rights Act.
[63]   Art. 70b(2) Political Rights Act.
[64]   Art. 70b(3) Political Rights Act.
[65]   Law of 17 September 1992 on the amendment of the Political Rights Act; LGBl. 1992.100.
[66]   See Marxer (n 6) 155–56.
[67]   Regierung des Fürstentums Liechtenstein, *Bericht und Antrag der Regierung an den Landtag des Fürstentums Liechtenstein betreffend die Vorprüfung der angemeldeten Volksinitiative auf Erlass eines Klimaschutzgesetzes* (BuA, 2004/79), Vaduz 2004, https://bua.regierung.li accessed 29 June 2020.
[68]   Landtag des Fürstentums Liechtenstein, *Landtagsprotokoll 2004*, 1093–1105, www.landtag.li accessed 29 June 2020.
[69]   Giovanni Biaggini, *Zur Verfassungsmässigkeit der Volksinitiative 'Klimaschutzgesetz'. Stellungnahme zum Bericht und Antrag der Regierung an den Landtag des Fürstentums Liechtenstein zuhanden des Initiativkomitees, 2004*; Anne Peters, *Gutachten zur Frage der Völkerrechtskonformität einer Initiative für ein Klimaschutzgesetz in Liechtenstein*, 2004.
[70]   StGH 2004/70.
[71]   See Marxer (n 6) 156.

Based on a report prepared by two experts,[72] the Government recommended that Parliament declare the initiative inadmissible.[73] The experts had concluded that the initiative proposal to reduce the pensions of state employees was too radical and therefore violated well-acquired rights and also violated the principle of equality due to unequal treatment of different state employees. The initiator appealed against the decision of Parliament[74] to declare the initiative inadmissible. The Constitutional Court found no reason for inadmissibility and ruled that the initiative was sufficiently balanced to be admissible.[75] Thus Parliament finally admitted the initiative in March 2014.[76]

3.2   Formal Limits

3.2.1   Clarity of the question
When registering or submitting a proactive initiative it must be clearly evident what form it takes: non-formulated or formulated initiative, launched as a popular or municipal initiative.[77] This is checked by the Government during the registration procedure. In the case of a rejective initiative, clear designation of the parliamentary resolution against which the rejective initiative is directed is required.[78]

In the case of proactive initiatives, the initiators often give names and titles to their request that are as appropriate or as mobilising as possible and may play some role in the debates leading up to the popular vote. The title is usually also adopted in the official governmental information on the forthcoming

---

[72]   Erich Peter and Peter Bussjäger, *Gutachten zur Frage der Vereinbarkeit der Volksinitiative Pensionskasse win-win zum Gesetz über die betriebliche Personalvorsorge des Staates (SBPVG) mit der Verfassung des Fürstentums Liechtenstein*, Zürich/Bendern 2013.

[73]   Regierung des Fürstentums Liechtenstein, *Bericht und Antrag der Regierung an den Landtag des Fürstentums Liechtenstein betreffend die Vorprüfung der angemeldeten Volksinitiative 'winwin50' zum Gesetz über die betriebliche Personalvorsorge des Staates (SBPVG)* (BuA, 2013/85), Vaduz 2013, https://bua.regierung.li accessed 29 June 2020.

[74]   Landtag des Fürstentums Liechtenstein, *Landtagsprotokoll 2013*, 1761–79, www.landtag.li accessed 29 June 2020.

[75]   StGH 2013/183, www.gerichtsentscheidungen.li accessed 29 June 2020.

[76]   Landtag des Fürstentums Liechtenstein, *Landtagsprotokoll 2014*, 72–84, <www.landtag.li> accessed 29 June 2020. The initiator had already started a second initiative while the Constitutional Court was still deciding on the first one. Finally, both initiatives were admitted and the initiator withdrew neither the first nor the second one. Thus, both initiatives were brought to the ballot on the same day and both were rejected. See also Marxer (n 6) 156, 161, 173, 260, 283, 408.

[77]   Art. 68(3), Art. 69(5) and Art. 80(2) Political Rights Act.

[78]   Art. 68(3)a and Art. 69(5) Political Rights Act.

popular vote and even on the ballot paper.[79] If the initiators do not include a title themselves, a neutral name is chosen by the Government (for example, 'Draft of the initiative committee to amend the law XY').

The wording on the ballot paper is defined by the Political Rights Act. In the case of proactive initiatives, the question on the ballot paper must be: 'Do you want to accept the draft XY?' If a counterproposal of Parliament is submitted as an alternative to the proactive initiative, two questions are put to the voters: 'Do you wish to accept the initiators' draft? or Do you wish to accept Parliament's counterproposal?'[80] If there are more proposals on the same subject, the law again provides for a predefined, clear wording.[81] For this reason, there is no scope for suggestive or manipulative action by the authorities on the voting issue.[82] In the case of a rejective initiative, there is also no leeway as the request is directed against a clearly formulated resolution of Parliament.[83]

In order to avoid manipulation by the authorities, the Government is obliged to give room for the arguments in favour and against the initiative in the official voting brochure, so that both sides can put forward their arguments. These are the initiators or the committee of a proactive or rejective initiative on the one hand and the Government, Parliament or other stakeholders on the other. According to decisions of the Constitutional Court, the authorities, including the Reigning Prince, are also obliged to act fairly in referendum campaigns.[84]

---

[79]   For example, voting questions on the ballot papers were: 'Do you want to accept the draft of the initiative committee "For Life" (*Für das Leben*)'? (2005); 'Do you want to adopt the draft of the initiative committee "Yes – so that your vote counts" (*Ja – damit deine Stimme zählt*) for the amendment of the national constitution?' (2012). The same titles were used in the official information sent to the voters before the popular vote (for example, Regierung des Fürstentums Liechtenstein, Information zur Volksabstimmung vom 29. Juni und 1. Juli 2012 über das Initiativbegehren zur Abänderung der Landesverfassung ('Ja – damit deine Stimme zählt') (Source: Archive of the author)).

[80]   Art. 83(1) and 83(2) Political Rights Act.

[81]   Art. 83(3)–(5) Political Rights Act.

[82]   There is no precedent for highly misleading titles chosen by initiators for their initiative. A legal entitlement that the title chosen by the initiators will be adopted by the authorities does not exist.

[83]   Parliamentary resolutions against which a rejective initiative may be taken are listed in public announcement after the parliamentary sessions. In the case of a rejective initiative, it must be clearly stated against which resolution the referendum is directed.

[84]   *StGH* 1990/6 of 2 May 1991, in: *Liechtensteinische Entscheidsammlung 1991*, 133. The Constitutional Court criticised the practice of not giving the initiators of the popular initiative for the introduction of the State Treaty referendum the opportunity to present their arguments in the Government's official voting brochure. Since then, equal space has been given to the pro and contra sides in the voting brochure. In another decision, the Constitutional Court criticised the unbalanced appearance of the Prime

3.2.2 Consistency of the subject matter

Liechtenstein law does not explicitly require unity of subject matter in the case of proactive initiative requests.[85] However, judgments of the Constitutional Court and the Administrative Court are partially contradictory on this issue.[86] In a judgment in 2002, the Administrative Court even explicitly distanced itself from a different assessment of the Constitutional Court.[87]

Irrespective of this, both a formulated proactive initiative and a rejective initiative must clearly show the will of the initiators. In the case of a rejective initiative, this means that it must be clearly evident which parliamentary resolution is targeted. Among other things, this rules out the possibility of a single rejective initiative directed against two parliamentary resolutions. If necessary, two separate signature sheets have to be used in order to give those entitled to vote the opportunity to express their opinion and wish on both proposals separately – when signing the rejective initiative as well as finally at the ballot box. This is to identify the clear will of those eligible to vote. Nevertheless, since a partial rejective initiative is not allowed, a rejective initiative can always only be directed against a resolution of Parliament as a whole, even if the resolution addresses different subject matters, which may be the case, for example, with a resolution amending numerous provisions of a law. Parliament is allowed to split a resolution into parts in order to announce them separately for the rejective initiative. However, the law does not provide for the bundling of different resolutions into a single bill, and this is therefore not permitted and has not occurred in practice.

The requirement that the request must be clear also applies to formulated initiatives. This rules out, above all, the possibility of two different concerns being taken up in a single initiative. This would undermine a clear and separate expression of intent on each issue raised. However, experience has shown that, for example, in a proactive initiative for a comprehensive constitutional review, numerous constitutional articles were drafted in a single proposal for adoption or rejection.[88]

Minister and the Reigning Prince on state television before the popular vote on the European Economic Area and demanded fairness and balance in the campaign (*StGH* 1993/8 of 21 June 1993, in: *Liechtensteinische Entscheidsammlung 1993*, 91). See also Marxer (n 6) 319–20; Wille (n 6) 400.

[85] Batliner (n 6) 148–51; VBI (Administrative Complaints Court) 2002/96 of 12 November 2002, 121.

[86] Marxer (n 6) 125–32.

[87] *VBI* 2002/96; see Marxer (n 6) 131.

[88] Popular initiative launched by the Prince and the hereditary Prince to amend the constitution; ballot on 16 March 2003; approved with 64.3 per cent Yes votes; voter turnout of 87.7 per cent (www.abstimmung.li).

3.2.3   Consistency of the form

The consistency of the form concerns the proactive initiative as well as the rejective initiative. According to Article 69(5) of the Political Rights Act, it is inadmissible to join together completely different types of requests in the same proposal. Thus, a proactive initiative must concern either the Constitution or an ordinary law, but not these two levels at the same time. A rejective initiative must be directed against only one clearly identifiable parliamentary resolution, be it a constitutional, legislative or financial resolution. Finally, it is not permitted to join together a rejective and a proactive initiative in the same submission.[89]

Government must reject requests that violate the consistency of the form. However, initiators are allowed to remedy the defect within a reasonable period of time.[90] According to a 1964 opinion of the Constitutional Court, a reasonable period is four weeks in the case of a rejective initiative and six weeks in the case of a proactive initiative.[91]

3.2.4   Proposal to cover the costs

At the national level, initiators are required to submit a financing proposal in case of a proactive initiative that has cost effects. According to Article 64(3) of the Constitution, if the initiative request concerns the enactment of a law that is not already provided for by the Constitution and its implementation would result either in a non-current expenditure not already provided for by the finance act or in an expenditure over a longer period, such request shall only be considered by Parliament if it is accompanied by a proposal on how to cover the necessary funds. The Political Rights Act specifies that this applies if a one-off new expenditure exceeds 500,000 Swiss francs and a recurrent annual expenditure exceeds 250,000 Swiss francs.[92]

In practice, the requirement of a cover proposal has had little effect, at least in recent times. The last inadmissibility decisions based on this ground date back very far.[93] In 1935, municipal initiatives for a reduction in the mortgage interest rate[94] and a reduction in the price of electricity were rejected because

---

[89]   See Marxer (n 6) 125–32, with reference to the decision of the constitutional court *StGH* 1964/3, in: *Entscheidsammlungen der Liechtensteinischen Gerichtshöfe*; ELG (Decisions of Liechtenstein Courts) 1962–1966, 224; and *StGH* 1986/10, in: *Liechtensteinische Entscheidsammlung*; LES (Collection of Court Decisions) 1987, 152–53.

[90]   Art. 69(6) Political Rights Act.

[91]   *StGH* 1964/3, in: ELG 1962–1966, 225.

[92]   Art. 80(3).

[93]   Marxer (n 6) 132–39.

[94]   Expert opinion of the Constitutional Court (*Staatsgerichtshof*, StGH) of 1 July 1935. Parliament took note of the expert opinion in the session of 30 August 1935 and consequently the initiative was not admitted.

there were no proposals for cover.[95] Most initiatives do not have cost implications, or at least do not entail expenditures in the amounts specified by the law. This applies, for example, to changes to the electoral law, equality issues, etc.

The law does not specify in which form a financing proposal must be made. An indication that the costs are to be covered from general tax revenues or financial assets may already be sufficient.[96] It should be borne in mind that the requirement for a financing proposal was formulated at a time when Liechtenstein was in an extremely weak financial position.

It is also unclear at what stage of the procedure a financing proposal should be made. In its ruling on the admissibility of the proactive initiative for climate protection, the Constitutional Court stated that the cover proposal does not already need to be provided when the initiative is registered, but only when it is submitted with the valid number of signatures.[97] However, the sense of such an interpretation can be doubted, as the purpose of a preliminary examination is to avoid unnecessary signature collection and voting. Finally, the cover proposal might also have an influence on the decision of those who are asked to sign an initiative. Therefore, it seems appropriate to include the coverage proposal, if at all necessary, simultaneously with the application for a proactive initiative.[98]

3.2.5 Blocking periods

Periods within which a direct-democratic request is inadmissible can also be counted among the formal limits. With regard to initiatives, such blocking periods only make sense in the case of the proactive, but not the rejective, initiative. If a proposal has been rejected in a popular vote, a proactive initiative concerning the same question may only be submitted after expiry of a period of two years.[99] A request to dismiss Parliament can only be made once every year.[100] In contrast, there are no blocking periods for the motion of no-confidence against the Reigning Prince and the other instruments which were introduced in 2003.

3.3 Limits at the Municipal Level

The municipal council is responsible for the examination and admission of proactive and rejective initiative applications. It examines the formal and substantive requirements and rejects a request if it is unlawful or relates to an issue

---

95 See Marxer (n 6) 136–37.
96 Marxer (n 6) 138–39.
97 StGH 2004/70, Rz 2.4.
98 See Marxer (n 6) 137–39.
99 Art. 70(3) Political Rights Act.
100 Art. 70(3) Political Rights Act.

that falls within the competence of other municipal authorities or a national authority.[101] Decisions of the municipal council on citizens' initiatives may be appealed to the Government and subsequently to the Administrative Court.[102]

Proactive initiatives at municipal level are inadmissible if the deadline for launching a rejective initiative concerning the same issue has passed unused or a rejective initiative concerning the same issue has been submitted. In the case of building regulations, zoning plans and other municipal council decisions of a general nature, a proactive initiative can only be launched once at least two years have passed since the relevant decision.[103] At municipal level, there is no requirement for a proposal to cover the necessary funds.

4.   INSTITUTIONAL AND PROCEDURAL FRAMEWORK

4.1   National Level

4.1.1   Proactive initiative and agenda initiative

In order to launch a proactive citizens' initiative, the initiators have to register the initiative with the Government.[104] The Government checks the compliance of the initiative with the formal limits set out above and rejects it if necessary. Initiatives which do not comply with the provisions shall be returned by the Government to the first signatory for the attention of all initiators, indicating the fault, and shall be invalid if the fault is not remedied within a reasonable time.[105] Appeals against governmental decisions can be brought before the Administrative Court.[106] If the initiative is deemed formally admissible, the Government examines whether it is in conformity with the Constitution and existing international treaties and forwards its report to Parliament for a decision on its substantive admissibility.[107] The report is not binding on Parliament. The initiators may hold informal discussions with the parties or provide them with documents, arguments and other material. These are eventually used by Members of Parliament during parliamentary sessions, but are not included in the parliamentary documents. If Parliament finds the initiative to be inadmis-

---

[101] Art. 43 Municipal Act.
[102] Art.   120   and   121   Municipal   Act;   State   Administration   Act (*Landesverwaltungspflegegesetz* vom 21. April 1922, LGBl. 1922.024).
[103] Art. 42(2) Municipal Act.
[104] Art. 80(4)(a) Political Rights Act.
[105] Art. 69(6) Political Rights Act.
[106] Art. 2(3) *Gesetz vom 21. April 1922 über die allgemeine Landesverwaltungspflege* (LGBl. 1922.024), www.gesetze.li accessed 29 June 2020.
[107] Art. 70b(1) Political Rights Act.

sible, the initiators are not heard by Parliament, but they may lodge an appeal with the Constitutional Court. If the initiative is ruled to be inadmissible, the collection of signatures may not be carried out.[108]

There are too few complaints against decisions on initiatives for a clear picture as to who is entitled to complain when and in what matters to emerge. Past complaints, however, do show that initiators are legitimised when an initiative is rejected[109] or when the authorities conduct an unfair referendum campaign.[110] Voters are also entitled to appeal against the Government's approval of what they consider to be an inadmissible initiative.[111] Furthermore, voters may also complain against the withdrawal of a vote if they discover irregularities, such as a one-sided and strongly opinion-forming campaign by the authorities or one-sided representations in the voting information prior to a vote.[112] Complaints are therefore possible in many ways and by various parties concerned.

Once a proactive initiative has successfully passed the preliminary examination, it is published by official announcement and the collection of signatures may begin.[113] The signatures that have been certified by the respective mayor's office must be submitted to the Government within six weeks.[114]

The Government reports to Parliament on the successful collection of signatures for the initiative. Parliament may approve the initiative and thus elevate it to a parliamentary resolution, which is subject to the rejective initiative.[115] If Parliament rejects the initiative, which is usually the case, a ballot vote is mandatory.[116] If the initiative contains a withdrawal clause, it may be withdrawn by the initiators as long as the date of the vote has not yet been fixed.[117] The voting date, which may not be later than three months after the debate in Parliament,[118] will be scheduled by the Government via official announcement

---

[108] Art. 70b(2) and 70b(3) Political Rights Act.

[109] StGH 2004/70 regarding the proactive initiative for climate protection; StGH 2013/183 regarding initiative on pension insurance for state employees.

[110] StGH 1993/8 regarding the legislature initiative on access to the European Economic Area.

[111] VBI 2002/96 and StGH 2002/73 regarding the proactive initiative on revision of the constitution. The courts had to rule whether the initiators – the reigning and the hereditary prince – were legitimised to register a proactive initiative.

[112] StGH 1990/6 regarding the proactive initiative for the introduction of the state treaty referendum, in which the Court ruled that an unbalanced information in the official voting leaflet was unlawful.

[113] Art. 80(4)(a) Political Rights Act.

[114] Art. 80(4)(b) Political Rights Act.

[115] Art. 82(1) Political Rights Act.

[116] Art. 82(2) Political Rights Act.

[117] Art. 82b Political Rights Act.

[118] Art. 72(1) Political Rights Act.

at least four weeks before the vote.[119] Parliament may submit a counterproposal for the vote.[120] In this case, a 'double or multiple yes' voting system applies, that is, voters who approve more than one proposal are also asked which proposal they prefer in case both/several proposals are approved by the majority.[121] The result of the vote shall be officially announced.[122]

If a bill is adopted by a majority of voters, the sanction of the Reigning Prince is required for it to enter into force. If the Prince refuses to sign it, the law cannot enter into force.[123] The entry into force of the enacted legal provisions must be communicated by promulgation and published in the Liechtenstein Legal Gazette.[124]

4.1.2 Legislature-initiated referendum and rejective initiative

Once Parliament has adopted a resolution (be it a constitutional amendment, a law, a financial resolution or assent to an international treaty), it may decide by majority vote to hold a referendum on it. If it does not do so and does not declare the resolution urgent, the resolution is published by means of an official announcement.[125] This triggers the deadline for launching a rejective initiative: the required number of signatures, which must be certified by the respective mayor's office, must be submitted to the Government within 30 days.[126] There is no need to register the collection of signatures against a parliamentary resolution before starting with the collection. As mentioned earlier, it must be clear against which publicly announced parliamentary decision the rejective initiative is directed.

If the collection of signatures has been successful, the Government must organise the popular vote,[127] the result of which it must publish. If the resolution does not obtain the majority of all valid votes in the ballot, it is definitely rejected. If it is approved by a majority, the Reigning Prince must sanction it in order for it to enter into force.[128] If the Prince refuses the sanction, the resolution cannot enter into force. If the Prince grants the sanction, the entry

---

[119] Art. 25(2) Political Rights Act.
[120] Art. 82(3) Political Rights Act.
[121] Art. 83(5) Political Rights Act.
[122] Art. 77(4) Political Rights Act.
[123] Art. 9 and 65 Constitution.
[124] Art. 3(a)–(c) Promulgation Act (*Kundmachungsgesetz* vom 17. April 1985, LGBl. 1985.041).
[125] Art. 70(1a) and 70a(1) Political Rights Act.
[126] Art. 70(1)(a) and 70a(1) Political Rights Act.
[127] Art. 72(1) Political Rights Act.
[128] Art. 65(1) and 66(5) Constitution.

into force must be promulgated by the Government and the relevant resolution must be published in the Liechtenstein Legal Gazette.[129]

4.2 Municipal Level

In the municipalities, resolutions that are subject to the rejective initiative are publicly announced[130] so that a rejective initiative can be launched within the set period of time by means of the required number of signatures of those entitled to vote in the municipality concerned. A request for a rejective initiative must be registered with the mayor of the municipality no later than 14 days after the announcement of the resolution, and it must be submitted within one month of the announcement.[131] The vote must take place within four months of the rejective initiative being submitted. The procedure for proactive initiatives largely corresponds to that for the rejective initiative.[132]

5. PRACTICAL RELEVANCE OF THE LEGAL LIMITS

The legal barriers to direct-democratic procedures are not discouraging in Liechtenstein. The people have decision-making rights in matters of the Constitution as well as concerning laws, finances and international treaties. At the national level, the most frequently used instruments of direct democracy are the rejective initiative directed against resolutions of Parliament and the proactive initiative. Further direct-democratic instruments, which have not attained any practical relevance yet, include the vote of no-confidence in the Reigning Prince, the abolition of monarchy and the right of the people of a municipality to secede from the union. In addition to popular votes triggered by the people, Parliament also has the right to submit its own decisions to a popular vote.

The formal and substantive examination of proactive initiatives is quite appropriate. The preliminary examination procedure at both the national and the municipal level prevents signatures from being collected for requests that are not admissible – be it at the national level, because they are in conflict with the Constitution or international treaties, or be it at the municipal level, because they are in conflict with national law or competences of other bodies. In practice, it rarely happens that a proactive initiative fails to pass the hurdle

---

[129] Art. 3(a)–(c) Promulgation Act.
[130] Art. 41(4) Municipality Act.
[131] Art. 41(3) Municipality Act.
[132] Art. 41(5) Municipality Act.

of preliminary examination. Furthermore, an appeal against an inadmissibility decision of the national Parliament can be lodged with the Constitutional Court, or with the Government and the Administrative Court in case of an initiative at the municipal level.

6.   CONCLUSION

Widely developed direct-democratic rights of those eligible to vote are in place in Liechtenstein, at both the national and the municipal level. This refers not only to the broad range of direct-democratic instruments, but also to the moderate legal hurdles imposed on them. Accordingly, popular votes take place quite frequently compared with most other countries. Moreover, most direct-democratic procedures have a binding effect on the representative bodies, that is, the Government and Parliament, which motivates citizens additionally to become politically active. The purpose of the preliminary examination procedure for proactive initiatives is to prevent direct-democratic proposals that contradict the Constitution or relevant international treaties. In the case of proactive initiatives at the municipal level, requests are to be avoided which contradict national law or do not fall within the competence of the municipality. In general, therefore, the principle of popular sovereignty does not dominate, but rather the compatibility of direct-democratic proce-dures with the rule of law.[133] This is accompanied by decision-making powers of the Constitutional Court, for example in questions of the admissibility of initiatives. The principle of sovereignty of the people is additionally weakened by the Reigning Prince's right of sanction, since most popular votes at national level require the Prince's sanction before a draft can enter into force. Direct democracy in Liechtenstein is therefore embedded in a complex system of Government and is shaped by the principle of rule of law.

---

[133] See Sabine Jung, *Die Logik direkter Demokratie* (Springer 2001) regarding the difference between the principle of popular sovereignty and the principle of the rule of law.

6. Italy

Henri Ibi

1. INTRODUCTION

Instruments of direct democracy were introduced in Italy for the first time with the entry into force of the Constitution of the Italian Republic (Italian Constitution or Constitution) of 1948.[1] The constitutional provisions on said instruments were implemented by means of an ordinary law of the Parliament (Law n. 352/1970 entitled 'Provisions on referendums provided for by the Constitution and on the citizen agenda initiative') over 20 years later in 1970.[2]

The Italian political climate at that time, in a certain way, encouraged the passing of the legislation on direct-democratic instruments. A few months after the entry into force of Law n. 352/1970, a controversial law was introduced by the Parliament: the Law n. 898/1970 regulating divorce. The largest Italian party at that time, that is, the Christian Democrats, was against this law but renounced obstructionism in Parliament, since it obtained 'in return' the approval of the law implementing the instruments of direct democracy provided for by the Constitution. The aim of the Christian Democrats was to launch an abrogative referendum against the law on divorce and entrust directly to the citizens the final political decision on a subject deemed to be 'sensitive'. In January 1971, the request for a referendum by the 'National Committee for the Referendum on Divorce', chaired by the Catholic lawyer

---

[1] The Italian Constitution was enacted by the Constituent Assembly – elected by universal suffrage on 2 June 1946 – on 22 December 1947, was promulgated on 27 December 1947 and entered into force on 1 January 1948. An English version of the Italian Constitution is available on the website of the Italian Constitutional Court: https://www.cortecostituzionale.it/documenti/download/pdf/The_Constitution_of_the _Italian_Republic.pdf, accessed 18 July 2020.

[2] The Italian version of the Law n. 352/1970 can be found at: https://www .normattiva.it/atto/caricaDettaglioAtto?atto.dataPubblicazioneGazzetta=1970-06-15 &atto.codiceRedazionale=070U0352&atto.articolo.numero=0&qId=b62dd618-7d5e -4feb-b8c0-5ca87a433f54&tabID=0.3033092646952269&title=lbl.dettaglioAtto, accessed 18 August 2020.

Gabrio Lombardi,[3] with the explicit support of the Christian Democrats and the Italian Social Movement, was filed with the Supreme Court.[4] The first abrogative referendum in Italian history was held three years later, on 15 May 1974. The referendum request to abolish the law regulating divorce was rejected by nearly 59.3 per cent of the voters and consequently the law remained in force. The abrogative referendum on divorce had the second highest turnout after the institutional referendum which was held in 1946: 87.72 per cent of the eligible voters participated in the popular vote. Since 1970,[5] 72 national referendums have been held in Italy, including 67 abrogative referendums, one consultative (advisory) referendum[6] and four constitutional referendums.[7]

With regard to the legal limits, the Constitution expressly regulates those imposed under Article 75(2) of the Constitution concerning the abrogative referendum. However, the most significant limits, both substantive and formal, have been introduced by the Italian Constitutional Court (Constitutional Court) as the latter is entitled to adjudicate on the constitutional admissibility of referendum requests by reviewing the compliance with those limits on the basis of the Constitutional Law n. 1/1953[8] and Law n. 352/1970.

---

[3]   A Manifesto on the Divorce was published explaining the reasons of such referendum: Un popolo al bivio. Referendum sul divorzio frontiera di libertà, Comitato nazionale per il referendum sul divorzio, Roma 1972.

[4]   The Ordinance of the Central Office of the Supreme Court which formally admitted the request of the promoters is available in Italian language at: http://www.cortedicassazione.it/cassazione-resources/resources/cms/documents/1971.12.06_divorzio.PDF, accessed 18 July 2020.

[5]   The list does not include the so-called 'institutional referendum' which took place on 2 June 1946 in order to determine the Italian state form. This is the first time Italian citizens were called to vote in a referendum. 54.27 per cent of the registered electors (out of 89.08 per cent of all voters) voted for the republican form of state. The statistics on referendums are available on the website of the Department for Internal and Territorial Affairs at: https://elezionistorico.interno.gov.it/index.php?tpel=F&dtel=17/04/2016, accessed 18 July 2020.

[6]   For the first and only time a consultative/advisory referendum was held in Italy on 18 June 1989, alongside European elections, on the European Economic Community. That was a non-binding referendum called by all main parties by means of an *ad hoc* constitutional law, because the Italian Constitution does not allow this type of direct-democratic instrument. It was a derogation to the Constitutional system as the entire Italian political system wanted to re-affirm the popular support of Italy to the process of European integration. The referendum question was approved by a very large percentage of the voters, that is, 80.03 per cent.

[7]   For a complete overview on referendum quorums and questions see: http://www.riformeistituzionali.gov.it/media/1241/storicoreferendumquorum.pdf, accessed 18 July 2020.

[8]   The Italian version of the Constitutional Law n. 1/1953 is available at: https://www.normattiva.it/atto/caricaDettaglioAtto?atto.dataPubblicazioneGazzetta=1953

Before the substantive admissibility check of the Constitutional Court takes place, an *ad hoc* judicial panel called Central Office for Referendums appointed within the Supreme Court (Central Office) is in charge of checking the formal admissibility of each referendum request by reviewing compliance, in closed session, of said requests with the requirements laid down in Law n. 352/1970. Once the decisions of the competent courts have been taken, the President of the Republic, symbol of the unity of the Republic,[9] in accordance with the existing legal provisions and by means of Presidential decrees, calls the referendum.[10]

2. EXISTING DIRECT-DEMOCRATIC INSTRUMENTS

The instruments of direct democracy provided for by the Constitution include – at national level – (i) the constitutional referendum, (ii) the abrogative referendum and (iii) the citizen-agenda initiative. According to the LIDD classification of direct-democratic instruments, both the Italian constitutional referendum and the abrogative referendum can be considered either as an institution-initiated referendum or a rejective citizen-initiated referendum, depending on the subject who submits the request for referendum. A popular initiative or – applying the LIDD distinction – a proactive citizen-initiated referendum which enables the citizens to make a proposal that is then submitted to a referendum is not foreseen.

With regard to the regional level, it is worth mentioning that consultative referendums are provided under Articles 132 and 133 of the Constitution for the possible merger between existing Regions, for the creation of new Regions and for the detachment and incorporation of the Provinces and Municipalities from one Region into another one. Furthermore, Article 123(2) of the Constitution states that Statutes, which are to be considered as the fundamental laws governing the functioning of the Regions, 'shall regulate the right to initiate legislation and promote referendums on the laws and administrative measures of the Region'. Typical examples of implementation of Article

---

-03-14&atto.codiceRedazionale=053C0001&atto.articolo.numero=0&qId=03a41bae
-8b97-4f56-a742-9f10dce7f0cf&tabID=0.3033092646952269&title=lbl.dettaglioAtto.

[9]   Art. 87 Constitution.
[10]   Art. 15 and 34 Law n. 352/1970.

123(2) of the Constitution are Lombardy[11] and Trentino Alto Adige,[12] which have expressly regulated the referendum in their Statutes.

Finally, a certain number of direct-democratic instruments are also provided for by sub-constitutional provisions at municipal and provincial level. A very interesting case is the City of Bolzano, which has a very extensive list of instruments of direct democracy in its Statute, with very detailed provisions with regard to the procedure.[13]

This chapter will cover only the national state level instruments of direct democracy in detail. As mentioned above, the requirements and the procedures governing the direct-democratic instruments are regulated not only by the Constitution, but also by Law n. 352 of 25 May 1970 and, to some extent, by significant rulings of the Constitutional Court which have become more and more decisive with specific reference to the interpretation of the legal limits.

2.1   Constitutional Referendum

Article 138(2) of the Italian Constitution provides that:

1.   laws amending the Constitution
2.   other constitutional laws

must be submitted to a popular referendum when, within three months of their publication, such request is made by either one-fifth of the members of a House or 500,000 voters or five Regional Councils, unless the constitutional amendment and/or law has been approved in the second voting by each of the Houses by a majority of two-thirds of the members according to Article 138(3). The constitutional referendum – which can be requested by the above-mentioned subjects in case of an approval of the constitutional amendment and/or law by less than a two-thirds majority – cannot be considered a law-initiated referendum, as a specific request to hold a referendum has to be submitted by the above-mentioned actors.

---

[11]   An Italian version of the Statute of the Region Lombardy is available at: http:// normelombardia.consiglio.regione.lombardia.it/NormeLombardia/Accessibile/main .aspx?exp_coll=lrst2008051400001&view=showdoc&iddoc=lrst2008051400001& selnode=lrst2008051400001, accessed 18 July 2020.

[12]   An Italian and German version of the Statute of the Region Trentino Alto Adige is available at: http://www.regione.taa.it/Moduli/933_STATUTO%202018.pdf, accessed 18 July 2020.

[13]   Both the Italian and the German version of the Statute of the City of Bolzano are available at: http://www.comune.bolzano.it/UploadDocs/8023_Statuto_ita_aggiornato _maggio_2015.pdf, accessed 18 July 2020.

In all cases, the President of the Chamber which has approved a law amending the Constitution or another constitutional law shall communicate to the Government whether the approval has been made by a two-thirds majority or less of the members of the Parliament. The request for a referendum under Article 138 of the Constitution must contain an indication of the law revising the Constitution or the constitutional law to be submitted to the popular vote, and must also mention the date of its final approval by the Chambers and the date and number of the Official Journal in which it was published.[14] In case no request for a referendum has been submitted within three months after the publication of the amendment and/or law, the President of the Republic shall promulgate the law which then enters into force.[15]

As the referendum can be requested by different subjects, the procedure regulating the referendum is structured differently depending on who is asking for the referendum.

According to Article 6 of Law n. 352/1970, if the request is made by one-fifth of the members of the Chamber, their signatures shall be authenticated by the secretariat of the Chamber to which they belong. It must attest that they are actually Members of Parliament in office. Three delegates chosen among the deputies requesting the referendum are in charge of filing such request with the Chancellor's office of the Supreme Court.

In case the request for a referendum is submitted by 500,000 citizens, it can be classified as a citizen-initiated rejective referendum. The promoters of the request, in number of not less than ten, must submit the request to the Chancellor's office of the Supreme Court, in order to start the procedure. Each initiative is announced in the Official Journal of the following day by the Office.[16] As far as the specific requirements of the signatures are concerned, it should be noted that the relevant sheets must have specific dimensions and must contain at the beginning of each side, whether printed or stamped, the declaration of the request for a referendum, with the indications as prescribed by the applicable law.[17]

Lastly, the constitutional referendum can be initiated by a formal request coming from five Regional Councils as well. Under Article 10(1) of Law n. 352/1970 the Regional Councils requesting a referendum must adopt a specific resolution in this regard. It has to be approved by a majority of votes of the councillors and must contain the indication of the law in respect of which the referendum is requested. Once the first Regional Council, which could be

---

[14] Art. 4 Law n. 352/1970.
[15] Art. 5 Law n. 352/1970.
[16] Art. 7 Law n. 352/1970.
[17] Art. 7 Law n. 352/1970.

called 'initiator', has adopted its resolution, it is officially communicated to the rest of the Regional Councils. They are requested, in case they adopt the identical resolution, to inform the first Regional Council that has taken the initiative, so that it can follow it up.[18] In case the identical resolution is adopted by at least four other Regional Councils, five delegates have to be nominated in order to draw up or sign the deed of request, and present it in person to the Supreme Court, together with certified copies of the decisions taken by each of the Regional Councils requesting the constitutional referendum.

For this type of referendum a turnout quorum is not provided for by the Constitution. The amendment and/or law submitted to the referendum shall not be promulgated by the President of the Republic if it has not been approved by a majority of valid votes of the citizens taking part in the popular vote.[19]

Only four constitutional referendums have taken place so far. The first constitutional referendum took place on 7 October 2001 on 'Title V of the Constitution'. The promoters aimed, by rewriting Title V of the Constitution, to give more power to the Regions by assigning them legislative competence in all matters not expressly reserved to the central State. The electors approved the referendum question by a large margin (64.21 per cent of the voters, despite a low turnout, that is, 34.05 per cent). The second constitutional referendum was held on 25 June 2006 asking for confirmation of several amendments relating to the second part of the Constitution aiming, among others, at reducing the number of the parliamentarians, overcoming equal bicameralism and increasing the powers of the Prime Minister. It was rejected by 61.29 per cent of the voters. On 4 December 2016, the constitutional referendum aiming at overcoming equal bicameralism, reducing the number of parliamentarians, containing the operating costs of the institutions and revising Title V of Part Two of the Constitution proposed by the Renzi Government was rejected by 59.12 per cent of the voters.[20] More recently, on 12 October 2019 the Parliament approved a constitutional amendment reducing the number of parliamentarians provided for in the Constitution to 400 deputies and 200 elective senators. As far as the instruments of direct democracy are concerned, no amendment to the system in force has been proposed. The text of the amendment was published in the Official Gazette of 12 October 2019.[21] As the amendment had not been approved by a two-thirds majority, a referendum under Article 138(3) of the

---

[18]   Art. 10 Law n. 352/1970.
[19]   Art. 138(3) Constitution.
[20]   For the percentages see the website of the Department for Internal and Territorial Affairs   at: https://elezionistorico.interno.gov.it/index.php?tpel=F&dtel=17/04/2016, accessed 18 July 2020.
[21]   https://temi.camera.it/leg18/provvedimento/tl18_riforme_costituzionali_ed _elettorali.html, accessed 18 July 2020.

Constitution was requested by the required number of the parliamentarians. The referendum request was declared admissible by the Central Office on 23 January 2020. The referendum was initially supposed to be held on 29 March 2020, but on 5 March 2020 the President of the Republic postponed the date of the constitutional referendum due to the Covid-19 pandemic. On 17 July 2020 the President recalled the referendum to be held on 20 and 21 September 2020[22]; the referendum question was approved by 69.96 per cent of the voters.

2.2 Abrogative Referendum

The abrogative referendum can be considered the most significant instrument of direct democracy in Italy. It requires a long and complicated procedure, and in many respects the Law n. 352/1970 regulating the procedure seems unclear. It can be initiated either by 500,000 citizens or five Regional Councils.[23] According to Article 75(1) of the Constitution 'a popular referendum shall be held to abrogate, totally or partially, a law or a measure having the force of law'. Under Italian law typical 'measures having the force of law' are legislative decrees and law decrees.[24] Article 75(2) of the Constitution imposes the express legal limits by excluding from the scope of the abrogative referendum certain types of laws: namely those relating to tax, budget, amnesty and pardon, and laws authorizing the ratification of international treaties. These limits will be covered in the next section dealing specifically with the legal limits.

The specific requirements of the referendum request are regulated by Law n. 352/1970, starting from Article 27 and the following. As far as the request

---

[22] The text of the referendum question was as follows: 'Do you approve the text of the constitutional law concerning amendments to Articles 56, 57 and 59 of the Constitution regarding the reduction of the number of parliamentarians, approved by Parliament and published in the Official Gazette of the Italian Republic – General Series – No. 240 of 12 October 2019?'

[23] Only once has the abrogative referendum been admitted to take place on a formal request of the Regional Councils. On 19 January 2016 the Constitutional Court admitted the referendum request concerning the 'Extension of oil extraction concessions within 12 nautical miles' jointly requested by the Regional Councils of the following regions: Basilicata, Calabria, Campania, Liguria, Marche, Molise, Puglia, Sardegna and Veneto.

[24] These are two different legislative instruments that are alternatives to the ordinary law passed by the Parliament. They are both legal acts having the force of law enacted by the Government in situations of necessity and urgency or for complex and articulated disciplines. The difference between these two measures is that the legislative decree can be adopted by the Government only if the Parliament has previously granted authorization for this purpose by means of an ordinary law, approved by an ordinary legislative procedure whereas the law decree can be adopted by the Government without express authorization and it enters immediately into force.

proposal and the signature gathering are concerned, reference can be made to the procedure relating to the constitutional referendum, apart from some peculiarities. In the case of the abrogative referendum the promoters can request to repeal not only the entire text of a law or of a measure having the force of law but also a partial abrogation. In the event they file a request to abrogate, for example, specific sections or specific parts of a section of a law, they must indicate the relevant sections and their full text.[25]

The filing of the signatures with the Chancellor's office of the Supreme Court has to be carried out within three months starting from the date of the stamp affixed to the sheets in accordance with the last paragraph of Article 7 of the Law n. 352/1970. However, in order to avoid possible overlapping with general elections, no request for a referendum can be filed in the 12 months prior to the end of the legislature or in the 6 months following parliamentary elections.[26] Requests for referendums may be deposited each year from 1 January to 30 September.[27]

As in case of the constitutional referendum, the request for a referendum under Article 75 of the Constitution can be submitted by five Regional Councils as well.[28] In this case, the request itself must contain, in addition to the question and the indication of the legal provisions to be abrogated, the indication of the Regional Councils which have decided to submit it, the date on which it is to be submitted and the respective decision taken by the Regional Council to hold the referendum.

Once both the preliminary legal review carried out by the Central Office[29] and the subsequent admissibility check of the Constitutional Court have taken place,[30] the President of the Republic calls the referendum by setting its date on a Sunday between 15 April and 15 June.[31] The decision takes the form of a decree upon a resolution of the Council of Ministers.

The abrogative referendum result is legally binding if the majority of citizens entitled to vote have participated in the popular vote. Unlike the constitutional referendum, the abrogative referendum thus requires a turnout quorum in order to be valid.[32] Once the turnout quorum has been reached and in the event the majority of the participants vote against the referendum request for abolishing a law or a measure of law having the force of law, then a new

---

[25]   Art. 27 Law n. 352/1970.
[26]   Art. 31 Law n. 352/1970.
[27]   Art. 32 Law n. 352/1970.
[28]   Art. 29 Law n. 352/1970.
[29]   Art. 32 Law n. 352/1970.
[30]   Art. 33 Law n. 352/1970.
[31]   Art. 34 Law n. 352/1970.
[32]   Art. 75(4) Constitution.

request for a referendum to repeal the same law cannot be submitted before the expiry of a period of five years.[33] It could also be the case that a law, or parts of it, are abrogated before the referendum already called takes place. In this particular circumstance, Article 39 of Law n. 352/1970 provides that the Central Office must withdraw the entire referendum process.

2.3 Citizen-agenda Initiative

The citizen-agenda initiative foreseen by Article 71 of the Constitution gives 50,000 persons eligible to vote the right to initiate legislation by proposing a bill drawn up in sections. This type of direct-democratic instrument is scarcely regulated by Law n. 352/1970 as the only provisions concerning the citizen-agenda initiative are provided by Articles 48 and 49 of said law.

The draft law must be submitted, accompanied by the signatures of the voters, to the President of one of the two Chambers.[34] The Chamber where the proposal is submitted is in charge of verifying and calculating the signatures of the promoters in order to ascertain the regularity of the submission of the draft law.[35]

With regard to the content of the request, the proposal must be presented in form of a draft law drawn up in sections and accompanied by a report explaining its aims and objectives.[36] As far as the signature gathering, the authentication process and the submission procedure are concerned, reference can be made to Articles 7 and 8 of Law n. 352/1970 which regulate the procedure for the other types of direct-democratic instruments. With specific reference to the legal limits, the legal provisions both on the constitutional and statute level do not expressly specify any limits imposed on the citizen-agenda initiative.

The citizen-agenda initiative is addressed to the Parliament, but neither the Constitution nor Law n. 352/1970 contain any provisions regarding the consequences in case the Chamber does not formally react by, for example, submitting it to a vote in Parliament. Even though there is no formal obligation to react to a citizen-agenda initiative, an obligation to complete the work on the proposed text within three months was introduced with the amendment of the Senate's regulations in 2018. After this deadline, the draft popular law is automatically entered in the calendar of the Assembly's work.[37] This is still not an obligation to put the draft to the vote of the members of the Parliament, but

---

[33] Art. 38 Law n. 352/1970.
[34] Art. 49(1) Law n. 352/1970.
[35] Art. 49(2) Law n. 352/1970.
[36] Art. 49(2) Law n. 352/1970.
[37] Art. 74 of the Senate's regulations at http://www.senato.it/1044?articolo=1066& sezione=150, accessed 18 July 2020.

at least it could be considered a first serious step to take into consideration the citizen-agenda initiative coming from the people.

In practice, this instrument of direct democracy has proved to have had a limited power. Parliamentary bodies are not obliged to give an opinion on citizen-agenda initiatives, nor are there mechanisms in place to guarantee significant procedural priorities. An exception is Article 74 of the Senate's Regulations, which requires the competent Commissions to start the examination of the citizen-agenda initiative drafts assigned to them no later than one month after the referral.

In order to make the citizen-agenda initiative more effective, the Chamber of Deputies has approved in its first deliberation a draft law for a constitutional law amending Article 71 of the Constitution in so far as it regulates the citizen-agenda initiative, introducing a 'reinforced' procedure that can be concluded, if certain conditions are met, by holding a referendum. This is to be considered only the first step of a very long procedure, but at least the legislator demonstrates that it is trying to better implement the instrument.[38]

3.   LEGAL LIMITS

The only substantive limits expressly provided for direct-democratic instruments in Italy relate to the abrogative referendum as specified in Article 75(2) of the Constitution. The Constitution itself does not provide for an admissibility procedure for the abrogative referendum. The admissibility procedure was introduced, as we have already seen, by means of *ad hoc* Constitutional Law n. 1/1953. In contrast, there is no explicit regulation of the formal limits of referendum questions. The Constitutional Court's case law relating to the legal limits has had unpredictable contours over the years.[39] Starting from a restrictive interpretation of what is excluded by Article 75(2) of the Constitution and the topic of the referendum proposed, the Court has extensively introduced new substantive and formal limits.

3.1   Substantive Limits Provided for under the Constitution

Article 75(2) of the Constitution sets out only a few cases of exclusion regarding the matters of the abrogative referendum:

1.   fiscal laws;

---

   [38]   The draft of the proposal of the relevant law can be found at: https://temi.camera
.it/leg18/provvedimento/tl18_riforme_costituzionali_ed_elettorali.html, accessed 18
July 2020.
   [39]   Bin-Pitruzzella, *Diritto Costituzionale* (Giappichelli Editore Torino 2018) 511.

2. budgetary laws;
3. amnesty and pardon laws;
4. laws authorizing the ratification of international treaties.

When the Constitutional Court decided on the constitutionality of the referendums relating to divorce and abortion – respectively in 1972 and 1975 – it adopted a restrictive interpretation in the sense that the request for an abrogative referendum is only declared inadmissible if the referendum refers to one of the topics expressly excluded under Article 75(2) of the Constitution.[40] The Court stated that since these two requests for a referendum did not concern one of the excluded matters falling within the scope of the Article 75(2) of the Constitution, they were to be considered constitutional and admitted them. In these very first decisions, the Court interpreted narrowly the exclusions of Article 75(2) of the Constitution as it considered that its role in connection with referendums was limited to verifying that the law subject to a referendum request belongs to one of the categories of law not explicitly covered by Article 75(2) of the Constitution.

A few years later, the Court started to use a wider interpretation of the exclusions under Article 75(2) of the Constitution. In its fundamental decision n. 16/1978[41] the Constitutional Court stated that the literal interpretation must be supplemented, if necessary, by a logical-systematic interpretation, in order to exclude from the referendum those provisions which are strictly connected to the scope of operation of the exempted laws expressly indicated in Article 75(2). Therefore, abrogative referendums are inadmissible not only with regard to laws authorizing the ratification of international treaties as expressly provided, but also with regard to those laws which are necessary to execute them (the Court specifically argued that the execution laws of the Lateran Treaty between the Italian Republic and the Vatican State could not be subject to the abrogative referendum).[42]

Furthermore, according to the Constitutional Court, the limits operate also in case of laws which the Italian State must enact as a result of an obligation under an international agreement, where there is a lack of discretion of the legislature. Such laws have been called 'internationally imposed laws'. They

---

[40] Decisions 10/1972 and 251/1975 of the Constitutional Court.

[41] The Constitutional Court was asked to determine if the eight different referendum questions were to be considered admissible and therefore to be put to a referendum in accordance with Art. 75(2) of the Constitution. The questions concerned the abrogation of specific provisions of the following laws relating to the military judicial system and the Military Criminal Code, the public funding of the political parties, the execution of the Lateran Treaty, the mental institutions, criminal law code and the public order and were decided together by the Court.

[42] Decision 16/1978 of the Constitutional Court.

are not technically executing laws of international treaties but produce effects that are closely linked to the scope of operation of the treaties themselves. Therefore, they can only be abrogated by an act of the Parliament.[43] The same reasoning has been made by the Court with reference to so-called 'necessary European laws', on which an abrogative referendum cannot be held because the Italian State could be held liable for failure to fulfil a specific obligation imposed by the European Union.[44]

As far as budgetary laws are concerned, the Constitutional Court, in numerous decisions, has stated that the express limits according to Article 75 apply – as strictly connected – also to the annual and multi-year budget laws, measures connected to budgetary laws and those laws which are deemed necessary for the implementation of financial and budgetary goals.[45]

3.2   Implicit Substantive Limits

Besides the expressly imposed limits provided by the Constitution, the case law of the Constitutional Court has introduced additional implicit limits which can be inferred from the constitutional system and especially from the nature of the abrogative referendum. The latter has been defined as an act which has the same force of law as the ordinary law.[46]

For example, according to the Court, the Constitution, the laws amending the Constitution and the other constitutional laws may not be subject to an abrogative referendum. The Court stated that, if it were otherwise, this would be in contrast with the characteristic of the Constitution itself which can be amended only by means of constitutional law or if the conditions are fulfilled for starting a constitutional referendum.[47] The same prohibition applies with regard to laws with a 'particular passive force' (*forza passiva peculiare*), which cannot be repealed by subsequent ordinary laws (such as the abrogative referendum, which, as said, is considered to have the same force of law as the ordinary law). For example, the execution laws of the Lateran Treaty between the Italian Republic and the Vatican State – entered into force in 1929 and revised in 1984 – have that particular passive force in the Court's view.[48] The laws with particular passive force are special, reinforced, atypical in form, strength and competence as they are enacted through special legislative

---

[43]   Decision 30/1981 of the Constitutional Court. See also Decisions 26/1993, 8/1995, 27/1997 of the Constitutional Court.

[44]   Decisions 4 and 45/2000 of the Constitutional Court.

[45]   Decisions 2/1994 and 12/1995 of the Constitutional Court.

[46]   Decision 29/1987 of the Constitutional Court.

[47]   Decision 16/1978 of the Constitutional Court.

[48]   Decision 16/1978 of the Constitutional Court.

procedures according to the Constitution. Therefore, the execution laws of the Lateran Treaty cannot be abrogated by means of an ordinary law of the Italian Parliament and subsequently cannot be subject to an abrogative referendum either.

In the same decision n. 16/1978 the Court argued that the abrogative referendum cannot be used with regard to those ordinary laws that have a content which is closely connected to the Constitution and thus have to be considered as 'mandatory constitutional laws'.[49] These are legal provisions that are so directly connected to the constitutional system that their elimination would affect the fundamental constitutional principles and the functioning of fundamental Organs of the State.[50] These types of law can only be repealed entirely by the elected Bodies of the Republic and cannot be challenged by an abrogative referendum as the latter is considered not to be an adequate instrument to take an appropriate decision with regard to such fundamental laws (such as electoral laws). In the Constitutional Court's view these rules can only be repealed as a whole by replacing them with new rules, a task which only the representative legislator, that is, the Parliament, is in a position to fulfil.[51]

A very interesting part of the case law of the Constitutional Court with regard to the limits concerns the electoral legislation. The electoral laws have always been considered as 'necessary constitutional laws'. The main reason for their importance is that a regulatory vacuum would occur in the legal system if they were repealed. The Court preliminarily stated that since the electoral laws are not comprised in the limits under Article 75(2), an abrogative referendum on these laws could be held.[52] But since the electoral laws are considered as 'necessary constitutional laws', they could not be repealed as a whole, but only partly, so that the renewal of the Constitutional Organ (the Parliament) or the election of its members is guaranteed at any time. As a result, in order to have an admissible abrogative referendum on electoral laws, the referendum has to necessarily be partial, in the sense that it may address only specific and connected parts of the law. Once the referendum has taken place, the resulting law in force must be able to eventually be applied in case of general elections.

Over the years many electoral referendums have been held and the case law of the Constitutional Court in dealing with them has developed fundamental principles of law which have had a huge impact also on the development of legal literature and the successive case law relating to the direct-democratic instruments in general. The electoral referendums have been characterized as

---

49 Decision 16/1978 of the Constitutional Court.
50 Decision 16/1978 of the Constitutional Court.
51 Decision 29/1987 of the Constitutional Court.
52 Decision 47/1991 of the Constitutional Court.

being in a certain way 'manipulative' as they have, in effect, 'introduced' new pieces of legislation by abolishing numerous provisions of existing electoral laws.[53] For example, in 1993, as a result of the referendum against specific parts of the electoral law regarding the Senate, the existing system was effectively replaced by a new one by eliminating single articles, sections, sentences or even only parts of them.[54]

3.3   Implicit Formal Limits

Neither the Constitutional provisions nor the ordinary laws provide for any formal limits with regard to the abrogative referendum. It has, again, been the Constitutional Court that has developed principles which the referendum questions must comply with. It is useful at this stage to point out that an abrogative referendum request submitted by the promoters can also contain different questions which can address also different laws. While the Central Office is in charge of the legality review of the request (see Section 4.2), a crucial part of the assessment of its constitutionality by the Constitutional Court concerns the interpretation of formal limits by addressing every single question that the referendum request contains.

According to the Constitutional Court's case law, the referendum question must be homogeneous, coherent and intelligible. Referendum requests which contain numerous and heterogenous questions (that is, questions with a lack of unity) have been declared inadmissible by the Court. It has stated that a lack of unity is contrary to the aim of the abrogative referendum itself, considered to be an instrument of genuine expression of popular sovereignty.[55] The referendum question must permit voters the possibility of choice. If, with the same referendum, a great number of questions lacking unity are posed to the voters, their freedom of vote is violated (by violating Articles 1 and 48 of the Constitution).[56] In fact, the very concept of the referendum implies the possibility of choice. Therefore, the essence of the referendum is undermined if the freedom of vote is violated because the wording of the referendum question is not clear.

The referendum question shall be simple, clear, not contradictory and complete. If the formulation of the referendum question is not clear and simple or even contradictory in the sense that it requests the removal of a certain law provision which is closely connected to others, it becomes impossible for the

---

[53] Decisions 47/1991, 5/1995 and 26/1997 of the Constitutional Court.
[54] Bin-Pitruzzella (n 39) 407.
[55] Decision 16/1978 of the Constitutional Court.
[56] Decision 16/1978 of the Constitutional Court.

citizen to choose. It cannot be argued that the referendum campaign could help in this regard, by simplifying or making coherent the referendum question, because in any case the choice of the voters would be to some extent affected since 'they are not given any other possibility of choice than either to express a vote that is not genuine, or to choose not to choose'.[57]

In a more recent decision concerning a referendum request for the abrogation of Law n. 883/1978 (regulating the Italian healthcare system), or more precisely specific sentences of its Article 63(2), the Constitutional Court stated that in the event the referendum request aims to repeal single parts of a law or single sentences of articles of a law, the requirements with regard to the clarity of the request are even stricter, so that the voters can effectively choose.[58] The aim of the referendum request was to maintain the principle of compulsory health insurance for all citizens, but to allow the alternative of using forms of insurance other than the National Health Service. With reference to the case at issue, the Court argued that the referendum question could not reach the goal of abrogating what the promoters effectively had in mind as even with the abrogation of the sentences they proposed the law would have had the same obligations. Consequently, the referendum question did not allow the electors to correctly express their will, as they were presented with a false alternative.[59]

One of the latest decisions of the Constitutional Court dealing with the limit of clarity of referendum questions should be mentioned as well.[60] On that particular occasion the promoters, by means of two differently formulated referendum questions, pursued the same objective: abolishing the electoral legislation in force by returning to the one that had been in force in 1993 (without expressly mentioning their intention in their request). The Court, with regard to the first question, argued that – also referring to its early case law on this specific matter[61] – electoral laws could be subject to a referendum on condition that a residual and immediately applicable electoral legislation still remains in force to ensure, even in the event of legislative inertia, the regular functioning of the elected bodies. As a consequence, the question to totally abolish the electoral law in force was declared not admissible by the Court because it did not allow the electors to distinguish which specific law would have come into force as a result of the abrogation of the existing electoral law. In fact, many electoral laws had been introduced and successively amended since 1993.

The Court considered inadmissible the second question of the referendum request as well. On the one hand, the question was considered to be contra-

---

[57] Decision 27/1981 of the Constitutional Court.
[58] Decision 39/1997 of the Constitutional Court.
[59] Decision 39/1997 of the Constitutional Court.
[60] Decision 13/2012 of the Constitutional Court.
[61] Decisions 13 and 32/1993 of the Constitutional Court.

dictory as it could not realize the purpose of abolishing the law it requested to repeal. On the other hand, it lacked clarity as it seemed impossible to exactly determine which laws the electors were called to abrogate or to interpret the abrogating effect produced by the removal of single paragraphs of articles of a law. Moreover, this latter circumstance would have led to certain difficulties with regard to the interpretation of the remaining law provisions, which according to the Court must be avoided.[62]

Lastly, it is worth mentioning that the Constitutional Court in one of its earliest and most important decisions has suggested that a preliminary check with regard to the simplicity, unity of the form and coherence of the referendum questions should occur even before the signature gathering in order to make citizens willing to sign the referendum request aware of the topic.[63] However, Law n. 352/1970 has clarified neither the criteria for preliminarily assessing the homogeneity of the referendum questions nor the body in charge of this assessment or its timing.

A future reform of the above-mentioned law should obviously address the crucial issues raised by the Court and at the same time incorporate the formal limits already introduced by the judgments of the Constitutional Court. The legislature has clearly failed in this regard so far.

4.   INSTITUTIONAL AND PROCEDURAL FRAMEWORK

4.1   Constitutional Referendum

In order to launch the constitutional referendum, no matter if the referendum request comes from either one-fifth of the members of the Parliament or five Regional Councils or 500,000 citizens, a formal request to the Chancellor's Office of the Supreme Court must be submitted. Once the request is registered, a specific *ad hoc* Office within the Supreme Court is established, composed of all the section presidents of the Supreme Court and presided over by the eldest of them.[64]

The Central Office is the only competent judicial body that verifies that the request for referendum is in accordance with the provisions of Article 138 of the Constitution and Law n. 352/1970.[65] The control of the Central Office is a legality review as it has to verify, for example, the authenticity and the

---

[62]   Decision 13/2012 of the Constitutional Court.
[63]   Decision 16/1978 of the Constitutional Court.
[64]   Art. 12 Law n. 352/1970.
[65]   Art. 12 Law n. 352/1970.

number of the signatures required in case the referendum request has been submitted by citizens and the validity of the resolutions passed by the Regional Councils or the validity of the request of the members of the Parliament entitled to request the referendum under Article 138 of the Constitution.

The Central Office shall decide, by ordinance, on the legality of the request for referendum within 30 days of its submission. It notifies, within the same period, the promoters of the referendum of any given irregularity of their request. If, based on the following clarifications of the promoters to be deposited within five days, the Central Office considers the request to be legal, it decides to admit it.[66]

The Central Office can either admit the request for constitutional referendum or reject it, if the requirements provided by law are not met. In the latter case and provided that the three-month deadline for launching the constitutional referendum provided by the Constitution has expired, the constitutional law and/or amendment must be promulgated by the President of the Republic.[67]

In case the referendum has been admitted, it is then called by decree of the President of the Republic, upon resolution of the Council of Ministers, within 60 days from the communication of the ordinance of the Central Office deciding on it. The date of the referendum is set on a Sunday between the 50th and the 70th day after the decree of the President.[68] The Central Office validates and officially declares the results of the popular vote.[69] Should complaints relating to voting operations emerge, they have to be addressed to the Central Office, which shall decide in public session before counting the ballot sheets.[70]

4.2   Abrogative Referendum

The abrogative referendum is subject both to a legality and an admissibility check. The Central Office is in charge of the legality check of the abrogative referendum request, which could be defined as a preliminary formal review.

The Central Office certifies that the referendum request is in conformity with the Law n. 352/1970. It has to verify – *inter alia* – that (i) the required

---

[66]   Art. 12 Law n. 352/1970.

[67]   Art. 14 Law n. 352/1970.

[68]   Art. 15 Law n. 352/1970. Art. 16 provides for the following formula submitted to the electors: 'The question to be put to the referendum consists of the following formula: "Do you approve the text of the law revising the article ..." (or articles ...) of the Constitution, concerning ... (or concerning ...), approved by Parliament, and published – in the Official Journal number ... of ...." or: "Do you approve the text of the constitutional law ... concerning ... approved by Parliament and published in the Official Journal number ... dated ...?'

[69]   Art. 24 Law n. 352/1970.

[70]   Art. 23 Law n. 352/1970.

number of signatures have been gathered, (ii) all the signatures have been authenticated and (iii) that the referendum request is addressed to a law or a measure having the force of law. If the request for abrogative referendum has been submitted by five Regional Councils, the Central Office verifies the validity of the resolutions passed by the Regional Councils requesting the referendum.

The preliminary legality check of the abrogative referendum carried out by the Central Office is broader than the one which occurs when the Central Office rules on the admissibility of the constitutional referendum. In fact, besides the already mentioned tasks, the Central Office can proceed to the merging of abrogative referendum requests which deal with very similar topics.[71] The promoters can challenge the preliminary decision regarding the merging of the requests by submitting additional written clarifications to the Central Office, but the latter must decide, by means of an ordinance and by 15 December of each year, whether the request for a referendum is legal or not.[72]

If the request is declared to be legal by the Central Office, the related ordinance is submitted to the President of the Constitutional Court. The admissibility check is up to the Constitutional Court in accordance with the Constitutional Law n. 1/1953[73] and Law n. 352/1970.[74] It consists of a substantive check which certifies that the law whose abrogation is requested does not fall into the exempted categories of Article 75(2) of the Constitution and the referendum request complies with the implicit substantive and formal limits. The Constitutional Court may rule on the admissibility of an abrogative referendum only after the Central Office has decided that the referendum request complies with the procedural requirements provided by Law n. 352/1970.

After receiving notice of the ordinance of the Central Office declaring the formal admissibility of the request for referendum, the President of the Constitutional Court shall fix the day when the decision of the Court must take place, which, in any case, shall not be later than 20 January of the year following in which the aforementioned ordinance was pronounced by the Central Office. No later than three days before the decision is taken in closed session by the Court, the promoters and the Government may, according to Article 33(1) and (2) of Law n. 352/1970, file with the Court memorandums on the constitutionality of the request for referendum. They are also entitled to

---

[71]   Art. 32 Law n. 352/1970.
[72]   Art. 32 Law n. 352/1970.
[73]   Art. 2 Law n. 1/1953: 'It is the task of the Constitutional Court to decide whether requests for a referendum to repeal submitted pursuant to Art. 75 of the Constitution are admissible under the second paragraph of the same Art. 75 of the Constitution.'
[74]   Under Art. 32 Law n. 352/1970 the Constitutional Court is empowered to decide on the admissibility of the abrogative referendum.

participate in the closed session of the Court and to discuss the already submitted written memorandums, even though this is not expressly provided by law.[75]

Moreover, in its decision n. 16 of 2008, the Court expressly allowed persons other than those referred to in Article 33 of Law n. 352/1970 – who are nevertheless interested in the decision on the admissibility – to submit memorandums containing additional arguments to those already submitted by the promoters and the Government. In contrast, these persons are not entitled to take part in the closed session. Nevertheless, if the Court deems it appropriate, it may grant them the right to present their memorandums, before the persons referred to in Article 33 of the Law n. 352/1970 could present their respective positions in front of the Constitutional judges.

According to Article 33(4) and (5) of Law n. 352/1970, the Constitutional Court decides by 10 February on the admissibility of the referendum request. Despite the possibility that a great number of referendum requests could be discussed in front of the Court, the Court decides separately but in the same decision about each of them by simply declaring each 'admissible' or 'not admissible'.[76] Within five days of its publication, the decision of the Court is communicated to the President of the Republic, then to the Presidents of the two Chambers, to the President of the Council of Ministers, to the Central Office, as well as to the promoters. Within the same period, the decision shall be published in the Official Journal of the Republic.

Once the popular vote has taken place, the Central Office certifies the votes and proceeds with the official proclamation of the results in a public hearing with the intervention of the Attorney General of the Supreme Court.[77] In case the majority of the voters approve the referendum request, the President of the Republic, by means of his or her own decree, declares the abrogation of the law.[78]

4.3   Citizen-agenda Initiative

Neither the Constitution nor Law n. 352/1970 provides for a legality and/or admissibility check with reference to the draft law submitted by means of a citizen-agenda initiative. According to Article 48(2) of Law n. 352/1970 only a signature check is required in order for the citizen-agenda initiative to be formally accepted by the Parliament.

---

[75]   Decision 16/2008 of the Constitutional Court.
[76]   Bin-Pitruzzella (n 39) 509.
[77]   Art. 36 Law n. 352/1970.
[78]   Art. 37 Law n. 352/1970.

5.   CONCLUSION

As has been shown above, the Italian legal system provides for a diverse range of instruments of direct democracy. Moreover, the practice shows that all of them have been used quite often. The abrogative referendum has certainly been the most significant of these instruments. In fact, it has represented a fundamental tool of minority political parties to request the abrogation of controversial laws introduced by the governing parties. But at the same time, it has been effective to challenge the lack of decision-making of the Parliament on crucial political matters such as, among others, public funding of political parties, electoral legislation, medically assisted procreation, and so on. In fact, requests for abrogative referendums have always been submitted to push and influence political decisions or accelerate the approval of laws delayed because of the obstructionism of the parties represented in Parliament.

Part of the legal literature has pointed out that over the last 20 years, there has been a crisis of the abrogative referendum, which seems to have lost its driving force.[79] Various factors have played a role in this crisis, such as the difficulties of the organized participation of citizens in political life and the invitation of the opponents of the referendum not to take part in popular votes. As a result, many abrogative referendums have failed to reach the turnout quorum provided for in the Constitution: seven out of eight abrogative referendums held between 1997 and 2016 did not reach the turnout quorum.[80] With reference to the total number of abrogative referendums held since 1974, the turnout quorum was reached in 58.2 per cent of the popular votes.[81] In those referendums where the turnout quorum was reached, the 'yes' vote prevailed in 59 per cent of the cases.[82]

The abrogative referendum has also been used as a substitute instrument for other types of direct-democratic instruments not provided for in the Constitution, such as the popular initiative or the consultative referendum.[83]

---

[79]   M. Volpi, Referendum e iniziativa popolare: quale riforma?, (Costituzionalismo. it, October 2016), https://www.costituzionalismo.it/download/Costituzionalismo _201602_567.pdf , accessed 18 July 2020.

[80]   M. Volpi, Referendum e iniziativa popolare: quale riforma?, (Costituzionalismo. it, October 2016), https://www.costituzionalismo.it/download/Costituzionalismo _201602_567.pdf , accessed 18 July 2020.

[81]   See online at, http://www.riformeistituzionali.gov.it/media/1241/storicorefere ndumquorum.pdf, accessed 18 July 2020.

[82]   See online at, http://www.riformeistituzionali.gov.it/media/1241/storicorefere ndumquorum.pdf, accessed 18 July 2020.

[83]   M. Volpi, Referendum e iniziativa popolare: quale riforma?, (Costituzionalismo. it, October 2016), https://www.costituzionalismo.it/download/Costituzionalismo _201602_567.pdf , accessed 18 July 2020.

During the 1990s the massive use of the abrogative referendum has transformed it, to some extent, from an abrogative instrument into a 'manipulative' one. In fact, the promoters – especially with regard to the electoral legislation – have submitted referendum requests for abolishing even single expressions or words of articles of electoral laws. The result was that through the abrogative referendum, by means of this 'manipulation' of the wording of laws, 'new' legal and binding norms have been introduced.

In those cases, the ultimate scope of the abrogative referendum was exceeded, because the Constitutional provisions and the numerous decisions of the Constitutional Court are very clear in this regard: the abrogative referendum is a citizen-initiated or institution-initiated referendum by means of which it is possible to repeal or reject laws, measures having the force of law or single provisions from the legal system. So the main purpose of the abrogative referendum is to abrogate, rather than to introduce pieces of legislation. As mentioned before, the popular initiative, a proactive citizen-initiated referendum, does not belong to the direct-democratic instruments available under Italian law.

The introduction of the popular initiative in the Constitution, enabling citizens to directly submit systematic proposals of laws that are then submitted to a popular vote, could be a concrete response in order to restrict the inappropriate use of the abrogative referendum. But so far, no political party has been able to submit proposals to the Parliament and effectively deal with the issue, even after long discussions and debates in the literature and society.

During the years, different initiatives in order to amend the Constitution have been proposed. Not all these Constitutional drafts have contained proposals to amend the direct-democratic system provided for by the Constitution already in force. But the constitutional reform proposed by the Renzi Government did contain some changes in this respect. This proposal provided for a new form of citizen-agenda initiative, introduced by at least 150,000 voters, with a guaranteed discussion within the limits set by parliamentary regulations.[84] With regard to the abrogative referendum, only a marginal amendment regarding the quorum was proposed. As we know, the constitutional amendment was approved by both Chambers of the Parliament by a less than two-thirds majority, and in 2016 a request for referendum was submitted in accordance with the provisions of Article 138 of the Constitution. On 4 December 2016, the extended constitutional reform was rejected by nearly 60 per cent of the voters.

---

[84] The Italian version of the constitutional reform proposed by Renzi's Government is available at: https://documenti.camera.it/leg17/dossier/pdf/ac0500n.pdf, accessed 18 July 2020.

7. Spain

Daniel Simancas

---

1. INTRODUCTION

Direct-democratic instruments were introduced in the Spanish constitutional system by the Constitution of 1931, which enabled the popular ratification of the Statutes of Autonomy of Catalonia (1931), the Basque Country (1933) and Galicia (1936). After the fall of the Second Republic, the instrument of the referendum was used by the Francoist dictatorship (1939–75): provided for by the Fundamental Law of 1945, it served for the popular ratification of two fundamental Francoist laws (Law of Succession in the Head of State of 1947 and Organic Law of the State of 1966) and the political transition to democracy (Law for Political Reform of 1976). Francoist referendums were, however, far from meeting democratic standards and reflecting faithfully public opinion, since they took place when freedoms of expression and the press were neither recognized nor protected. Instead, they were used to lend democratic legitimacy to the dictatorship.

The authoritarian use of the referendum during the dictatorship, as well as the intention to establish a system in which citizens participate in public affairs mainly through their political representatives, led direct-democratic instruments to be viewed with distrust during the drafting of the Constitution of 1978 (Spanish Constitution or Constitution).[1] Thus, the Socialist Gregorio Peces-Barba, one of the *fathers* of the Spanish Constitution, maintained that 'the referendum may entail the manipulation of the question; may divide, in some aspects, the country into two large blocks – which is not positive at this moment [transition from the dictatorship to democracy].'[2] For his part, the

---

[1] The Spanish Constitution was ratified in the referendum of 6 December 1978 and entered into force on 29 December 1978, <https://www.boe.es/buscar/act.php?id=BOE-A-1978-31229>, English translation, https://www.boe.es/legislacion/documentos/ConstitucionINGLES.pdf, accessed 8 August 2020.

[2] Official Journal of the Congress of Deputies (Lower House; hereinafter: BOCD), 6 June 1978, no 81, 2943, http://www.congreso.es/public_oficiales/L0/CONG/DS/C_1978_081.PDF, accessed 8 August 2020.

illustrious framer José Pedro Pérez-Llorca, a member of the centrist party, stated that 'basically we are facing an evaluative problem of whether it is more worthwhile to establish the parliamentary system in all its purity in our Constitution or we can make it coexist with other systems whose effectiveness in a parliamentary system is not proven.'[3]

Despite these concerns, the drafters finally opted for the regulation of direct-democratic instruments in the Constitution, a decision that, as will be seen later, does not seem to have negatively affected the settlement of the party system in Spain. These instruments were later developed through Organic Law 2/1980, 18 January 1980, on the Referendum (Referendum Act) and Organic Law 3/1984, 26 March 1984, on the Popular Legislative Initiative (Popular Initiative Act). This chapter will mainly focus on the analysis of these two laws as they regulate the exercise of these instruments at the national level.

2. DIRECT-DEMOCRATIC INSTRUMENTS IN SPAIN

The Spanish Constitution regulates four types of direct-democratic instruments at the national level, namely, the mandatory referendum (law-initiated referendum), the consultative referendum (executive-initiated referendum), the legislature-initiated referendum and, finally, the popular initiative (citizens' agenda initiative). Other mechanisms, such as the subnational entity-initiated referendum or the citizen-initiated referendum, do not exist in Spain.

To explain the direct-democratic instruments existing at the regional level, it is necessary to make a distinction between *popular consultations* and *referendums*. This distinction is also essential to determine the competent body for the regulation of said instruments: whereas the central government has the competence to regulate the instrument of the referendum, popular consultations are placed within the regional competency framework. The Spanish Constitutional Court has provided some clues to distinguish the two instruments, stating that, regardless of its binding or advisory nature, the referendum is characterized by its formal guarantees: strict procedural rules, official register of voters, supervision by the Electoral Administration and judicial control.[4] The relevance of this distinction has also been defined by the Constitutional Court, which maintains that the holding of a referendum involves a call to the holder of the sovereignty for participating in political decision-making.[5] The Constitutional

---

[3]   BOCD, 13 July 1978, no 109, 4213, http://www.congreso.es/public_oficiales/L0/CONG/DS/C_1978_109.PDF, accessed 8 August 2020.

[4]   Decision 137/2015, 11 June 2015, 4th Legal Ground (hereinafter: LG).

[5]   Decision 137/2015, 11 June 2015, 4th LG.

Court adds that this participation constitutes a way of exercising the fundamental right of political participation (Article 23.1 of the Constitution), which entails the activation of judicial mechanisms for the protection of fundamental rights (Article 53 of the Constitution).[6] In contrast, popular consultations that do not meet the formal guarantees mentioned above cannot be included in the concept of the referendum; they are not a way of exercising the fundamental right of political participation but an expression of participatory democracy (Article 9.2 of the Constitution).[7]

The Autonomous Communities can regulate as many types of popular consultations as they desire, provided that they do not have the features of the referendum.[8] Besides popular consultations, the direct-democratic instruments existing at the regional level are the citizens' agenda initiative, the law-initiated referendum and the executive-initiated referendum.[9]

Finally, even though the Constitution does not regulate the municipal referendum, the Spanish legal system also allows mayors to submit municipal issues to the vote of their residents as long as these issues satisfy, as will be seen below, a series of conditions.

3.   REFERENDUM

Only two years elapsed from the promulgation of the Constitution to the approval of the Referendum Act. This legislative velocity does not stem from the interest of the legislator in regulating direct-democratic instruments to compensate for the constitutional predominance of the party system, but rather from the role that the Constitution gave to citizens in shaping the new territorial model. The building process of the autonomous system demanded the urgent regulation of this instrument, especially one of its types: regional law-initiated referendums. This explains the noteworthy role of this type of referendum in the Referendum Act, as well as its use during the first years

---

[6]   Decision 137/2015, 11 June 2015, 4th LG.

[7]   Decision 137/2015, 11 June 2015, 4th LG.

[8]   For example, Catalonia provides for the holding of popular consultations whose promoters can be citizens (citizen-initiated), the regional parliament (legislature-initiated) or, even, a group of municipalities that represents a certain number of voters (subautonomous entity-initiated): Art. 29.6 Statute of Autonomy of Catalonia and Art. 4 Catalonian Law 10/2014, 26 September 2014.

[9]   Nevertheless, the Statute of Autonomy of Extremadura includes a legislature-initiated referendum similar to that which is provided for by Art. 167 Spanish Constitution: Art. 91.2 of this Statute states that its modification can be submitted to a regional referendum if so demanded by two-thirds of the autonomous parliamentarians.

of the Constitution and its gradual decline as the bases of the new territorial system were established.

The data reveal that, during the first years of the Constitution, six supra-municipal referendums were held in Spain – five regional and one national. The national referendum was held on 12 March 1986. The Government asked its citizens about Spain's membership in the North Atlantic Treaty Organization (NATO), given that the ruling party (Socialist Party) had advocated, while it was in opposition, the rejection of NATO. Its change of opinion when it came to power led to the holding of a consultative referendum, which finally resulted in 56.85 per cent votes in favour of remaining within NATO.[10] Although municipal referendums were held in the following years, the next national referendum did not arrive until 20 February 2005, when Spanish people endorsed the Treaty that provided the European Union with a Constitution.[11] In this case, both the ruling party (Socialist Party) and the main opposition party (People's Party) campaigned for a 'yes' vote.

The results of these referendums show ultimately that the decrease of national and regional referendum calls is not owing to bad experiences in the use of this mechanism during the early years of democracy but rather to the completion of the new territorial model; all the issues that have been submitted to national or regional referendums have been approved by the voters.[12]

3.1 Law-initiated or Mandatory Referendum

The Constitution imposes the holding of a referendum in four cases: first, when a constitutional amendment affects the 'hardest' provisions of the Constitution;[13] second, when a territory becomes an Autonomous Community through the procedure of Article 151.1 of the Constitution; third, for the approval or modification of the Statutes of Autonomy of those Communities that had been constituted through Article 151.1 or the Second Transitory Provision;[14] and, finally, for a hypothetical incorporation of Navarra into the Basque Country.[15] This chapter will focus exclusively on the first type of

---

[10]   The results of the NATO referendum can be consulted at https://app.congreso.es/consti/elecciones/referendos/ref_otan.htm, accessed 8 August 2020.

[11]   The results of the European Constitution referendum can be consulted at https://app.congreso.es/consti/elecciones/referendos/ref_europa.htm, accessed 8 August 2020.

[12]   This trend has not changed in the following years as the approval rate for national and regional referendums currently remains at 100 per cent, https://app.congreso.es/consti/elecciones/referendos/index.htm, accessed 8 August 2020.

[13]   Art. 168 Spanish Constitution.

[14]   Arts. 151.2.3 and 152.2 Spanish Constitution.

[15]   Fourth Transitory Provision Spanish Constitution.

Table 7.1   Referendums held in Spain

Decade	National referendum		Subnational referendum			Authorized Municipal Referendum*
	Constitutional amendment	Executive-initiated or consultative	Approval of Statute of Autonomy	Modification of Statute of Autonomy	Others	
1978–90	–	1	4	–	1	5
1990–2000	–	–	–	–	–	12
2000–10	–	1	–	2	–	11
2010–20	–	–	–	–	–	36
TOTAL	0	2	4	2	1	64

Note: * The data correspond to the number of municipal referendums authorized from 1985 to May 2020; they have been obtained from <http://www.senado.es/web/expedientdocblobservlet?legis=12&id=86165> accessed 8 August 2020, and through a consultation (nº 001-43637) formulated to the transparency portal of the Government of Spain.

Source: Congress of Deputies and Senate. The data have been obtained from <https://app.congreso.es/consti/elecciones/referendos/> and <http://www.senado.es/web/expedientdocblobservlet?legis=12&id=86165> accessed 8 August 2020.

mandatory referendum, that is, the referendum on the amendment of 'hard' constitutional provisions, since the other types of referendums are only held in the Community concerned rather than the whole of the nation.

A constitutional amendment entails a mandatory referendum if either a total revision of the Constitution is proposed or a partial revision affecting the constitutional system's fundamental principles (Preliminary Title), fundamental rights (First Section of the Second Chapter of the First Title) or the Crown's regulation (Second Title).[16] In these cases, the Parliament will have to communicate the draft amendment to the Government, which will be in charge of adopting the referendum call decree.[17] The communication will not have to be accompanied by any request since, in this case, the holding of the referendum is imperative. The result of the referendum is binding, so that if the draft amendment is rejected, it cannot be carried out.[18]

3.2 Institution-initiated Referendums

3.2.1 Legislature-initiated referendum

Article 167 of the Constitution includes the only case in which Parliament can initiate a referendum. This referendum is again connected to the constitutional amendment procedure. A draft constitutional amendment may be submitted to a referendum, provided that at least 10 per cent of either deputies or senators request it. The request must be made to the President of the Spanish Government (Prime Minister) within 15 days following parliamentary approval of the draft amendment.[19] Even though the Spanish Constitution and the Referendum Act use the word 'request', the Government cannot refuse to call a referendum if it has the required parliamentary support.[20] In short, the holding of this referendum, unlike the mandatory one, does not result from the Constitution but from the will of Parliament. Its result will equally be binding on the state authorities.[21]

---

[16]   Art. 168 Spanish Constitution.

[17]   Art. 7 Referendum Act. A part of Spanish doctrine has criticized this provision, arguing that the call decree should not be countersigned by the Prime Minister but by the President of the Congress of Deputies: Eva Sáenz Royo, *El referéndum en España* (Marcial Pons 2018) 39.

[18]   Art. 168.3 Spanish Constitution.

[19]   Art. 7 Referendum Act.

[20]   José Antonio Alonso de Antonio and Ángel Luis Alonso de Antonio, *Derecho Constitucional Español* (5th edn, Dykinson 2013) 296.

[21]   Art. 167.3 Spanish Constitution.

3.2.2   Executive-initiated or consultative referendum

This referendum is set out in the chapter of the Constitution related to the drafting of laws, more specifically in Article 92 of the Constitution. Its peculiar location is due to the fact that the original text of the preliminary constitutional draft did not only establish the possibility that certain political decisions could be submitted to citizens' approval, but also provided for both types of legislative referendum – abrogative and confirmative. However, an oral amendment posed by the Communist deputy Solé Tura and supported by the majority of parliamentary parties removed the legislative referendum, leaving only the executive-initiated referendum.[22]

Article 92 of the Constitution allows the Prime Minister to consult citizens' opinions – without being bound by the results of the referendum – on 'political decisions of special importance'. These decisions are not, however, defined either in the Constitution or in the Referendum Act, giving a wide margin of discretion to the executive. Nevertheless, the drafters of the Constitution have compensated for that margin by requiring that consultative referendums must be authorized by the (absolute) majority of the Congress of Deputies. The Prime Minister must send the final draft of the text to be proposed to the citizens so that it can be debated and voted on in the plenary session.[23]

This type of referendum also exists at regional and municipal levels. In both cases it has to be authorized by the Spanish Government.[24] The municipal referendum requires, in addition, the agreement of the plenum of the local council.[25]

4.   CITIZENS' AGENDA INITIATIVE

The Spanish Constitution allows citizens to submit legislative proposals, provided that they meet a series of formal and substantive requisites.[26] Although the official name of this instrument is 'popular legislative initiative', it has also been defined as 'propositional legislative instrument', given that the participation of citizens in the law-making procedure ends with the proposal.[27]

---

[22]   BOCD, 6 June 1978, no 81, 2937, http://www.congreso.es/public_oficiales/L0/CONG/DS/C_1978_081.PDF, accessed 8 August 2020.

[23]   Art. 6 Referendum Act and Art. 161 Congress of Deputies' Standing Orders.

[24]   Art. 149.1.32 Spanish Constitution and Art. 2.2 Referendum Act.

[25]   Art. 71 Law 7/1985, 2 April 1985, on the Bases of Local Regime (Local Regime Act).

[26]   Art. 87.1 Spanish Constitution.

[27]   Joan Vintró Castells, 'Un punto de partida: el marco normativo de la iniciativa legislativa popular en España', in Joan Vintró Castells and Juan María Bilbao Ubillos (eds), *Participación ciudadana y procedimiento legislativo: de la experiencia española*

Only the Parliament has the power to decide on the transformation of a popular legislative proposal into a law initiative.

This instrument was first regulated by Article 66 of the Constitution of 1931. At that time, Spanish people were empowered to submit legislative proposals to Parliament as long as they were endorsed by 15 per cent of voters. Fifty years later, the drafters of 1978 considered that, albeit the popular initiative should be included in the new constitution, it was necessary to make some changes regarding the legal limits:

On the one hand, the launching of initiatives was facilitated by reducing the required number of signatures to 500,000 (Article 87.3 of the Spanish Constitution).[28] However, a part of Spanish doctrine argues that the current number of required signatures still complicates the submission of popular iniatives to Parliament.[29] Authors usually allude to the number of signatures required in other European countries such as Italy, where the number required is ten times less than in Spain, even though Italy's population is significantly greater than Spain's.[30] The need to review this hurdle certainly finds support in the data provided,[31] as almost 33 per cent of the registered initiatives expired as a result of not reaching the minimum number of signatures.

On the other hand, Article 87.3 of the Spanish Constitution excludes certain issues from the scope of the instrument and enables the introduction of further limits through the Popular Initiative Act.[32] Thus, the legislator has increased the list of prohibited issues, further restricting the exercise of the popular initiative. The original preamble of the Referendum Act revealed the reasons for the constrictive spirit of its provisions, noting that historical experiences demonstrated that direct-democratic instruments can serve *demagogic manipulations* and legitimize the will of the minority through *false popular consensus*.[33]

---

a la iniciativa ciudadana europea (Centro de Estudios Políticos y Constitucionales 2011) 19.

[28]   As of 1 March 2020, this number was equivalent to 1.35 per cent of the electoral roll (36,966,163). The data have been obtained from https://www.ine.es/ss/Satellite ?c=Page&cid=1254735793323&pagename=CensoElectoral%2FINELayout&L=0, accessed 30 May 2020.

[29]   Tomás Vidal Marín, *Regeneración democrática e iniciativa legislativa popular* (Indret 2015) 20, among others.

[30]   Vidal Marín (n 29) 20.

[31]   See Table 7.2.

[32]   The Constitution of 1978 states, just as the Constitution of 1931 did, that the popular legislative has to be regulated by an organic law, which ensures a certain consensus on the regulation of the instrument as the approval of the law requires a reinforced parliamentary majority.

[33]   The expressions in italics were finally removed from the preamble by Organic Law 4/2006, 26 May 2006.

This perception of the instrument changed after the approval of the Organic Law 4/2006, 26 May 2006, when the legislator made some amendments that facilitated the use of the mechanism – among other changes, the deadline for collecting signatures was extended, signatures could now be collected electronically and a financial compensation for the expenses of promoters of initiatives was introduced.

The data show a progressive increase in the submission of popular initiatives until 2016 and a sudden decrease from that year. However, this decrease can be explained by the end of the bipartisanship in Spain – the incorporation of new political parties has not only modified the organization of the Spanish party system, but it has also served to address citizens' demands through the functioning of the representative system.

The agenda initiative also exists at the regional level. The Autonomous Communities have included in their Statutes of Autonomy the possibility that their citizens can present initiatives to the respective regional parliaments. Some Communities, such as Andalusia, Catalonia and Aragon, have even approved their own regional laws, based on national legislation, adapting the exercise of the mechanism to the regional scope.[34]

5.   LEGAL LIMITS

5.1   Referendum

5.1.1   Substantive limits

Neither the Constitution nor the Referendum Act contain a list of issues that are excluded from the scope of the referendum. The limitation of consultative referendums to 'political decisions of special importance' has not been considered as a substantive limit since, due to its vagueness, it does not really work as a restriction. However, if it was considered as a limit, it could be regarded as being controlled by the plenary session of the Congress of Deputies.

There are at least three reasons that could explain the absence of substantive limits. The first reason is the absence of intangible constitutional clauses. The Spanish Constitution allows the modification of all its provisions, so that all draft constitutional amendments approved by Parliament can be subject to referendum. Second, the Constitution submits national executive-initiated referendums to prior authorization by the Lower House. This requirement not only reinforces the dialogue between the legislative and the executive powers but also guarantees a certain consensus in the decision on those political issues

---

[34]   Thus, for instance, they have reduced the number of signatures required for the submission of initiatives.

Table 7.2   *Citizens' agenda initiatives of the Congress of Deputies of Spain since 1989*

Terms	Initiatives	Results								Unresolved initiatives
		Inadmissable	Expired	Withdrawal	Rejected by Plenum	Rejected for budgetary reasons	Approved with modifications	Subsumed in other bill	Passed to next term	
1989–93	7	2	4	1	–	–	–	–	–	–
1993–96	6	3	1	–	–	–	–	–	2	–
1996–2000	11	1	2	–	3	–	–	1	4	–
2000–04	13	3	3	–	4	–	–	–	3	–
2004–08	13	3	7	–	1	–	–	–	2	–
2008–11	23	8	6	2	–	–	–	–	7	–
2011–16	36	14	13	1	2	–	1	1	4	–
2016–16	6	–	1	–	–	–	–	–	5	–
2016–19	20	8	7	–	–	–	–	–	5	–
2019–19	8	–	1	–	–	–	–	–	7	–
2019	8	–	–	–	–	1	1	–	–	7
TOTAL	151	42	45	4	10	1	1	2	39	7

Note: Since the focus of the LIDD project is on the period from 1990 onwards, the table only reveals the data for the last 30 years.
Source: Central Electoral Board and Congress of Deputies. The data have been obtained from <http://www.juntaelectoralcentral.es/cs/jec/ilp/legislaturas> and <http://www.congreso.es/portal/page/portal/Congreso/Congreso/Iniciativas> accessed 8 August 2020.

that may be subject to a referendum and impedes its unlawful use by the Government. The deliberative and parliamentary authorization regime could, ultimately, be the reason behind the absence of substantive limits on national executive-initiated referendums. Third, regional law-initiated referendums, that is, those which are regulated in Articles 151.1, 152.2 and the Fourth Transitory Provision, are substantively delimited either by the Constitution or by the bill of approval or modification of the Statute of Autonomy. In other words, the subject of these referendums can only consist in the constitution of a group of provinces as an Autonomous Community or in the approval of the bill of Statute of Autonomy. Thus, given that there is no substantive margin for the elaboration of call decrees in this category of referendums, the addition of further substantive limits seems to be unnecessary.

On the contrary, the competency framework gives some clues to determine the substantive limits that are imposed on regional consultative popular votes. The Constitutional Court has indicated that regional consultations, irrespective of whether they are *referendums* or *popular consultations*, cannot be held on issues that fall within the competence of the central government.[35] This was the case of Catalonian Law 19/2017, 6 September 2017, on the self-determination referendum in Catalonia, which was declared unconstitutional for competency and substantive reasons, among others.[36] The Constitutional Court held that the Law ignored the exclusive competence of the central government for the regulation of the instrument of referendum and aimed at holding a (secessionist) referendum without its mandatory authorization (Article 149.1.32 of the Constitution).[37] Besides, the Law contravened the constitutional system's fundamental principles, such as the national sovereignty that resides in the Spanish people, the unity of the nation and the supremacy of the Constitution that binds all public powers, including Catalonian ones. Thus, the Law was placed above the rules of the Spanish legal system, including the Spanish Constitution, and declared the sovereignty of the Catalonian people to decide on the separation of Catalonia from Spain. It purported to make a constitutional amendment outside the constitutional channels provided for by Article 168 of the Constitution. The Constitutional Court therefore reiterated that regional popular consultations can neither concern subjects that belong to the competence of the central gov-

---

[35]   Decision 51/2017, 10 May 2017, 4th LG.

[36]   Decision 114/2017, 17 October 2017. The Constitutional Court had previously declared unconstitutional some provisions of the Catalonian Law 10/2014, 26 September 2014, on non-referendum popular consultations and other ways of citizen participation (Decision 31/2015, 25 February 2015) and the Catalonian Law 4/2010, 17 March, on popular consultations by way of referendum (Decision 51/2017, 10 May 2017).

[37]   Decision 114/2017, 17 October 2017, 3rd LG.

ernment nor deal with issues that were resolved by the constituent power and are removed from the decision of the constituted powers.[38] Despite the fact that the Law was declared unconstitutional, the Catalonian government approved the Call Decree 139/2017, 6 September 2017, for the self-determination referendum in Catalonia. Although the call decree was immediately suspended and subsequently declared unconstitutional[39] for the same defects as the Law 19/2017, 6 September 2017, Catalonian authorities disobeyed, once again, the decision of the Constitutional Court, and the 'referendum' was finally held on 1 October 2017 without formal guarantees.

Ultimately, certain substantive limits can also be observed at the municipal level. Article 71 of the Local Regime Act establishes that municipal consultative referendums must deal with subjects of municipal scope that are relevant to residents' interests but cannot be related to local treasury issues. According to Spanish legal doctrine, this substantive limit aims to prevent the demagogic use of this type of referendum with regard to municipal finances.[40]

5.1.2   Formal limits

The Referendum Act states that the call decree must contain the entire text of the constitutional provision that is required to be approved or, if it is a consultative referendum, the relevant political decision subject to the consultation.[41] This requirement safeguards the free will-formation of citizens since it allows them to know the subject of the referendum well in advance. The decree must also specify the date of the referendum, which must take place between 30 and 120 days after its publication in the State Official Gazette and the official gazettes of those territories in which the referendum is to be held.[42]

Besides the former requisites, the call decree has to indicate 'clearly' the question or questions of the referendum.[43] However, the adverb 'clearly' could lead to diverse interpretations: it could imply that the call decree has to establish unambiguously the questions on which citizens are called to express their opinion, or it could refer to the intelligible drafting of the questions. Nevertheless, according to the very express wording of Article 3.1 of the Referendum Act, the clarity requirement has to be understood according to the

---

[38]   Decision 114/2017, 17 October 2017, 5th LG.

[39]   Decision 122/2017, 31 October 2017. The Constitutional Court had also declared unconstitutional the Call Decree 129/2014, 27 September, for the popular consultation on political future in Catalonia (Decision 32/2015, 25 February 2015).

[40]   Joan Oliver Araujo, *El referéndum en el Sistema constitucional español* (no 15, Cuadernos de la Facultad de Derecho 1986) 147.

[41]   Art. 3.1 Referendum Act.

[42]   Art. 3.1 Referendum Act.

[43]   Art. 3.1 Referendum Act.

former interpretation, so that the call decree of the referendum has to formulate expressly the questions of the referendum. There is therefore no limit concerning the intelligibility of the referendum questions.

On the other hand, citizens can express their opinion by voting 'yes', 'no' or in blank to the question or questions of the referendum.[44] Thus, one might wonder if a single vote on a multiple-questions referendum is legally permitted. Articles 3.1 and 16.2 of the Referendum Act do not provide for an unequivocal answer. However, given that voting is not a constitutional duty in Spain, it can be stated that a single vote on multiple questions is allowed.

Likewise, it is not clear if a unity of substance requirement for the holding of referendums exists. Although neither the Referendum Act nor the relevant practice provide an indisputable answer, a systematic interpretation of Article 4.2 of the Referendum Act, which disposes a minimum period of 90 days between the holding of referendums, could serve as basis to maintain that this requirement is implicitly provided.

5.1.3   Time limits

The Referendum Act also includes time limits on the holding of referendums. They cannot take place during a state of emergency or siege, or within 90 days after its cessation.[45] Likewise, the holding of any type of referendum, except for those on constitutional amendments, is forbidden in the period between 90 days before and after the date of parliamentary or municipal elections, or that of another referendum.[46] In these cases, a referendum will be automatically suspended, so that it will have to be called again.[47] In the opinion of Spanish legal doctrine, these limits hinder the holding of national referendums as the multitude of electoral processes (European Parliament, Spanish Parliament, regional parliaments and councils) and the lack of synchrony among them make finding available dates complicated. They reflect, once again, the preference for representative democracy over direct-democratic mechanisms as the Referendum Act clearly prioritizes elections over referendums.[48]

5.2   Citizens' Agenda Initiative

5.2.1   Substantive limits

There are two categories of issues that are excluded from the scope of the popular initiative. The first category comprises those subjects that can only

---

44   Art. 16.2 Referendum Act.
45   Art. 4.1 Referendum Act.
46   Art. 4.2 Referendum Act.
47   Alonso de Antonio and Alonso de Antonio (n 20) 296.
48   Oliver Araujo (n 40) 147.

be regulated by organic law, such as fundamental rights, the organization of the judiciary and the electoral system. The second one includes economic or tax issues, as well as those subjects that belong to the prerogatives of the Government, that is, international affairs, the national budget, the planning of economic activity and the granting of pardons.[49]

One of the most disputed substantive limits is the exception of fundamental rights. The Constitutional Court has repeatedly stated that the principle of organic law reservation regarding fundamental rights has to be interpreted restrictively, which means that popular initiatives are only impermissible if they concern the 'direct regulation' or the 'minimum core content' of fundamental rights.[50] A part of the doctrine maintains that the present definition of the limit grants a wide margin of discretion to the Bureau to decide on the admissibility of popular initiatives.[51] In their opinion, the redefinition of this limit would ensure that the Bureau exercises its power properly without the risk of decisions based on political reasons.[52]

Otherwise, the Constitutional Court has added, through a systematic interpretation of the Constitution, one more issue to the previous lists: the constitutional amendment.[53] Article 166 of the Constitution grants the right to propose constitutional amendments to the Government, the Lower House, the Upper House and regional parliaments. The restrictive nature of the provision gives no opportunity for citizens to propose constitutional amendments via popular initiatives. Moreover, the Constitutional Court has held that this prohibition also extends to those popular initiatives that, trying to circumvent it, urge the respective bodies to exercise their right to initiate the constitutional amendment procedure.[54] This interpretation of the Court is respectful of the Constitution as the participation of citizens is not completely excluded, but postponed until popular ratification of the draft amendment approved by Parliament.

5.2.2 Formal limits

Popular initiatives must meet a number of formal requirements to be admitted by the Bureau of the Congress of Deputies (Article 5 of the Popular Initiative Act): first, the initiative has to contain a text articulating the legislative pro-

---

[49]   Art. 87(3) Constitution and Art. 2 Popular Initiative Act.
[50]   Decisions 160/1987, 21 October 1987, 93/1988, 8 November 1988 and 173/1998, 23 July 1998.
[51]   Vidal Marín (n 29) 48–49 and Aitor Martínez Jiménez, *La iniciativa legislativa popular como instrumento de participación ciudadana en el siglo XXI* (Fundación Ideas 2012) 15, among others.
[52]   Vidal Marín (n 29) 48–49 and Martínez Jiménez (n 51) 15, among others.
[53]   Decision 76/1994, 14 April 1994, 5th LG.
[54]   Decision 76/1994, 14 April 1994, 5th LG.

posal and an explanation of the motives for the referendum; second, it has to include the personal details of its promoters and the reasons why they consider that their initiative should be processed and approved by Parliament; third, the initiative cannot concern the same subject as another bill that is in the phase of amendment or a more advanced phase; fourth, the subject of the initiative may not coincide with that of another popular initiative that has already been presented in the same term; and, finally, the issues it covers must have a certain homogeneity.

The last requirement, set forth in Article 5.2 (c) of the Popular Initiative Act, has been criticized on the basis that, besides the concept of homogeneity being ambiguous, there are no convincing reasons for demanding more internal coherence from popular initiatives than from government and parliamentary legislative proposals.[55] This criticism may have inspired the modification made by Organic Law 4/2006, 26 May 2006, which has restricted its application to those initiatives that deal with 'manifestly' different subjects. The doctrine considers that this modification advises a restrictive interpretation of the unity of substance requirement,[56] so that this requirement does not consist in a review of legislative technique but serves to reject those popular initiatives that deal with different subjects without logical relation.[57]

6.   INSTITUTIONAL AND PROCEDURAL FRAMEWORK FOR THE REVIEW OF COMPLIANCE WITH THE LEGAL LIMITS

6.1   Referendum

As discussed in previous sections of this chapter, substantive limits exist neither for national referendums (Articles 92, 167 and 168 of the Constitution) nor for regional law-initiated referendums (Articles 151, 152 and Fourth Transitory Provision of the Constitution). However, the constitutional framework of competencies and Article 71 of the Local Regime Act establish certain substantive limits for the holding of regional and municipal consultative referendums. Compliance with them is initially controlled by the Government, which will only authorize such referendums if these substantive limits are

---

[55]   Juan Alfonso Santamaría Pastor, 'Comentario al artículo 87', in Fernando Garrido Falla (dir), *Comentarios a la Constitución* (2nd edn, Civitas 1985) 1264 and Vidal Marín (n 29) 24.

[56]   Enrique Arnaldo Alcubilla, Manuel Delgado-Iribarren García-Campero and Ángel José Sánchez Navarro, *Iniciativa Legislativa Popular* (1st edn, La Ley 2013) 98.

[57]   Arnaldo Alcubilla, Delgado-Iribarren García-Campero and Sánchez Navarro (n 56) 98–99.

respected.[58] The decision of the Government can be challenged either through a conflict of jurisdiction[59] before the Constitutional Court, if the referendum promoter is an Autonomous Community, or through an administrative appeal before the Supreme Court, if the referendum is initiated by a council.[60]

If an Autonomous Community disregards the governmental decision and calls a consultative referendum without the pertinent authorization, the Government can react through the appeal provided for by Article 161.2 of the Constitution before the Constitutional Court; this entails an automatic suspension of the effects of the referendum call decree. Suspension is without prejudice to criminal responsibilities that regional public authorities may incur for the illegal holding of a referendum. This possibility must be noted especially after recent events in Catalonia.[61]

The formal limits of call decrees of referendums are controlled by the judiciary. Thus, those decrees that do not contain the elements provided for by Article 3 of the Referendum Act or do not respect the time limits set by Article 4 of the Referendum Act can be challenged by an administrative-contentious appeal.[62] The power to decide on such appeal will vary depending on the scope of the referendum: in the case of national referendums, the competence is assumed by the Supreme Court.[63] If the call decree has been adopted by a regional government, the High Court of Justice of the respective Autonomous Community is competent to decide.[64] The decisions of both judicial bodies may be appealed

---

[58] Art. 2.1 and 2 Referendum Act.

[59] The conflict of jurisdiction is a constitutional procedure that can be used by certain territorial entities (State and Autonomous Communities) to react when their competences are infringed by others (Art. 161.1 (c)) Spanish Constitution and Art. 60–67 Organic Law 2/1979, 3 October 1979, on the Constitutional Court. It is not only a mechanism to claim the titularity of competences, but also to react to damaging conducts of the exercise of said competences, even when they do not strictly entail an infringement and provided that they have immediate legal effects. See Pablo Pérez Tremps, *Sistema de Justicia Constitucional* (2nd edn, Aranzadi 2016) 103–104 and Decision 44/2007, 1 March, 9th LG.

[60] Art. 12.1 (a) Law 29/1998, 13 July 1998, on the Contentious-Administrative Jurisdiction.

[61] See Section 5.1.1 above.

[62] The Referendum Act does not provide a specific proceeding to appeal call decrees for referendums. So if a call decree does not meet the former requirements, it may be challenged through the general appeal provided to contest the activity of the Administration (Art. 25.1 Law 29/1998, 13 July 1998). The procedural capacity, legitimacy and representation rules are provided by Art. 17–24 Law 29/1998, 13 July 1998.

[63] Art. 12.1 (a) Law 29/1998, 13 July 1998.

[64] Art. 25 Law 29/1998, 13 July 1998.

before the Constitutional Court in accordance with the general provisions of the constitutional complaint.[65]

6.2   Citizens' Agenda Initiative

The Bureau of the Congress of Deputies[66] is one of the bodies in charge of reviewing popular initiatives for their compliance with the legal limits.[67] During this administrative procedure, the Bureau will review whether a popular initiative satisfies the limits set out in Section 5.2. Thus, its decision on admissibility must be based on legal considerations, not political reasons.[68] If the initiative is submitted without the requisites provided for by Article 5 of the Popular Initiative Act – articulated text, memorandum, personal data of its promoters and the reasons why the initiative is, in their opinion, necessary or beneficial for the citizenry – the Bureau will grant one month to rectify the formal defect with the caveat that otherwise the initiative will definitively be declared inadmissible.[69] The promoters of the initiative can appeal the inadmissibility decision through a constitutional complaint,[70] claiming a violation of the right to political participation guaranteed by Article 23.1 of the Spanish Constitution. The Constitutional Court will review whether the initiative violates any material or formal limits and, if this is the case, whether the deficiency extends to the entire proposal or only certain of its provisions.[71] In the latter case, the Bureau shall ask the promoting committee whether it wants to withdraw the initiative or make the appropriate modifications.[72]

Given that there is no specific proceeding designed to challenge inadmissibility decisions of popular initiatives, the review of the Constitutional Court will be carried out in accordance with the provisions of the constitutional complaint.[73] Article 46 of the Constitutional Court Act establishes that persons

---

[65]   Art. 41–58 Organic Law 2/1979, 3 October 1979.

[66]   The Bureau of the Congress of Deputies is a collective body that governs and organizes the day-to-day of the Chamber (Art. 30.1 Congress of Deputies' Standing Orders). It is composed of the President, four Vice-presidents and four Secretaries (Art. 30.2 Congress of Deputies' Standing Orders) and among its functions are to qualify parliamentarian documents and to establish the agenda of the Plenary and Committees (Art. 31 Congress of Deputies' Standing Orders).

[67]   Art. 4 Popular Initiative Act.

[68]   Art. 5 Popular Initiative Act.

[69]   Art. 5.2 (b) Popular Initiative Act.

[70]   Article 6.1 Popular Initiative Act does not establish any instrument to challenge an admissibility decision.

[71]   Art. 6 Popular Initiative Act.

[72]   Art. 6.3 Popular Initiative Act.

[73]   Art. 6.1 Popular Initiative Act and Art. 42 Organic Law 2/1979, 3 October 1979.

who benefit from the object of the constitutional complaint or have a legitimate interest in it can participate as defendants or co-adjuvants in the proceeding. In application of this provision, the promoters of the popular initiative, the Prosecution Service and the Parliament that would have made the challenged decision can participate in the proceeding against an inadmissibility decision.

If the initiative meets all the limits, the period for collecting the signatures begins.[74] The promoting committee then has nine months, exceptionally extendable for another three, to collect 500,000 signatures and present them to the National Electoral Commission, which is in charge of verifying and counting them.[75] If, at the end of this period, the promoters have not collected the required amount of signatures, the popular initiative expires. If the initiative has received the required number of signatures, the Electoral Commission informs the Bureau so that it can, in turn, inform the Government and convene the Plenum to decide about the processing of the initiative.[76]

The plenary decision of the Congress of Deputies is preceded by a parliamentary debate, in which the representative designated by the promoting committee has the opportunity to participate and persuade parliamentarians of the necessity of the initiative.[77] If the plenary session endorses its processing, the appropriate regulatory channels will be followed so that parliamentarians can make changes to the initial draft of the initiative.[78] On the contrary, rejection by the Plenum entails the end of the initiative and, unlike the decisions of the Bureau, this pronouncement cannot be appealed through a constitutional complaint before the Constitutional Court.[79]

There is another possibility that popular initiatives may not be finally processed, despite complying with the aforementioned legal limits and without being rejected by the plenary session. This possibility is provided for by Article 134.6 of the Constitution, as well as by Articles 126.2 and 127 of the Congress of Deputies' Standing Orders. These articles determine that proposals or amendments that entail an increase in expenses or a reduction in incomes need the consent of the Government. Thus, after receiving notification that an initiative has obtained the required number of signatures, the

---

[74] Art. 7.1 Popular Initiative Act.

[75] Art. 7.3 Popular Initiative Act; the signatures need to be authenticated by the public notary, legal secretary or municipal secretary of the municipalities in which the respective signatories of the initiative are registered (Art. 9.2 Popular Initiative Act).

[76] Art. 12.3 Popular Initiative Act and Arts 126 and 127 Congress of Deputies' Standing Orders.

[77] Art. 13 Popular Initiative Act.

[78] Arts. 126.5 and 127 Congress of Deputies' Standing Orders.

[79] Arts. 126.5 and 127 Congress of Deputies' Standing Orders; Decision 140/1992, 25 May 1992, 3rd LG.

Government may exercise its 'veto prerogative', reasoning that the initiative would alter the budget plan. In this case, the Bureau will adopt a resolution to decide on the processing of the initiative. This resolution can be appealed through a constitutional complaint before the Constitutional Court.[80] Although this governmental prerogative could be very detrimental to popular initiatives, there is no evidence of an abusive exercise of it.[81]

7.   LEGISLATIVE PROPOSALS FOR REFORMING DIRECT-DEMOCRATIC INSTRUMENTS

In the last ten years, several proposals have been submitted to reform the regulation of direct-democratic instruments. In this section, we will try to outline and analyse some of them.[82]

The first proposal was presented on 18 July 2012 by two parliamentary groups – the Mixed Parliamentary Group and 'La Izquierda Plural' Parliamentary Group – in the Lower House. Unlike the two following, more comprehensive proposals, this one focused on making mandatory the holding of consultative referendums on those decisions of the Government that harm the economic, social and labour rights of citizens. The proposal was made at a time when the Spanish population was suffering from social and labour cutbacks as a result of the crisis that had struck southern European economies. Its aim therefore was for citizens to have a say in some of the difficult decisions that were being taken at that moment. Nevertheless, this proposal posed several problems as it would have led to a slowdown in regulatory activity when Spain was demanding quick and effective responses. It was finally rejected by Parliament.

On 13 May 2013, the same parliamentary groups registered a new proposal that made some changes to the constitutional provisions regulating the referendum and the popular initiative. With regard to the referendum, it was proposed, on the one hand, that every constitutional amendment should be submitted to

---

[80]   Art. 23.2 Spanish Constitution and Art. 42 Organic Law of the Constitutional Court.

[81]   Nevertheless, this prerogative has recently been used in the 'legislative proposal for the equal salary and equipment of the Security Forces in Spain'. This case can be consulted at http://www.juntaelectoralcentral.es/cs/jec/ilp/legislaturas/Legislatura ?idDocNumExp=3&p=1379061558559&template=ILP/JEC_DetalleBD, accessed 8 August 2020.

[82]   These proposals can be found at <http://www.congreso.es/public_oficiales/L10/ CONG/BOCG/B/BOCG-10-B-91-3.PDF>; <http://www.congreso.es/public_oficiales/ L10/CONG/BOCG/B/BOCG-10-B-122-1.PDF> and http://www.congreso.es/public _oficiales/L10/CONG/BOCG/B/BOCG-10-B-194-1.PDF#page=1, accessed 8 August 2020.

a referendum. On the other hand, two new types of referendum were to be introduced: a citizen-initiated referendum and a legislature-initiated referendum that, unlike the one provided for by Article 167 of the Constitution, was not connected to the constitutional amendment procedure. Regarding popular initiatives, the proposal removed the regulation of the number of signatures and the list of prohibited issues from the Constitution and confined it to the Popular Initiative Act. This proposal was formulated when citizens, especially young people, were denouncing a lack of representation and demanding greater participation in political life. However, the proposal expired without a decision of the Plenum of the Lower House.

Finally, on 16 May 2014, the Parliament of Asturias registered a constitutional amendment proposal to modify the regulation of direct-democratic instruments with a view to facilitating their exercise, after citizen platforms had collected thousands of signatures asking regional parliaments to initiate the constitutional amendment procedure for this purpose. Regarding the popular initiative, it was suggested that the provision that prohibits popular initiatives on organic law issues (fundamental rights and the electoral system, among others) should be removed. With regard to the referendum, the reform proposals were more far-reaching: it was proposed that 500,000 citizens should be able to initiate consultative and rejective referendums, as well as that a referendum and elections could be held on the same date. This proposal, unlike the previous ones, is still pending resolution.[83]

8.   CONCLUSIONS

Spanish citizens have the possibility of participating in political decision-making either through their representatives or, despite the distrust of the framers of the Constitution, through direct-democratic instruments. This distrust also existed during the first years of democracy, which explains why the legislator introduced new limitations in the regulation of these instruments to prevent their exercise from jeopardizing the establishment of the representative system in Spain.

However, as the Spanish party system matured, the initial restrictive legislative trend has been reversed – a process that has been accentuated given the

---

[83] It can be consulted at http://www.congreso.es/portal/page/portal/ Congreso/Congreso/Iniciativas?_piref73_2148295_73_1335437_1335437.next _page=/wc/servidorCGI&CMD=VERLST&BASE=IW14&PIECE=IWA4&FMT =INITXD1S.fmt&FORM1=INITXLUS.fmt&QUERY=%28I%29.ACIN1.+%26+ %28%22PROPOSICI%C3%B3N-DE-REFORMA-CONSTITUCIONAL-DE -COMUNIDADES-AUT%C3%B3NOMAS%22%29.SINI.&DOCS=3-3, accessed 8 August 2020.

political, economic and social events of the last ten years. The disaffection of citizens towards the political class due to the effects of the economic crisis and the disclosure of corruption cases led to a crisis of representativeness, causing direct-democratic instruments to play an unparalleled role in Spain's recent democratic history. Citizen movements urged the introduction of new types of referendum and the relaxation of the legal limits on the submission of popular initiatives. Even though some citizens saw the solution to Spain's serious problems in a further and more generous regulation of these instruments, the crisis of representativeness was resolved through its very functioning. Citizens' demands were addressed through the adaptation of the party system to incorporate new parties, so that the historical bipartisanship was replaced by a more fragmented multi-party system.

The future of the regulation of direct democracy in Spain may depend on the evaluation of the former events. If, after more than 40 years of constitutional democracy, the party system is seen as robust enough to support a less restrictive regulation of direct-democratic instruments, then the proposals analysed in Section 7 could be implemented. On the contrary, if the representative system is considered as able to satisfy citizens' demands in such a delicate political situation and without yielding ground to direct democracy, the legislator will lean towards a minor revision of these instruments. In this exercise of reflection, the Spanish legislator may take into account the results of the referendums held in other countries, such as the United Kingdom, Italy and Colombia.

8.   France

Marthe Fatin-Rouge Stefanini[1]

1.   INTRODUCTION

France builds on a representative democratic system with few direct-democratic instruments. The popular initiative does not exist but referendums can be organized at the local and national levels by various procedures. However, the referendum practice is scarce at national level. The legal limitations imposed on direct-democratic instruments are weak at national level, especially when the referendum is initiated by the two chambers of parliament or by government and it is called by the President of the French Republic. The Constitutional Council (*Conseil constitutionnel*) is not prepared to assess the constitutionality of the referendums triggered by the President. So, in fact, the President is not subject to any legal requirements when deciding about a referendum. A minority of parliamentarians associated with a minority of citizens can also propose a law to the Parliament that may be submitted to a referendum, but the procedure is too complicated and the required number of petitioning citizens too high for this procedure to be effective. In this procedure, the legal requirements are more stringent and compliance with these requirements is checked by the Constitutional Council.

2.   THE DIFFERENT INSTRUMENTS OF DIRECT DEMOCRACY

At the national level, four different instruments of direct democracy are provided for by the Constitution. They are all initiated by state institutions except for the constitutional referendum, which is triggered automatically if certain conditions laid down by the Constitution are met. The Constitution does not

[1]   ILF-GERJC, Aix-Marseille Univ, Université de Toulon, Univ Pau & Pays Adour, CNRS, DICE, Aix-en-Provence, France. I thank Vanessa Richard for her translation assistance.

provide for any direct-democratic instrument initiated by citizens on their own. A citizens' agenda initiative does not exist either at the national level.

2.1 Instruments at the National Level

2.1.1 Constitutional referendum

The Constitution of the Fifth Republic, as the one of the Fourth Republic, was submitted to the approval of the people by referendum. The Constitution was approved with 79.25 per cent of the votes cast.[2] As provided for by the Constitution, a referendum can be organized to decide upon a constitutional amendment.

Article 89 of the Constitution provides that:

> The President of the Republic, on the recommendation of the Prime Minister, and Members of Parliament alike shall have the right to initiate amendments to the Constitution.
>
> A Government or a Private Member's Bill to amend the Constitution must be considered within the time limits set down in the third paragraph of Article 42 and be passed by the two Houses in identical terms. The amendment shall take effect after approval by referendum.
>
> However, a Government Bill to amend the Constitution shall not be submitted to referendum where the President of the Republic decides to submit it to Parliament convened in Congress; the Government Bill to amend the Constitution shall then be approved only if it is passed by a three-fifths majority of the votes cast. The Bureau of the Congress shall be that of the National Assembly (…).

The use of a referendum procedure to reform the Constitution is optional in case of Government Bills, while mandatory for Private Member's Bills.[3] Most of the constitutional revisions were approved by the Congress. This has principally happened because when the President chooses between approval by the Congress and by referendum, they, in line with their political majority, favour the Congress. The Congress's approval is considered to be more reliable than approval by referendum, even though the required qualified majority is more stringent in the Congress. One may note that so far, every constitutional amendment that was submitted to the Congress has been adopted, although in most cases the constitutional revision procedures fail before this last step. The only example of the use of a referendum to amend the Constitution is from

---

[2]   Francis Hamon, *Le référendum. Etude comparative* (2nd edn, LGDJ 2012) 110.

[3]   Laurence Morel classifies it as a 'mandatory referendum' but she adds that mandatory referendums concern 'not all revisions but only those initiated by Parliament'; Laurence Morel, 'Types of Referendums, provisions and practice at the national level worldwide', in Laurence Morel and Matt Qvortrup (eds), *The Routledge Handbook to Referendums and Direct Democracy* (Routledge 2018) 40.

2000, when the constitutional amendment which set the duration of the presidential mandate to five years was approved through a popular vote.[4] In this particular case the referendum was not mandatory since the constitutional draft submitted to the popular vote was actually a Government Bill.

2.1.2 Executive- and legislature-initiated referendum
Article 11(1) and (2) of the Constitution provide that:

> The President of the Republic may, on a recommendation from the Government when Parliament is in session, or on a joint motion of the two Houses, published in the *Journal Officiel*, submit to a referendum any Government Bill which deals with the organization of the public authorities, or with reforms relating to the economic, social or environmental policy of the Nation, and to the public services contributing thereto, or which provides for authorization to ratify a treaty which, although not contrary to the Constitution, would affect the functioning of the institutions.
>
> Where the referendum is held on the recommendation of the Government, the latter shall make a statement before each House and the same shall be followed by a debate.

The referendum procedure evolved following two constitutional reforms of 1995 and 2008, which allowed to submit to a referendum a Government Bill which deals with 'reforms relating to the economic, social or environmental policy of the Nation, and the public services contributing thereto (...)'.[5] This provision was essentially used at the beginning of the Fifth Republic by General De Gaulle to propose constitutional amendments. Its use then dwindled and the last referendum based on this provision was held in 2005.[6]

This type of referendum has been subject to extensive discussions since the very beginning of the Fifth Republic. Although the initiative to use this procedure does not clearly belong to the President but either to the Government or the two Houses of the Parliament, this referendum has always been used by the President as a means to secure the support of the French people on different matters. Besides, this provision appears under Title II of the Constitution, which deals with the powers of the President. Resorting to a referendum is thus a prerogative of the President and it is not subjected to any ministerial countersignature. So, this referendum procedure was conceived primarily as a prerogative of the President and not as a mechanism for citizen participation.[7]

---

[4] Loi constitutionnelle no. 2000-964 du 2 octobre 2000 relative à la durée du mandat du Président de la République.

[5] The word 'environmental' was added in 2008.

[6] Referendum on the ratification act of the Treaty establishing a Constitution for Europe held on 29 May 2005.

[7] Gérard Conac, 'Les débats sur le référendum sous la Ve République' (1996) no 77 Pouvoirs 101.

The President used this referendum procedure in 1962 and 1969 to amend the Constitution. Such use was heavily criticized by the Senate and the parliamentarian opposition in 1962.[8] President De Gaulle wanted to revise the Constitution so that the President would no longer be elected indirectly but by direct universal suffrage. Instead of using the procedure under Article 89 of the Constitution, he initiated a referendum based on a broad understanding of the notion of 'organization of the public authorities' mentioned by Article 11(1) of the Constitution. This allowed the President to bypass the Senate, which was opposed to the proposed amendment, and to directly put the reform to the popular vote without requesting the vote of the Houses. French voters approved the constitutional revision with a 61.75 per cent majority of the votes cast. This approval is considered by part of the legal literature to be also an approval of the possibility to review the Constitution based on Article 11 of the Constitution.[9]

In 1969, President De Gaulle used this procedure in order to pass a constitutional amendment aimed at creating regions but at the same time also at weakening the Senate. This constitutional draft law was rejected by French voters.[10]

Despite the heavy criticism levelled against the use of Article 11 of the Constitution to amend the Constitution, this provision has never been amended to rule out this contentious practice. Although this issue was mentioned during the 1995 and 2008 constitutional reform processes, the governing majority has constantly decided to keep this provision's interpretation in limbo. Thus, one cannot describe this referendum as a 'legislative referendum' because its use remains ambiguous and, for the last 50 years, no other draft constitutional revision has been submitted to referendum based on this provision.[11]

The acute crisis of 1962, with the use of Article 11 to amend the Constitution, and the rejection of the text proposed in 2005 (Ratification of the Treaty establishing a Constitution for Europe) by a majority of 54.7 per cent of votes cast against the Government Bill, may explain the resistance to resort to referendums which still exists nowadays. Indeed, no referendum has been held at the national level since that date.

---

[8]   Fabien Conord, 'De la "République sénatoriale" à la "forfaiture". Le Sénat et la Ve République 1959–1962', (2010) no 12 Histoire@Politique 4. The author evokes the opposition of the President of the Senate, Gaston Monnerville, and of most jurists and political staff.

[9]   Johanna Noël, 'Pour une analyse épistémologique de la querelle autour de l'article 11: de la dénonciation à la réhabilitation d'une violation de la Constitution', (2016) Revue française de droit constitutionnel 391.

[10]   53.18 per cent of the votes cast were against the project, Hamon (n 2).

[11]   Laurence Morel, *La question du référendum* (Les presses de SciencesPo 2019) 117.

The following referendums have been held since the beginning of the Fifth Republic at the national level on the basis of Article 11 of the Constitution:

- On 8 January 1961, the referendum on the self-determination and organization of the government in Algeria was approved by 75.26 per cent of votes cast.
- On 8 April 1962, the referendum relating the approval of the Evian Accord (end of the war in Algeria and self-determination) was supported by 90.7 per cent of the votes cast.
- On 28 October 1962, the referendum concerning the election of the President of the Republic by direct universal suffrage was approved with 61.75 per cent of the votes cast.
- On 23 April 1969, the referendum concerning the extension of the European Community was approved by 67.7 per cent of the votes cast.
- On 27 September 1969, the referendum on the creation of regions and the reform of the Senate was rejected by 53.18 per cent of the votes cast.
- On 6 November 1988, the referendum on the statutory and preparatory provisions for self-determination in New Caledonia was supported by 80 per cent of the votes cast.
- On 20 September 1992, the referendum on the ratification of the Maastricht Treaty obtained 51 per cent of the votes cast.
- On 29 May 2005, the referendum on the ratification of the Treaty establishing a Constitution for Europe was approved by 54.7 per cent of the votes cast.

2.1.3 'Shared referendum initiative'

The constitutional revision of 23 July 2008 introduced a new instrument of direct democracy. The scope of this newly introduced referendum is the same as the referendum initiated by the Government or the Parliament provided under Article 11(1) of the Constitution. The 'shared initiative' is an optional legislative referendum with citizen support. This procedure is prescribed by Article 11(3)–(7) of the Constitution:

> A referendum concerning a subject mentioned in the first paragraph may be held upon the initiative of one fifth of the Members of Parliament, supported by one tenth of the voters enrolled on the electoral register. This initiative shall take the

form of a bill proposal and shall not be applied to the repeal of a statutory provision promulgated for less than one year.

The conditions by which it is introduced and those according to which the Constitutional Council monitors the respect of the provisions of the previous paragraph, are set down by an Institutional Act.

If the bill proposal has not been considered by the two Houses within a period set by the Institutional Act, the President of the Republic shall submit it to a referendum.

Where the decision of the French people in the referendum is not favourable to the bill proposal, no new referendum proposal on the same subject may be submitted before the end of a period of two years following the date of the vote.

Where the outcome of the referendum is favourable to the Government Bill or to the bill proposal, the President of the Republic shall promulgate the resulting statute within fifteen days following the proclamation of the results of the vote.

Although the referendum procedure provided for by Article 11(3) of the Constitution is called 'shared referendum initiative' by part of the literature[12] and on official websites,[13] these words do not exactly describe the reality. This referendum procedure can only be initiated by a minority of members of the parliament.[14] If their initiative complies with constitutional requirements, then it can be backed by citizens. Although this procedure was established in France by means of the constitutional change of 2008, the implementing regulations have only been adopted at the end of 2013[15] and the procedure has only been in use since 1 January 2015.

---

[12] Francis Hamon, 'Le référendum d'initiative partagée sera bientôt opérationnel mais l'on s'interroge encore sur son utilité', (2014) Revue française de droit constitutionnel 253; Marine Haulbert, 'Le référendum d'initiative "partagée": représentants versus représentés? Commentaire des dispositions législatives et organiques visant à l'application de l'article 11 de la Constitution', (2014) Revue de droit public et de sciences politiques 1650. It is now commonly called 'Référendum d'initiative partagée' (RIP).

[13] See, for example: https://www.referendum.interieur.gouv.fr/contenu/comment -ca-marche, accessed 13 September 2020.

[14] Some authors qualify this procedure as a parliamentary minority referendum and I agree with these opinions: Stéphane Diémert, 'Le référendum législatif d'initiative minoritaire dans l'article 11, révisé, de la Constitution', (2009) Revue française de droit constitutionnel 55; Christophe Geslot, 'La mise en oeuvre du referendum d'initiative minoritaire', (2014) Actualité juridique Droit administratif 893; Olivier Beaud, 'Remarques sur le référendum d'initiative parlementaire et sur les arguments de ceux qui ont voulu en bloquer la procédure', (*Juspoliticum Le Blog*, 23 May 2019) http://blog .juspoliticum.com/2019/05/23/remarques-sur-le-referendum-dinitiative-parlementaire -et-sur-les-arguments-de-ceux-qui-ont-voulu-en-bloquer-la-procedure-par-olivier -beaud/, accessed 13 September 2020.

[15] Loi organique no 2013-1114 du 6 décembre 2013 portant application de l'article 11 de la Constitution, JORF, no. 284, 7 Dec. 2013, 19937 and Loi no 2013-1116 du 6 décembre 2013 portant application de l'article 11 de la Constitution, JORF, no. 284, 7 Dec. 2013, 19939.

RIP

It is a legislative referendum procedure since commitment of the bill proposal with the Constitution is clearly mentioned. If Parliament does not consider the bill proposal, the President must call the referendum. The Constitution does not specify whether the President retains the possibility of calling a referendum if Parliament examines the request but rejects it.

The first bill proposal supported by the required number of members of the parliament in order to start the 'shared initiative' was issued in May 2019. The proposal was directed against the privatization of the Paris Airport company. Citizens were encouraged to support this proposal until the end of February 2020. However, the required number of signatures is very high – 10 per cent of the voters equals to over 4.7 million signatures. Since only 1,093,030 signatures were collected within the time limit, the referendum was not held.

2.1.4 Referendum on accession of a state to the European Union

Article 88-5 of the Constitution provides that:

> Any Government Bill authorizing the ratification of a treaty pertaining to the accession of a state to the European Union shall be submitted to referendum by the President of the Republic.
>
> Notwithstanding the foregoing, by passing a motion adopted in identical terms in each House by a three-fifths majority, Parliament may authorize the passing of the Bill according to the procedure provided for in paragraph three of Article 89.

The procedure under Article 88-5 of the Constitution was originally established in 2005 in a slightly different version, when the Constitution was modified in order to ratify the Treaty establishing a Constitution for Europe. In the first version, the referendum was mandatory with regard to every new treaty of accession to the EU.[16] This provision aimed at reassuring the people who feared an arbitrary imposition of an enlargement of the EU to the East, in particular the adhesion of Turkey. The people called to vote in the referendum on 29 May 2005 rejected the new bill which ratified the Treaty establishing a Constitution for Europe and the provisions which had been incorporated into the Constitution with a view to ratification of the Treaty establishing a Constitution for Europe have lapsed. Nevertheless, a new version of the Treaty was negotiated which became the Treaty of Lisbon. Instead of being

---

[16]   It was then Art. 88-7 of the Constitution, which provided that: 'Tout projet de loi autorisant la ratification d'un traité relatif à l'adhésion d'un État à l'Union européenne est soumis au référendum par le Président de la République' (our translation: 'Any government bill authorizing the ratification of a treaty relating to the accession of a State to the European Union is submitted to a referendum by the President of the Republic'). This Article was, together with other provisions, introduced by the Loi constitutionnelle no. 2005-204 modifiant le titre XV de la Constitution, 1 March 2005.

put to a referendum, this treaty was directly proposed to the ratification by the French Parliament. Therefore, a 'tidying-up' of the Constitution was performed in 2008. In the framework of the constitutional revision of 4 February 2008,[17] the referendum became optional. It is thus only if the President decides so that the electoral body is called to a referendum to decide on a new accession. So far, no referendum has been organized based on the above-mentioned procedure since no decision with regard to accession to the EU has been taken.

2.2　　Instruments at the Local Level

At the local level, binding or advisory referendums can vary considerably. Some of them are regulated by the Constitution, others are provided for by law. The main procedure is provided for by Article 72-1(2) of the Constitution, which states that: 'In the conditions determined by an Institutional Act, draft decisions or acts within the powers of a territorial community may, on the initiative of the latter, be submitted for a decision by voters of said community by means of a referendum.' Thus, the deliberative assembly of any local community may request a local referendum on a matter within its jurisdiction. Based on Article 72-1(1) of the Constitution[18] and Articles LO 1112–16 *et seq.* of the General Local Authorities Code (*Code général des collectivités territoriales (CGCT)*), an advisory referendum may be requested by the voters of a municipality. They can submit this request to the deliberative assembly by exercising their collective right of petition.[19] This right is larger than a citizens' initiative because there is no provision for the content or form of the petition. Texts simply state that the matter must fall within the jurisdiction of the local authority.

---

[17]　Loi constitutionnelle no. 2008-103 modifiant le titre XV de la Constitution, 4 February 2008.

[18]　Art. 72-1(1) of the Constitution provides that: 'La loi fixe les conditions dans lesquelles les électeurs de chaque collectivité territoriale peuvent, par l'exercice du droit de pétition, demander l'inscription à l'ordre du jour de l'assemblée délibérante de cette collectivité d'une question relevant de sa compétence'. (Our translation: 'The law sets the conditions under which the electors of each local authority may, by exercising the right to petition, request the inclusion in the agenda of the deliberative assembly of that authority a question falling within its competence').

[19]　Art. 1112-16 CGCT provides that: 'Dans une commune, un cinquième des électeurs inscrits sur les listes électorales et, dans les autres collectivités territoriales, un dixième des électeurs, peuvent demander à ce que soit inscrite à l'ordre du jour de l'assemblée délibérante de la collectivité l'organisation d'une consultation sur toute affaire relevant de la décision de cette assemblée ...' (Our translation: 'In a municipality, one fifth of registered voters and, in other local authorities, a tenth of registered voters, may request that a consultation regarding any question within their scope be included in the agenda of the deliberative assembly of the local authority').

At local level, a participation quorum of 50 per cent of registered voters is required so that the result is mandatory for the local authority.[20]

Other types of direct-democratic instruments are directly provided under the Constitution. The Constitution prescribes mandatory consultations for a status change of overseas local authorities[21] and when an authority supersedes overseas departments and regions or in case of the establishment of a single deliberative assembly for these two authorities.[22] Meanwhile facultative consultations may be held on the creation of a local authority granted with a special status or of a review of its organization[23] and on the change in the overseas local authority's organization, competences or legislative regime.[24]

Specifically, on the New Caledonia situation, as a transitional provision Article 76 of the Constitution required the organization of a local consultation in order to approve the Nouméa Accords of 5 May 1998. This consultation took place on 8 November 1998 and the Accords were approved by a 71.86 per cent majority. Article 77 of the Constitution provides for the adoption of an organic law which allows the organization of referendums regarding independence.[25] The first referendum was organized on 4 November 2018, on the question: 'Do you want New Caledonia to become fully sovereign and independent?' The question was rejected with a 56.67 per cent majority of the votes cast. A second referendum on self-determination was held on 4 October 2020 and independence was rejected with 53.6% of the vote.

Besides the procedures provided for by the Constitution, other local referendums are established by laws. As regards the local community governed by Article 74 of the Constitution (Saint Barthélémy Island, for example), citizens have a right to submit collective or individual petitions to the deliberative assembly.[26] This deliberative assembly, the territorial council, may decide to organize a referendum or a consultation, including when it is requested by a tenth of the voters.[27]

In 2016, in the context of heated objections to the construction of a new airport on the Notre-Dame-des-Landes site, a new consultation was created aiming at consulting the people on projects having a significant environmental impact. Such a consultation could not be organized at national level, since it was not within the scope of Article 11 of the Constitution. Neither was it

---

[20] Art. LO 1112-7 CGCT.
[21] Art. 72-4(1) Constitution.
[22] Art. 73(7) Constitution.
[23] Art. 72-1(3) Constitution.
[24] Art. 72-4(2) Constitution.
[25] See Organic Law of 19 March 1999.
[26] Art. LO 6321-1, LO 6331-1, LO 6441-1, CGCT.
[27] LO 6233-1, LO 6333-1, LO 6446-1 CGCT.

within the framework of a local consultation or referendum, since the project was of national interest. This new procedure was thus specifically established by Ordinance no. 2016-488 of 21 April 2016 regarding the local consultation of citizens on projects likely to have an environmental impact and Decree no. 2016-491 of 21 April 2016 regarding the local consultation of citizens on projects likely to have an environmental impact. The consultation was organized on 26 June 2016 and the airport project on the controversial site was adopted by a 55.17 per cent majority of the public consulted. However, because of the change of President of the Republic in 2017, the airport project was abandoned.

There is no official data on the number of local referendums or consultations organized.

3.   LEGAL LIMITS ON REFERENDUMS

The limits are very different depending on the type of referendum or consultation envisaged. Some of these limits are prescribed by the Constitution, others are specified by laws, others are deduced from the jurisprudence of the Constitutional Council. Indeed, there is no single legislation regulating referendums and consultations in France. Some laws have clarified the system of referendums and local consultations[28] or the framework of the 'shared referendum initiative'.[29] On the other hand, no law was adopted concerning the implementation of the referendum of Article 11(1) (optional referendum) or the referendum provided under Article 89 (constitutional referendum).

Three types of limitations can be distinguished for each procedure: substantive, formal and circumstantial or temporal limitations. Some of these limits are vague and, for lack of relevant practice, an interpretation of the respective texts has not been able to develop.

3.1   Substantive Limits

3.1.1   Executive and legislature-initiated referendum and shared initiative

The positive scope of the referendum under Article 11(1) of the Constitution is rather broad, therefore, there is really no forbidden subject. Three different

---

[28]   Loi organique no 2003-705 du 1er août 2003 relative au référendum local, JORF no 177, 2 August 2003, 13218 and loi no 2004-809 du 13 août 2004 relative aux libertés et responsabilités locales, JORF no 190, 17 August 2004, 14545.

[29]   Organic law and ordinary law, 6 December 2013, implementing Art. 11 Constitution, cited above.

issues may be the subject of a draft bill that can be submitted to a referendum, namely:

- the organization of the public authorities;
- reforms relating to the economic, social or environmental policy of the Nation, and to the public services contributing thereto;
- authorization to ratify a treaty which, although not contrary to the Constitution, would affect the functioning of the institutions.

The notion of 'organization of the public authorities' has raised issues of interpretation. Could, for example, the referendums regarding the status of Algeria and its independence really be considered as an issue of 'organization of the public authorities'? Likewise, as happened in 1962 and 1969, could the election of the President by universal suffrage, or the creation of regions as a type of local authority, be considered to fall within the scope of this notion? Such uses of the referendum were criticized by the opposition in Parliament[30] and the legal literature.[31] The term is voluntarily vague and the uncertainties regarding its contours have given the President a lot of discretionary power.

Similarly, the notion of 'reforms relating to the economic, social or environmental policy of the Nation, and to the public services contributing thereto' is very broad as well. It generated debates in 1995, in particular in relation to the protection of fundamental rights.[32] It was debated whether this provision could serve as a basis for organizing referendums on questions such as the death penalty or abortion. Questioned about the potential risk of such an expansion of Article 11 of the Constitution to cover fundamental rights and freedoms, the Minister of Justice explained that no freedom could ever be the subject of this procedure.[33] In practice, however, no topic is explicitly excluded from the scope of the referendum under Article 11 of the Constitution.

The only clear issue is that of treaty ratification. The Constitution provides that treaties cannot be contrary to the Constitution. Consequently, the ratification bill and – logically – the treaty itself must be brought into compliance with the Constitution before being submitted for ratification by the people.

---

[30] In particular the Presidents of the Senate Gaston Monnerville in 1962 and Alain Poher in 1969, taking the head of the opposition to the recourse to the referendum of Article 11.

[31] See Gérard Conac, 'Les débats sur le référendum sous la Ve République', (1996) no 77 Pouvoirs 105.

[32] Francis Hamon, 'L'extension du référendum: données, controverses, perspectives' (1996) no 77 Pouvoirs 111; Marthe Fatin-Rouge Stefanini, 'Le référendum et la protection des droits fondamentaux' (2003) Revue française de droit constitutionnel 77.

[33] Débats parlementaires, Assemblée nationale, 1ère séance du 11 juillet 1995, Journal officiel de la République Française, p. 920.

Beyond the vague terminology, it is also not clear whether, based on Article 11 of the Constitution, a constitutional revision could be effected in derogation of the procedure of Article 89 of the Constitution. The 1962 practice, although it gave rise to criticism, has never been questioned afterwards. None of the constitutional revisions has ever clarified the scope of referendums initiated by the government or the assemblies in the framework of Article 11 of the Constitution. By contrast, the 23 July 2008 constitutional amendment, which introduced 'the shared initiative', expressly specifies that the draft bills that may be the subject of this procedure cannot provide for any constitutional change.[34] Besides, there is a specific constitutionality assessment for this type of referendum proposal.[35]

During the assessment of the organic law on the implementation of the shared initiative,[36] the Constitutional Council specified an additional limitation, which also applies to ordinary draft bills presented by parliamentarians: financial inadmissibility. Accordingly, the draft bill cannot be admitted if its adoption leads to either a decrease of public resources or the creation or worsening of a public burden. The Constitutional Council considered itself to have jurisdiction to assess compliance with this limitation which, with regard to ordinary bills, is directly assessed by the assemblies.[37]

Since Article 11(1) may enable the President of the Republic to amend the Constitution, limitations which apply to constitutional revisions should also be applied to referendums organized in this framework.

3.1.2   Constitutional referendum

For constitutional revisions, Article 89(5) provides that: 'The republican form of government shall not be the purpose of any amendment.' When this limitation was introduced in the Constitution, in 1884 during the Third Republic, it was aimed at preventing a return to monarchy. In a decision of 1992, the Constitutional Council re-affirmed this limitation and clarified additional

---

[34]   Art. 61(1) Constitution, which states that: 'The organic laws, before their promulgation, the legislative proposals referred to in Article 11 before they are submitted to the referendum, and the rules of the parliamentary assemblies, before their implementation, must be submitted to the Constitutional Council, which decides on their conformity with the Constitution' (our translation).

[35]   Art.61(1) Constitution and Organic law no. 2013-1114 implementing Art. 11 Constitution, 6 December 2013, which specifies the competencies of the Constitutional Council.

[36]   Organic law no. 2013-1114 implementing Art. 11 Constitution, 6 December 2013.

[37]   Conseil Constitutionnel, Decision no. 681 DC, 5 December 2013, Loi organique portant application de l'article 11 de la Constitution, para. 8.

circumstantial limitations as well.[38] Such limitations must in principle apply to Article 11 referendums if their purpose is to amend the Constitution.

3.1.3 Referendum on accession of a state to the European Union

The limits which apply to the procedure under Article 88-5 of the Constitution are related to its very narrow scope: the ratification of an accession treaty with a new Member State. When the Constitution imposed a mandatory referendum for any new accession of a State to the European Union (see Section 2.1.4 above), the question arose of whether this procedure should be followed for the States with which negotiations for accession had been conducted. The Constitutional Law of 23 July 2008 clarified that Article 88-5 of the Constitution does not apply to accessions following an intergovernmental conference the convocation of which was decided by the European Council before 1 July 2004.[39] Indeed, the question of Turkey's accession was at the heart of the debates in France during the 2005 referendum campaign on the ratification of the Treaty establishing a Constitution for Europe.[40] Turkey has been applying for membership since 1959 and was officially accepted as a candidate by the European Union in 1999, but public opinion in Europe, particularly in France, has been increasingly hostile to this enlargement.[41] Other applications for accession have been examined by the European Union since that date, but Article 88-5 of the Constitution was never implemented. In 2019 France vetoed the opening of the accession negotiations for both North Macedonia and Albania.[42]

3.1.4 Local referendums

With regard to local referendums, their scope is defined either by the Constitution itself or by the respective implementing laws.

---

[38] See in this chapter Section 3.3.

[39] Constitutional Law No. 2008-724 of 23 July 2008 Article 47 III: 'Article 88-5 of the Constitution, in its drafting resulting from both Article 44 of this Constitutional Law and 2 of the I of this Article, shall not apply to accessions following an intergovernmental conference the convocation of which was decided by the European Council before 1 July 2004'.

[40] Dorothée Schmid, 'La Turquie aux portes de l'Union : vers une négociation politique!', (2005) Revue du Marché commun et de l'Union européenne 73; Cengiz Aktar, 'Et si l'Europe puissance passait par la Turquie', (2005) Revue du Marché commun et de l'Union européenne 303.

[41] Chantal Kafyeke, 'L'adhésion de la Turquie à l'Union européenne : enjeux et état du débat', (2006) Courrier hebdomadaire du CRISP 5.

[42] Alain Buzelay, 'Les défis de l'élargissement de l'Union européenne à l'est', (2020) Revue de l'Union européenne 256.

As far as local referendums under Article 72-1 of the Constitution are concerned, the referendum can only address a deliberation or an act which falls within the jurisdiction of the local authority concerned. This is a significant limitation since it entails the illegality of all deliberations which are related to national projects or concern several local authorities.

3.2   Formal Limits

3.2.1   National referendums

Regardless of the type of direct-democratic instrument, the only formal requirement is that the proposal must be drafted.[43] The case law of the Constitutional Council[44] provides additional details in this regard.

Since 1987, it has gradually imposed the requirement of clear and fair consultations for all types of referendums. In Decision 226 DC of 2 June 1987, the Constitutional Council stated that:

> The question put to the populations concerned must satisfy the double requirement of loyalty and clarity of the consultation; (…) if it is permissible for the public authorities, within the framework of their competences, to indicate the envisaged orientations, the question put to the voters must not contain any ambiguity, particularly as regards the scope of these indications.[45]

The scope of the requirement of clarity and fairness of consultations was not detailed by the Constitutional Council.[46] However, some aspects can be deduced from the few cases in which the Constitutional Council applied them in response to the applicants' arguments. In general, it is clear from the case law that the Constitutional Council's review of compliance with this double requirement is minimal and therefore very favourable to the government. The clarity of the consequences of voting obliges public authorities to propose an 'unequivocal'[47] question and to recall the purely consultative scope of voting

---

[43]   In Arts. 11 and 89 of the Constitution the words 'Government's Bill' or 'Private Member's Bill' are used.

[44]   On the competencies of the Constitutional Council, see para 4.

[45]   Decision no. 87-226 DC, 2 June 1987, para. 7.

[46]   The Constitutional Council uses the generic term '*consultations*' referring to as referenda or '*consultations référendaires*'.

[47]   Decision no. 87-226 DC, 2 June 1987, para. 7 to 9. The Constitutional Council decision was about the constitutionality of a law organizing a consultation on the evolution of New Caledonia towards an independent status of the French State. The question was 'Do you want New Caledonia to become independent or to remain within the French Republic with a status whose essential elements have been brought to your attention?' This consultation was organized on the basis of Article 53(3) Constitution. The Constitutional Council considered that the wording of the question was 'ambigu-

when this is the case.[48] In the case of the referendum on the status of New Caledonia, the Constitutional Council held that the question was ambiguous because it led voters to believe that the essential elements of the status were already fixed when they were not.[49]

The Constitutional Council has indicated that clarity and loyalty of consultations requires that election documents are communicated to the electors in advance[50] and that the administration implements 'all means at its disposal to ensure that electors are able to read it before the election'.[51] Finally, with regard to the documents which are sent to voters, the transmission of recitals of the bill (recitals being 'inseparable' from the bill itself) is not contrary to the requirement of clarity and loyalty of the vote in so far as its content 'does not exceed' its purpose, which is twofold: 'to present its main characteristics, but also (…) to highlight the interest which is attached to its adoption'.[52]

It can be underlined that clarity and loyalty are rarely distinguished by the Constitutional Council even at the request of the applicants. In the decision '*Consultation de la population de Mayotte*', it held that the loyalty related to the process that preceded the drafting of the text submitted to the electors

---

ous' because 'it may, in the minds of the voters, give rise to the erroneous idea that the elements of the statute are already fixed, whereas the determination of this status is, pursuant to Article 74 of the Constitution, a law taken after consultation of the territorial assembly' (our translation). The law was found unconstitutional.

[48] Decision no. 2000-428 DC, 4 May 2000, *Consultation de la population de Mayotte*, para. 16 and 17. In this decision, the Constitutional Council was reviewing the constitutionality of the law organizing the consultation of the people of Mayotte. Section 3 of the Act stipulated that 'voters will have to answer with a "yes" or "no" to the following question: "Do you approve of the agreement on the future of Mayotte, signed in Paris on January 27, 2000?"' This wording came out from a government bill. The applicants' criticisms focused on the ambiguities of the government and the conditions under which this 'agreement' was obtained (without a real consensus). Regarding the advisory nature of the vote, the Constitutional Council expressed a reservation of interpretation of the law by considering that, although the law uses the words 'avis' (as opinion), and that Parliament has the right to choose to do such consultation concerning the future of a territorial community, 'it will be up to the competent authorities, in particular the regulatory authority, to make all necessary provisions to remind the people of Mayotte of the purely consultative scope of their vote'. If the Constitutional Council had found that the principle of clarity and loyalty was not respected, it would have declared the legislative provision to be unconstitutional. In this case, the law could not have been enacted.

[49] Decision no. 87-226 DC, 2 June 1987, para. 7 to 9.

[50] Decision no. 33-REF, 7 April 2005, *De Villiers et Peltier*, para. 5.

[51] Decision no. 31-REF, 24 March 2005, *Hauchemaille et Meyet*, para. 11.

[52] Decision no. 33-REF (n 11) para. 9.

and the clarity concerned the text itself and its consequences.[53] In the decision *'Consultation de la Nouvelle-Calédonie'* (1987) the law was found unconstitutional because of a lack of clarity of the consultation.[54]

Finally, it should be noted that the legal basis of this double requirement is not entirely clear.[55] It is argued here that it can be deduced from Article 3 of the Constitution and in particular from the freedom of vote, which clearly implies the sincerity of the vote.[56]

3.2.2 Local referendums

According to Article 72-1 of the Constitution, either a draft deliberation of the local assembly or a draft executive act can be submitted to a referendum. Individual draft acts cannot be submitted.

The requirement of clarity and fairness in referendums is also assessed by the administrative courts.[57]

---

[53] Decision no. 2000-428 DC, 4 May 2000, *Consultation de la population de Mayotte*. According to the applicants, the law was contrary to the requirement of clarity of consultation because the persons consulted would not be able to understand the consequences of their votes ('yes' and 'no'). They argued that the agreement did not offer a clear solution on the status of Mayotte. Similarly, they objected that the drafting of certain articles of this agreement would be too complex and their understanding would be reserved for experts. They also criticized the very process of drawing up the agreement as being unfair because there would have been no consensus on its vote and the two Mayotte members of the French Parliament were opposed to the text. In addition, according to the applicants, 'by planning to give Mayotte the status of "departmental community", the Government would deliberately maintain confusion with "the clear and constant departmental claim of the population of Mayotte".'

[54] Decision no. 87-226 DC, 2 June 1987, para. 9.

[55] In Decision no. 87-226 DC, 2 June 1987, *Consultation des populations intéressées de la Nouvelle-Calédonie*, the Constitutional Council had based the double requirement on para. 2 of the Preamble to the 1958 Constitution, dealing with the free determination of the peoples of the overseas territories and the free expression of their will, and on Art. 53(3) Constitution, which states that 'No assignment, no exchange, no addition of territory is valid without the consent of the populations concerned.' This requirement could therefore be interpreted as imposing itself only on the overseas populations as former colonies.

[56] Marthe Fatin-Rouge Stefanini, 'La sincérité de l'expression référendaire', in Sophie De Cacqueray and others (eds), *Sincérité et démocratie* (PUAM 2011) 347–377.

[57] See Marthe Fatin-Rouge Stefanini, 'L'exigence constitutionnelle de clarté et de loyauté des consultations', in *Renouveau du droit contitutionnel*, Mélanges en l'honneur de Louis Favoreu (Dalloz 2007) 1525–1552.

3.3 Circumstantial or Temporal Limits

3.3.1 Constitutional referendum

Regarding constitutional revisions, Article 89(4) of the Constitution provides that: 'No amendment procedure shall be commenced or continued where the integrity of national territory is placed in jeopardy.' On 2 September 1992, a decision of the Constitutional Council noted that other constitutional provisions specify some similar circumstantial limits which forbid a constitutional revision during certain periods.[58]

First, Article 7(11) of the Constitution provides that no constitutional change procedure can be triggered 'during the vacancy of the Presidency of the Republic or during the period between the declaration of the permanent incapacity of the President of the Republic and the election of his successor'. Vacancy describes the situation where the position of President is not filled as a result of death or resignation. Incapacity describes the situation where the President cannot perform his or her functions anymore, due to physical or mental health problems, for example, but he or she has not officially resigned.

Second, Article 16 of the Constitution deals with the implementation of the President's exceptional powers. This provision does not expressly forbid a constitutional change during the exercise of such powers but the restriction stems from its interpretation.[59]

These provisions could also apply to institution-initiated referendums when used to amend the Constitution.

3.3.2 Shared referendum initiative

Article 11(3) of the Constitution provides that the referendum initiative 'may not be applied to the repeal of a legislative provision promulgated for less than one year'. This limit aims at protecting a bill which has just been adopted. In practice, in 2019 the parliamentary opposition found a way to bypass this limitation by submitting a draft referendum bill just before the final adoption of another law, the PACS law. This draft referendum bill directly called into question one of the purposes of the PACS law, the privatization of the *Aéroport de Paris* company, by declaring it a national public service. Even though the adopted PACS law could have entered into force, the draft referendum bill resulted – in practice – in the suspension of its application pending the

---

[58] Decision no. 92-312 DC, 2 September 1992, *Traité sur l'Union européenne*, para. 19.
[59] Decision no. 92-312 DC, 2 September 1992, *Traité sur l'Union européenne*, para. 19.

statutory period for collecting citizens' signatures. This situation had not been considered by the 2008 Constitution revision at all.

A second limitation is based on Article 11(6) of the Constitution, stating that 'no new referendum proposal on the same subject may be submitted before the end of a period of two years following the date of the vote'.

3.3.3   Local referendums

There are many circumstantial limitations to the organization of local referendums specified by Article LO 1112-6 CGCT. The organization of a referendum is prohibited before elections and during election campaigns: six months before an election; during the election campaign until the polling day as regards part or total renewal of the deliberative assembly of a local authority; during the election campaign or on the voting day for a consultation under Article 72-1(3) Constitution, for a consultation by referendum under Article 72-4 of voters from an overseas territory, or else for an Article 73 referendum.

Likewise, no local referendum can be organized during the campaign or the voting day of any legislative, senatorial, presidential or European election, or a referendum initiated by the President of the Republic.[60]

Moreover, resignation, cancellation of the election of the members of a deliberative assembly or its dissolution cancel the deliberation providing for the referendum.

Finally, more than one local referendum cannot be organized in the same local authority on the same subject during a time period of less than a year.[61]

The scale of these limitations can be debated for two reasons. First, the great diversity of the elections, consultations and referendums concerned significantly decreases the periods when a local referendum can be organized. Second, the multiplication of polling days instead of their batching encourages abstention, since voters prefer to spend their weekend elsewhere and will only participate in the polls that they regard as the most important.

4.   INSTITUTIONS AND PROCEDURES FOR REVIEWING THE LIMITS OF REFERENDUMS

The Constitutional Council ensures the proper conduct of referendum proceedings (Article 60 of the Constitution) and it is the competent state organ to check the constitutionality and legality of the 'shared referendum initiative' (Article 61-1 of the Constitution).

---

[60]   Arts. 11, 73, 88-5, 89 Constitution.
[61]   Art. LO 1112-6 CGCT.

The Council is an independent constitutional judicial body with constitutional status.[62] It is composed of nine members appointed respectively by the President of the Republic (three members), the President of the Senate (three members) and the President of the National Assembly (three members). The decisions of the Constitutional Council are not subject to appeal. As constitutional judge, the Constitutional Council is competent for carrying out a judicial review of the organic laws, the bills proposed by a parliamentary minority submitted in a 'shared referendum initiative' procedure and the rules of procedure of parliamentary assemblies (Article 61-1 of the Constitution). The judicial review is mandatory and occurs before the coming into force of the legal acts mentioned above. The Constitutional Council is also competent for the judicial review of the constitutionality of ordinary laws before their enactment (Article 61(2) of the Constitution) if it is requested by the President of the Republic, the Prime Minister, the President of the Senate, the President of the National Assembly, 60 members of the National Assembly or 60 members of the Senate. Since 2010, the Constitutional Council can also rule on a question of constitutionality[63] raised during a trial before a court under the judicial or administrative order (Article 61-1 of the Constitution and organic law implementing this article).[64] The question is raised by one of the parties to the trial. If the Constitutional Council deems the legislative provision to be unconstitutional, it will declare it unconstitutional and the provision will be repealed (Article 62 of the Constitution).

As a judge of elections and referendums, the Constitutional Council monitors all national elections (that is, presidential elections, elections of deputies and senators and referendums). The powers of the Constitutional Council in electoral matters vary depending on the election in question.[65] The jurisdiction that derives from Article 60 of the Constitution, in the matter of a referendum, has been broadened in the course of its jurisprudence as it is permitted the legality review of decrees organizing a referendum.[66] Since the introduction of the 'shared referendum initiative' in 2008,[67] the Constitutional Council also

---

[62] Art. 56 to 63 Constitution.

[63] This procedure is called 'QPC' as 'Question prioritaire de constitutionnalité'.

[64] Organic Law no. 2009-1523, 10 December 2009, implementing article 61-1 Constitution, JORF 11 December 2009, 21379.

[65] Constitutional Council competencies are specified by the Organic Law on the Constitutional Council: *Ordonnance no 58-1967 du 7 novembre 1958 portant loi organique sur le Conseil constitutionnel*, Art. 30–51 (*Organic Law on Constitutional Council*).

[66] Decision no. 2000-21 REF, 25 July 2000, *Hauchemaille*, para. 5.

[67] Art. 11(3) and 61(1) Constitution specified by Organic law no. 2013-1114 implementing Art. 11 Constitution, 6 December 2013 and law no. 2013-1116 implementing

has new powers starting from the moment when the initiative is submitted by a parliamentary minority to when it is placed on the ballot for the referendum.

4.1   Institution-initiated, Constitutional and EU Accession Referendums

The issue of the review of the referendum bills submitted under Article 11(1) of the Constitution has been one of the most debated issues in French constitutional law since 1962.[68]

As mentioned, the President used the referendum procedure in 1962 to bypass the assemblies, in particular the Senate. The Constitutional Council was petitioned to give its advisory opinion on the decrees which organized the referendum and to review the constitutionality of the draft referendum bill.

The advisory opinion issued by the Constitutional Council on the decrees organizing the referendum is part of its jurisdiction under Article 60 of the Constitution, which provided in its initial version that 'the Constitutional Council shall ensure the proper conduct of referendum proceedings and shall proclaim the results of the referendum'. The organic law on the Constitutional Council specifies the scope of the Council's jurisdiction.[69] Its Article 46 provides that 'the Constitutional Council shall be consulted by the Government on the holding of referenda. It shall immediately be informed of all measures taken for that purpose.' Consequently, the Government consulted the Constitutional Council as well as the Council of State (*Conseil d'État*) – the French administrative supreme court – on the referendum. Both issued (but did not publish[70]) unfavourable opinions and considered that the use of this

---

Art. 11 Constitution, 6 December 2013. These details are contained in the Organic Law, 7 November 1958, on the Constitutional Council: Art. 45-1 to 45-6.

[68]   See Marthe Fatin-Rouge Stefanini, *Le contrôle du référendum par la justice constitutionnelle* (Economica 2004) 381; Georges Berlia, 'Le problème de la constitutionnalité du référendum du 28 octobre 1962' (1962) Revue de droit public et de sciences politiques 936; Bernard Branchet, 'L'article 11 et le respect de la Constitution de 1958', (1990) Revue de droit public et de sciences politiques 1705; Jean-François Flauss, 'Le contrôle de la constitutionnalité des lois référendaires' (1987) Les Petites Affiches 7; Francis Hamon, 'L'extension du référendum: données, controverses, perspectives', (1996) no 77 Pouvoirs 113; Benoît Mercuzot, 'La souveraineté de l'expression référendaire: un principe nécessaire au droit constitutionnel' (1995) Revue de droit public et de sciences politiques 661; Jean-François Prévost, 'Le droit référendaire dans l'ordonnancement juridique de la Constitution de 1958', (1977) Revue de droit public et de sciences politiques 6.

[69]   Organic Law on Constitutional Council.

[70]   The Constitutional Council provided an opinion on 2 October 1962, which was unofficial. The Council of State gives an opinion on all bills, but they are not published. The general assembly of the Council of State rendered an unfavourable opinion on 29

procedure to amend the Constitution was unconstitutional[71] because the only one provided by the Constitution was the procedure of Article 89.

Once the referendum had been approved with a 61.75 per cent majority, the President of the Senate made an application to the Constitutional Council based on Article 61(2) of the Constitution which empowers the Constitutional Council to adjudicate the constitutionality of laws. In its Decision 20 DC of 6 November 1962, the Constitutional Council declared itself '*forum non conveniens*' since it has only subject-matter jurisdiction and such jurisdiction only includes laws voted by the Parliament and not those laws which have been adopted by the people by means of a referendum and thus are a direct expression of national sovereignty. This position has never been contradicted thereafter, even with regard to a treaty ratification law which can only be subordinated to the Constitution[72] or a law assessed in the framework of a *a posteriori* constitutionality judicial review (Article 61-1 of the Constitution).[73] In the latter two cases, the provisions subject to the Constitutional Council judicial review were indeed laws in nature and did not proceed to a revision of the Constitution as in 1962. One would have thought that the Constitutional Council would have changed its jurisprudence and accepted to control laws approved by referendums[74] by departing from the tense context of the 1962 referendum.[75]

Henceforth, the sole authority who has the power to check compliance with the limitations imposed by Article 11 of the Constitution is the President. The

---

September 1962. See the Constitutional Council unofficial Opinion on the referendum on the election of the President of the Republic by direct universal suffrage, in Bertrand Mathieu and others, *Les grandes délibérations du Conseil constitutionnel, 1958–1983* (Dalloz 2009) 99–100.

[71] On debates within the Constitutional Council on the use of referendum Art. 11 (1), see Bertrand Mathieu and others, *Les grandes délibérations du Conseil constitutionnel, 1958–1983* (Dalloz 2009) 99–112.

[72] Decision no. 92-313 DC, 23 September 1992, *Loi autorisant la ratification du Traité sur l'Union européenne*. According to Art. 11 Constitution, only 'Government Bill (…) which provides for authorization to ratify a treaty which, although not contrary to the Constitution, would affect the functioning of the institutions' may be submitted to a referendum.

[73] Decision no. 2014-392 QPC, 25 April 2014, *Province Sud de Nouvelle-Calédonie*. In this case, the legislative provision subject to the Constitutional Council judicial review was adopted by referendum.

[74] Marthe Fatin-Rouge Stefanini, *Le contrôle du référendum par la justice constitutionnelle* (Economica 2004) 95–102.

[75] The 1962 referendum came at the end of the Algerian War and its declaration of independence. General De Gaulle was perceived as the man likely to stabilize the institutions. The Constitutional Council had a very weak legitimacy at that time and very limited competences.

President has complete discretion in calling the referendum and he or she is considered to act as the main guardian of the Constitution following the mandate stemming from Article 5 of the Constitution: 'The President of the Republic shall ensure due respect for the Constitution.'

Unfortunately, this interpretation of the Constitution has never been challenged on the occasion of subsequent constitutional reforms, despite the legal literature's criticism[76] and the unease of the Constitutional Council itself. Since 2000, the latter has accepted to check on an exceptional basis the legality – and thus the constitutionality – of the preparatory acts of referendums, which include the presidential decrees to organize a referendum. Before that, these decrees had eluded all controls since both the Constitutional Council and the Council of State declared themselves *forum non conveniens*.[77] In 2000, in the *Hauchemaille* decision, the Constitutional Council based itself on its general referendum surveillance mandate under Article 60 of the Constitution to expand its jurisdiction over other acts. It considered that:

> by virtue of Article 60, it is part of its mandate to decide on requests bearing allegations on the regularity of forthcoming operations, in cases where the inadmissibility of these requests could seriously compromise the efficiency of its referendum operations compliance check, vitiate the general execution of the vote or adversely affect the normal functioning of public powers.[78]

This means that the principle of an advisory opinion of Constitutional Council over preparatory acts remains, but exceptionally requests about these acts can be admitted by the Constitutional Council and may be examined in judicial proceedings before it when potential irregularities could have seriously damaging consequences.

In 2005 several requests related to the organization of the referendum on the Treaty establishing a Constitution for Europe were submitted to the Constitutional Council. In one of its decisions, it agreed to check compliance with the formal framework of Article 11 of the Constitution. The appellant, *Hauchemaille*, asked for the cancellation of the decree based on the reason that the Prime Minister had not signed it and that the decree had not been sent to one of the two assemblies and did not give rise to a declaration followed by a debate before the assemblies. The Constitutional Council accepted to check these grievances and thus assessed compliance with the formal and

---

[76]   See n 64.

[77]   Constitutional Council, decision no. 62-20, 6 November 1962; Council of State, Assembly, 19 October 1962, *Brocas* in which the Council of State refused to control the decree of the President of the Republic deciding to hold a referendum because it considered it an 'act of government' (political decision).

[78]   Decision no. 2000-21 REF, 25 July 2000, *Hauchemaille*, para. 5.

procedural framework as provided by the Constitution. As a result, it dismissed the arguments put forward by the appellant. Another grievance was substantive: the appellant argued that the ratification law on the Treaty establishing a Constitution for Europe submitted to referendum was contrary to the Charter for the Environment which had been granted constitutional status a few days before. The Constitutional Council declined to pronounce itself on its jurisdiction but nevertheless stated that 'in any case, the Treaty is not contrary to the Constitution'.[79]

Despite the request addressed to parliamentarians by some legal authors[80] to clarify the scope of Article 11 of the Constitution, the ambiguity of this provision remains. The 23 July 2008 constitutional reform does not deem the Constitutional Council competent, as a constitutional judge, to review the constitutionality of draft laws introduced under Article 11(1). With this amendment, the scope of Article 60 of the Constitution only has been clarified so that the Constitutional Council is competent, as an electoral judge, for ensuring the proposer conduct of national referendums and not local referendums. Article 60 of the Constitution provides that 'The Constitutional Council shall ensure the proper conduct of referendum proceedings as provided for in Articles 11 and 89 and in Title XV and shall proclaim the results of the referendum.' These provisions are detailed in the organic law on Constitutional Council.[81]

This reasoning also applies to referendums organized in the framework of Article 89 and as a consequence to all the referendums whose purpose would be a constitutional change. Indeed, if the Constitutional Council admitted that there are limitations to constitutional amendments,[82] it considers itself to be incompetent to control compliance with them.[83] Again, the sole check remains the political one performed by the President of the Republic at the time when he or she decides to have the constitutional change ratified by the Congress or a referendum.

Within the framework of its mandate to ensure 'proper conduct of referendum proceedings', the Constitutional Council could assess alleged violations of the two-fold requirement of clarity and loyalty of the consultation (see Section 3.2.1 above). As we have seen above, the control of compliance with

---

[79] Decision no. 2005-31 REF, 24 March 2005, *Hauchemaille et Meyet*. Marthe Fatin-Rouge Stefanini, 'La décision Hauchemaille et Meyet du 24 mars 2005: un nouveau pas en matière de contrôle des référendums', (2005) Revue française de droit administratif 1040.

[80] See n 64.

[81] Organic law on Constitutional Council, arts. 46–50.

[82] Decision no. 312 DC, 2 September 1992, *Traité sur l'Union européenne*.

[83] Decision no. 2003-469 DC, 26 March 2003, *Loi de révision constitutionnelle sur l'organisation décentralisée de la République*.

this requirement is nevertheless not systematic since it is only conducted if a request is submitted to the Constitutional Council and if it exceptionally accepts to review it before the popular vote takes place (Decision no. 2000-21 REF, 25 July 2000, *Hauchemaille*, cited above).

4.2   'Shared Referendum Initiative'

With regard to the 'shared initiative', judicial control takes place at all steps of the procedure. Article 61(1) of the Constitution provides that at the very beginning of the process the referendum draft bill is sent to the Constitutional Council. Article 61(1) of the Constitution states that 'institutional Acts, before their promulgation [and] proposal Bills mentioned in Article 11 before they are submitted to referendum (…) shall, before coming into force, be referred to the Constitutional Council, which shall rule on their conformity with the Constitution'.

This compulsory prior check entrusted to the Constitutional Council is clarified by an organic law of 6 December 2013.[84] It covers the control of the threshold number of parliamentarians required to initiate the procedure (one-fifth of the members of the Parliament), compliance with the framework of the referendum as provided for by Article 11(1) of the Constitution and compliance with the prohibition to submit a referendum draft bill about a legislative provision promulgated for less than one year[85] or a new referendum proposal on the same subject before the end of a period of two years following the date of the vote.[86] Compliance check of the referendum draft bill with the constitutional provisions is also included in the control of the admissibility of the referendum.[87]

The first shared initiative proposal was submitted in May 2019 and resulted in the first shared initiative decision of the Constitutional Council of 9 May 2019.[88] The decision found that all the formal, substantive and procedural requirements were complied with. The Constitutional Council allowed the collection of signatures to start.

---

[84] Organic law no. 2013-1114 implementing Art. 11 Constitution, 6 December 2013.

[85] Art. 11(3) Constitution.

[86] Art. 11(6) Constitution.

[87] Art. 61(1) Constitution and Art. 45-2 (2) and (3) Organic law on the Constitutional Council.

[88] Decision, no. 2019-1 RIP, 9 May 2019.

This first decision has been heavily criticized by part of the literature[89] but also by the Government itself,[90] because the Constitutional Council accepted that parliamentarians may bypass the prohibition to ask for the abrogation of a law passed less than a year ago. However, the Constitutional Council strictly adhered to the provisions of the Constitution and the organic law on referendum. Another interpretation would have resulted in a restriction of the constitutional right granted to the parliamentarian minority and to citizens by the 23 July 2008 constitutional reform.

---

[89] See Olivier Duhamel and Nicolas Molfessis, 'ADP: Avec le RIP, le Conseil constitutionnel joue avec le feu' (*Le Monde*, 14 May 2019) https://www.lemonde .fr/idees/article/2019/05/14/adp-avec-le-rip-le-conseil-constitutionnel-joue-avec-le -feu_5461684_3232.html, accessed 13 September 2020; Anne Levade, 'Privatisation d'ADP: le Conseil constitutionnel comme si de rien n'était !' (*L'Express*, 23 May 2019) https://www.lexpress.fr/actualite/privatisation-d-adp-le-conseil-constitutionnel -comme-si-de-rien-n-etait_2078634.html, accessed 13 September 2020; Jean-Eric Schoettl, 'De quelques questions épineuses sur le RIP "Aéroports de Paris" (*Lextenso*, 7 June 2019) https://www.lextenso-etudiant.fr/article-à-la-une-constitutionnel/ de-quelques-questions-épineuses-sur-le-rip-«-aéroports-de-paris-», accessed 13 September 2020.
  See also Contra: Denis Baranger, 'Notre Constitution démocratique donne au peuple la possibilité de s'exprimer' (*lepoint.fr*, 16 May 2019) https://www.lepoint.fr/ editos-du-point/laurence-neuer/adp-notre-constitution-democratique-donne-au-peuple -la-possibilite-de-s-exprimer-16-05-2019-2313090_56.php, accessed 13 September 2020; Olivier Beaud, 'Remarques sur le référendum d'initiative parlementaire et sur les arguments de ceux qui ont voulu en bloquer la procédure' (*Juspoliticum Le Blog*, 2 May 2019) http://blog.juspoliticum.com/2019/05/23/remarques-sur-le-referendum -dinitiative-parlementaire-et-sur-les-arguments-de-ceux-qui-ont-voulu-en-bloquer-la -procedure-par-olivier-beaud/, accessed 13 September 2020; Paul Cassia and Patrick Weil, 'Sur ADP, le Conseil constitutionnel n'a pas commis de faute' (*Le Monde,* 17 May 2019) https://www.lemonde.fr/idees/article/2019/05/16/referendum-sur-adp -le-conseil-constitutionnel-n-a-commis-ni-faute-juridique-ni-faute-politique_5462653 _3232.html, accessed 13 September 2020; Jean-Philippe Derosier, 'Complémentarité démocratique' (*La Constitution décodée*, 15 May 2019) <https://constitutiondecodee .fr/2019/05/15/complementarite-democratique/> accessed 13 September 2020; Marthe Fatin-Rouge Stefanini, 'Le RIP pourrait devenir une nouvelle forme de veto suspensif' (*LeMonde.fr*, 17 May 2019) https://www.lemonde.fr/idees/article/2019/05/17/marthe -fatin-rouge-stefanini-le-rip-pourrait-devenir-une-nouvelle-forme-de-veto-suspensif _5463514_3232.html, accessed 13 September 2020; Marthe Fatin-Rouge Stefanini, 'La décision n° 1-2019 RIP ou quand un mécanisme voué à l'échec devient un véritable atout pour l'opposition', (2019) Revue française de droit constitutionnel 999.
[90] Franc Lemarc, 'Référendum ADP: le gouvernement demande au Conseil constitutionnel "d'interrompre" la procédure' (*Maire info*, 17 May 2019) https:// www.maire-info.com/test-2/referendum-adp-le-gouvernement-demande-au-conseil -constitutionnel-d%27interrompre-la-procedure-article-23058, accessed 13 September 2020.

Once the period of signature collection is over, the Constitutional Council checks whether the threshold of citizens' support as required by the Constitution is reached, so that the initiative can be submitted to the Parliament. It ensures the regularity of voters' signature collection and has competence regarding all related grievances.

Finally, if the threshold of citizens' support is reached and the resort to referendum is decided, the Constitutional Council exercises its competences as it does for every referendum within the framework of its mandate under Article 60 of the Constitution – ensuring the regularity of referendum-related operations.

Shared initiative referendums are thus subjected to multiple checks stemming from the specificity of the way the procedure is triggered. This is in stark contrast with the minimal mandate entrusted to the Constitutional Council by Article 60 of the Constitution for the other types of national referendums.

5.   CONCLUSION

In late 2018, the main demand of a huge social protest called the 'yellow jackets' (*gilets jaunes*) was the introduction of a citizen-initiated referendum in order to submit proposals regarding ordinary laws and constitutional amendments, to ask for the abrogation of ordinary laws (rejective citizen-initiated referendum) and for the revocation of elected officials (recall).[91]

The President of the Republic, and his government, also organized a nationwide discussion which pointed to the will of the French citizens to be more involved in decision-making on public affairs.[92] A constitutional reform proposal which takes these demands into account was presented in August 2019.[93] It would extend the scope of Article 11(1) of the Constitution to the organization of *territorial* public authorities. However, no judicial review of draft referendum bills would be provided for.

Besides, and above all, a new title on 'citizen participation' would appear in the Constitution. The shared initiative would be part of this title and the number of required signatures would be reduced to 1 million. Furthermore, the temporal limit for proposing a shared initiative whose purpose is the abroga-

---

[91]   Anthony Berthelier, 'Les gilets jaunes réclament le "RIC", le référendum d'initiative citoyenne' (*Huffington Post*, 6 December 2018) https://www.huffingtonpost.fr/2018/12/06/les-gilets-jaunes-reclament-le-ric-le-referendum-dinitiative-citoyenne_a_23610454/, accessed 13 September 2020; Raul Magni-Berton and Clara Egger, *RIC. Le référendum d'initiative citoyenne expliqué à tous* (Limoges FYP éditions 2019).

[92]   See https://granddebat.fr

[93]   Constitutional draft bill, no 2203, 29 August 2019, *Pour un renouveau de la vie démocratique.*

tion of a law that has just been enacted would be raised from one to three years. A Citizen Participation Council (*Conseil de participation citoyenne*) would be established as well.

This reform of the Constitution is unlikely to be approved as it lacks sufficient support in parliament. However, sooner or later, a reform will definitely be required to modernize the institutions of the Fifth Republic in order to allow citizens to be more directly involved in political decision-making.

PART III

'New' European democracies

9. Slovenia

Bruna Žuber and Igor Kaučič

1.   INTRODUCTION

All of the most common instruments of direct democracy, that is, the referendum, the citizens' agenda initiative and the town meeting, are established in the Republic of Slovenia (Slovenia). Citizens can directly participate in the process of forming and deciding on different legal acts as well as regarding other important decisions on both the national and local levels. Judged by the number and diversity of these instruments, Slovenia ranks among the states with the most developed systems of direct democracy in Europe. This holds true also in terms of the practical application of direct-democratic instruments, particularly referendums.[1]

Slovene legal doctrine distinguishes between formal and substantive legal limits of direct democracy. The substantive limits may be explicit or implicit.[2] Explicit limits are provided in legislation and in the constitution, whereas the implicit limits of direct democracy derive from the principle of constitutional democracy. The idea of this principle is that values of constitutional importance prevail over the democratically taken decisions of the majority. The principle of constitutional democracy thus prevents unnecessary direct decision-making by voters in situations where it is already clear that the outcome of such decision-making would be unconstitutional.[3]

A reasonable number of legal limits are imposed on direct-democratic instruments in Slovenia. Explicit substantive legal limits are determined only for the referendum, while implicit legal limits are inherent to all instruments

---

[1]   Ciril Ribičič and Igor Kaučič, 'Constitutional Limits of Legislative Referendum: The Case of Slovenia' (2014) 12 Lex Localis – Journal of Local Self-Government 900. See also Bruna Žuber, 'The Concept of Constitutional Democracy in Referendum Decision-Making' in Manuel Carrasco Durán and Blanca Rodriguez-Ruiz (eds), *La participación ciudadana como pilar del estado democrático: posibilidades y límites en el marco de la democracia representativa* (Thomson Reuters Aranzadi 2019) 212.
[2]   See Ribičič and Kaučič (n 1) 916.
[3]   See Žuber (n 1) 206–212.

of direct democracy. The objective of this contribution is to analyse the legal limits of direct democracy in Slovenia and to open a discussion on their need, dimensions, scope and content. The chapter also offers an overview of the mechanisms for the legal protection of voters with regard to restrictions of direct-democratic rights.

2. INSTRUMENTS OF DIRECT DEMOCRACY IN SLOVENIA

The Constitution of the Republic of Slovenia[4] (Constitution) and relevant legislation provide the following instruments of direct democracy at the national and local levels:

- the referendum;
- the citizens' agenda initiative;
- the town meeting;
- the right to file a petition.

The Constitution regulates only those instruments of direct democracy that are within the competence of the National Assembly (the general legislative body of Slovenia),[5] namely the referendum on joining international organizations, the legislative referendum, the constitutional referendum, the referendum on the establishment of a municipality, the constitutional initiative, the legislative initiative and the right to file a petition, which is defined as a human right.[6] Furthermore, the Constitution only regulates the fundamental characteristics of these direct-democratic instruments, whereas detailed regulation is provided in the Referendum and Popular Initiative Act (RPIA).[7] All other instruments of direct democracy are regulated in the RPIA, in the Law on Local Self-Government (LSGA)[8] and in the Self-Imposed Contributions Act.[9] Some

---

[4]   Official Gazette RS No. 33/91-I, 42/97, 66/00, 24/03, 69/04, 69/04, 69/04, 68/06, 47/13, 47/13, 75/16, https://www.us-rs.si/en/about-the-court/legal-basis/constitution/, accessed 2 June 2020.

[5]   In addition to the National Assembly, the Slovene Parliament also comprises the National Council, which represents diverse local and other (especially professional) interests.

[6]   According to Art. 45 of the Constitution, every citizen has the right to file petitions and to pursue other initiatives of general significance.

[7]   Official Gazette RS No. 15/94 as amended http://www.pisrs.si/Pis.web/cm ?idStrani=prevodi, accessed 2 June 2020.

[8]   Official Gazette RS No. 72/93 as amended http://www.pisrs.si/Pis.web/cm ?idStrani=prevodi, accessed 2 June 2020.

[9]   Official Gazette RS No. 87/01.

procedural rules for applying different instruments of direct democracy are provided in the Rules of Procedure of the National Assembly.[10]

2.1   Referendum

The Slovene legal system regulates, at the national and local level, the following types of referendums:

- constitutional referendums;
- legislative referendums;
- referendums on joining international organizations;
- consultative referendums;
- local referendums.[11]

2.1.1   Constitutional referendum
Article 170 of the Constitution[12] provides that:

1. The National Assembly must submit a proposed constitutional amendment to voters for adoption in a referendum if so required by at least 30 deputies.
2. A constitutional amendment is adopted in a referendum if a majority of those voting voted in favour of the same, provided that a majority of all voters participated in the referendum.

A constitutional referendum is a facultative phase in the procedure for amending the Constitution and is characterized by the voters' ratification of the constitutional amendment. A constitutional referendum is also referred to as a minority or oppositional referendum, its key purpose being to prevent the entry into force of the constitutional amendment until the voters' decision in the referendum.

A constitutional referendum is a subsequent and suspensive legislature-initiated referendum: it takes place after the constitutional amendment has been adopted by the National Assembly[13] and before its promulgation and entry into force if the conditions determined by the Constitution and the RPIA are met. It is called if at least 30 deputies of the National Assembly so

---

[10]   Official Gazette RS No. 35/02 as amended.

[11]   Ciril Ribičič and Igor Kaučič, *Referendum and the Constitutional Court of Slovenia* (Universitätsverlag Regensburg 2016) 13–16.

[12]   Detailed regulation of the constitutional referendum is provided in Art. 4-8 RPIA and in Art. 108, 182 and 184–186 Rules of Procedure of the National Assembly.

[13]   The National Assembly adopts acts amending the Constitution by a two-thirds majority vote of all deputies (60 out of 90 deputies have to vote in the affirmative).

require. Voters cannot initiate it. The fact that exclusively deputies can initiate a constitutional referendum is the main reason why one has never been held, despite the fact that ten constitutional amendments have been adopted thus far.

For a constitutional amendment to be adopted in a referendum, a dual majority is required: majority participation of all voters (a turnout quorum) and a majority of the participating voters voting in the affirmative.[14]

2.1.2   Legislative referendum

Article 90 of the Constitution[15] provides that:

1. The National Assembly shall call a referendum on the entry into force of a law that it has adopted if so required by at least 40,000 voters.
2. A referendum may not be called:
    •   on laws on urgent measures to ensure the defence of the state, security, or the elimination of the consequences of natural disasters;
    •   on laws on taxes, customs duties, and other compulsory charges, and on the law adopted for the implementation of the state budget;
    •   on laws on the ratification of treaties;
    •   on laws eliminating an unconstitutionality in the field of human rights and fundamental freedoms or any other unconstitutionality.
3. The right to vote in a referendum is held by all citizens who are eligible to vote in elections.
4. A law is rejected in a referendum if a majority of voters who have cast valid votes vote against the law, provided at least one fifth of all qualified voters have voted against the law.
5. Referendums are regulated by a law passed in the National Assembly by a two-thirds majority vote of deputies present.

The Slovene legislative referendum is a rejective citizen-initiated referendum. The constitutional regulation of the legislative referendum completely changed in 2013.[16] A legislative referendum is subsequent to the adoption of the law and suspensive. The subject of a legislative referendum is the question of the entry into force of a law. The voters cannot decide on a particular issue regulated by a specific law but only on the law as a whole. A request for the calling of a legislative referendum defers the entry into force of the law until

---

[14]   Art. 170 Constitution. See also: Ribičič and Kaučič (n 11) 16–18.

[15]   Detailed regulation of the legislative referendum is provided in Art. 9-25 RPIA and in Art. 108, 184–186 and 222 Rules of Procedure of the National Assembly.

[16]   From 1994 until today there have been twenty legislative referendums held in Slovenia, out of which the voters initiated ten. For details, see the official website of the National Electoral Commission: https://www.dvk-rs.si/index.php/si/arhiv-referendumi, accessed 8 July 2020.

a decision has been made in the referendum.[17] The new regulation emphasizes the role of the referendum as an instrument of control by the people over the work of parliament, while at the same time it limits the possibility of using it to resolve internal parliamentary conflicts.

Voters have the exclusive competence to call a legislative referendum. According to Article 90(1) of the Constitution, a legislative referendum can be initiated by at least 40,000 voters, representing approximately 2.4 per cent of the entire electorate, which is less than in comparable European states. The procedure for collecting voters' signatures is regulated by the RPIA (see Section 4.1.1).[18]

A law is rejected in a referendum if the majority of voters who cast valid votes voted against it, provided that at least one-fifth of all voters vote against the law.[19]

2.1.3   Referendum on joining international organizations

Article 3.a of the Constitution[20] provides that:

1. Pursuant to a treaty ratified by the National Assembly by a two-thirds majority vote of all deputies, Slovenia may transfer the exercise of part of its sovereign rights to international organizations (…) and may enter into a defensive alliance with states (…).

2. Before ratifying a treaty referred to in the preceding paragraph, the National Assembly may call a referendum. A proposal is passed in the referendum if a majority of voters who have cast valid votes vote in favour of the same. The National Assembly is bound by the result of such referendum. If such referendum has been held, a referendum regarding the law on the ratification of the treaty concerned may not be called.

Article 3.a(2) of the Constitution provides a special form of legislature or executive-initiated referendum that enables voters to decide on Slovenia joining the European Union, or possibly joining any other international organization to which Slovenia wishes to transfer the execution of its sovereign rights, and joining defence organizations (such as NATO). The subject

---

[17]   Since its purpose is to prevent the entry into force of a law, it is also called a 'popular veto'.

[18]   Art. 16.a and 16.b RPIA. See also Igor Kaučič, 'Referendumska iniciativa' in Igor Kaučič (ed.), *Zakonodajni referendum – pravna ureditev in praksa v Sloveniji* (Inštitut za primerjalno pravo, GV Založba 2010) 83–93.

[19]   Art. 90(4) Constitution.

[20]   Detailed regulation of the referendum on joining international organizations is provided in Art. 25.a–25.g RPIA and in Art. 108 and 184–186 Rules of Procedure of the National Assembly.

of this referendum is neither the treaty in question itself nor the law on its ratification, but an individual question that is of key significance in the treaty. A referendum on joining international organizations is optional. The National Assembly may call it by its own decision on the proposal of the government, at least ten deputies or a deputy group. A proposal for calling a referendum may be made before or after the signing of the treaty, but must be made before the adoption of the law on the ratification of the treaty by the National Assembly.[21] Referendums on joining international organizations have been held only twice so far, both times in 2003, regarding joining the European Union and NATO.[22]

2.1.4   Consultative referendum

The consultative referendum is regulated in Articles 26–29 of the RPIA. The National Assembly may call a consultative referendum on questions within its competence that are of wider significance to citizens. The National Assembly may hold a consultative referendum in the whole country or in a specific area in cases where the referendum question concerns only part of the electorate. The consultative referendum is optional and preliminary. The National Assembly is not bound by the result of a consultative referendum. A consultative referendum was held nationally only once, in 2008, concerning the establishment of regions in Slovenia.

2.1.5   Local referendums

There are various types of local referendums: referendums on general legal acts of a municipality, referendums on the establishment and territorial reorganization of a municipality, consultative referendums of a municipality, referendums on statutory issues and referendums on self-imposed contributions. The Self-Imposed Contributions Act governs the latter, while other local referendums and other forms of direct democracy at the local level are governed by the LSGA.

A referendum on a general legal act of a municipality is a fundamental form of direct decision-making by voters residing in the municipality.[23] It is subsequent and either optional (held on the proposal of the mayor or a member of the municipal council at the request of at least 5 per cent of the municipality's voters) or compulsory (if required by law or the municipal charter). A referendum proposal is approved if a majority of participating voters vote in favour of

---

[21]   See Ribičič and Kaučič (n 11) 21–23.
[22]   The referendum questions were 'Do you agree for the Republic of Slovenia to become a member of the North Atlantic Treaty Organization (NATO)?' and 'Do you agree for the Republic of Slovenia to become a member of the European Union (EU)?'
[23]   Art. 46 LSGA.

the proposal, making this decision binding on the municipal council until the end of its term.[24]

2.2 Citizens' Agenda Initiative

The citizens' agenda initiative (in Slovenian law: the popular initiative) allows voters to place an issue on the agenda of the state authorities but does not lead to a referendum. The authorities are obliged to consider the voters' proposal and carry out the prescribed procedure; however, if they decide not to implement the proposal, they are not obliged to call a referendum on it.[25]

There are three types of agenda initiatives in Slovenia, namely the constitutional initiative, the legislative initiative and the local initiative.

The constitutional initiative is provided in Article 168 of the Constitution.[26] A proposal for a constitutional amendment may be requested by at least 30,000 voters (representing less than 2 per cent of the electorate). Along with the required signatures, the proposal must also provide a draft of the constitutional amendment. The National Assembly first decides whether to accept the proposal by a two-thirds majority vote of the deputies present. For the actual adoption of the constitutional amendment, a two-thirds majority vote of all deputies is required. If the proposal is not adopted, the procedure for amending the Constitution is terminated. The same proposal cannot be resubmitted during the same term of office.[27]

The legislative initiative is regulated in Article 88 of the Constitution.[28] The legislative proposal may be submitted by at least 5,000 voters (representing approximately 0.3 per cent of the electorate). The National Assembly decides on the adoption of a legislative proposal by a majority of the votes of the deputies present if a greater majority is not prescribed.[29] If the National Assembly decides that the legislative proposal is suitable for the further procedure, the legislative procedure continues, otherwise it ends.[30]

The citizens' agenda initiative is regulated in a similar way at the local level. Article 48 of the LSGA provides that at least 5 per cent of the voters in

---

[24] Ribičič and Kaučič (n 11) 24–25.
[25] Ibid. 28.
[26] Detailed regulation of the constitutional initiative is provided in Art. 57 and 59 RPIA and Art. 173 and 177 Rules of Procedure of the National Assembly.
[27] Art. 177 Rules of Procedure of the National Assembly.
[28] Detailed regulation of the legislative initiative is provided in Art. 58 and 59 RPIA and in Art. 114, 115.a and 122 Rules of Procedure of the National Assembly.
[29] Art. 84 Rules of Procedure of the National Assembly.
[30] Art. 122 Rules of Procedure of the National Assembly.

a municipality may request the abrogation of a general legal act or any other decision of the municipal council or other municipal authorities.

As the citizens' agenda initiative in Slovenia does not directly lead to a referendum, citizens do not pay much attention to it. So far, there have been only a few legislative initiatives and only one constitutional initiative. In contrast, the agenda initiative is more common on the local level.[31]

2.3   Town Meeting

The LSGA provides that at a town meeting the members of a municipality are entitled to discuss individual issues, form standpoints, submit proposals, initiatives and opinions as well as make decisions. A meeting can be convened for the entire municipality or just a particular part thereof. The LSGA provides two ways of calling a town meeting, namely an obligatory and a facultative way. A town meeting is obligatory if so determined by either a law or the charter of the municipality or if so required by at least 5 per cent of the voters of the municipality (or the respective particular part of it). A facultative town meeting can be initiated by the mayor, the municipal council or the council of a narrower part of the municipality. The municipal charter of each municipality determines the course and process of decision-making at town meetings.[32]

3.   LEGAL LIMITS ON DIRECT DEMOCRACY

3.1   Limits on Referendums

3.1.1   Substantive limits

Substantive limits on referendums are provided only for the legislative referendum and the referendum on a general legal act of a municipality.

Before its amendment in 2013, the Constitution did not determine any limits for the legislative referendum. In principle, a legislative referendum was permissible with regard to any law adopted by the National Assembly. Nevertheless, in order to avoid referendums that might cause unconstitutional consequences, Article 21 of the RPIA prescribed proceedings for a review of the constitutional admissibility of legislative referendums. The Constitutional Court of the Republic of Slovenia (Constitutional Court) was authorized to assess whether suspending the entry into force of a law due to a referendum procedure or rejection of a law in a referendum might result in unconstitutional consequences. The Constitutional Court only carried out such a constitutional

---

review at the request of the National Assembly, not *ex officio*. The National Assembly would request a constitutional review only if it deemed that suspending the entry into force of a law or its rejection might result in unconstitutional consequences. If the Constitutional Court decided that this is the case, it would prohibit the referendum. 'Unconstitutional consequences' was an undefined legal term and it was up to the Constitutional Court to define it, taking into consideration Article 21 of the RPIA. At first, the Constitutional Court built up its case law regarding such matters; however, in 2011 it changed its doctrine and thereby narrowed its interpretation of Article 21 of the RPIA arguing that the existing legal basis is not appropriate and sufficient for carrying out the review of the constitutional admissibility of legislative referendums. From then until the new constitutional regulation of the legislative referendum in 2013 only one legislative referendum was prohibited.[33]

The constitutional regulation in force lists, in Article 90(2), four types of laws that are excluded from the scope of the legislative referendum.

First, the inadmissibility of referendums on laws on urgent measures to ensure the defence of the state, security or the elimination of the consequences of natural disasters arises from the need for rapid and effective action. The Constitution does not exclude any laws in these areas, but only those pertaining to urgent measures, from the scope of the referendum.[34]

Second, referendums on laws on taxes, customs duties and other compulsory charges and on laws adopted for the implementation of the state budget are prohibited because of the need to ensure the financial basis of the state. This referendum prohibition does not apply to all laws that affect public expenditure, public guarantees and so on. Such a broad exclusion of all laws that may, even if only indirectly, affect government expenditure would amount

---

[33] On the basis of the previous regulation that is no longer in force, the Constitutional Court prohibited legislative referendums in four out of eight cases. The Constitutional Court decided that due to the suspension of the entry into force of the law or by its rejection in a referendum, unconstitutional consequences could occur in the following cases: U-II-1/09 of 5 May 2009 (prohibition of referendum on the Act Amending the Attorneys Act), U-II-2/09 of 9 November 2009 (prohibition of referendum on the Act Amending and Supplementing the Public Sector Salary System Act and the Act Amending and Supplementing the Judicial Service Act), U-II-1/10 of 10 June 2020 (prohibition of referendum on the Act Amending the Act Regulating the Legal Status of Citizens of Former Yugoslavia Living in the Republic of Slovenia), and U-II-1/12, U-II-2/12 of 17 December 2012 (prohibition of referendum on the Act Regulating Measures of the Republic of Slovenia to Strengthen the Stability of Banks and the Slovenian Sovereign Holding Act). On this see also Bruna Žuber, *Ustavnosodni nadzor zakonodajnega referenduma* (GV Založba, Lexpera, 2018) 122–150.

[34] Ribičič and Kaučič (n 1) 917.

to an almost complete prohibition of referendums, since most laws also touch upon fiscal issues and, at least indirectly, influence the state budget.[35]

Third, laws on the ratification of treaties are exempt from the referendum due to the particularity of the Slovenian system whereby the National Assembly ratifies treaties by a law and not by a decree or similar act. Any concerns about the content or constitutionality of a treaty should be resolved prior to ratification.[36] Accordingly, Article 160(2) of the Constitution provides for a preventive review of the constitutionality of treaties, which may be triggered by the President of the Republic, the Government or a third of the deputies of the National Assembly. The Constitutional Court's opinion on the conformity of a treaty with the Constitution is binding on the National Assembly. This limit does not, however, apply to the treaties referred to in Article 3a(2) of the Constitution. These treaties can be subject to a referendum on joining international organizations or a legislative referendum.[37]

Fourth, a legislative referendum may not be called on laws eliminating an unconstitutionality in the field of human rights and fundamental freedoms or any other unconstitutionality. This prohibition is designed to protect other constitutional values: it ensures that violations of constitutional values, including human rights and fundamental freedoms, or unconstitutional legislation may be eliminated. As constitutional democracy is established in Slovenia, inclusion of such provision in the Constitution can be seen as underlining the importance of the protection of constitutional rights and freedoms.[38]

The Constitution thus makes a distinction between laws whose adoption is in the exclusive competence of the National Assembly and those where the legislative power is divided between the National Assembly and the voters who can reject the law in a referendum. This constitutional regulation introduced in 2013 is more appropriate than the previous one as it explicitly lists the laws that are excluded from the referendum. Nevertheless, the limits can never be fully defined in advance and thus remain interpretatively open.[39]

Since 2013 the Constitutional Court has ruled on the admissibility of legislative referendums in two instances.

In one instance, Decision No. U-II-2/15 of 3 December 2015, the Constitutional Court decided that the Order of the National Assembly rejecting

---

[35]   Ibid.

[36]   Ibid. 917, 918.

[37]   However, it should be noted that if referendum on joining international organizations has been held, a legislative referendum regarding the law on the ratification of the treaty concerned may not be called (Art. 3(2) Constitution).

[38]   Ribičič and Kaučič (n 1) 918.

[39]   Ibid. 916. See also Igor Kaučič, 'Ustavnosodna presoja zakonodajnega referenduma po novem' [2015] Podjetje in delo 1345–1357.

a request to call a legislative referendum on the Act Amending the Defence Act is in conformity with the Constitution. In this case the Constitutional Court had to decide whether the Act Amending the Defence Act is a law concerning the field of security and a law on urgent measures to ensure security. The Constitutional Court stated that 'the statutory regulation which entails the basis for the implementation of urgent measures for ensuring security that could not be carried out without a law corresponds to the notion of a law on urgent measures referred to in the first indent of Art. 90(2) of the Constitution.' It further explained that 'the authority competent to assess the urgency of measures to ensure security due to which a law has to be adopted is the National Assembly. The Constitutional Court may only assess whether the National Assembly demonstrated reasonable grounds for the assessment that it adopted.'[40]

In contrast, by Decision No. U-II-1/15 of 28 September 2015,[41] the Constitutional Court abrogated the Order of the National Assembly rejecting a request to call a legislative referendum on the Act Amending the Marriage and Family Relations Act (AAMFRA) and thus allowed the referendum to go ahead. The AAMFRA modified the definition of a marriage by stipulating that a marriage is a regulated community of two people, introducing same-sex marriage in place of same-sex civil partnership and equating same-sex non-marital partnerships with heterosexual non-marital partnerships. The AAMFRA eliminated unconstitutionalities established by the Constitutional Court in its Decision No. U-I-425/06 of 2 July 2009[42] and, in addition, also comprehensively regulated and equated same-sex and heterosexual couples in all rights and obligations at general and systemic levels.[43] The National Assembly declared the referendum inadmissible, stating that the AAMFRA was a law eliminating an unconstitutionality and, thus, the referendum fell under the prohibition of the fourth indent of Article 90(2) of the Constitution. The proposers of the referendum initiated proceedings for a review of the constitutional admissibility of a legislative referendum before the Constitutional Court. The Constitutional Court abrogated the order of the National Assembly, arguing that the AAMFRA did not simply eliminate unconstitutionalities but also regulated further questions. It held that:

> the wording of the fourth indent of the second paragraph of Art. 90 of the Constitution, which refers to the elimination of an unconstitutionality, is to be

---

[40] Decision of the Constitutional Court of the Republic of Slovenia No. U-II-2/15 of 28 September 2015, § 15.

[41] Official Gazette RS No. 80/15.

[42] Official Gazette RS No. 55/09.

[43] Bruna Žuber, Igor Kaučič, 'Referendum Challenges in the Republic of Slovenia' [2019] Białostockie Studia Prawnicze 145.

understood in a manner such that it is not admissible to call a referendum only with regard to laws that eliminate an unconstitutionality that the Constitutional Court has already established by a decision and also with regard to laws eliminating a violation of human rights established by a judgment of the European Court of Human Rights. The fourth indent of the second paragraph of Art. 90 of the Constitution cannot be interpreted in such a manner that it is not admissible to call a referendum in cases where the legislature adopts a statutory regulation by which it indirectly, by means of the effects that such statutory regulation produces in other legal fields, eliminates an unconstitutionality that the Constitutional Court or the European Court of Human Rights has already established.[44]

The decision was severely criticized by legal scholars who argued that it interprets Article 90(2) of the Constitution too narrowly, making this interpretation inadmissible in a constitutional democracy.[45]

The Constitutional Court has repeatedly emphasized that decisions causing unconstitutional consequences cannot be adopted in a referendum. This would suggest that Article 90(2) of the Constitution, which explicitly excludes some types of laws from the referendum, does not prevent the Constitutional Court from rejecting a legislative referendum in certain other cases.[46] The Constitutional Court has not yet explicitly ruled whether the constitutional list of limits on the legislative referendum is exhaustive or not. However, in its decision on the AAMFRA it stated in an *obiter dictum* that it is.[47] This position can be problematic as in some cases it would be necessary to prohibit a referendum on a law that is not listed in Article 90(2) of the Constitution to protect another important constitutional value. In this regard, it seems Slovenia might follow the practice of the Italian Constitutional Court, which is particularly interesting. Initially the Italian Constitutional Court treated the constitutionally determined limits as exhaustive and interpreted them narrowly, but later began to interpret them more broadly.[48]

The legal arrangement of referendums on general legal acts of a municipality equally imposes certain legal limits. According to Article 46(1) of

---

[44]   See Section B-I. of Decision of the Constitutional Court of the Republic of Slovenia No. U-II-3/11 of 28 September 2015.

[45]   Žuber and Kaučič (n 43) 147. See also Žuber (n 33) 193–199; Bruna Žuber, 'Presoja dopustnosti izključevanja referenduma o nekaterih zakonih' [2018] Podjetje in delo 1241–1253.

[46]   See Ribičič and Kaučič (n 1) 899–928.

[47]   § 44 of the Decision of the Constitutional Court of the Republic of Slovenia No. U-II-1/15 of 21 October 2015.

[48]   For more on the case law of the Italian Constitutional Court, see Massimo Luciani, *La formazione delle leggi: Il referendum abrogativo* (Zanichelli editore, Soc. ed. del foro italiano 2005) 322–524; Luigi Arcidiacono et al, *Diritto Costituzionale* (Cedam 2013) 190–197.

the LSGA, referendums on the budget and the annual financial statement of a municipality as well as on general legal acts that determine municipal taxes and other charges provided by a law are prohibited.

3.1.2 Formal limits

The legislation in force does not establish formal requirements as to unity of substance or unity of form. However, in previous years, a legislative referendum could also be held before the adoption of a given law (the so-called preliminary legislative referendum). In this case, the Constitutional Court could review the admissibility of the referendum question, which had to be clear, precise and in conformity with the Constitution.[49]

The referendum question is now defined by law. Article 16.c of the RPIA determines:

> A request to call a referendum, an initiative to the voters and an initiative to the National Assembly shall contain the referendum question, which shall read: 'Are you in favour of the entry into force of the Act (indicate the title of the Act) adopted by the National Assembly at its session of...?'

If the referendum question is not formulated in accordance with this provision, the President of the National Assembly has to correct it with the consent of the proposer of the initiative or (if no consent is obtained) call on the proposer of the legislative referendum to supplement or to correct it as appropriate within a period that may not be less than three days. If the proposer fails to supplement or correct the referendum question, the referendum request is deemed to have been withdrawn.[50]

The RPIA also defines the wording of the questions for constitutional referendums and determines the procedure for correcting them and the legal consequences in case of non-compliance.[51] Article 25.b of the RPIA similarly determines that a proposal to call a referendum on joining international organizations must clearly specify the question that is to be the subject of the referendum and establishes the procedure for correcting questions as well as the legal consequences in the event the proposer fails to do.

---

[49] Art. 15 and 16 RPIA (1996). The Constitutional Court considered unclear and imprecise referendum questions as contrary to the principle of the rule of law (Art. 2 Constitution) as well as to the very essence of a referendum. It stated that voters must be precisely informed of the contents of the question on which they are voting and that a referendum question must form a whole. See Decision of the Constitutional Court of the Republic of Slovenia No. U-I-121/97 of 23 May 1997, § 39.

[50] Art. 20 RPIA.

[51] Art. 5.c and 5.č RPIA.

3.1.3   Temporal limits

There are certain temporary bans on holding a referendum on the same issue. For the constitutional referendum, Article 8 of the RPIA determines that for a period of two years after promulgation of the referendum decision, the National Assembly may not adopt a constitutional amendment whose content is contrary to the decision of the voters. Similarly, the National Assembly may not adopt a law whose content is contrary to the decision of the voters in a legislative referendum for a period of one year after the referendum.[52] The decision of voters in a local referendum on a general act of a municipality is binding on the municipal council until the expiry of its term of office.[53] Finally, Article 3.a(2) of the Constitution states that if a referendum on joining an international organization has been held, a legislative referendum regarding the law on the ratification of the treaty concerned may not be called.

3.2   Limits on Citizens' Agenda Initiatives and Town Meetings

There are no explicit substantive limits on citizens' agenda initiatives and town meetings. The only implicit substantive limit on these two forms of direct democracy is the principle of constitutional democracy, meaning that citizens' proposals and decisions should not conflict with values of constitutional importance. If the proposal of a citizens' agenda initiative is not in accordance with constitutional values or with higher-ranking norms, the National Assembly will reject it.[54] Similarly, the proposals, opinions, petitions and decisions adopted at a town meeting that conflict with the most important legal values will not be implemented and will therefore remain without legal effect.

The formal requirements of the citizens' agenda initiative are provided by the RPIA. Its Article 57 provides that a proposal to initiate the procedure for amending the Constitution has to state the subject and manner of amending the Constitution as well as the reasons therefor. In addition, it must be accompanied by the signatures of at least 30,000 voters. Similarly, a legislative proposal must comprise all the elements laid down in the Rules of Procedure of the National Assembly of Slovenia and must be accompanied by the signatures of at least 5,000 voters.[55] While the RPIA does not determine any legal consequences in the event of non-compliance with the formal requirements, the Rules of Procedure of the National Assembly do so. Compliance with the

---

[52]   Art. 25 RPIA.
[53]   Art. 46(4) LSGA.
[54]   See Art. 122 Rules of Procedure of the National Assembly.
[55]   Art. 58 RPIA.

formal requirements is reviewed by the President of the National Assembly.[56] There is no legal remedy provided against the decision of the President of the National Assembly on the formal inadmissibility of an initiative.

4. PROCEDURE FOR THE REVIEW OF REFERENDUMS

4.1 Legislative Referendums

Contrary to some other European states (such as Italy, France and Austria), in Slovenia the Constitution does not contain any rules on the constitutional and judicial review of legislative referendums. Basic rules are, however, provided by the RPIA. In addition, some further requirements have been established by the relevant case law.[57] The Administrative Court of the Republic of Slovenia and the Supreme Court of the Republic of Slovenia are competent to provide judicial protection of the right to vote in a legislative referendum.[58] The Constitutional Court conducts a constitutional review of legislative referendums. Legal reviews of legislative referendums must take into account the principles of the separation of powers, constitutional democracy and the protection of human rights and fundamental freedoms. The reviews must be effective, efficient and fair.[59]

The legal review of a legislative referendum is carried out as a preliminary review, as a review of the process for implementing the referendum and as a subsequent review.

4.1.1 Preliminary review

The purpose of a preliminary review is to ensure that voters' right to file an initiative to request the calling of a referendum and the right to require the calling of a referendum are exercised in conformity with the Constitution and the relevant legislation. In addition, a preliminary review also focuses on preventing

---

[56] See Art. 115.a and 172(5) Rules of Procedure of the National Assembly. It should be noted that the applicable laws do not explicitly determine who checks the signatures. From the Rules of Procedure of the National Assembly and the RPIA it can be inferred that the President of the National Assembly checks them. However, only the number of signatures is checked systematically.

[57] See for instance the Decision of the Constitutional Court of the Republic of Slovenia No. U-I-191/17 of 25 January 2018.

[58] Art. 53 and 53.a RPIA.

[59] Bruna Žuber, 'Judicial Review of the Legislative Referendum' [2019] Revista General de Derecho Constitucional 19. See also Bruna Žuber, 'Ustavnosodni nadzor zakonodajnega referenduma z vidika nekaterih temeljnih ustavnih načel' [2017] Pravnik, 623–652.

abuse of the legislative referendum (that is, attempting to carry out a legislative referendum in order to achieve goals that have no connection to the subject of the referendum) and on preventing abuse of legislative competences (for example, if the National Assembly includes in a law that is excluded from referendum decision-making issues that are not excluded from referendum decision-making with the only intent to prevent referendum decision-making on these questions).[60]

The National Assembly shall call a legislative referendum if so required by 40,000 voters. A request to call a referendum may be submitted by at least 40,000 voters, provided that within seven days of the adoption of the law the initiator of the request notifies the President of the National Assembly of his or her request.[61] The initiative must include a defined request and must be supported by the signatures of at least 2,500 voters.[62]

If an initiative is submitted in accordance with the provisions of the RPIA, the President of the National Assembly determines the period during which the signatures of 40,000 voters are to be collected in support of the request to call a referendum.[63] However, the President of the National Assembly can also reject the referendum initiative if the formal requirements determined by the RPIA are not met.[64] Consequently, the period during which voters' signatures are to be collected in support of the request to call a referendum is not determined and the law enters into force. The referendum initiator or other persons with a legal interest may initiate a review of the constitutionality of the law that has entered into force to prove that the rejection of the referendum initiative was unlawful. If the Constitutional Court finds that there were infringements in the referendum procedure and that the referendum initiative should not have been rejected, it abrogates the law.[65] It can be concluded that the formal admissibility review (compliance with the procedural requirements) is carried out by the President of the National Assembly, whereas the Constitutional

---

[60] Žuber (n 59) 19. For more on a preliminary review in this regard, see: Žuber (n 33) 71–103. See also Decision of the Constitutional Court of the Republic of Slovenia No. U-I-85/16, Up-398/16, dated 14 July 2016, Official Gazette RS No. 52/16.

[61] Art. 12.a RPIA.

[62] Art. 16 RPIA.

[63] Art. 16.a RPIA.

[64] It has to be noted that formal requirements are not equal to formal limits. Formal requirements require that the referendum initiative is lodged in time, that it refers to the correct subject, that it is clear and that it contains a question formulated in accordance with the RPIA. If the referendum question is not formulated in accordance with the RPIA, the President of the National Assembly has to either correct it with the consent of the proposer of the initiative or call on the proposer to correct it. If the proposer fails to do so, the referendum request is deemed to have been withdrawn (Art. 20 RPIA).

[65] See Žuber (n 33) 83–93.

Court is authorized to review the constitutionality and legality of the formal admissibility review.

Within the preliminary review, assessment of the admissibility of the legislative referendum (compliance with the substantive limits) is carried out. In accordance with Article 21 of the RPIA, the National Assembly has to decide on the constitutional admissibility of a legislative referendum within 14 days of the lodging of the referendum initiative. The National Assembly acts as the legislative body and not as a court in this procedure. It decides the matter on the basis of the Constitution, the RPIA and the Rules of Procedure of the National Assembly. If the National Assembly decides that the proposed referendum is not in conformity with the Constitution, it declares it inadmissible by an order, which has to state the reasons for doing so. The proposer of the referendum can challenge the order before the Constitutional Court within 15 days. The Constitutional Court has to adopt a decision on the admissibility of the referendum within 30 days.[66] If it finds that the order of the National Assembly is not in conformity with the Constitution, the referendum procedure is continued. If it confirms the order, the referendum procedure terminates and the law is sent for promulgation and publication.[67]

The Constitutional Court performs a preventive control whereby the admissibility of a referendum is resolved before it is held. This approach is in accordance with the provisions of Section III.3 of the Code of Good Practice on Referendums adopted by the Venice Commission. However, a preventive control is inappropriate in the case of urgent laws as it delays the entry into force of a law by at least a month or two. Therefore, the only exception where control over the admissibility of a legislative referendum is conducted subsequently concerns laws on urgent measures to ensure the defence of the state, security or the elimination of the consequences of natural disasters.

The procedure for legislative referendums relating to these laws is provided in Article 21.a of the RPIA, which was adopted in April 2020 in order to speed up the entry into force of laws designed to alleviate the consequences of the Covid-19 pandemic. In accordance with Article 21.a of the RPIA, at the request of the Government, the National Assembly adopts an order declaring the inadmissibility of a legislative referendum concerning laws on urgent measures to ensure the defence of the state, security or the elimination of the consequences of natural disasters irrespective of whether a referendum initi-

---

[66]   In this procedure, the rules of the Constitutional Court Act apply. In most cases, the National Assembly and the petitioner are parties to the procedure and there is no public hearing, although Art. 29 of the Constitutional Court Act contains a legal basis for conducting public hearings. The decision of the Constitutional Court is therefore in most cases adopted on the basis of the written procedure.

[67]   Art. 21 RPIA.

ative has been lodged or not. The National Assembly adopts this order seven days after the adoption of the urgent law or even earlier if the National Council decides not to require the National Assembly to decide again on such law.[68] If the National Council requires the National Assembly to decide again on such law, the National Assembly adopts an order declaring the inadmissibility of a legislative referendum as soon as the law is passed again. The order has to state the reasons for limiting referendum decision-making. After the National Assembly has adopted an order declaring the inadmissibility of a legislative referendum, the law is sent for promulgation and publication. In the event a referendum initiative is lodged, it is deemed to not have been lodged. In this case, the legal protection of voters' referendum rights is provided subsequently, after the law has entered into force. Each voter may submit a request to the Constitutional Court to initiate the procedure for a review of the constitutionality of the law by alleging a violation of Article 90(2) of the Constitution within 15 days of the entry into force of the law. The Constitutional Court has to decide thereon within 30 days. If the Constitutional Court finds that Article 90(2) of the Constitution was violated, it only abrogates the law and does not decide whether the referendum should go forward.[69]

4.1.2 Review of the process for implementing a legislative referendum

The review of the process for implementing a referendum focuses on the constitutional review of the legal act that represents the legal basis for holding the legislative referendum (the so-called ordinance on calling a referendum adopted by the National Assembly), control over the referendum campaign and protection of the right to vote in a legislative referendum.[70]

4.1.3 Subsequent review of a legislative referendum

In two instances, a specific subsequent review applies. First, there is the subsequent review over the admissibility of legislative referendums on laws on urgent measures to ensure the defence of the state, security or the elimination of the consequences of natural disasters in accordance with Article 21.1 of the RPIA (see Section 4.1.1 above). Second, it is possible to control whether, after

---

[68] In line with Art. 91 of the Constitution, the National Council may within seven days of the passing of a law and prior to its promulgation require the National Assembly to decide again on such law (suspensive veto). In deciding again, a majority of all deputies must vote for such law to be passed unless the Constitution envisages a higher majority for the passing of the law under consideration. The new decision by the National Assembly is final.

[69] As Art. 21.a of the RPIA was adopted in April 2020, there is no case law relating to this procedure yet.

[70] Žuber (n 59) 20.

the rejection of a law in a referendum, the National Assembly has adopted a new law that is contrary to the referendum decision of the voters (see Section 3.3.3 above). Furthermore, all laws passed in a legislative referendum can be subject to the procedure for a review of constitutionality.

4.2 Referendums on General Legal Acts of a Municipality

If the municipal council is of the opinion that the content of the submitted request to call a referendum is not in conformity with the Constitution or a law, it may request that the Constitutional Court review the admissibility of the referendum. The municipal council may initiate proceedings before the Constitutional Court from the day of the submission of the request until the closing date for calling a referendum. The Constitutional Court must decide on the municipal council's request within 15 days.[71] The Constitutional Court prohibits referendums on general legal acts of a municipality that are explicitly excluded from referendum decision-making in accordance with Article 46(1) of the LSGA or are not in conformity with another law or the Constitution.[72]

5. CONCLUSION

Slovenia is a relatively well-developed country with regard to direct-democratic instruments and their legal review. Slovenia is also a relatively young democracy, and it will take some time to settle the application of limits of direct democracy in practice.

The new constitutional regulation of the legislative referendum, which explicitly imposes limits on the legislative referendum, was accepted with a high degree of approval among constitutional experts. As anticipated, in the general public the imposition of limits on the legislative referendum was controversial. The criticism focused especially on the prohibition of referendums on taxes, customs and other obligatory charges and on the law adopted for the implementation of the state budget. The existing case law shows that fears that the new constitutional regulation would render any referendum decision-making practically impossible were unfounded.[73] Nevertheless, as in other cases, here too we will have to wait for the case law to provide answers to some questions that remain open.

---

[71] Art. 47.a(2) LSGA.

[72] See Igor Kaučič, 'Pravna ureditev lokalnega referenduma', in Kukovič Simona, Haček Miro, Ferfila Bogomil and Brezovnik Boštjan (eds): *Petindvajset let lokalne samouprave v Republiki Sloveniji* (University of Ljubljana, Faculty of Social Sciences 2019) 47.

[73] Ribičič and Kaučič (n 1) 916, 921.

Other instruments of direct democracy existing at the national level are rarely used in practice. Therefore, the legal limits on these instruments, as well as the procedures for reviewing compliance with these limits, do not raise too many questions in either theory or practice.

10. Croatia

Robert Podolnjak

1. INTRODUCTION

The Croatian constitution provides for various instruments of direct democracy at the national as well as the local and regional levels, which, at least at
first glance, makes Croatia one of the countries with significant opportunities
for direct decision-making by the people. However, these instruments have
become part of the Croatian constitutional order at different times, with some
of them having been designed more or less without due deliberation and with
no enthusiastic support of the representatives in Parliament. They are inconsistent in some essential aspects and, in the case of the popular initiative, fraught
with significant procedural hurdles and legal loopholes, which makes their
practical application difficult. The most severe constitutional problem related
to the functioning of direct democracy in Croatia has been the legal deficiency
of constitutional and statutory regulation of the popular initiative. The second
crucial problem has been the absence of legal limits in the Constitution as to
the issues which may be the subject of a referendum. As a consequence, only
three referendums have been held at the national level (of which just one upon
the request of the citizens) and not many more at the local and regional levels
since the establishment of the Croatian state some 30 years ago.

2. DIRECT-DEMOCRATIC INSTRUMENTS IN THE CROATIAN CONSTITUTION AND STATUTORY LAW

All democratic constitutions express, in similar formulations, the principle of
popular sovereignty. The Croatian Constitution specifies this principle in the
very first article, stating that power in the Republic of Croatia derives from the
people and belongs to the people as a community of free and equal citizens.

The people shall exercise this power through the election of representatives and direct decision-making.[1]

The original Constitution from 1990 contained only provisions related to the mandatory and the optional (facultative) referendums on the national level. The popular initiative was constitutionalized as part of a comprehensive constitutional reform in 2000 and, finally, the provision on an advisory referendum was added by an amendment of the Constitution in 2010.[2]

As to the instruments of direct democracy on the regional (counties) and local (municipalities and cities) level, the constitutional amendment in 2000 established the constitutional right of the citizens to participate directly in the administration of local affairs, through meetings, referendums and other forms of direct decision-making, in compliance with law and local ordinances.[3] The Local and Regional Self-Government Act prescribes several instruments of direct democracy: an optional local referendum, called by the representative body, the popular initiative and the recall procedure for removal of directly elected mayors/county governors.[4] However, these instruments of local direct democracy are used very rarely and their influence on the overall state of direct democracy in Croatia is negligible.[5] Therefore, this chapter shall analyse only the instruments of direct democracy on the national level.

2.1   Mandatory Referendum

The Constitution prescribes a mandatory referendum (*law-initiated referendum*) for only one instance, that is, in case of association (or disassociation) of the Republic of Croatia into alliances with other states. Article 142 of the

---

[1]   Art. 1 (2)–(3) Constitution of the Republic of Croatia (consolidated text published in the Official Gazette No. 85/2010) in Jefri Jay Ruhti (ed.), *World Constitutions Illustrated – Croatia* (William S. Hein & Co. 2010).

[2]   Art. 87 (6) Constitution. Currently an advisory referendum may be held on the reorganization of local self-government units. See Art. 57 Act on Referendum and Other Forms of Individual Participation in the Functioning of State Authority and the Local Self-Government 1996 (the Official Gazette, No 33/96, 92/01, 44/06, 58/06, 38/09, 100/16 and 73/17).

[3]   Art. 133(3) Constitution.

[4]   Local and Regional Self-Government Act, the Official Gazette, No. 33/2001, 60/2001, 129/2005, 109/2007, 36/2009, 125/2008, 36/2009, 150/2011, 144/2012, 123/2017, 98/2019.

[5]   Since 1999, only 15 local referendums were held in 555 local government units, mostly in smaller municipalities. Most of them failed because the turnout quorum of participation of the majority of the voters in a local government unit was not reached. The turnout quorum is prescribed in Art. 6 (2) Referendum Act. See: Anita Blagojević and Ana Sesvečan, 'Ustavnopravni okvir referendum u Republici Hrvatskoj: Trenutno stanje i budući izazovi' (2019) 56 Zbornik Pravnog fakulteta u Splitu 835, 866–67.

Constitution stipulates that any association of the Republic of Croatia shall first be decided upon by the Parliament by a two-thirds majority of all deputies. Then the final decision concerning the association of the Republic of Croatia shall be made in a referendum by a majority vote of all voters voting in the referendum.[6]

The approval quorum, according to which the decision on the referendum shall be made by a majority vote of the total number of electors in Croatia, for the mandatory referendum was eliminated by the 2010 constitutional amendment. It was the prevalent opinion of constitutional scholars and the representatives in the Parliament that the approval quorum for the referendum on accession to the European Union (EU) should be removed 'since it contained a practically impossible requirement in light of the disorder of the list of voters due to a large number of persons with double citizenship'.[7] In the Croatian EU membership referendum, held on 22 January 2012, 1,299,008 voters (66.67 per cent) voted for the accession of Croatia to the EU, with a turnout of only 43.51 per cent.[8]

2.2   Optional Referendum

The optional referendum is regulated in Article 87 of the Constitution. The Parliament may call a referendum on a proposal to amend the Constitution, a bill or any other issue within its competence (*legislative-initiated referendum*). The President of the Republic (President) may, at the proposal of the Government and with the countersignature of the Prime Minister, call a referendum on a proposal for the amendment of the Constitution or any other issue which the President considers to be important for the independence, unity and existence of the Republic of Croatia (*executive-initiated referendum*).[9]

The pre-2010 Constitution prescribed that decisions shall be made by the majority of voters who voted in a referendum, provided that the majority of the total number of voters have taken part in the referendum.[10] The 2010 constitutional amendment has abolished the turnout quorum and now a simple majority

---

[6]   Art. 142(3)–(4) Constitution.

[7]   Branko Smerdel, 'Republic of Croatia' in Leonard Besselink and others (eds), *Constitutional Law of the EU Member States* (Kluwer 2014) 199–200.

[8]   Državno izborno povjerenstvo, Izvješće o državnom referendum o pristupanju Republike Hrvatske Europskoj Uniji (The State Electoral Commission, Report on the state referendum on the accession of the Republic of Croatia to the European Union) https://www.izbori.hr/arhiva-izbora/data/referendum/2012/izabrani/i_81_000_0000 .pdf, accessed 10 December 2019.

[9]   Art. 87(1)–(2) Constitution.

[10]   Art. 87(3) Constitution of 1990.

of voters is sufficient for accepting proposals in a national referendum. The referendum decision is binding. The Referendum Act[11] stipulates further that a state authority does not have the right to pass a legal act or decision which contradicts the referendum decision within one year after the referendum. Another referendum cannot be called about the same issue or issues before a deadline of six months expires from the day when the referendum was held.[12]

The Parliament has never called an optional referendum on its initiative. The President called the first national referendum on an issue vital for the independence, unity and existence of the Republic of Croatia – it was the referendum on Croatian independence held in May 1991.

2.3   Popular Initiative

The popular initiative (*proactive citizen-initiated referendum*) became part of the Constitution in 2000. The then Article 86 (now Article 87) was amended, prescribing that the Parliament shall call a referendum on any issue that may be put to a referendum by the Parliament or the President when so demanded by 10 per cent of all voters of the Republic of Croatia. With this constitutional provision, Croatian citizens have acquired the full-scale popular initiative to request a constitutional or legislative referendum or a referendum on some other issue important for the independence, integrity and existence of the Republic of Croatia. A citizen-initiated referendum can also be called with the goal to abrogate an existing law or some part of a law, or to replace existing law with a new one, or to enact a completely new law. Formally speaking, no issues are excluded from the citizen-initiated referendum.

In the last 20 years, since the popular initiative has been a part of the Constitution, only one citizen-initiated referendum has been held. It was the most successful popular initiative to date in Croatia by the 'In the Name of the Family' association, calling for a referendum on the question: 'Do you agree that a provision be added to the Constitution of the Republic of Croatia whereby marriage constitutes a living union between a woman and a man?' (the so-called 'marriage referendum'). In May 2013, the initiative collected almost 750,000 signatures,[13] thereby fulfilling the necessary condition to call the first citizen-initiated constitutional referendum in Croatia.

---

[11]   The Act on Referendum and Other Forms of Individual Participation in the Functioning of State Authority and Local Self-Government, the Official Gazette, No 33/96, 92/01, 44/06, 58/06, 38/09, 100/16 and 73/17, hereinafter: Referendum Act.

[12]   Art. 8(2) Referendum Act.

[13]   Officially, only 683,948 signatures were valid, but that was also more than was needed to call a referendum.

At the time, there were different constitutional interpretations concerning the possible consequences of a decision taken in a citizen-initiated constitutional referendum.[14] The most important constitutional questions were whether the Parliament is obliged to call a referendum in all cases when a popular initiative meets the constitutional requirements and whether it can in any way obstruct the will of the people expressed in a referendum.

The opinion of some leading MPs from the governing coalition was that the Parliament could not be forced to call a referendum whose goal is to diminish the rights of same-sex partners and that the constitution-making power belongs, under the Constitution, solely to the Parliament.[15]

In a joint statement, all professors of constitutional law from the law faculties in the country stated the fundamental principles of the Constitution regarding the popular initiative and the consequences of the referendum decision:

> The Croatian Parliament is obliged to hold a constitutional referendum if one is requested by 10 per cent of the total number of voters /.../ Rejection by the Croatian Parliament to call a referendum when an initiative has fulfilled all the necessary formal and legal requirements would be a denial of the very essence of a citizen-initiated referendum. It could have incalculable consequences for the constitutional stability of the country. Any decision made by the citizens in a constitutional referendum would be, by its very nature, constitutional in character, and would be binding on all state bodies. It would represent a change in the Constitution and come into force upon confirmation that the referendum was held according to the Constitution.[16]

Nevertheless, the Committee on the Constitution, Standing Orders and Political System of the Parliament proposed a decision to call a national referendum only 'to *begin* the procedure to amend the Constitution'. Second, the Committee suggested that in the referendum 'a decision will be made on

---

[14]   The following passages are adapted from Robert Podolnjak, 'Constitutional Reforms of Citizen-Initiated Referendum: Causes of Different Outcomes in Slovenia and Croatia' (2015) 26 Revus – Journal for Constitutional Theory and Philosophy of Law 129, 138–39.

[15]   See the opinion of Pedja Grbin, the chairperson of the Committee on the Constitution, Standing Orders and Political System in 'Građani na referendumu ne mogu izmijeniti Ustav!' (Citizens cannot change the Constitution in a referendum!), https://www.tportal.hr/vijesti/clanak/gradani-na-referendumu-ne-mogu-izmijeniti-ustav-20131024, accessed 22 May 2020.

[16]   The statement (in Croatian) is published in Robert Podolnjak and Branko Smerdel (eds), *Referendum narodne inicijative u Hrvatskoj i Sloveniji: Ustavnopravno uređenje, iskustva i perspektive* (*Referendum of Popular Initiative in Croatia and Slovenia: Constitutional Regulation, Experience, and Prospects*) (Croatian Association for Constitutional Law 2014) 233–235.

beginning the procedure to amend the Constitution'.[17] In the Committee's opinion, the referendum decision would only be the first step in the process of changing the Constitution, which could only be made, in the Committee's view, by a two-thirds majority of MPs and not directly by the people in the referendum.

Before this proposed decision was debated by the Parliament, the Constitutional Court issued, for the first time, an 'unusual and unprecedented act'[18] called 'Warning' to the Parliament, stating that parts of the proposed decision were contrary to Croatian constitutional law.[19] The Court grasped the real intention of the proposed decision of the Constitution Committee – that the referendum decision, based on the popular initiative, would be just a first phase in the process of amending the Constitution and not a decision with the effect of a regular constitutional amendment. That would be, in the Court's opinion, constitutionally unacceptable. The Constitutional Court emphasized:

> (T)he voters in a national constitutional referendum called based on a people's constitutional initiative within the meaning of Article 87 of the Constitution ... (in relation to Article 1 of the Constitution), always decide on the merits of the case, that is, on the very referendum question, which means: the people directly decide to change the Constitution, which is proposed – in the form of a referendum question – by at least 10 per cent of the total number of voters, by voting for or against the proposal ... Accordingly, a decision where the Constitutional Court confirms that a specific popular referendum to amend the Constitution – where the people ... had voted FOR a proposed referendum question – was conducted in conformity with the Constitution also means that the Constitution is amended on the day the referendum is held with immediate legal effect.[20]

After the Court's Warning, the Parliament changed the disputable parts of the decision to call the referendum according to the Court's opinion. The Court's Warning to the Parliament to respect the Constitution was of utmost impor-

---

[17]   Committee on the Constitution, Standing Orders and Political System, Draft of the Decision on the calling of the State Referendum, 24 October 2013 https://www.sabor.hr/hr/radna-tijela/odbori-i-povjerenstva/prijedlog-odluke-odbora-za-ustav-poslovnik-i-politicki-sustav-8, accessed 22 June 2020.

[18]   Sanja Barić, *The Transformative Role of the Constitutional Court of the Republic of Croatia: From ex-Yu to the EU* (Analitika, Center for Social Research 2016) 24.

[19]   See the 'Warning concerning the Proposal of a Decision by the Committee on the Constitution, Standing Orders and Political System of the Croatian Parliament to call a national referendum of 24 October 2013', Constitutional Court, No. U-VIIR-5292/2013, 3–4 https://sljeme.usud.hr/usud/prakswen.nsf/fOdluka.xsp?action=openDocument&documentId=56FBA104F615D85AC1257E5F003E9519, accessed 15 December 2019. See also *Bulletin on Constitutional Case-Law* (The European Commission for Democracy through Law 2014) 477–78.

[20]   Ibid., 5.

tance not only by stressing its obligation to call a citizen-initiated referendum but also in recognizing the results of the referendum vote. It has significance also for future citizen-initiated referendums in Croatia.

The first referendum demanded by a popular initiative was held on 1 December 2013. With a relatively modest turnout of 37.9 per cent, almost two-thirds of voters (946,433, or 65.87 per cent) voted for amending the Constitution with the inclusion of the definition of marriage as a union of man and woman.[21]

Besides the 'marriage referendum', there have been several other important popular initiatives that had either collected the necessary number of signatures for triggering the referendum or claimed that they had done so but this was not confirmed by the authorities. For instance, two popular initiatives, 'The People Decide' and 'The Truth about the Istanbul Convention', claimed that they had collected the necessary number of signatures in May 2018, but this was not confirmed after the signatures' verification made by the Ministry of Administration.

In all these cases, the Constitutional Court had the final word. In some cases, the Court decided that the initiatives had not collected enough signatures (accepting the respective official reports that the formal condition of the signatures of 10 per cent of voters in Croatia had not been fulfilled).[22] In other instances, it decided that the referendum question was not in accordance with the Constitution.[23] In one particular case, the referendum was not called because the Constitutional Court ruled that it is not necessary to conduct a formal referendum because the Government had accepted the popular initiative demands by withdrawing a bill from the parliamentary procedure. The Court emphasized that 'this conduct of the Croatian Government proves that in a democratic society, direct voter participation in political decision-making can be realized just by meeting the requirements for holding a referendum and that the administration of a referendum is not even necessary.'[24]

---

[21] State Electoral Commission of the Republic of Croatia, Report on the National Referendum held on 1 December 2013, http://www.izbori.hr/2013Referendum/rezult/rezultati.html, accessed 20 December 2019.

[22] See Constitutional Court's rulings U-VIIR-3620/2018, U-VIIR-2626/2019, and U-VIIR-114/2019/U-VIIR-1623/2019 (dismissing the complaints of two popular initiatives on procedural grounds).

[23] On the Court's decisions on the constitutionality of the referendum questions of popular initiatives see Djordje Gardasevic, 'Constitutional Interpretations of Direct Democracy in Croatia' (2015) 17 Iustinianus Primus Law Review, 1 and Sanja Barić (n 18) 22–26.

[24] The decision No U-VIIR-4696/2010 https://sljeme.usud.hr/usud/prakswen .nsf/fOdluka.xsp?action=openDocument&documentId=6937DFB8D37F 2A2FC1257E5F003E9712, accessed 15 December 2019 (para. 23).

The last (successful) popular initiative from 2019 is the best example of the shortcomings in the constitutional and statutory regulation of the institution. Several Croatian trade union confederations initiated the collection of signatures for the popular initiative '67 is too much', directed against the government pension reform of 2018. The key demands of the trade unions were the reduction of the retirement age from 67 to 65 years and the lowering of the penalization of early retirement from 0.3 to 0.2 per cent per month. The referendum question was formulated as a specifically worded draft law (the Draft Act Amending the Pension Insurance Act). In May 2019, the popular initiative collected almost 750,000 signatures (approximately 20 per cent of all registered voters in Croatia). The Parliament did not ask the Constitutional Court to decide whether the referendum question is in accordance with the Constitution, but neither did it call the referendum, as it should have done. Instead, on the Government's proposal, the Parliament enacted the Act Amending the Pension Insurance Act, with the same text that was contained in the referendum question.[25] In that way, the goal of the popular initiative was accomplished without the formal referendum decision-making process. However, such a procedure is prescribed neither in the Constitution nor in any other legal act.[26] It was based on an analogy with the Constitutional Court's decision of 2010 holding that there is no reason to call a referendum if the goal of the initiative can be achieved without it. Responding to the request of the parliamentary Committee on the Constitution, the Standing Orders, and the Political System, the Constitutional Court answered in May 2020 two questions regarding the initiative '67 is too much'. The first question related to the further course of the referendum procedure after the Parliament enacted the bill proposed by the popular initiative. The Court stated that by the enactment of the new law, which is identical in its content to the bill proposed in the referendum question, the popular initiative 'achieved the goal for which the voters gave their signatures for calling the referendum, so in such a situation the implementation of the referendum lacks legal meaning and objective and reasonable justification.'[27] The second question related to the legal interpretation of the one-year limit for not changing the decisions enacted at the referendum. The Court repeated its standpoint from 2010 that in this concrete case no bill could be submitted to the parliamentary procedure which would change any

---

[25]   Pension Insurance Act amended https://www.sabor.hr/en/press/news/pension -insurance-act-amended, accessed 15 December 2019.

[26]   Such a procedure was, for example, specified in the Weimar Constitution (Article 73(3)–(4)), but was never implemented.

[27]   U-VIIR-343/2020, 5.

part of the bill contained in the referendum question of the popular initiative '67 is too much' during the one-year period.[28]

3.   LEGAL LIMITS

The Constitution does not specify any legal limits for optional referendums or popular initiatives, except that a referendum question must be within the competences of the Parliament or the President, respectively. However, the Constitution does not clarify whether 'any issue within the competence of the Parliament' could indeed be a matter for a referendum.[29] For example, does that mean that enacting the state budget could be put to a referendum by a popular initiative?

The only substantive legal limit is that a referendum question must be in accordance with the Constitution. This limit applies only to popular initiatives; it is prescribed by the Constitutional Act on the Constitutional Court (Constitutional Court Act),[30] which has the same legal force as the Constitution.[31] Because of the lack of proper regulation of the popular initiative, it has been up to the Constitutional Court to develop its constitutional interpretations regarding the role and legal limits of referendums initiated by the citizens.[32]

---

[28]   Ibid, 6.

[29]   Formally speaking, yes; however, leading constitutional lawyers argue that 'you cannot decide on a referendum, for example, on the responsibility of the President of the Republic for violating the Constitution (Article 105), because it is a quasi-judicial procedure that requires adequate guarantees (it is a matter of establishing the material truth). Nor could a referendum be called on the issues that belong to the foundations of the legal order, such as the affiliation of the Republic of Croatia to the international community (historical foundations of the Constitution), national equality or gender equality (Article 3). A referendum cannot be initiated on the abolition of political pluralism and multi-party system, nor, for example, on the abolition of taxes ... Equally, on a referendum cannot be decided on the political responsibility of the government or its individual members, nor collect signatures for such a referendum.' See Branko Smerdel, *Ustavno uređenje europske Hrvatske* (The Constitutional Order of the European Croatia) (Narodne novine 2013) p. 391.

[30]   The Constitutional Act on the Constitutional Court of the Republic of Croatia (consolidated text) https://www.usud.hr/sites/default/files/dokumenti/The_Constitutional _Act_on_the_Constitutional_Court_of_the_Republic_of_Croatia_consolidated_text _Official_Gazette_No_49-02.pdf, accessed 15 December 2019.

[31]   Article 95 Constitutional Court Act.

[32]   Professor Jasna Omejec, the former President of the Croatian Constitutional Court, confirmed this: 'So far, the legislator has not developed the rules of procedure and the method of implementation of popular constitution-making initiatives within the /.../ constitutional norms. Accordingly, the Croatian Constitutional Court had to, in its practice, build the rules which must be followed when it comes to the implementation

Formally, the Constitutional Court's legal basis for dealing with popular initiatives at the national level is contained in Article 95 of the Constitutional Court Act. This provision was inserted in the Constitutional Court Act in 2002, two years after the popular initiative had been constitutionalized. It states that:

> upon the request of the Croatian Parliament, the Constitutional Court shall, in the case when 10 per cent of the total number of voters in the Republic of Croatia request calling a referendum, establish whether the question of the referendum is in accordance with the Constitution and whether the requirements in Article 87, paragraphs 1–3, of the Constitution of the Republic of Croatia for calling a referendum, have been met.[33]

The Court must reach its decision within a term of 30 days from the day the Parliament has requested the Court's opinion.[34]

3.1   Substantive Limit: Conformity with the Constitution

Two weeks before the 'marriage referendum' was held, the Constitutional Court had issued another important opinion called the 'Communication on the citizens' constitutional referendum on the definition of marriage'.[35] This stated its views on the constitutional limits of the referendum by citizen initiative and the Constitutional Court's general supervisory authority over the conformity of a referendum initiated by citizens with the Constitution.

In the Communication, the Constitutional Court formulated the most important substantive limit regarding referendum questions submitted to voters by a popular initiative. The referendum question should not threaten to destroy the structural characteristics of the Croatian constitutional state, that is, its constitutional identity, including the highest values of the constitutional order of the Republic of Croatia (Articles 1 and 3 of the Constitution). Article 1 establishes the Republic of Croatia as a unitary and indivisible democratic and social state. It also proclaims the principle of popular sovereignty. Article 3 lists the highest values of the Croatian constitutional order: freedom, equal rights, national

---

of popular constitution-making initiatives.' See Jasna Omejec, 'Narodna ustavotvorna inicijativa i razgraničenje nadležnosti između Hrvatskog sabora i Ustavnog suda' (The Popular Constitutional Initiative and the Delimitation of Competences between the Croatian Parliament and the Constitutional Court) (2014) Informator No. 6258, 1–3.

[33]   Art. 95(1) Constitutional Court Act.
[34]   Art. 95(2) Constitutional Court Act.
[35]   The Communication on the Citizens' Constitutional Referendum on the Definition of Marriage, SuS-1/2013, 14 November 2013, https://sljeme.usud.hr/usud/prakswen.nsf/fOdluka.xsp?action=openDocument&documentId=56C91B7316EAF361C1257E5F003D7476, accessed 17 December 2019.

equality and equality of genders, pacifism, social justice, respect for human rights, inviolability of ownership, conservation of nature and the environment, the rule of law and a democratic multi-party system. These highest values serve as the basis for the interpretation of the Constitution.

The doctrine of the unconstitutional constitutional amendment in Croatia was a *novum*, at least in the context of a popular initiative for amending the Constitution and as a case of preventive constitutional review. The long-standing doctrine of the Court was expressed in its ruling in 2001 that it does 'not have the jurisdiction to review the constitutional provisions on substantive grounds'. Only the 'procedure of the adoption and changes to the Constitution may be subject to constitutional review in terms of whether the Constitution is adopted or amended in accordance with the provisions of the Constitution'.[36] In a recent report, the Constitutional Court stated that the 'Constitution does not provide for unamendable (eternal) provisions. Nevertheless, the Constitutional Court, indirectly, through its powers to monitor the constitutionality of referendum questions, has succeeded in arriving at constitutional interpretation, opening the door to the thesis that in the Croatian Constitution, there are values that must be considered as an eternal Croatian clause.'[37]

---

[36] Case U-I-1631/2000, See also the Constitutional Court of Croatia, National Report – Answers to the Questionnaire for the XVIIth Congress of the Conference of European Constitutional Courts (Batumi, 29 June to 1 July 2017) 29–30, https://www.usud.hr/sites/default/files/dokumenti/Questionnaire_and_the_topic_of_the_XVIIth_Conference_of_European_Constitutional_Courts_Batumi_Georgia_28_June_-_1_July_2017.pdf, accessed 10 December 2019.

The former President of the Constitutional Court wrote in a scholarly article in 2010 that the Croatian Constitution does not foresee the power of the Court to review constitutional norms for their constitutionality. The Croatian Constitution does not contain an explicit eternal clause (like the German *Grundgesetz* does), nor is this power 'inherent to the Croatian constitutional law tradition'. See Jasna Omejec, 'Kontrola ustavnosti i ustavnih normi (ustavnih amandmana i ustavnih zakona)' (Control of Constitutionality of Constitutional Norms (Constitutional Amendments and Constitutional Laws)) (2010) 1 Yearbook of Croatian Academy of Legal Sciences, 1, 21–22, 26.

[37] The Court also admitted that 'there is a tendency of enhancing the authority of the Constitutional Court in terms of its jurisdiction to review amendments to the Constitution.' It also recognized that 'academic scholars openly advocate the expansion of the Constitutional Court's jurisdiction and its authority to review substantive amendments as well'. See 'Role of Constitutional Courts in upholding and applying constitutional principles, Report of the Constitutional Court of Croatia – Summary', XVIIth Congress of the Conference of European Constitutional Courts (Batumi, 29 June to 1 July 2017) 4–5 available at https://www.confeuconstco.org/reports/rep-xvii/croatia_S_EN.pdf), accessed 15 December 2019. See also Biljana Kostadinov, 'Constitutional Identity' (2011) 4 Iustinianus Primus Law Review, 1, 17–20; Anita Blagojević, 'Procedures Regarding National Identity Clause in the National Constitutional Court's

However, the Court did not find that inserting a definition of marriage as a heterosexual union in the Constitution would be in conflict with the highest values of the Croatian constitutional order. In its Communication, the Court stated that the content of the referendum question is already a positive legal provision contained in the Family Act.[38] The Court acknowledged that it had received a proposal to review the constitutionality of the entire Family Act and also regarding the definition of marriage, but had not acted upon it. It stated that in the specific procedure of assessing the constitutionality of the referendum question it cannot conduct the procedure of abstract review of the conformity of a legal provision in an existing act with the Constitution. Therefore, the Court concluded that its:

> (d)ecision in finding a referendum question not to be in conformity with the Constitution would not only lead to a prohibition to call the referendum, but it would spill over into the existing legislative order in the legal area to which that question related.
> In view of Article 5 of the Family Act, this is precisely the case with the referendum question on the definition of marriage: 'Do you agree that a provision be added to the Constitution of the Republic of Croatia whereby marriage constitutes a living union between a woman and a man?' With the possible establishment of the unconstitutionality of the content of this referendum question, the Constitutional Court would, in fact, be finding Article 5 of the Family Act to be unconstitutional.[39]

In the Court's reasoning that would be contrary to the principle of the rule of law, one of the highest values of the constitutional order of the Republic of Croatia.

On the other hand, after an analysis of the existing regulation of marriage and same-sex civil unions 'within the framework of today's European legal standards' in the legislation of the Council of Europe member states and the Croatian legislation,[40] the Court stated that Croatia legally recognizes marriage, common-law marriage and same-sex unions and thus 'Croatian law is today aligned with the European legal standards regarding the institutions of marriage and family life'.[41] The Court stressed that Article 35 of the Constitution

---

and CJEU's Case-Law', in Dunja Duić and Tunjica Petrašević (eds), *Procedural Aspects of EU Law* (Faculty of Law, Josip Juraj Strossmayer University of Osijek 2017) 210–237.

[38]   Art. 5 Family Act: 'Marriage is a legally governed life union between a woman and a man.'

[39]   The Communication on the Citizens' Constitutional Referendum on the Definition of Marriage 8–9.

[40]   Act on Same-sex Civil Unions and the Anti-discrimination Act.

[41]   The Communication on the Citizens' Constitutional Referendum on the Definition of Marriage, 12.

protects the rights of all persons, regardless of gender and sex, to respect for and legal protection of personal and family life and human dignity. Therefore, according to the Court, the 'marriage referendum' was not a referendum on the right to respect for family life; this right was guaranteed by the Constitution for all persons, regardless of gender and sex, and was under the direct protection of the Constitutional Court and the ECtHR.[42]

There is one more important statement in the Court's Communication. That is the warning of the Court that it 'could not accept as a rule the new aspect that in a citizen's constitutional referendum already existing legislation would be transformed into constitutional law'. A possibility of 'systematic "constitutionalization" of legislation' is unacceptable for the Court and could be used as a specific argument in assessing the constitutionality of future popular initiatives.[43]

Besides the Court's statements regarding the 'marriage referendum', there are three crucial Court decisions relevant for the formulation of constitutional limits of referendum questions submitted by popular initiatives. In the respective cases, popular initiatives had collected enough signatures for calling a legislative referendum and the Parliament asked the Court to determine the constitutionality of the questions. In all three cases, the Court decided that the referendum questions were not in conformity with the Constitution.

In December 2013, several war veterans' associations (officially, the Committee for the Defence of Croatian Vukovar) succeeded in collecting the necessary number of signatures for a referendum to amend the Constitutional Act on the Rights of National Minorities. More specifically, they intended to change minority language rights in the sense that a minority language can be granted only in local self-government units where at least half of the population is from an ethnic minority. Under the current legislation in Croatia, national minorities must comprise at least one-third of the population to claim these rights. The problem with the minority language rights escalated with the instalment of bilingual public signs in Vukovar, where, according to the last census, the Serbian minority constitutes more than one-third (but less than half) of the total population. At the request of the Parliament, the Constitutional Court decided that the referendum question was constitutionally inadmissible.[44] The Court emphasized that such a 'general intervention of national dimensions in the threshold already achieved for the official use of languages and scripts, which form the very essence of the identity of the national minorities in the

---

[42]   Ibid, 8.

[43]   Ibid, 8–9.

[44]   Decision No. U-VIIR-4640/2014 of 12 August 2014. https://sljeme.usud.hr/usud/prakswen.nsf/fOdluka.xsp?action=openDocument&documentId=D79E16416D87711AC1257E5F003E99B2, accessed 15 December 2019.

Republic of Croatia', has no clear and rational basis. In the Court's opinion, 'there are no relevant or sufficient reasons deriving from recognized and precisely defined urgent social needs' for a general increase in the threshold.[45]

Two further popular initiatives by several trade unions were successful in collecting the requisite number of signatures in 2014, but the Constitutional Court decided that their referendum questions, formulated as specifically worded draft laws, were also constitutionally inadmissible.[46] The first initiative demanded a referendum on preventing the outsourcing of non-core services in the public sector, the second a referendum against the monetization of the Croatian motorways. Although, due to the Constitutional Court's decisions, the requested referendums were not held, the Government nevertheless abandoned its plans for the outsourcing of services in the public sector and the monetization of the motorways.[47]

In the outsourcing decision, the Court established an additional legal limit for referendum questions submitted by popular initiatives. The Court stated that the fundamental goal of the proposed bill was to prescribe two general prohibitions. One is the prohibition of outsourcing auxiliary and non-core activities in the public sector and the second is the prohibition of performing these activities in any other way except by workers who are employed in the public sector. In the Court's opinion, 'blanket prohibitions' foreseen by the draft act 'a priori, automatically, unselectively and permanently prevent changes in organizing optimum labour-law models for auxiliary and non-core activities in the public sector'. Additionally, these prohibitions would also directly affect the functionality of the state and the budget framework in processes of economic, social, political and administrative reforms. The Court concluded that 'blanket legal prohibitions whose aim is to prevent changes in such a legal model permanently … do not have a legitimate goal, and are contrary to the purpose and constitutional concept of state and public services in a democratic

---

[45]   Ibid, 12. See also Endre Dudas, 'Croatian Constitutional Court: The Referendum on the Cyrillic Script' (2015) 9 Vienna Journal on International Constitutional Law / ICL Journal, 126–33.

[46]   See the Constitutional Court's Decisions No. U-VIIR-1159/2015 of 8 April 2015   https://sljeme.usud.hr/usud/prakswen.nsf/fOdluka.xsp?action=openDocument &documentId=9393347C501C6FA7C125800B002B0806, accessed 16 December 2019, and No. U-VIIR-1158/2015 of 21 April 2015 https://sljeme.usud.hr/usud/ prakswen.nsf/fOdluka.xsp?action=openDocument&documentId=1B89597C08C3 BA87C125800B002B12EA, accessed 16 December 2019.

[47]   See, e.g., 'Deputy PM regrets halting of reform by the anti-outsourcing initiative', https://vlada.gov.hr/news/deputy-pm-regrets-halting-of-reform-by-anti-outsourcing -initiative/16719, accessed 20 December 2019, and 'Croatia backs up from monetization of highways' http://www.globalpost.com/dispatch/news/xinhua-news-agency/ 150313/croatia-backs-monetization-highways, accessed 20 December 2019.

society.' The Court emphasized that the drafters of the Constitution did not explicitly state questions that are in the exclusive jurisdiction of representative bodies and cannot be the subject of a referendum, so they must be derived from the Constitution as a whole. Based on that, the Court stated that the blanket prohibitions foreseen by the proposed draft law would affect the exclusive authorities of the Government and the Parliament concerning issues relevant to the state budget. Therefore, they were unconstitutional.[48]

In its decision concerning the referendum on the motorways, the Court similarly held that a blanket legislative measure that includes an absolute prohibition to award concessions on all existing public roads in Croatia impinges upon the very essence of the economic system stipulated in Article 49.1 of the Constitution (free enterprise and free markets as the foundation of the economic system).[49]

3.2 Formal Limits

3.2.1 Statement of reasons

In its decision on the official use of languages and scripts of national minorities, the Constitutional Court noticed that 'current legislation does not contain rules on the obligation to explain the request to call a referendum'.[50] Considering that such an explanation of the request would be relevant for the Parliament and eventually for the Court, especially in terms of deliberating on the issue of the constitutionality of a referendum question, the Court declared:

> Each future request to call a referendum submitted to the Croatian Parliament pursuant to Article 87.3 of the Constitution must contain a detailed presentation of the facts and circumstances which were the reason for setting the referendum question in the proposed content, and a sufficient and relevant statement of reasons for the request to call a referendum.
>
> Any new submissions which organizing committees for voting on the need to request the calling of a referendum may prepare and send to the Constitutional Court after the Croatian Parliament has requested the Court to proceed pursuant to Article 95 of the Constitutional Act cannot be deemed to be a part of their request since they have not been previously sent to the Croatian Parliament. The Constitutional Court will not consider such submissions.[51]

---

[48] Constitutional Court's Decision No. U-VIIR-1159/2015 of 8 April 2015.
[49] Constitutional Court's Decision No. U-VIIR-1158/2015 of 21 April 2015.
[50] Decision No. U-VIIR-4640/2014 of 12 August 2014.
[51] Decision No. U-VIIR-4640/2014 of 12 August 2014, 13–14. See also Biljana Kostadinov, 'Direct Participation of the People in Public Power – Advantages and Disadvantages of a Referendum, Croatian and European Perspective' in Reiner Arnold and JI Martinez-Estay (eds), *Rule of Law, Human Rights and Judicial Control*

A detailed explanation of reasons for a referendum must be prepared and published by the organizing committee not later than at the time of submitting the collected signatures to the Parliament.

3.2.2   Unity of form, unity of content and unity of hierarchical level

Neither the Croatian Constitution nor the relevant legislative acts prescribe detailed requirements of procedural validity for texts submitted to a referendum, such as elaborated in the Code of Good Practice on Referendums of the Venice Commission (Code of Good Practice).[52] The Referendum Act prescribes only that the decision of the organizing committee of a popular initiative to call a referendum must contain 'a clear question on which it wants the calling of a referendum'.[53] This clarity requirement does not have an extensive practice, because in all cases where the Court had to decide on the constitutionality of a referendum question, this question was related to a specific law (a legislative referendum). Therefore, in each case, there was a simple and clear referendum question: 'Are you in favour of passing the following law in a referendum?'

Starting with the popular initiatives regarding the outsourcing of non-core services in the public sector and the monetization of the Croatian motorways, the Constitutional Court has tested the procedural validity of a proposed text of the referendum questions, with specific reference to the Code of Good Practice.[54] In several cases, it concluded that the respective proposals did have the required form and included all the necessary elements of a legal text – that they satisfy the unity of form, content and hierarchical levels.[55]

---

of Powers: Some Reflections from National and International Law (Springer 2017) 119–120.

[52] See the 'Code of Good Practice on Referendums' (CDL-AD(2007)008rev-cor, point III. 2), 12–13. https://www.venice.coe.int/webforms/documents/default.aspx?pdffile=CDL-AD(2007)008rev-cor-e, accessed 15 December 2019.

[53] Art. 8b Referendum Act.

[54] U-VIIR-1159/2015 of 8 April 2015 and U-VIIR-1158/2015 of 21 April 2015.

[55] Decision No. U-VIIR-1159/2015 of 8 April 2015, 11–12, and Decision No. U-VIIR-1158/2015 of 21 April 2015, 20–21.

4.   THE INSTITUTIONAL AND PROCEDURAL FRAMEWORK

4.1   Popular Initiative

Procedural issues relevant for holding a referendum on the initiative of voters are regulated in the Referendum Act.[56] First of all, the voters have to set up an organizing committee. The committee makes a decision which must contain a clear referendum question and the deadline for collecting voters' signatures, which must not exceed 15 days. This decision has to be published in daily newspapers and other public media.[57]

In 2018 a popular initiative was denied setting up stands to collect signatures in a major city. The organizing committee filed a complaint to the State Electoral Commission (SEC). The SEC held that the Commission controls the legality of referendums *after* the decision of the competent body on calling a referendum had been made and that the authority of the SEC does not extend to pre-referendum activities. The organizing committee of the popular initiative appealed to the Constitutional Court because under Article 49 of the Referendum Act, 'the constitutionality and legality of the state and local referendums are monitored by the State Referendum Commission and the Constitutional Court of the Republic of Croatia.'

However, the Court rejected the appeal, claiming that its competences, like the SEC's, do not extend to the pre-referendum phase. The Court declared that it does not exclude, exceptionally, its intervention also in the pre-referendum period, but only in a situation of a drastic breach of a democratic procedure that would derogate or seriously violate the right of citizens to request a referendum. In the concrete case, the Court did not find the circumstances to be of such character. In a vigorous dissent, one justice claimed that the Court should intervene and force the mayor to respect the legal order because a 'basic common sense leads to the conclusion that preventing the collection of signatures for a referendum initiative undermines the very essence of the right to a referendum'.[58]

The law does not say anything about verifying the voters' signatures. As a rule, the Parliament requires the Government to check the number and credibility of signatures. In recent cases, the Constitutional Court has given up its competence to determine whether the formal prerequisites for calling a ref-

---

[56]   The Local and Regional Self-Government Act also regulates the popular initiative on the local and regional levels.
[57]   Art. 8a and 8b Referendum Act.
[58]   See Decision of the Court U-VIIR/1960/2018 of 5 June 2018.

erendum on popular initiative, namely whether there are enough valid signatures, have been fulfilled.[59] In previous cases, the Court had always determined whether the formal conditions for calling a referendum had been met, regardless of Parliament's earlier statements that there were enough valid signatures. Consequently, the Court left it to the Government and the Parliament to freely choose a procedure of checking voters' signatures of future popular initiatives, apply their standards of (non)transparency of the procedure and reach a final decision on the fulfilment of formal conditions for calling a referendum.

If enough signatures have been collected, the organizing committee shall deliver the signatures to the Parliament and ask for the calling of the referendum.[60] There is no deadline in the law for delivering the collected signatures to the Parliament and also no deadline for the Parliament to call the referendum.

Based on Article 95 of the Constitutional Court Act, Parliament can make a request to the Constitutional Court regarding the fulfilment of the conditions for calling a referendum on the popular initiative: whether the question is in accordance with the Constitution and whether the formal conditions have been met. However, the Court has established that, exceptionally, it can intervene and decide on the constitutionality of the referendum question even if not asked by the Parliament. In its 'Communication on the citizens' constitutional referendum on the definition of marriage', the Court admitted that, because of Article 95, it can deal with the constitutionality of the referendum question and whether the requirements have been met to call a national referendum only at the request of the Croatian Parliament and that 'any other conduct by the Constitutional Court would border on inadmissible voluntarism'. But then the Court proclaimed:

> [The Constitutional Court] … has the general constitutional task to guarantee the respect of the Constitution and to oversee the conformity of a national referendum with the Constitution, right up to the formal conclusion of the referendum procedure.
>
> Accordingly, after the Croatian Parliament had rendered a decision to call a national referendum based on a citizens' constitutional initiative, and it had not before that acted on Article 95.1 of the Constitutional Act, the Constitutional Court's general supervisory authority over the conformity with the Constitution of a referendum called in this way does not cease.
>
> However, out of respect for the constitutional role of the Croatian Parliament as the highest legislative and representative body in the state, the Constitutional Court believes that it is only permissible to make use of its general supervisory authorities in that situation as an exception when it establishes the formal and/or substantive unconstitutionality of a referendum question, or a procedural error of such severity

---

[59]   The relevant Court's decisions regarding these two popular initiatives are U-VIIR/3592/2018 of 18 December 2018, U-VIIR/3260/2018 of 18 December 2018 and U-VIIR/2626/2019 of 4 September 2019.

[60]   Art. 8g Referendum Act.

that it threatens to destroy the structural characteristics of the Croatian constitutional state, that is, its constitutional identity, including the highest values of the constitutional order of the Republic of Croatia (Articles 1 and 3 of the Constitution). The primary protection of those values does not exclude the authority of the framer of the Constitution to expressly exclude some other questions from the circle of permitted referendum questions.[61]

After the Communication of 2013, the Constitutional Court has not made use of its 'general supervisory authority over the conformity with the Constitution' of a referendum question. Still, the reason for this is simple – in the cases of subsequent popular initiatives which had collected enough signatures (except the last one regarding the pension reform), the Parliament has always invoked Article 95 and asked the Court to determine whether the referendum question is in accordance with the Constitution.

Participation rights are not regulated in any law or the parliamentary standing orders. The Referendum Act is completely silent about the procedures related to the popular initiative between the delivery of voters' signatures to the Parliament and the calling of a referendum. The parliamentary Committee on the Constitution, the Standing Orders, and the Political System is responsible for all issues-related popular initiatives. This Committee makes all draft decisions and conclusions for the Parliament regarding every matter concerning a particular popular initiative. This includes the verification of the necessary number of signatures, the evaluation of the Government's report on the fulfilment of the requisite number of signatures, the assessment of the constitutionality of a referendum question and the request to the Constitutional Court to decide on the matter. The representatives of a particular popular initiative may be present at a Committee session. It is up to the chairperson of the Committee to let them participate and speak on the relevant issues. However, in the latest case of two popular initiatives in 2018 the representatives were not allowed to speak at the Committee session. The representatives of popular initiatives have no legal right to participate in any of the proceedings regarding the verification of voters' signatures or in the parliamentary deliberation.

4.1.1 Mandatory and optional referendum

There are no particular provisions either in the Constitution or in the Referendum Act that would prescribe any kind of control of the process for calling a referendum on the initiative of the Parliament or the President. As stated before, Article 95 of the Constitutional Court Act gives the Court the explicit authority to determine the fulfilment of the formal and substantial

---

[61] The Communication on the Citizens' Constitutional Referendum on the Definition of Marriage 2–3.

conditions only in case of the popular initiative, and only when asked by the Croatian Parliament. However, if the constitutional provisions which make up the Croatian 'constitutional identity' cannot be changed in a referendum demanded by a popular initiative, as stated by the Court, the same should also logically apply to all other possible ways of amending the Constitution.[62]

5.   CONCLUSION

In the past 30 years since Croatian independence, only three national referendums have been held, just one of which was called as a result of the popular initiative. Although Croatia belongs to the small group of countries having a 'large popular initiative on constitutional and legislative matters',[63] the full potential of the popular initiative has not been realized. The reasons for that are twofold: first, the very high number of signatures required and the procedural difficulties in collecting these signatures and, second, the decisions of the Constitutional Court on the constitutionality of popular initiatives.

There is an 'ever more restrictive practice of the Constitutional Court related to referendums requested by way of the popular initiative', which 'are leading to considerable closure of the route of citizen-initiated referendums'.[64] In the cases related to the popular initiatives against outsourcing and monetization of highways, the Constitutional Court has proclaimed that it would apply a more stringent test of constitutionality for bills proposed by popular initiatives as compared with similar laws enacted in the Parliament. The reason for this, according to the Court, is the fact that bills proposed by popular initiatives are not prepared, written, controlled, corrected and discussed in a democratic procedure, which would make them substantively different from bills enacted in the Croatian Parliament.[65] However, it is difficult to accept that the Court's

---

[62]   See Ana Horvat Vuković, 'U ime ustava – materijalne granice promjene ustava' (In the Name of the Constitution – Substantive Limits of Constitutional Change), (2015) 65 Collected Papers of the Zagreb Law Faculty, 481, 492–93.

[63]   Laurence Morel, 'Types of referendums, provisions and practice at the national level', in Laurence Morel and Matt Qvortrup (eds), *The Routledge Handbook to Referendums and Direct Democracy* (Routledge 2018) 44.

[64]   See Ana Horvat Vuković, 'Ustavni sud Republike Hrvatske i referendum narodne inicijative 2013–2015: Analiza i prijedlozi' (Constitutional Court of the Republic of Croatia and Citizen-Initiated Referenda in the 2013–2015 Period: Analysis and Proposals) (2016) 37 Collected Papers of the Faculty of Law of the University of Rijeka 805, 806.

[65]   In one case, the Court stated that 'as opposed to the abstract review of the constitutionality of a law, where the Constitutional Court examines whether a law conforms to the Constitution, in the procedure of referendum review, bills must have

controlling powers are substantially different depending on the identity of the body proposing and/or enacting the legislative act.[66]

The fact is that whenever the Court has been asked by the Parliament to determine whether the formal conditions have been fulfilled or whether the referendum question is in accordance with the Constitution, its decision has been negative. The greatest successes of popular initiatives have been achieved when the Parliament had not asked the Court to determine whether the referendum question was in accordance with the Constitution. That occurred in 2013, when the Parliament called the 'marriage referendum' and in 2019, when the Parliament enacted the act proposed by the popular initiative, instead of calling the referendum.

It should also be stated that some other popular initiatives have achieved political success without the formal implementation of a referendum.[67] When these initiatives had collected enough signatures for calling a referendum, the Government gave up its bills or other measures that were the reason for the organization of the popular initiatives in the first place, before the formal decisions of the Constitutional Court that the referendum questions were unconstitutional. In those cases, the popular initiatives had functioned as a sort of people's veto, despite the absence of the formal referendum decisions.

Finally, it must be emphasized that several attempts of the Parliament to solve the pressing problem of the exceptionally dysfunctional constitutional (and legislative) framework of the institution of the popular initiative have come to nothing so far.[68] The fact is that these attempts have only been made in response to some successful initiatives and because the issues that these successful initiatives brought into the public eye became much more severe once all quorums prescribed for the validity of referendum decisions had been eliminated in 2010.[69]

---

the highest degree of substantive alignment with the Constitution'. See the Decision U-VIIR-1159/2015, 7.

[66] See Vuković, 'Ustavni sud' (n 64) 825.

[67] All were the popular initiatives of the Croatian trade unions: against the Amendment of Labour Act, the outsourcing of auxiliary services and the monetization of highways. See also the 2019 '67 is too much' initiative.

[68] See the Proposal to Amend the Constitution regarding the referendum from 2013 https://www.sabor.hr/sites/default/files/uploads/sabor/2019-0118/080622/PRIJEDLOG%20PROMJENE%20USTAVA%20RH.pdf, accessed 9 July 2020.

[69] More on these attempts, Podolnjak, 'Constitutional Reforms' (n 14) 143–147.

11. Slovakia

Kamil Baraník

1. INTRODUCTION TO THE CONCEPT OF THE REFERENDUM IN SLOVAKIA

Before 1992, the direct exercise of state power by the citizens in the territory that is now the sovereign Slovak Republic was a purely hypothetical possibility. Technically, the Czechoslovak Constitution of 1920 introduced limited prospects of direct involvement of the people into decision-making for the first time. The statutory regulation that would specify this constitutional commitment and would allow the Czechoslovak citizens to exercise this power in practice, however, was never adopted.[1] Therefore direct democracy, especially in the form of the referendum, had never become prevalent in the first Czechoslovak constitutional regime. Many decades later, in 1992, the Act on Referendum, the first signal after 1920 that would encourage direct democracy, was adopted. This statutory device, however, came into force only in the dying seconds of the existence of the Czecho-Slovak Federation. Consequently, the envisioned instrument was never used in practice. Therefore, no referendum had been organized until 1992.[2]

The constitutional entrenchment of the referendum by the newly established Slovak Republic was, thus, a continuation of a trend to take the direct will of the people into consideration in specific cases of national (or local) significance. Based on this experience, the inclusion of the referendum into the constitutional framework of the young republic could be denoted as an important historical event.

Despite theoretical unfamiliarity and utter practical inexperience with the forms of direct democracy, several leading academics have started to indicate that the Slovak Republic has been constitutionally constructed as a semi-direct

---

[1] Ľudmila Somorová, 'Referendum ako forma výkonu štátnej moci' (2000) Pocta Jaroslavovi Chovancovi (Procom) 248–255.
[2] Dušan Nikodým, 'Referendum v Ústave Slovenskej republiky' (1997) Právny obzor 21–22.

democracy.[3] This bold statement has been anchored to Article 2(1) of the Constitution of the Slovak Republic (Constitution), which stipulates that 'state power originates from citizens, who exercise it through their elected representatives or directly'.[4] After 27 years of constitutional development, the reality, however, has proved that the exercise of the state power was far from an equal division between the citizens and their elected representatives. As the further text reveals, the cumbersome nature of some constitutional provisions regulating the referendum, combined with the political unwillingness to cooperate, have created major obstacles to the more frequent use of this traditional constitutional tool.

2.   EXISTING DIRECT-DEMOCRATIC INSTRUMENTS

Theoretically, the Slovak constitutional regulation of the referendum can be divided into several categories. The most obvious one is to distinguish referendums on the basis of their territorial scope. In that regard, the Constitution differentiates between a referendum at the national[5] and a referendum at the subnational level. A subnational referendum can be a municipal referendum or a referendum in a self-government regional unit.[6]

The most important (and constitutionally obvious) difference between these two groups is their legal force. While the referendum at the national level has been constitutionally designed as a legally binding tool of direct democracy, the Constitution remains completely silent on the effects of the referendum at the subnational level.[7] The obligatory and optional forms of local referendums recognized under the statutory scheme have so far produced extremely limited consequences. Most commentators have suggested that this type of referen-

---

[3]   Marián Giba et al., *Ústavné právo* (Wolters Kluwer 2019) 209.
[4]   The Constitution of the Slovak Republic in English language is accessible here https://www.constituteproject.org/constitution/Slovakia_2017?lang=en, accessed 10 June 2020.
[5]   Art. 7(1) and Art. 93–100 Constitution.
[6]   Art. 67(1) Constitution.
[7]   Ján Drgonec, *Ústava Slovenskej republiky. Teória a prax. 2. vydanie* (C.H. Beck, 2019) 1122.

dum may aspire to legally binding consequences.[8] This, however, has not been reflected appropriately in a corresponding statutory regulation.[9]

At the national level, the Constitution distinguishes between the mandatory referendum (a law-initiated referendum that confirms the decision of the constitution-making body) and the optional referendum[10] (that can be initiated either by the legislative body or by a specific number of citizens).[11] At the subnational level, the Constitution only creates a distinction between a municipal referendum and a referendum in a self-government regional unit.[12] The statutory regulation implicitly recognizes the existence of a mandatory and an optional referendum at the subnational level.

The national referendum is constitutionally framed in Article 2(1), Article 7(1) and in a separate subchapter titled 'Referendum' (Articles 93–100) of Chapter Five ('Legislative Power'). The specificities of the referendum process are stipulated in Act no. 180/2014 Coll. on the conditions of the exercise of the right to vote (Articles 196–215). The subnational referendum is constitutionally outlined in Article 67(1) and statutorily regulated in Act no. 369/1990 Coll. on the municipal establishment (the referendum at the municipal level) and in Act no. 302/2001 Coll. on the self-government regional units (the referendum on the level of self-government regional unit).

Since the introduction of the original Constitution in 1992, the wording of the provisions dealing with the issue of the national referendum has been quite ambiguous and offered various, often contradictory interpretations.[13] Therefore, it has been imperative to follow the case law of the Constitutional Court of the Slovak Republic (SCC). Despite the fact that the SCC dealt with this issue only three times,[14] it sought to clarify the textually vague constitutional provisions. It succeeded only to a certain extent, thus the confusion about fundamental issues of the functioning of the referendum still remains.

Nowadays, the referendum symbolizes an ever-appealing option for direct decision-making by citizens in various relevant and sometimes controversial disputes. It is regularly elevated to national attention by heterogenous groups

---

[8]　　See Ján Drgonec, *Ústavné právo hmotné* (C.H. Beck, 2018) 248–249; Lívia Trellová, *Ústanoprávne aspekty územnej samosprávy* (Wolters Kluwer, 2018) 141–147; Marek Domin, 'O adresátovi miestneho referenda. Nielen toho gabčíkovskeho' (2016) 68 Justičná revue 8–9, 879–882.

[9]　　Radoslav Procházka, 'Miestne referendum a krajské referendum – 1. časť' (2009) 61 Justičná revue 10, 1159–1166.

[10]　　Peter Kresák, 'The Government Structure in the New Slovak Republic' (1996) 4 Tulsa Journal of Comparative and International Law 1, 30–32.

[11]　　Art. 95(1) Constitution.

[12]　　Art. 67(1) Constitution.

[13]　　Giba (n 3) 209.

[14]　　Decisions PL. ÚS 42/95 (1996); II. ÚS 31/97 (1997); PL. ÚS 24/2014 (2014).

of politicians, specialists, interest groups and NGOs. However, for many reasons that will be elaborated further in the text, the referendum epitomizes an example of a currently dysfunctional constitutional instrument that has been, perhaps opportunistically, mostly blocked by the politicians. They have not been willing to live up to the promise of Article 2 of the Constitution that stipulates the power-sharing between the citizens and their representatives in the exercise of the state power.

2.1 Mandatory (Law-initiated) Referendum

The Constitution distinguishes two main types of the referendum at the national level – mandatory and optional. According to the Constitution, there is only one possibility of how the mandatory referendum can be initiated. Article 7(1) stipulates that if the Slovak Republic decides to enter into (or withdraw from) a state union with other states, the decision shall be made by a constitutional law which has to be subsequently confirmed by a (mandatory) referendum. The very same rationale is reconfirmed in Article 93(1) of the Constitution, instructing: 'A referendum is used to confirm a constitutional law on entering into a union with other states, or on withdrawing from that union.' Therefore, this type of referendum is triggered by the decision of the Slovak Parliament to enter into (or withdraw from) a state union taken in the form of a constitutional law.

The requirement to confirm a constitutional statute by a referendum is argu-ably deduced from the highest democratic magnitude of the decision that could diminish or even terminate the sovereignty of the Slovak Republic. Therefore, this decision must be imperatively 'consulted' with the ultimate source of all state power and legitimacy, that is, with the people in a referendum.

This provision was introduced in the original wording of the Constitution in 1992,[15] that is, before the termination of the Czech and Slovak Federation on 31 December 1992. It was a reflection of the situation, in which the possibility of splitting up the existing federation was being constitutionally expected. At that time the referendum represented the only acceptable legal avenue for how to consult an issue of such significance directly with the people.[16] Despite the importance of the issue and the constitutional obligation to hold a ref-erendum, the separation of the Federation at the end of 1992 did not trigger a

---

[15]   The Slovak Constitution was adopted on 1 September 1992 by the Slovak National Assembly. However, the Slovak Constitution only became fully operational on 1 January 1993 when the independent Slovak Republic was established.

[16]   Art. 1(2) Constitutional Statute no 327/1991 on referendum ('The proposal to withdraw the Czech Republic or the Slovak Republic from the Czech and Slovak Federal Republic can only be decided by referendum').

'mandatory' referendum. The decision to split up the former 'brother nations' remained purely political.[17]

Nowadays, the constitutional provision relating to the mandatory referendum has become relevant again, as legal scholars[18] and even the SCC itself[19] discuss it in connection to the constitutional limits of the ongoing EU integration. In the future in this process, the Slovak Republic could hypothetically lose certain fundamental qualities and powers that define its state sovereignty. That procedure could, thus, reach the threshold of Article 7(1) of the Constitution in regard to 'entering into a union with other states', which would then require to be consulted directly with the Slovak citizens in a mandatory referendum.

2.2   Optional (Citizen-initiated or Institution-initiated) Referendum

All other forms of referendums at the national level are optional, which means that they may be held if specified constitutional pre-conditions are met. The power to call a referendum is an exclusive competence of the President of the Slovak Republic (the President).[20] The President may only execute this power if he or she is 'requested by a petition signed by at least 350,000 citizens, or on the basis of a resolution of the National Council of the Slovak Republic, within 30 days after receiving the petition, or the resolution of the National Council of the Slovak Republic'.[21] The presidential power to call a referendum is, therefore, conditioned upon the delivery of the petition of citizens (citizen-initiated referendum) or the resolution of the Slovak Parliament (institution-initiated referendum).

The National Council of the Slovak Republic (National Council or Parliament) decides about the initiation of a referendum by a simple majority of votes. Under Article 96(1) of the Constitution the motion to pass a resolution of the National Council on calling a referendum may be introduced by members of parliament or by the Government.

The popular initiative of 350,000 citizens is not conditioned upon a decision of any other state organ. The right to initiate a referendum cannot be invoked individually, only by a constitutionally specified number of citizens. Interestingly, there is no time limit for collecting signatures. On the other hand,

---

[17]   It took place on the basis of the Constitutional Statute no 542/1992 on the dissolution of the Czech and Slovak Federal Republic adopted by the Federal Assembly.

[18]   See: Daniel Krošlák et al., *Ústavné právo* (Wolters Kluwer, 2016) 134–139.

[19]   Decision II. ÚS 171/05.

[20]   If there is no President in office or the President cannot execute his or her powers within the meaning of the Constitution, the power to call a referendum is temporarily executed by the Government of the Slovak Republic (Art. 105 Constitution).

[21]   Art. 95(1) Constitution.

the number of citizens required to initiate a referendum is tremendously high, since 350,000 signatures represent almost 8 per cent of all voters (approximately 4.45 million people). If the initiative fulfils all constitutional prerequisites, the President is constitutionally obliged to call a referendum.[22]

The subject of an optional referendum must avoid certain specific constitutional limitations (see section 3.2.). It is, however, not constrained to be either proactive or rejective. Therefore, the referendum can introduce new issues or it can be aimed specifically against certain legislative acts.

The results of a referendum can only be considered valid if the participation of citizens reaches the constitutionally stipulated threshold, which is at least one half of eligible voters (a turnout quorum) and if the majority of the participating citizens endorses the proposed question(s) (an approval quorum). Under Article 94 of the Constitution only citizens of the Slovak Republic have the right to participate in a referendum: 'Every citizen of the Slovak Republic who has the right to vote in elections of the National Council of the Slovak Republic is entitled to participate in the referendum.' Without achieving these formal procedural prerequisites, no referendum can be considered valid and thus produce legal effects.

2.3   Citizens' Agenda Initiative

The right to petition is recognized under Article 27 of the Constitution. It stipulates that 'everyone has the right, alone or with others, to address requests, proposals and complaints to the state and local authorities in matters of public or other common interest.'

The SCC declared that this right embodies one of the forms of direct democracy in Slovakia. It is part of the principle of the sovereignty of citizens, which empowers them to participate in the administration of public affairs.[23] The purpose of this right is to allow citizens to express their opinion directly and in relation to the legislative activity of the National Council. If the petition is signed by at least 100,000 citizens, it must be discussed in the National Council.[24] The Parliament, however, is not obliged to legislate upon this citizens' proposal.[25] Therefore, the right to petition does not limit the legislative power of the National Council.[26] The only constitutional limitation of this right

---

[22]   Art. 95(1) Constitution.
[23]   Decision PL. ÚS 42/95.
[24]   Art. 133 (3) Rules of Procedure of the National Council of the Slovak Republic. Accessible (in Slovak language) here https://www.nrsr.sk/web/Static/sk-SK/NRSR/Doc/zd_rokovaci-poriadok-20190821.pdf, accessed 10 June 2020.
[25]   Decisions III. ÚS 266/08, I. ÚS 38/94.
[26]   Decision IV. ÚS 409/2010.

is that the petition cannot be aimed at restricting the fundamental rights and freedoms.[27]

3.   LEGAL LIMITS

3.1   Substantive Limits

The Constitution prescribes one positive and three negative pre-conditions for the subject of a national optional referendum.

The positive pre-condition for questions posed in a referendum is formulated in Article 93(2) of the Constitution: 'A referendum can be used to decide also on other important issues of public interest.' What exactly could be understood as 'other important issues of public interest' was explained by the SCC in PL. ÚS 24/2014. It stated that:

> the term 'public interest' is an uncertain legal expression ... However, without the necessity for a more or less precise definition of this concept, the Constitutional Court emphasizes that ... the requirement that a referendum can be organized on the basis of a petition supported by at least 350,000 citizens must be taken into account. The prerequisite of 350,000 or even more citizens asking for a referendum in a particular issue is a strong indication that this (question) is being transformed into an important issue of public interest.

In other words, the SCC requires the support of 350,000 citizens for an issue to satisfy the definition of an 'important issue of public interest' under Article 93(2) of the Constitution. That kind of support potentially elevates any issue into the scope of an optional national referendum.

In another important judgment, concerning the feasibility of revising the Constitution via the questions posed in the referendum, the SCC declared that the constitutional provisions did not contain any restrictions that would limit a constitutional revision initiated by a referendum.[28]

The negative substantive limits of the referendum are prescribed in Article 93(3) and in Article 99(2) of the Constitution. Even though these issues may be 'important issues of public interest', that is, be within the scope of Article 93(2) of the Constitution, they are temporarily or permanently excluded from the purview of an optional referendum.

Temporarily excluded from the scope of the optional referendum are those issues that were the subject of a referendum in the recent past. Article 99(2) of the Constitution stipulates that a referendum on the same subject matter

---

[27]   Art. 27(2) Constitution.
[28]   Decision II. 31/97.

may be repeated only after three years from the day it was held. The provision prevents the same issue from being repeatedly put on the ballot, which could diminish the relevance of results achieved in a referendum.

Issues that are permanently excluded from the scope of the optional referendum are, according to Article 93(3) of the Constitution, 'the fundamental rights and freedoms, taxes, levies, and the state budget'. While shielding questions that deal with taxes, levies and the state budget from being consulted in referendums has been quite uncontroversial and understandable in regard to the preservation of a stable and predictable state income, the matter of 'fundamental rights and freedoms' caused certain interpretative complications. The constitutional protection of fundamental rights and freedoms is based on their individual character. The main purpose of excluding fundamental rights from direct democracy is to protect individuals against a majoritarian interference. Therefore, it should not be feasible to discuss their (non)existence in a referendum. Otherwise, the entire concept of individual protection could be undermined by a majoritarian decision. Ultimately, putting human rights to the vote in a referendum could lead to a legal repudiation of their existence.

The issue gained attention in 2014, when the President articulated doubts that the scope of proposed questions for the upcoming same-sex marriage referendum may be interfering with the constitutional limitation on 'fundamental rights and freedoms'. His doubts revolved around the question whether the fundamental rights and freedoms were completely banned from any consideration in a referendum. Therefore, the President filed the case with the SCC, asking whether the subjects of the referendum were in compliance with the Constitution.

In the PL. ÚS 24/2014 decision the SCC reviewed the constitutionality of the four proposed questions:[29] (1) 'Do you agree that no cohabitation of persons other than a union between one man and one woman could be named marriage?' (2) 'Do you agree that neither same-sex couples nor groups shall be allowed to adopt children and subsequently raise them?' (3) 'Do you agree that no other cohabitation of persons than marriage should be granted special protection, rights and duties which are only granted to marriage and married couples by standards as of 1 March 2014 (especially acknowledgement or registration as a life partnership at a public authority, possibility to adopt a child by the second husband/wife of a parent)?' (4) 'Do you agree that schools should not require participation of children in classes dedicated to sexual

---

[29] For more details on this case see Daniel Krošlák, 'The Referendum on the So-Called Traditional Family in the Slovak Republic' (2015) Central and Eastern European Legal Studies 149–167; Lucia Berdisová, 'K ne/súladu referenda o ochrane rodiny s Ústavou Slovenskej republiky' (2014) Justičná revue 1246–1255.

behaviour or euthanasia if their parents or the children themselves do not agree with the content of the lessons?'

In regard to the constitutional limitation on referendum questions dealing with fundamental rights and freedoms, the SCC held that it:

> tends to understand Art. 93(3) of the Constitution as a ban to referendums on issues that could undermine the concept of fundamental rights and freedoms by lowering their standards resulting from international law, as well as from the national legal system to an extent that would threaten the rule of law principle. However, it is not possible to reject every question that concerns as little as possible the content of one of the fundamental rights and freedoms. Otherwise, this understanding would indeed deny the meaning and purpose of the referendum.

This statement was supplemented by a formulation that fundamental rights and freedoms were allowed to be expanded by a question posed in a referendum, but their understanding should never be restricted. The SCC also added that '[it] must always ensure that a possible extension of the standard of a particular fundamental right or freedom does not lead in parallel to a restriction of another fundamental right or freedom.' This assertion is again quite unclear and raises several other problems of interpretation. The most complicated issue is to ascertain how to raise 'the standard' of one fundamental right, while at the same time not influencing or diminishing the standard of another fundamental right – especially since so many fundamental rights are conflicting in their nature.

In reaching this conclusion, the SCC reviewed the Slovak legislation, as well as the ECtHR's case law in connection to the legal status of same-sex marriages and adoption. The SCC stated that the first and the second questions did not interfere with then-legislative *status quo*, already banning the marriages between the persons of same sex, as well as prohibiting the adoptions of children by unmarried couples. Therefore, these two questions were held constitutional.

The formulation of the third question was cumbersome, but it was generally understood that it implicitly dealt with the legal status of unmarried same-sex couples. The SCC, however, stated that the phrase 'no other cohabitation of persons' represents a broad range of relationships and it could not be suggested that it categorizes persons on the basis of their sexual orientation. The SCC declared that the case at hand only distinguished marriage and all 'other cohabitation of persons', which includes relations of both same-sex and opposite-sex couples. The formulation of the question clearly omitted the fact that the Slovak law already recognized several categories of cohabitation. The initiators of the referendum tried to constitutionally entrench an exclusive legal status of marriage against all other forms of cohabitation. That would, according to the SCC, result in lowering the standards of the fundamental right of protection against unauthorized interference with the family life. Therefore, the SCC declared this question unconstitutional.

The fourth question was found constitutionally irrelevant, as it was not imperative. Even if approved, it would require further statutory implementation, which would offer various possibilities for the legislator. Therefore, the question was not held unconstitutional.

The issue of fundamental rights has not been further elaborated or addressed in another SCC decision, thus many questions still remain unresolved.

3.2   Formal Limits

There are no requirements of unity of substance, unity of form, or unity of hierarchical level concerning the questions posed in a referendum recognized either by the Constitution or by the SCC case law.

However, the SCC held impermissible a question in the form of a specifically worded draft of a legislative enactment.[30] The SCC stipulated that in the Constitution the legislative power was fashioned in two ways. It belongs not only to the National Council but also directly to the Slovak citizens.[31] The referendum, however, cannot serve as a complete substitution for the legislative power of the Parliament. In that regard, the past practice that involved an attachment of a specifically worded draft of a legislative enactment, in order to limit involvement of the Parliament, if the referendum was successful, was declared unconstitutional.[32] In other words, a successful referendum cannot generate a bill that the Parliament then has to promulgate without any deliberation or possibility to modify it. That practice would completely side-step the legislative power of the Parliament. Under Article 72 of the Constitution, the National Council is the only constitution-making and legislative body in the Slovak Republic and, therefore, the only channel through which the Slovak legal order can be modified. Thus, a successful referendum can only serve as a constitutional trigger that activates the power of the National Council to legislate. Implementation of the result of the referendum must remain within the discretion of Parliament. In other words, the SCC has banned specifically worded proposals from being subject to a referendum. Therefore, only *questions of principle* are generally permissible in referendums. This constitutional ban, however, places the enormously important power of implementation back in the hands of parliamentarians.

---

[30]   Decision PL. ÚS 31/97.
[31]   Decision II. ÚS 31/97.
[32]   Decision II. ÚS 31/97.

3.3   Core Constitutional Values as the Subjects of Referendums

The referendum has reached an almost mythical pre-eminence in the Slovak constitutional discourse. The high turnout requirement[33] has elevated the referendum in Slovakia to the heights of the ultimate will of the people, which is capable of any change within the constitutional realm. The reflection of this extraordinary character of a valid referendum has been formulated in a recent landmark decision of the SCC,[34] in which the existence of an implicit (unamendable) material core of the Constitution has been announced.[35] The decision formulated several constitutional principles as foundational: that the Slovak Republic is a democratic state based on the rule of law and the separation of powers forms the implicit core of the Constitution. These foundational principles can never be undone by any legislative power of the Parliament. The SCC, however, articulated one single exception through which an alteration of the material constitutional core would still be possible. It outlined that a modification would be possible 'by the decision of the original constitution-making body (the people) in the referendum'.[36] The SCC, thus, declared that the results of a referendum may not be subject to further constitutional limits. Even the material constitutional core is not immune against a change or complete annihilation by the results of a valid referendum. Thereby, the results of a referendum have been essentially equalled to the mythical 'pouvoir constituant'. This SCC declaration was an embodiment of a prevailing doctrinal position on the potential power of referendum in Slovakia. Thus, it is now almost unthinkable to fashion any additional substantive constitutional constraints on the results of a referendum. Similarly, any subsequent constitutional challenge of a valid referendum has been considered absurd. The only practical check against this 'nuclear' power of the referendum in Slovakia has been the elevated turnout quorum that historically prevented referendums from being successful. This threshold itself has produced a continual avalanche of public condemnation.[37] Even though this criticism may seem appropriate, any modification of the

---

[33]   Slovakia's high constitutional turnout requirement for a valid referendum is not unique in the Central European region, see Anneli Albi, *EU Enlargement and the Constitutions of Central and Eastern Europe* (Cambridge University Press, 2005) 140.

[34]   Decision PL. ÚS 21/2014 [177].

[35]   For more details about this case see Simon Drugda, 'Slovak Constitutional Court Strikes Down a Constitutional Amendment – But the Amendment Remains Valid' (Blog of the International Journal of Constitutional Law, 25 April 2019) http://www.iconnectblog.com/2019/04/slovak-constitutional-court-strikes-down-a-constitutional-amendment-but-the-amendment-remains-valid, accessed 10 June 2020.

[36]   Decision PL. ÚS 21/2014 [177].

[37]   Marek Domin, 'A Part of the Constitution Is Unconstitutional, the Slovak Constitutional Court has Ruled' (Verfassungsblog, 8 February) https://verfassungsblog

turnout quorum must be accompanied by a complete reconsideration of the potential 'pouvoir constituant' consequences of the referendum. Otherwise, the referendum could produce unimaginably damaging results that could either diminish or even destroy the nature of the Slovak Republic as a democratic state based on the rule of law and the separation of powers.

4. INSTITUTIONAL AND PROCEDURAL FRAMEWORK FOR REVIEWING COMPLIANCE WITH THE LEGAL LIMITS

Both avenues of an optional referendum (by a vote of the National Council and by a popular initiative) are fully autonomous. The President has an obligation to examine whether the popular or parliamentary initiative fulfils all constitutional prerequisites. If it meets the procedural and substantive constitutional limits outlined above, the President has a straightforward constitutional duty to call a referendum within a period of 30 days. If the President has doubts regarding the constitutional conformity of the proposed referendum, he or she may refuse to call it.

Additionally, if the President has specific reservations about the subject of a referendum, that is, about the substantive framing of the question(s), he or she may initiate an *ex ante* judicial review before the SCC.[38] The SCC will then decide upon its constitutionality. Article 95(2) of the Constitution stipulates that 'the President may, before calling a referendum, file with the Constitutional Court a petition for a decision whether the subject of the referendum, which should be organized on the basis of a citizens' petition or a resolution of the National Council … is in compliance with the Constitution or constitutional statutes.' It is not the President's constitutional duty to initiate this type of proceeding. Such initiation rests fully upon his or her consideration.

This type of judicial review is further regulated in Article 102–109 of Act no. 314/2018 on the Constitutional Court. In addition to the general requirements, the proposal must contain the subject(s) of the referendum; the legal basis for the referendum (mandatory or optional; citizen-initiated or institution-initiated); the reasons which lead the President to doubt the constitutional conformity of the subject of the referendum; and an indication of the constitutional provision(s) that is (are) according to the President incompatible with the subject of the referendum.[39] The parties to the subsequent proceedings

---

.de/a-part-of-the-constitution-is-unconstitutional-the-slovak-constitutional-court-has -ruled/, DOI: https://doi.org/10.17176/20190211-212614-0, accessed 10 June 2020.

[38] For further elaboration see Milan Ľalík, Tomáš Ľalík, *Zákon o Ústavnom súde Slovenskej republiky, Komentár* (Wolters Kluwer SR, 2019) 340–341.

[39] Art. 103 Act no. 314/2018 on the Constitutional Court.

before the SCC are the President and the National Council. If the referendum was initiated by a citizens' petition, the parties to the proceedings are the President and the petition's committee.[40] Before deciding, the President of the Court requests the opinion of the National Council and, if a referendum is to be called on the basis of a citizens' petition, the opinion of the petition's committee. Other experts may also submit their opinions without request. The SCC, however, is not obliged to take them into account.[41]

Article 125b(3) of the Constitution indicates a 60-day period during which the SCC is obliged to decide on the issue.[42] The SCC's constitutional review suspends the time limit for the President to call a referendum. If the SCC declares the subject of a proposed referendum unconstitutional, it cannot take place.

The operative part, the reasoning and the instruction on the legal effects of the ruling, together with the dissenting opinions, shall be published in the Collection of Laws. The SCC decides which part of the reasoning of the judgment shall be promulgated in the Collection of Laws.[43]

Ultimately, if a referendum is called, it shall be held within 90 days from the day it was called by the President according to Article 96(2) of the Constitution. A referendum may not take place within 90 days prior to elections to the National Council of the Slovak Republic.[44] But a referendum may be held on the day of elections to the National Council.[45]

5. LEGAL EFFECTS OF REFERENDUMS

The legal impact of a valid referendum can be vaguely deduced from the constitutional text. Consequently, the legal ramifications of the relevant constitutional provisions have been highly disputed. Several uncertainties have been previously addressed in the SCC's case law, but many others still remain.

First, the most obvious impact of a valid referendum is its generally binding character. This consequence can be deduced from the wording of Article 93(2) of the Constitution, which specifies that 'a referendum can be used to decide …'. The formulation implies the decisive character of a successful referendum. Therefore, its results should enjoy conclusive, not only counselling, effect(s). In 2014 the SCC reconfirmed that the results of a referendum do have

---

[40] Art. 104 Act no. 314/2018 on the Constitutional Court.
[41] Art. 105 Act no. 314/2018 on the Constitutional Court.
[42] Similarly, Art. 106 Act no. 314/2018 on the Constitutional Court.
[43] Art. 108 Act no. 314/2018 on the Constitutional Court.
[44] Art. 97(1) Constitution.
[45] Art. 97(2) Constitution.

legal consequences and thus a valid referendum cannot be regarded as a vote without any legal relevance.[46]

Based on Article 98(2) of the Constitution, if a referendum is successful, the National Council has a constitutional duty to promulgate the proposals adopted in the referendum in the same way as it promulgates statutes. The constitutional construction 'in the same way as it promulgates statutes' generated numerous academic debates.[47] The literal interpretation of this provision could suggest that by the promulgation of the results of a successful referendum in the official gazette for the publication of legal norms, they become instantaneously legally binding and directly applicable in the Slovak legal order.

According to one group of Slovak jurists, however, the results of a referendum can never be directly applicable.[48] The constitutional expression 'in the same way as it promulgates statutes' should not be understood in the sense that a valid referendum (and its results) becomes legally binding immediately after it was published in the official gazette. Under this consideration, it ought to be rejected that the results of a successful referendum would become legally binding in the same manner as 'ordinary' statutes adopted by the Parliament, that is, to be generally and directly binding.

Other Slovak academics have been pleading for the direct applicability of certain results of a successful referendum. The applicability is limited, however, to those results that are capable of being directly applicable. The directly applicable results would include mostly, but not exclusively, those that could directly determine (clearly and precisely) the duties and obligations of individuals or legal entities. These referendum results would then create a separate source of law that would be enforceable. Consequently, the questions posed in a referendum should be (intentionally) formulated in a directly applicable manner. If not, they say, these questions do not fulfil the basic substantive precondition of Article 93(2) of the Constitution ('other important issues of public interest'), and thus cannot be posed in a referendum.[49]

The debate was conceptualized by the SCC in 1997, when it declared that 'a successful referendum has a constitutional relevance in the sense that participating citizens are instructing the Parliament to act in accordance with the proposal adopted in the referendum'.[50]

---

[46] Decision PL. ÚS 24/2014.
[47] Drgonec (n 7) 1264–1265; Tomáš Ľalík, 'Tracing constitutional changes in Slovakia between 2008–2016' (2017) 58 Hungarian Journal of Legal Studies 2, 122–124; Marek Domin, 'Formálno-právna povaha výsledku referenda' (2010) 62 Justičná revue 11, 1247–1255.
[48] For the discussion see Giba (n 3), 223–225.
[49] Drgonec (n 8) 248–249.
[50] Decision II. ÚS 31/97.

The articulated constitutional obligation to legislate, however, produced another source of constitutional discrepancy, this time linked to the incoherency between the mentioned constitutional command to legislate instigated by a successful referendum and the representative mandate of the member of parliament, which assumes that each member of parliament should be free from any influence or coercion. Under Article 73(2) of the Constitution the members of parliament 'execute their mandate personally according to their conscience and conviction and are not bound by any orders'. The prevailing interpretation of this obvious contradiction among academics indicated that the constitutional duty to accept the results of a successful referendum should exceptionally bind the MPs despite the constitutional nature of their mandate.[51] Under this view, the constitutional obligation of the MPs should follow the general will of the people expressed in a referendum.

In contrast, the SCC rejected the possibility that the citizens are capable of enforcing their will upon the parliamentarians in 2014. The SCC stipulated that 'It is constitutionally impossible to instruct the MPs how to vote on a proposal adopted in a referendum'.[52] Consequently, there is no exception of the MPs' representative mandate and the citizens can only hold them accountable politically, that is, during the next parliamentary elections.

Therefore, the legal force of the results of a successful referendum should hinge upon the nature of the implementing act adopted by the National Council. There are, however, several specificities of this rationale that must be taken into consideration.

Article 99(1) of the Constitution stipulates that '(t)he National Council of the Slovak Republic may amend or annul the result of a referendum by means of constitutional statute no sooner than three years after the result of the referendum came into effect.' This provision explicitly shields the results of a referendum against any legislative intervention within three years. After this period, the results based on a successful referendum are protected against any legislative amendment that does not have constitutional relevance. Only a constitutional statute, approved by a constitutionally required parliamentary super-majority, is capable of reversing the will of the people expressed in a successful referendum.

The limited untouchability of the results of a referendum is fragile and deserves further elaboration. This logic would constitutionally protect even ordinary statutes that implement the results of a successful referendum into the legal system. How would a constitutionally permissible method to change the

---

[51]   Boris Balog, Lívia Trellová, 'Povinnosť parlamentu prijať zákon?/!' (2012) Právny obzor, 33
[52]   Decision PL. ÚS 24/2014.

sub-constitutional legislation by a constitutional statute look? What would that mean for the legal system? These are the constitutionally relevant queries that ought to be addressed by the SCC in the future.

6.   REFERENDUMS AT THE SUBNATIONAL LEVEL

The constitutional foundations of the referendum at the subnational level (that is, the municipal referendum and the referendum in the self-government regional units) are stipulated in Article 67 of the Constitution. It specifies that the territorial self-administration is performed at meetings of municipality residents, by a municipal referendum, by a referendum in a self-government regional unit, by the municipality bodies or the bodies of self-government regional unit. The execution of the local referendum and the referendum on the territory of a superior territorial unit shall be specified by statute.

The implementing statutes are Act no. 369/1990 Coll. on a municipal establishment (referendum at the municipal level) and Act no. 302/2001 on the self-government regional units (referendum at the level of self-government regional units). In regard to these legal acts, the SCC declared that the statutory regulation of the referendum at the subnational level has been inconsistent and lacks proper implementation.[53] Therefore, it can be stated that the issue of direct democracy at the subnational level did not gain the appropriate attention of the national legislator that should regulate the issue comprehensively.

The referendum at the subnational level is being utilized to ascertain popular support for issues of municipal significance or vital importance for the self-government regional unit. The obligatory municipal referendum is called by the municipal council in case of (a) a merger or a dissolution of municipalities; (b) a recall of the mayor; (c) a petition request of 30 per cent of municipal inhabitants; (d) a change of the name of the municipality; or (e) if it is statutorily required.[54] The municipal council may also call an optional referendum on any other important issue of local governance.[55]

The obligatory referendum in the self-government regional unit takes place in case of a recall of the chairman of the self-government regional unit. The optional referendum may be called by the council of the self-government regional unit on any other important issue concerning the exercise of self-governance. It can be initiated either by a resolution of the council or by a petition of at least 30 per cent of inhabitants of the self-governance unit.[56]

---

[53]   Decision PL. ÚS 4/2016.
[54]   Art. 11a(2) Act no. 369/1990 Coll. on a municipal establishment.
[55]   Art. 11a(4) Act no. 369/1990 Coll. on a municipal establishment.
[56]   Art. 15(1) Act no. 302/2001 on the self-government regional units.

The results of all mentioned subnational referendums are considered valid, if the turnout quorum reaches at least one half of the population of the particular subnational unit and simultaneously if the majority of the participating inhabitants endorses the proposed question(s).[57]

Regrettably, the legal duty of the municipal and regional bodies to follow the results of a successfully conducted referendum at the subnational level has been highly disputed.[58] The results of subnational referendums are not regulated constitutionally and mostly remain in full disposal of local representatives.

7.   CONCLUSION

The referendum in the Slovak Republic has been considered a highly relevant tool of direct decision-making mostly by constitutional scholars and other academics. The promise to involve the public opinion into important decision-making at the subnational or even at the national level has not yet lived up to the original expectations of the public.

The Constitution provides a quite amenable and loosely fashioned framework that constructs several possibilities of how and when to conduct a referendum. The previous pages identified three main reasons that have enormously complicated the practical usage of the referendum.

First, the initiation requirement of a petition signed by 350,000 citizens. This extremely high threshold (8 per cent of all eligible citizens) has not allowed to bring many diverse topics to the public discourse.

The second impediment has been the extremely high turnout quorum (50 per cent of all voters). The referendum has been regularly used by politicians who had not been capable of passing their proposals through the legislative process in the Parliament. Therefore, their counterparts have been consistently discouraging their constituents from participation in referendums. The high turnout threshold has made it relatively easy for the political parties to effectively torpedo any referendum attempts. Only once, in case of the 2003 EU referendum, did all major political parties join their forces and heavily encouraged citizens to participate. That was the only time in history when a referendum was successful.[59] The referendum has, therefore, never been a platform for a societal debate, but has mostly only been used as a tool of currently marginalized political representatives.

---

[57]   Art. 11a(8) Act no. 369/1990 Coll. on a municipal establishment; Art. 15(5) Act no. 302/2001 on the self-government regional units.

[58]   Trellová (n 8) 141–46.

[59]   See further Albi (n 33) 138–62.

Lastly, as formulated by the SCC case law, the legal effects of valid referendums rest primarily in the hands of politicians in the process of implementation of the results. This necessary reconfirmation of the results in Parliament did not help to persuade citizens of the viability of popular initiatives.

The combination of these factors in three different stages of the referendum process have contributed to the merely hypothetical importance of its constitutional existence. The ambiguities of the constitutional text could have been slowly diminished or even removed by the practical usage of the referendum. This clarification could have made the requirements of a successful referendum more transparent, predictable and its results more acceptable to the general public. This process, however, has not happened. Numerous interpretative possibilities that are mentioned in this chapter have only been hypothetically constructed. The reasons for that are quite simple. Only eight referendum events have been held in the history of the Slovak Republic.[60] Moreover, only one of them – the referendum on the accession to the EU – was successful. This was undoubtedly caused by the rigid initiation process that has not created more interpretative opportunities for the SCC to clarify the discrepancies of the constitutional text. The constitutional jurists and commentators have produced various opinions that sketch different avenues of how to construe the relevant constitutional provisions. Unfortunately, without the authoritative decisions of those actors that are constitutionally involved in the process of referendum, the hypothetical solutions simply cannot provide the much-needed predictability and clarity of the legal framework. Slovakia, therefore, lacks not only historical experience, but also its own practice with this instrument of direct democracy.

In the light of the latest SCC landmark decision,[61] the shortcomings of the referendum process may gain a new light. According to the SCC's reasoning in this decision, even the implicit material constitutional core could be transformed by the results of a referendum. Therefore, a potentially simple relaxation of the turnout quorum could enable a minority of citizens to annihilate the constitutional foundations of the republic. That would be unacceptable. Therefore, if any change of the referendum will be proposed in the future, it is imperative to rethink the entire mechanism, especially those constitutional provisions that deal with the legal effects of a referendum. Any 'cosmetic' modifications that would just enable a referendum to be more effective without reconsidering its further impacts could have tragic consequences.

---

[60] The second (failed) referendum in 1997 was even prevented from happening as the government left the last question off the ballot paper. For a list of referendums, see the official webpage of the Statistical Office of the Slovak Republic (https://slovak .statistics.sk/) accessed 8 May 2020.

[61] PL. ÚS 21/2014.

The historical experience with referendums in Slovakia has been quite gloomy so far. This, however, should not predict the future. Possibilities still exist for the people as well as for their representatives to approach referendums differently, not as a polarizing tool, but as a vital device for a direct and deep societal discussion, in which collaboration rather than division will be promoted. Undoubtedly, that would require the involvement of public education and the support from national and local authorities as well as from civil society. These are, however, indispensable pre-conditions for a referendum to function properly, not only in the Slovak Republic but worldwide.

12. Hungary

Anna Forgács

1. INTRODUCTION

Direct-democratic instruments were introduced in Hungary in 1989, as part of the process of democratic transition,[1] when they were put to a test at once by the so-called 'four-yes' referendum about demolishing the remains of the communist party structure and the election of the President. Even though direct democracy has a short history in Hungary, already the second legal regime is in force, as after the adoption of the new Constitution in 2011 (Fundamental Law)[2] a new act on referendums (Referendum Act)[3] was also created.

The constitutional system builds on representative democracy as the main pillar of the exercise of popular sovereignty. From the early days of Hungarian democracy, direct democracy has been regarded as an exceptional form of popular sovereignty, which is exercised seldom but on such occasions it presides over representative democracy.[4] This exceptionality also shows in numbers: Hungarian voters have been asked to answer 13 referendum questions on seven occasions[5] since 1989, even though the number of referendums initiated annually is well in the hundreds since 2006–2007.[6]

---

[1] They were first introduced by the Act XVII of 1989 even before the major democratic constitutional reform. For a summary of the historical evolution of direct democracy in Hungary (including current trends) see László Komáromi, 'Milestones in the History of Direct Democracy in Hungary' (2013) 9(4) Iustum Aequum Salutare 41.

[2] The Fundamental Law of Hungary was adopted on 25 April 2011 and entered into force on 1 January 2012 http://njt.hu/translated/doc/TheFundamentalLawofHungary _20190101_FIN.pdf, accessed 1 April 2020.

[3] Act CCXXXVIII of 2013 on Initiating Referendums, the European Citizens' Initiative and Referendum Procedure https://www.valasztas.hu/web/national-election -office/act-ccxxxviii-of-2013-on-initiating-referendums-the-european-citizens -initiative-and-referendum-procedure, accessed 1 April 2020.

[4] 52/1997 (X. 14.) Constitutional Court (CC) decision, 2/1993 (I. 22.) CC decision.

[5] See http://c2d.ch/country/HU, accessed 1 April 2020.

[6] For the reasons behind the rise of initiatives see: Zoltán Tibor Pállinger, 'Potentials of Direct Democracy in an Extremely Majoritarian System: The Case of Hungary' (2016) Andrássy Working Papers zur Demokratieforschung 1/2016,

The National Election Office has provided statistical overviews since 2002,[7] but in the 1990s the number of initiatives per year did not reach 50.[8] The available statistical information shows that between May 2002 and December 2019 the number of questions submitted for authorization was 2,153 at national level. Out of these 2,153 questions, the election authorities validated only 186 questions, which is 8.6 per cent of all questions.

One of the main reasons behind this huge contrast between the number of referendums initiated and actually taking place lies in the elaborate system of substantive and formal limits imposed on direct-democratic initiatives, coupled with a rigorous administrative and judicial review procedure. The Fundamental Law explicitly prohibits referendums in ten subject matters, while the Referendum Act adds the formal limit of clarity to the restrictions, which is the most common ground for refusing validation.

2.   DIRECT-DEMOCRATIC INSTRUMENTS

Article 8 of the Fundamental Law contains the main provisions regarding nationwide referendums. A referendum can be initiated by citizens or the executive (President or Government) and it can be proactive or rejective (abrogative). Although this is not specified in the legal provisions,[9] the consistent practice of the election bodies has been to authorize both questions that are generally phrased and those proposing to amend or abrogate specific legal provisions.[10]

Most of the initiatives are submitted by private individuals or political parties, with the recent exception of the 2016 quota-referendum,[11] which was

---

17 https://www.andrassyuni.eu/pubfile/de-209-1-2016-wp-1-def.pdf, accessed 1 April 2020.

[7]   See https://www.valasztas.hu/documents/20182/305738/Statisztik%C3%A1k+az+elb%C3%ADr%C3%A1lt+n%C3%A9pszavaz%C3%A1si+kezdem%C3%A9nyez%C3%A9sekr%C5%91l.pdf/a0655454-ecd7-412f-ab08-8a23dc419f5e, accessed 1 April 2020.

[8]   Gabriella Antalicz, 'Magyarországi Országos Népszavazási Kezdeményezések Statisztikai Elemzése' (2019) 15(1) Iustum Aequum Salutare 171, 172.

[9]   The old Constitution contained a provision about confirmatory referendums in Art. 26(1), which is not part of the current system. See 64/2009 (VI. 18.) CC decision.

[10]   Most recently the 15/2017 (VI. 30.) CC decision clarified that the Fundamental Law does not limit the aim or form of the referendum initiative. It can be aimed to amend, abrogate or create a legislative act or other legislative decision; the question can be the summary of its content, an actual legislative provision or a reference to a legal act or proposed legal act. See 15/2017 (VI. 30.) CC decision, paragraph 32.

[11]   Andrew MacDowall, 'Voters back Viktor Orbán's rejection of EU migrant quotas' *Politico* (Brussels, 2 October 2016) https://www.politico.eu/article/hungary-referendum-eu-migration-viktor-orban/, accessed 1 April 2020.

a plebiscite initiated by the Government. The only other referendum initiated by state actors was the referendum on the accession to NATO, while the referendum on the accession to the EU was specifically mandated by law. In case a referendum is initiated by 200,000 citizens, it is obligatory to call the referendum, while in case a referendum is proposed by the President, the Government or 100,000 citizens, the parliament may order a referendum but is not obliged to do so.[12] In the Hungarian jurisprudence this distinction is referred to as that between 'mandatory' and 'facultative' referendums.

The legal provisions governing referendums – including limits and procedures – are the same for all direct-democratic instruments regardless of whether they are initiated by citizens or state institutions. After the referendum question is formulated, it has to be submitted to the National Election Commission, which reviews its compliance with formal and substantive limits. A legal remedy against the validation decision is provided by the supreme court (Curia), against which a constitutional complaint procedure may be initiated at the Constitutional Court. After the validation, citizens have 120 days to collect signatures. In all cases, the simple majority of the members of parliament (National Assembly) makes the decision on calling the referendum, and the President sets its date. The same quorum applies for all types of direct-democratic instruments: the majority of people with voting rights have to participate, with the majority of participants approving the referendum in order for it to be valid. If the quorum is met, the referendum results are binding and must be implemented.[13]

The citizen-initiated referendum is the only type of referendum that exists both at local and national level. Law-initiated referendums and legislature-initiated referendums are only present at local level,[14] while agenda initiatives have been abolished in the new constitutional system.

This chapter will analyse only national-level referendums in further detail. Even though there have been some interesting local cases in Budapest,[15] the

---

[12] The Constitutional Court analysed the relationship between the two types in 52/1997 (X. 14.) CC decision, English summary http://www.codices.coe.int/NXT/gateway.dll/CODICES/precis/eng/eur/hun/hun-1997-3-009?fn=document-frameset.htm$f=templates$3.0, accessed 1 April 2020.

[13] See Art. 8 Fundamental Law.

[14] Art. 98-105 Act CLXXXIX of 2011 on the Local Self-Governments of Hungary. The only exception is the referendum regarding the accession to the EU, where Art. 79 of the old Constitution mandated that a referendum has to be held on this specific issue and also that the referendum has to take place on 12 April 2003.

[15] In recent years there have been a number of initiatives related to the new Museum district to be built in City park and related to Budapest applying for the organization of the Summer Olympics. See: Knk.VII.37.644/2017/2, Knk.VII.37.306/2017/2, Knk.IV.37.298/2017/4, Knk.IV.38.143/2015/6.

most relevant referendum experience comes from national referendums and initiatives. The so-called 'national consultation' is also excluded from the analysis. It is a non-binding public questionnaire circulated by the government on various topics; however, it does not have any constitutional or legal basis. It is an ad hoc political tool which could not be considered a genuine instrument of direct democracy.[16]

3.   SUBSTANTIVE LEGAL LIMITS ON REFERENDUMS

Article 8(2)–(3) of the Fundamental Law contains the substantive limits of referendums, which consist of the positive scope of referendums and the prohibited subjects:

> National referendums may be held about any matter falling within the functions and powers of the National Assembly, while no national referendum may be held on:
> (a)   any matter aimed at the amendment of the Fundamental Law;
> (b)   the content of the Acts on the central budget, the implementation of the central budget, central taxes, duties, contributions, customs duties or the central conditions for local taxes;
> (c)   the content of the Acts on the elections of Members of the National Assembly, local government representatives and mayors or Members of the European Parliament;
> (d)   any obligation arising from international treaties;
> (e)   person- and organization-related matters falling within the competence of the National Assembly;
> (f)   the dissolution of the National Assembly;
> (g)   the dissolution of a representative body;
> (h)   the declaration of a state of war, state of national crisis and state of emergency; furthermore, on the declaration and extension of a state of preventive defence;
> (i)   any matter related to participation in military operations;
> (j)   the granting of amnesty.

Statistically the most commonly used substantive limits are, apart from the positive scope of referendums, the prohibition on constitutional amendments, the fiscal exemption and the prohibition relating to international obligations.[17]

---

[16]   See: Zoltán Pozsár-Szentmiklósy, 'Direct democracy in Hungary: from popular sovereignty to popular illusion' (European Constitutional Democracy in Peril: People, Principles, Institutions Conference, Budapest, June 2016) https://www.academia.edu/ 28770995/Direct_democracy_in_Hungary_from_popular_sovereignty_to_popular _illusion, accessed 1 April 2020.

[17]   A thorough analysis was carried out about the decisions of the National Election Commission between January 2014 and December 2017 based on 227 questions by

3.1 Positive Scope of Referendum Issues

Under Hungarian law any matter can be put to a referendum that falls within the functions and powers of the National Assembly and is not prohibited. A valid referendum creates an obligation for the National Assembly to execute the will of the people, thus the legislature needs to have the respective competence. Before the adoption of the new Fundamental Law, the Constitutional Court interpreted this provision widely. Basically, any national issue could be the subject of a referendum, as the powers of the National Assembly were, according to the Constitutional Court, complete and open.[18] After the review powers were transferred to the Curia, it rather swiftly limited this wide interpretation and departed from the previous practice of the Constitutional Court.[19] In the Knk.37.807/2012 case the Curia reviewed the decision of the election commission in which it had refused to validate the question 'Do you agree that no football stadium should be built by 31 December 2014 in Felcsút using public funds?' The election commission and the Curia agreed that the question falls within the powers of the executive and thus outside the positive scope of referendums. Interpreting the competence to decide on building a stadium also as a legislative competence would make this positive condition fictitious as all questions could be interpreted as such. According to the Curia this would be in violation of the exceptionality of referendums based on the popular sovereignty clause of the Fundamental Law.[20] This narrow interpretation of legislative competences was criticized by the legal literature,[21] as it is not well founded in the principles of separation of powers and hierarchy of norms, while it also creates a possibility for the Government to shield some issues from referendums by simply regulating them.

Neither the Fundamental Law (or previously the Constitution), nor the Referendum Act contains any additional positive condition on the issues that could be put to a referendum. However, the Constitutional Court concluded relatively early on that other restrictions on referendums can be inferred from

János Mécs, 'Az egyértelműség követelménye az országos népszavazási kérdések hitelesítése során' (Jogi Tanulmányok, ELTE Állam-és Jogtudományi Kar Állam-és Jogtudományi Doktori Iskola, 2018); similar results in Antalicz (n 8) 185–187.

[18] 53/2001 (XI. 29.) CC decision and later: 46/2006 (X. 5.) CC decision, 90/2008 (VI. 19.) CC decision.

[19] This is also worth noting because the Curia made it clear from the beginning that it would adhere to the previous practice of the Constitutional Court, see: Kvk.O.37.300/2012/2.

[20] This interpretation was consistently upheld by the Curia in Knk.VII.37.647/2018/2, Knk.IV.38.258/2018/2, Knk.VII.37.695/2016/3, Knk.IV.37.222/2016.

[21] See László Komáromi, 'A Kúria határozata a felcsúti labdarúgó-stadionról szóló népszavazási kezdeményezésről' [2013] 4 JeMa 37.

the Constitution.[22] As one consequence, restrictions have started to emerge in the judicial practice based on the 'constitutional functions' of referendums.

One line of argument is based on the importance of the question, which is clearly linked to the positive scope of referendums.[23] The preamble of the Referendum Act states that 'it is part of the democratic exercise of power that when deciding the most important issues affecting the country, the citizens are involved directly, through referendum.' It is rare that the sole legal base for not validating a question is that the question is not important enough, usually this is a supporting argument.[24] In the 9/2012. (III. 9.) CC decision, however, the lack of importance argument was the only reason for rejecting an initiative. The initiative proposed that the Constitutional Court should be legally mandated to create a database showing which legal expert works on which decision. The State Election Commission, which was the predecessor of the National Election Commission, refused to authorize the question, stating that it is contrary to the constitutional functions of direct democracy, as it was clearly not a question that belongs to the most important issues affecting the country. The Constitutional Court upheld this decision by a one-line reasoning stating that the plea was unfounded. In the jurisprudence of the Curia, the importance of the question requirement is also traceable,[25] although its practice is not consistent. In two recent decisions, the Curia reached contradictory conclusions on whether the importance of the question could be a ground for refusing validation.[26] In both cases the referendum initiatives were about whether the highest state officials shall be entitled to special health care. In the Knk.IV.38.258/2018/2 decision the Curia used the lack of importance of the question as a supporting argument for refusing the initiative. In the Knk. VII.38.256/2018/2 decision, in contrast, it held that even though the preamble of the Referendum Act contains a reference to the importance of referendum questions, the refusal of the validation of an initiative could only be based on the grounds explicitly contained in the Constitution and the Referendum Act.

The other line of argument stems from the principle of exercising rights in good faith in accordance with their purpose. However, this ground for refusal is not connected to the content of the question, but rather to the conduct of the

---

[22] 25/1999 (VII. 7.) CC decision, which upheld the practice that constitutional amendments are prohibited, even though the limits on referendums had been reformed in 1997 and the then new rules did not contain such a limitation.

[23] See 18/2008 (III.12.) CC decision or Curia decision Kvk.III.37.223/2016/2 about the infamous case of the concurrent Sunday shop closing initiatives (also in: Pállinger (n 6) 21–22).

[24] Mostly to support the clarity requirement, see 75/2009 (VII. 10.) CC decision.

[25] See Knk.IV.37.484/2013/2.

[26] Knk.VII.38.256/2018/2 and Knk.IV.38.258/2018/2.

initiators. This principle first appeared in the height of the referendum frenzy in 2006–2007. A number of questions were submitted to validation that were deemed frivolous or contained the same issue in different versions of wordings. The Constitutional Court held in the 18/2008. (III.12.) CC decision that the practice of submitting a question and then withdrawing and resubmitting it without the real intention of having a referendum is in violation of this principle. Similarly, in a recent decision the Curia held that submitting the same questions with only minor differences in wording revealed the intent of the organizers to leave it up to the election commission to choose the proper version, which could also be in violation of the principle.[27]

3.2 Constitutional Amendments as Prohibited Issues

One of the most important changes to the provisions on referendums in the new Fundamental Law was that the list of prohibited subjects was expanded to include constitutional amendments. This change codified a respective practice of the Constitutional Court. Since 1993 the Constitutional Court had consistently held that an issue cannot be allowed to be submitted to a referendum if it envisages an implied amendment of the Constitution.[28] The Court differentiated between ordinary legislative and constitutional competences of the parliament and held that amending the Constitution falls within the exclusive competence of the National Assembly. Citizens could not deprive the National Assembly from this exclusive authority, as popular sovereignty is exercised directly only in exceptional circumstances and within the framework of the Constitution. Nevertheless, the 25/1999. (VII. 7.) CC decision of the Constitutional Court also emphasized that this prohibition only applies to citizen-initiated referendums, while the state institutions can decide to ask for a confirmative referendum on constitutional amendments. In contrast, the new Fundamental Law prohibits constitutional amendments for all types of referendums. This prohibition has far-reaching implications: it is virtually impossible to initiate a referendum on any issue related to fundamental rights or state institutional settings.

In case of fundamental rights, the Curia rather consistently applies the same judicial test. It first examines if the question may envisage the restriction of a fundamental right and then analyses the question based on the necessity–proportionality test created by the Constitutional Court and now enacted in

---

[27] Knk.VII.37.959/2017/3; see also Knk.VII.37.520/2017/2 and Knk. VII.37.523/2017/2 and, in a different context, Kvk.III.37.223/2016/2 about the infamous case of the concurrent Sunday shop closing initiatives; see also Pállinger (n 6) 21–22.

[28] 2/1993 (I. 22.) CC decision.

Article I (3) of the Fundamental Law. According to this test 'a fundamental right may only be restricted to allow the effective use of another fundamental right or to protect a constitutional value, to the extent absolutely necessary, proportionate to the objective pursued and with full respect for the essential content of that fundamental right'.[29] If the collision between fundamental rights or values can only be lifted through the amendment of the Constitution, the referendum question cannot be authorized. The Curia has applied this test in a series of anti-corruption questions.[30] In the Knk.IV.37.416/2015 case, the initiators aimed to oblige the family members of politicians and government leaders to publicly declare their assets. The Curia held that this would be a disproportionate restriction of the protection of personal data. First, the Curia stated that in the current regulatory framework both high-level state officials and their family members are obliged to declare their assets, with the one major distinction that only the declarations made by state officials are public information. Making information on private assets public presents a conflict between the protection of personal data encompassed in the respect for private life and the transparency (and accountability) of public life. The Court held that even though the latter fundamental value can necessitate the restriction of private life, the publication of private assets is not a proportionate restriction in case of family members. While high-level state officials voluntarily accept their position, knowing that it entails the obligation to make their private assets transparent, this voluntary element is missing in the case of family members. Thus, they would be obliged to publish private information without their consent or control, which would be a disproportionate restriction of their private sphere.

The National Election Commission applies the same test to deal with questions of fundamental rights – for instance, when questions regarding the reinstatement of the death penalty resurface from time to time.[31] In these cases, the National Election Commission cites the landmark case of the Constitutional Court on the abolishment of the death penalty, which held that the death penalty not only restricts the right to life and human dignity but amounts to a complete and irreversible elimination of their essential content.[32] It follows that the reinstatement of the death penalty would require the amendment of

---

[29]   See for example 64/1991. (XII. 17.) CC decision, 22/2003. (IV. 28.) CC decision.

[30]   Knk.IV.37.386/2015/3, Knk.IV.37.387/2015/3, Knk.IV.37.388/2015/3, Knk. IV.37.416/2015/2, Knk.IV.37.488/2015/3.

[31]   See for example Decisions 130/2015, 122/2015, 99/2015, 50/3013 or Decisions 1/1999 (I. 14.), 49/2005 (XII. 15.).

[32]   23/1990. (X. 31.) CC decision http://www.codices.coe.int/NXT/gateway.dll/ CODICES/precis/eng/eur/hun/hun-1990-s-003?fn=document-frameset.htm$f= templates$3.0, accessed 1 April 2020.

the constitutional guarantees of the right to life and human dignity and thus falls within the referendum exception.[33] Interestingly, the State Election Commission used a different argument before 2013 to refuse such questions: it based the refusal on the prohibition of holding referendums on obligations arising from international treaties, as Hungary has ratified the Second Optional Protocol to the International Covenant on Civil and Political Rights, aiming at the abolition of the death penalty.[34]

To my knowledge, the Curia has validated only one question where the claim was based on fundamental rights and values. In the Knk.VII.37.424/2017/2 decision it upheld the validation decision of the National Election Commission regarding a question that aimed at increasing the limitation periods for corruption crimes. A citizen challenged the validation decision and argued that the *ratione temporis* of the question was not clear, which violated the principles of rule of law and *nulla poena sine lege*, as the longer limitations could apply for crimes already committed. The Curia argued that the principle of non-retroactivity is part of the criminal legislation, so in case of a successful referendum, the new provisions on the statute of limitations could be adopted and interpreted only in a way to adhere to these principles. This implies that the referendum would not result in amendment of these constitutional values.

Questions on institutional settings are equally rare to reach a vote. In recent years there have been a series of attempts to limit the re-election of the prime minister to the maximum of two government cycles.[35] Although the Constitution is silent about this question, the Curia held each time that the introduction of such a limit would require the amendment of the Constitution. According to its reasoning, the position of the prime minister is a key element in a parliamentary system, as the parliament has the sovereignty to elect the prime minister who is then accountable to the representative body. Introducing a term limit would encroach on the liberty of parliament to choose a prime minister and change the state structure envisaged by the Constitution and thus cannot be the subject of a referendum. These decisions are particularly *[sic!]* interesting as they equate the Constitution being silent about a question with its being implicitly regulated, thus widening the scope of this prohibition.[36]

---

[33] See for example Decision 99/2015.

[34] See for example Decisions 353/2009 or 1/1999 (I. 14.).

[35] Knk.IV.37.790/2013/2, Knk.IV.37.394/2017/3, Knk.IV.37.394/2017/3 and Knk. IV.37.567/2018/2.

[36] See also Csaba Erdős, 'A Kúria két határozata a miniszterelnöki ciklusok számának maximalizálására irányuló népszavazási kezdeményezésekről' [2017] 4 JEMA 41.

3.3 Obligations Arising from International Treaties as Prohibited Issues

Since substantive prohibitions on referendums have existed in the Hungarian system, international obligations have always been among them. However, the wording of this prohibition has changed with the Fundamental Law. Under the old Constitution, the prohibition attached only to valid, ratified international obligations, which meant that it was possible to have referendums about future international obligations or even an international treaty that had already been signed by Hungary but not yet ratified.[37] The Fundamental Law left out the reference to 'valid' international treaties, so that it is now questionable whether an international treaty not yet in force can be the subject of a referendum.[38] By contrast, referendums about leaving international organizations to which Hungary is a party (EU, NATO, UN) can never be the subject of a referendum.[39]

The case law shows that the prohibition of holding referendums about international obligations is usually clear when international treaties are affected.[40] However, placing EU law obligations within this system still poses challenges. While in cases about primary sources of EU law the Curia emphasizes their international legal character, in cases about secondary legal sources their 'special legal status' is highlighted. Regarding a question about prohibiting foreign nationals from acquiring agricultural land, the Curia stated that even though all provisions of EU law have become part of the Hungarian legal system, it shall not be forgotten that the Treaty of Accession is still an international treaty and thus the question was prohibited.[41]

Meanwhile the Curia reached a different conclusion in case of the quota-referendum. After the National Election Commission had authorized the government-initiated question 'Do you want the European Union to be able to mandate the obligatory resettlement of non-Hungarian citizens into Hungary even without the approval of the National Assembly?', the Curia upheld the validation in the Knk.IV.37.222/2016/9 decision. The Curia argued that the

---

[37] The question has arisen in relation to the Constitutional Treaty of the EU and the confirmatory vote initiated on the subject; see 58/2004 (XII. 14.) CC decision.

[38] Pállinger (n 6) 11 and László Komáromi, 'A népszavazásra vonatkozó szabályozás változásai az Alaptörvényben és az új népszavazási törvényben' [2014] 35 MTA Law Working Papers 6.

[39] Kvk.II.37.186/2012/2, Kvk.II.37.185/2012/2, Kvk.II.37184/2012/2 or Knk. IV.37.712/2016/2.

[40] See cases about blocking the expansion of the Paks nuclear power plant: Knk. IV.37.358/2015/3, Knk.37.178/2014/3.

[41] Knk.IV.37.446/2014/3.

question was related to the Council Decision (EU) 2015/1601 on establishing provisional measures in the area of international protection for the benefit of Italy and Greece,[42] which was part of the secondary legal sources of EU law. As such it was part of the special legal order of the EU, which cannot be equated with obligations arising from international treaties. The Fundamental Law regulates the sovereignty transfer to the EU (Article E) and international treaty obligations (Article Q) separately, and according to the Curia only the latter belong to the prohibited issues.

All parties challenging the quota-decision argued that the question did not even belong to the competences of the National Assembly, as the Government was allowed to take part in the EU decision-making procedures and the National Assembly had no influence on EU decisions reached in the Council. The Curia laconically refused these arguments by stating that the legislative competences of the National Assembly are open towards any social relation and can regulate any issue.[43] In contrast, in a later case about joining the European Public Prosecutor's Office, the Curia emphasized that the decision to participate in the Council Regulation on the establishment of the European Public Prosecutor's Office[44] was left to the Government as the main actor of the Council and outside the scope of functions of the National Assembly.[45]

3.4 Fiscal Legislation as a Prohibited Issue

A large number of initiatives are refused in Hungary because they would affect the content of fiscal legislation. The Constitutional Court laid down the main principles that govern this prohibited subject in its 51/2001 (XI. 29.) CC decision.[46] The Court emphasized that prohibited issues should be interpreted

---

[42] Council Decision 2015/1601 of 22 September 2015 establishing provisional measures in the area of international protection for the benefit of Italy and Greece [2015] OJ L 248.

[43] Here the decision quotes the Knk.IV.37.807/2012/2. decision, which reached significantly different conclusions about legislative and executive power.

[44] Council Regulation 2017/1939 of 12 October 2017 implementing enhanced cooperation on the establishment of the European Public Prosecutor's Office ('the EPPO') [2017] OJ L 283.

[45] Knk.VII.37.942/2018/2.

[46] Additionally, the 2008 'three-yes' or 'social' referendum was surrounded by debates about this principle, more specifically, about the distinction between the revenue and the expenditure side of the budget and the type of revenues that can be the subject of referendums. See 15/2007 (III. 9.) CC decision, 16/2007 (III. 9.) CC decision, 32/2007 (VI. 6.) CC decision, 33/2007 (VI. 6.) CC decision, 34/2007 (VI. 6.) CC decision, 58/2007 (X. 17.) CC decision, 59/2007 (X. 17.) CC decision, 60/2007 (X. 17.) CC decision and later: Knk.IV.37.339/2015/3.

narrowly and the fiscal restriction could not be interpreted in a way to cover all legislative acts with fiscal-monetary impact as virtually all issues within the functions of the National Assembly have such an impact. It held that this restriction covers three cases: a referendum cannot oblige the National Assembly to amend the current annual acts on the central budget or acts on the implementation of the central budget, and it cannot aim to precisely determine single fiscal expenditures of future acts on the central budget. This interpretation has been upheld by consequent decisions, although the narrow interpretation of these budgetary acts has widened over the years. In general, it is usually a clear case of a prohibition when the current budget is affected. However, when future revenues or expenditures are in question, the election commission and the courts are not always consistent in determining how close the connection between the question and the budgetary issue must be to warrant refusal of the validation.[47]

4.   FORMAL LEGAL LIMITS ON REFERENDUMS

Article 9 of the Referendum Act states that 'the question proposed for referendum shall be worded in such manner that it allows a straightforward response, and permits the National Assembly to decide – on the basis of the outcome of the referendum – whether it has the obligation to make a law, and if so, what kind of a law.' Over 70 per cent of the referendum questions are not validated due to violation of this clarity of question requirement.[48]

Based on the landmark 52/2001 (XI. 29.) CC decision a question proposed for a referendum has to fulfil two – sometimes contradictory – conditions: clarity for voters and clarity for legislation. A question has to be clear and straightforward for the voters, without requiring the use of legal or other scientific terms. At the same time, it must be clear for the legislator if and what kind of legislative obligations the question creates. These two requirements often contradict each other, as the more precisely the question is formulated, the easier it is for the legislature to implement the results, but the more difficult it is for the voters to understand it.[49] A proposed issue can consist of several questions. However, if they contradict each other or their internal connection is not clear or they are not connected substantively to each other, then the clarity

---

[47]   See Knk.IV.37.467/2015/2 Decision annulled by 28/2015 (IX. 24.) CC decision; see also László Komáromi, 'Az Alkotmánybíróság határozata a nőkre vonatkozó kedvezményes nyugdíjba vonulási feltételek férfiakra történő kiterjesztésére irányuló népszavazási kezdeményezésről' [2016] 1–2 JEMA 5.

[48]   Mécs (n 17) 110–111.

[49]   See   at   Curia   Knk.VII.37.371/2017/2,   Knk.VII.37.336/2017/3,   Knk. IV.37.333/2017/5, Knk.VII.37.326/2017/3.

of question requirement is violated.[50] As it can be seen, this interpretation of the clarity requirement basically contains a unity of substance requirement as well and implicitly excludes longer legal texts or whole legislative acts as questions.

When reviewing questions, the election commissions and courts tend to look beyond the wording of the question and examine the whole legal environment that the question touches upon, including the legal consequences. An example for this trend is the question of free beer. In the first major influx of referendum questions in 2006–2007, the now still existing Two-tailed Dog Party submitted the question 'Do you agree that the customers of restaurants and pubs should not pay for beer?' The Constitutional Court held in the 26/2007. (IV. 25.) CC decision that the question is neither clear for the legislator nor for the people, because it does not point to a source of revenue that should cover the cost of free beer. The voters could not foresee the consequences of their decision and thus it would be not clear for them what they would vote about. This decision is a landmark case because it opened the door to a very searching review under the criterion of clarity. Another great example of this judicial attitude is a more recent decision of the Curia upholding the refusal of the National Election Commission to authorize the question 'Do you agree that all places of business should be closed on Sunday?', because voters could not foresee the changes such a ban would bring to everyday life.[51] Involving the foreseeable consequences of a question opens up the analysis to a level that virtually any question can be deemed unclear, as any issue can have multiple legal, economic or social consequences.

This expansive review is coupled with a tendency to overly 'protect' voters from complex issues, regardless of the publicity of the issue. In recent years there has been a tendency to submit referendum questions in reaction to current political events. For example, a number of questions were submitted about the status of the Central European University (CEU) and, even more recently, about an amendment of the Labour Act that started a wave of street protests in the winter of 2018. The initiators of the CEU referendums submitted variously worded proposals that all aimed at abrogating the new conditions of the Act on National Higher Education for foreign higher education institutions which CEU could no longer fulfil. One of these initiatives contained CEU specifically, but the others were worded in a more general manner. None of them were authorized by the National Election Commission, and the Curia upheld the refusal decisions. The one mentioning CEU was refused due to the fact that it would create an unconstitutional discriminatory situation if only CEU was

---

[50] 52/2001 (XI. 29.) CC decision.
[51] Knk.IV.37.174/2015/2.

exempted,[52] while the more generally worded proposals were refused based on the requirement of clarity: the questions would require voters to have such a deep understanding of complex legal issues that only experts or directly affected persons could have.[53] This argument could be true if these questions existed in a vacuum. However, they were submitted at the highpoint of political debate and protests. Similar arguments were raised about the amendment of the Labour Act initiative.[54] By contrast, the Curia used a rather lenient approach to clarity in the quota-referendum,[55] even though the legal challenges against the authorization decision of the National Election Commission all raised different concerns about clarity. The Curia held that the question does not violate the requirement of legislative clarity, because the National Assembly could fulfil its obligation not only by the adoption of a legal act, but also by other regulatory instruments. Furthermore, the term 'resettlement' contained in the referendum question was clear as it meant to voters that non-Hungarian citizens would be moved to Hungary for a longer period.[56]

5.   INSTITUTIONS AND PROCEDURES FOR REVIEWING THE LIMITS OF REFERENDUMS

5.1   Institutions Reviewing the Limits of Referendums

The initial decision about authorizing a referendum is an administrative decision in the Hungarian system. Before 2013 the State Election Commission was in charge of validating referendum questions, now it is the National Election Commission. A common feature of both the former and the current central election commissions is that they include(d) elected as well as delegated members. The idea behind this construction is to create an independent body through the elected members, while at the same time providing for participation and representation of the candidates of elections and the political groups elected to the National Assembly. This, however, creates a fragile balance within the commission that changes from election to election.

The rules about the National Election Commission are laid down by the Act on Electoral Procedure.[57] The National Election Commission shall have at least

---

[52]   Knk.IV.37.427/2017/3.

[53]   Knk.IV.37.425/2017/3 and Knk.IV.37.426/2017/3.

[54]   In Knk.IV.37.164/2019/3 the Curia hold that without a knowledge of the system of the Labour Act the question is not clear for voters.

[55]   See: Pállinger (n 6) 24.

[56]   Knk.IV.37.222/2016/9.

[57]   Act XXXVI of 2013 on Electoral Procedure https://www.valasztas.hu/documents/538536/548702/Act+XXXVI+of+2013+on+Electoral+Procedure.pdf/2e82a257-b592-4819-923f-eac4a18cfec6, accessed 1 April 2020.

seven elected members, who all have to have university-level law degrees.[58] Conflict of interests rules guarantee that the elected members are neither high-level state or local government officials, nor members or candidates of political parties.[59] The members are elected for nine years by the National Assembly with the vote of two-thirds of the members of parliament present.[60] Even though the elected members have always been elected by parliament, it is a new element of the regulation that the term of their mandate is longer than an election cycle. Prolonging their terms can be seen both as a sign of ensuring their independence and as a way to lock in future election decisions. The number of delegated members depends on the number of political groups in the National Assembly (currently also seven), while before general elections or elections to the European Parliament it depends on the number of nominating organizations putting forward national candidate lists.[61] The mandate of the delegated members from the parliamentary groups lasts from the inaugural session of the National Assembly until the date of the general elections are set. From then until the inaugural session of the new National Assembly, the nominating organizations delegate the members. For instance, at the last general elections in 2018, in total 23 organizations put forward a national candidate list, which meant that 23 organizations gained the right to delegate a member to accompany the seven elected members during the election campaign.

The work of the National Election Commission is assisted by the National Election Office, which is an autonomous government agency with a president appointed by the President of the Republic on a proposal of the prime minister.[62]

The availability of judicial review (by the Constitutional Court) was first introduced in 1997 as part of the then-new Act on Electoral Procedure.[63] Initially, review was only provided against decisions related to citizen-initiated referendums. However, the Constitutional Court held in the 64/1997. (XII. 17.) CC decision that legal certainty as part of the rule of law requires that a preliminary constitutional review shall be available for all types of referendums. When the new Fundamental Law was adopted in 2011, the review powers were transferred to the Curia, which as a regular court was more equipped to deal with the heavy referendum caseload. The Curia is the highest regular court in Hungary, which provides extraordinary remedy in criminal, civil and

---

[58] Art. 14, 17 Act on Electoral Procedure.
[59] Art. 18 Act on Electoral Procedure.
[60] Art. 20 Act on Electoral Procedure.
[61] Art. 27 Act on Electoral Procedure.
[62] See at https://www.valasztas.hu/web/national-election-office/national-election -office, accessed 1 April 2020.
[63] Act C of 1997 on Electoral Procedure.

administrative law cases as well as ensures the uniformity of the application of law by ordinary courts. The review of referendum decisions belongs to the Administrative Department of the Curia.

Until 2012, a single-level judicial review was available against the decisions of the election commission. However, the transfer of review powers to the Curia opened the door to a further extraordinary remedy procedure to the Constitutional Court. The decision of the Curia to uphold or change the authorization decision is considered to be a regular judicial decision, which means that a constitutional complaint procedure is available.[64] This remedy procedure is rare, because the Constitutional Court applies a strict admissibility test.

5.2   Procedures for Reviewing the Limits of Referendums

All referendum initiatives must be submitted to the National Election Commission, which checks both the formal and substantive admissibility of the question. Article 10 of the Referendum Act empowers the President of the National Election Office to reject an initiative that is obviously contrary to the constitutional purposes of the legal institution of the national referendum or does not comply with some basic formal requirements.[65] There is no remedy against this decision, but the question can be resubmitted and then it must be put on the agenda of the National Election Commission.

Under Article 11 of the Referendum Act, the National Election Commission decides about the validation of the question within 30 days of its submission, preliminary to signature collection. The Commission meetings are open to the public, so the initiators can participate in the meeting. However, the election commission is free to decide what kind of evidence it uses to support its decision. It may – on request – allow the initiators to present an oral statement,[66] but it is not obliged to do so. The Commission either certifies or refuses the question as a whole; it does not have a competence to modify the wording of the initiative or to validate parts of it.

Anyone affected by the decision can apply for a remedy at the Curia within 15 days of the publication of the resolution.[67] According to the consistent practice of the Curia, 'affectedness' must be widely interpreted and can encompass basically anyone. The legal interest in the outcome of the ref-

---

[64]   See Art. 233 Election Procedure Act, Art. 24(2) Fundamental Law and Art. 27 Act on the Constitutional Court.

[65]   For instance, the organizer has not provided personal information or signatures from 20–30 supporters, the question was not submitted by mail or in person, or the moratorium to submit a question with same content applies.

[66]   Art. 43 Election Procedure Act.

[67]   Based on Art. 1, 29 Referendum Act and Art. 222 Election Procedure Act.

erendum case exists based on the right to vote in the referendum. In the Knk. IV.37.222/2016/9 decision on the quota-referendum, the Curia stated that affectedness is always determined based on the content of the question, so in the instance of the quota-referendum all Hungarian inhabitants were affected.[68]

The referendum procedure at the Curia is considerably different from other administrative law remedy procedures. The Referendum Act determines a 90-day deadline for reaching a decision (30 days if the election commission resolution was not on the merits of the question). The decision is reached in a non-trial procedure, which means that the three-judge panel decides in chambers based on written submission. A trial or an open hearing cannot be held in referendum procedures, thus parties do not have a right to be heard. The Curia decides the merits of the case by the adoption of a resolution, either upholding or altering the resolution of the National Election Commission.[69] This is a crucial point with regard to the enforcement of due process guarantees. In other administrative law cases, if the Curia notices that the administrative body or the lower-level court conducted a procedure in serious violation of procedural rules, it annuls the lower-level decision and instructs the administrative body or court to conduct a new procedure that adheres to the due process guarantees. In referendum cases, the Curia does not have cassation powers. Furthermore, the design of its procedure is not equipped to substitute for violations of due process. This means that if the National Election Commission conducts a procedure that is in violation of due process (for instance, it does not decide by majority vote) or if there are other procedural shortcomings (for example regarding affectedness), the Curia has no means to correct the violation.[70] It can observe in its resolution that procedural rights have been violated, but it cannot offer an effective remedy.

Based on Article 233 of the Election Procedure Act, a constitutional complaint to the Constitutional Court can be submitted against the decision of the Curia. This is an extraordinary remedy procedure, so the Constitutional Court adheres to strict standards when deciding about the admissibility of the case. In the 3195/2014. (VII. 15.) CC decision, the Constitutional Court clarified that the constitutional complaint cannot be admitted if it only contests the interpretation of the prohibited subjects by the Curia. Instead, the applicants have to show that the Curia's decision is significantly affected by a violation of the Fundamental Law or that the case raises constitutional law issues of fundamental importance.[71] In addition, the applicants only have standing if the judicial

---

[68] See also Knk.IV.37.002/2018/2, Knk.VII.37.427/2017/3.
[69] Art. 30 Referendum Act.
[70] Knk.VII.37.868/2018/2 or Knk.IV.37.222/2016/9.
[71] Art. 29 Act on the Constitutional Court.

decision is contrary to the Fundamental Law because it violates their rights laid down in it.[72] If admitted, the Constitutional Court decides 'within reasonable time' based on the petition and other written submissions available.[73]

6.   TRENDS AND CONCLUSIONS

As mentioned earlier, more than 90 per cent of referendum initiatives are rejected by the election commission and the courts. The Hungarian legal system imposes many restrictions on referendums and these restrictions are usually interpreted widely. Thus, the institutional positions and practices of the election commission and the courts also play a crucial role in the rejection rates.

The decision-making practice is strongly influenced by the former decisions of the Constitutional Court.[74] Today, the Curia also actively shapes the judicial practice of referendums, which the National Election Commission follows. Even though the National Election Commission is a special administrative body whose constantly changing composition of elected and delegated members could politically influence its decisions, the existence of judicial review constrains such trends. It could not even be said that the National Election Commission follows a stricter or a more lenient practice than the courts.[75] All referendum authorities follow a very restrictive practice.

Both the Constitutional Court and the Curia have expanded the formal and substantive limits, usually as a reaction to an unexpected development in practice. For instance, the influx of 'not serious' questions[76] in 2007 gave way to analysing legal consequences in clarity review or requiring referendum questions to cover 'important issues' or to be submitted 'in good faith in accordance with their purpose'. However, these additional requirements have been built into the practice and have started to expand themselves.[77]

---

[72]   Art. 27 Act on the Constitutional Court; see for instance 3130/2016 (VI. 29.) CC decision or 3117/2019 (V. 17.) CC decision.

[73]   Based on Art. 57 Act on the Constitutional Court, the Court may order a hearing, but it has never done so in a referendum case.

[74]   The 31/2013 (X. 2.) CC decision explicitly upheld the previous practice.

[75]   Since the power of judicial review has been transferred to the Curia, the Curia has reversed a refusal decision of the National Election Commission (and thus authorized the respective referendum question) in only 11 cases out of the 198 cases decided between 2012 and August 2019. In four cases it has reversed an acceptance decision.

[76]   The free-beer question was followed by questions like 'Do you want to have a mountain on Hortobágy?'

[77]   For instance, in a recent decision the National Election Commission argued that a referendum question about the term limit of the attorney general was in violation of exercising rights in good faith in accordance with their purpose because of its political

Additionally, the interpretation of the explicit limitations has also widened over time. For example, the prohibition of holding referendums on constitutional amendments can be now interpreted in a way that also the silence of the Fundamental Law on a specific issue falls under it, while the monetary-fiscal prohibition can cover even very indirectly related questions.[78] Even though both the Constitutional Court and the Curia have created judicial tests to analyse the applicability of the limits, these tests leave a large margin of discretion to the National Election Commission and to the courts themselves. This leeway shows especially in the inconsistencies of the practice, as for example the strict interpretation of clarity breaks down in the quota-decision.[79]

The judicial review unifies the practice, but also juridifies the referendum process. In general, judicial decision-making adheres only to legal standards of review. As a trend, the Curia even overemphasizes the legal character of review in order to distance itself from the political realities behind the questions and from the possible political attacks. A judicial review is a legal review and should not take account of political reasons, but referendum cases – and especially cases about clarity – should not be decided completely in the abstract, as if they did not exist in a social-political reality.

The heightened scrutiny of legal limits blocks almost all initiatives before citizens could become aware of them and show their support. However, the validation of more questions would not necessarily lead to more referendums, let alone to more successful referendums. The Hungarian referendum practice shows that only political parties with strong support can gather the necessary amount of signatures, and the heightened quorum requirements are almost impossible to reach. Only two of the seven referendums held since 1989 would be valid under the current quorum requirements.[80] Even the Government could not reach them in the quota-referendum, despite spending more money on the campaign than both sides of the Brexit campaign together.[81]

---

motivations. The Curia rightly held that neither the National Election Commission nor the Curia itself has the authority to inquire into the political motivations of a question (Knk.VII.37.959/2017/3).

[78]   28/2015 (IX. 24.) CC decision.

[79]   See Pozsár-Szentmiklósy (n 16).

[80]   Voter turnouts in the seven referendums: 1989: 58.03%, 1990: 14.01%, 1997: 49.25 %, 2003: 45.62%, 2004: 37.49%, 2008: 50.51%, 2016: 44.08%. See https://www .valasztas.hu/orszagos-nepszavazasok, accessed 1 April 2020 and István Kukorelli, *Kell-e nekünk népszavazás – Elrendelt népszavazások Magyarországon 1989–2019* (RETÖRKI, Antológia Kiadó, 2019).

[81]   See Tamás Lattmann, 'Referendum on the refugee quotas in Hungary – protection of sovereignty or much ado about nothing?' (*International Law Reflection #7*, 4 October 2016) http://www.dokumenty-iir.cz/ILR/Reflection_7.pdf, accessed 1 April 2020.

13. Latvia

Mārtiņš Birģelis

1. INTRODUCTION

The constitution of Latvia (*Satversme*) sets out a number of ways for citizens to express their will. The people elect the unicameral parliament (*Saeima*) and can also recall it.[1] In addition, they can act as legislator themselves by submitting draft laws and deciding on them in national referendums.[2] Likewise, citizens can decide in a referendum on the laws or amendments to the *Satversme* adopted by the *Saeima*,[3] as well as on other issues put to a national referendum.[4] While the constitution provides for both citizens' legislative initiatives and referendums, it does not comprehensively regulate them. This has been done by the legislator by means of a separate law, namely, the Law on National Referendums and Initiation of Legislation, which was in force until 2012, and, since then, the Law on National Referendum, Legislative Initiative and European Citizens' Initiative[5] (Law on Referendums). Finally, the agenda initiative, regulated by the Rules of Procedure of the *Saeima*,[6] allows 10,000 citizens to place their concerns on the agenda of parliament. While there are no direct-democratic instruments at the local level, new draft legislation that

---

[1] Art. 6–9, 14 *Satversme* (1922. gada 15. februāra Latvijas Republikas Satversme. 'Latvijas Vēstnesis', 1 July 1993 (No 43)). An English version of the *Satversme* is available on the website likumi.lv which ensures free access to systematised (consolidated) legal acts of the Republic of Latvia: https://likumi.lv/ta/en/en/id/57980-the -constitution-of-the-republic-of-latvia, accessed 10 September 2020.

[2] Art. 64, 65, 78–80 *Satversme*.

[3] Art. 72–75, 77, 79, 80 *Satversme*.

[4] Art. 48, 68(3), 68(4) *Satversme*.

[5] 1994. gada 31. marta likums Par tautas nobalsošanu un likumu ierosināšanu. 'Latvijas Vēstnesis', 20 April 1994 (No 47). An English version of the Law on Referendums is available on the website likumi.lv: https://likumi.lv/ta/en/en/id/58065, accessed 10 September 2020.

[6] 1994. gada 28. jūlija Saeimas kārtības rullis. Publicēts oficiālajā laikrakstā 'Latvijas Vēstnesis', 18 August 1994 (No 96). An English version of the Rules of Procedure of the Saeima is available on the website of the *Saeima*: https://www.saeima .lv/en/legislative-process/rules-of-procedure, accessed 10 September 2020.

would provide for a local referendum is currently working its way through the parliamentary process.[7]

Although a number of instruments of direct democracy are thus foreseen by the *Satversme* and various pieces of legislation, recent public polls indicate that around 80 per cent of Latvians do not feel that they have a real opportunity to influence the decisions made by the government or the parliament.[8]

2. EXISTING DIRECT-DEMOCRATIC INSTRUMENTS

2.1 Mandatory Referendum

2.1.1 Amendment of certain constitutional provisions

According to Article 77 of the *Satversme*, amendments of certain constitutional provisions by the *Saeima* must be submitted to a national referendum. These fundamental provisions determine the following:

- Latvia is an independent democratic republic (Article 1 of the *Satversme*);
- The sovereign power of the State of Latvia is vested in the people of Latvia (Article 2 of the *Satversme*);
- The territory of the State of Latvia, within the borders established by international agreements, consists of Vidzeme, Latgale, Kurzeme and Zemgale (Article 3 of the *Satversme*);
- The Latvian language is the official language in the Republic of Latvia. The national flag of Latvia shall be red with a band of white (Article 4 of the *Satversme*);
- The *Saeima* shall be elected in general, equal and direct elections, and by secret ballot based on proportional representation (Article 6 of the *Satversme*);
- Articles 1 to 4 and 6 are subject to a mandatory referendum (Article 77 of the *Satversme* itself).

Since they are regarded as the basis of the legal and political order of the Latvian state, these provisions of the *Satversme* are especially difficult to

---

[7] See database of parliamentary documents (in Latvian): http://titania.*Saeima*.lv/LIVS13/*Saeima*livs13.nsf/webSasaiste?OpenView&restricttocategory=162/Lp13, accessed 6 August 2020.

[8] See Latvijas Sabeidriski Mediji, 'Aptauja: 80% neredz iespējas ietekmēt *Saeima*s un valdības lēmumus' (Survey: 80% do not see opportunities to influence the decisions of the *Saeima* and the government), https://www.lsm.lv/raksts/zinas/latvija/aptauja-80-neredz-iespejas-ietekmet-*Saeima*s-un-valdibas-lemumus.a366282/, accessed 6 August 2020.

amend. Articles 4 and 77 were added to the list in 1998 – Article 4 in order to cement the fundamental value of the Latvian language after Latvia had regained its independence, Article 77 in order to ensure that parliament cannot circumvent the requirement for a referendum by amending this provision itself.

According to the Constitutional Court, a referendum must also be held if the *Saeima* infringes upon the essence of one of these fundamental constitutional provisions by adding new provisions to the *Satversme* or amending legislative acts.[9] For instance, there were extensive debates in Latvia on whether or not joining the European Union (EU) would infringe upon the independence and sovereignty of Latvia as guaranteed by Articles 1 and 2 of the *Satversme*. Eventually, it was concluded that Article 77 of the *Satversme* was not triggered.[10] A similar discussion concerned the treaty on the State Border of Latvia and Russia. In 2007 the Constitutional Court confirmed that a mandatory referendum could be triggered not only by an amendment of the text of Article 3 of the *Satversme* but also by amendments of other regulatory acts. Furthermore, the court held that Article 73 of the *Satversme*, stating that agreements with other nations may not be submitted to a national referendum, is not applicable to the mandatory referendum according to Article 77. Therefore, in general such a treaty may trigger the mandatory referendum. However, the Constitutional Court concluded that the specific treaty in question did not infringe upon Article 3, so that a mandatory referendum was not required.[11]

According to Article 79 of the *Satversme*, an amendment to the constitution submitted for national referendum shall be deemed adopted if at least half of the electorate has voted in favour. In practice, this high threshold makes it very difficult to change the *Satversme*.

So far, the *Saeima* has never amended one of the fundamental articles that would trigger the mandatory referendum. However, a citizens' legislative initiative under Article 78 of the *Satversme* was intended to amend Article 4, according to which the Latvian language is the official language in the Republic of Latvia. The initiative proposed amendments of Articles 4, 18, 21, 101 and 104 of the *Satversme* by introducing Russian as a second official language. Had the initiative been accepted, Latvian and Russian would have become the working languages for self-government institutions and everyone would have had the right to receive official information in Latvian and Russian. However, in the referendum held on 18 February 2012 only 273,347 voters supported the constitutional amendments, while 821,722 voted against

---

[9]   Judgment of 29 November 2007, case No. 2007-10-0102.
[10]   Satversmes grozījumu izstrādes darba grupa, 'Kādēļ Latvijas konstitūcijā nepieciešami labojumi' Jurista Vārds, 15 May 2001, No 14(207).
[11]   Judgment of the Constitutional Court of 29 November 2007, case No. 2007-10-0102.

them. This referendum once again underlined the fundamental value of the Latvian language, sparked discussions on the inviolable core of the *Satversme* and eventually led to the addition of a preamble to the *Satversme* that stresses the constitutional identity of Latvia.

2.1.2 Membership in the European Union

Another mandatory referendum is envisaged by Article 68(3) of the *Satversme*, according to which 'membership of Latvia in the European Union shall be decided by a national referendum, which is proposed by the *Saeima*.' Therefore, joining or leaving the EU will trigger a referendum. This form of the mandatory referendum was only introduced once Latvia had received the invitation for accession to the EU. In May 2003, the Parliament of Latvia adopted amendments to the constitution and the Law on National Referendum and Legislative Initiatives. Importantly, the turnout quorum for this type of mandatory referendum was set considerably lower than that according to Article 77 of the *Satversme*: a decision regarding membership of Latvia in the EU is adopted if the number of voters is at least half of the number of electors who participated in the previous *Saeima* election and if the majority of them have voted in favour of the membership of Latvia in the EU.[12] At the time of writing, the required majority is 497,543 votes. In the referendum held on 20 September 2003, Latvians voted in favour of joining the EU by 66.97 per cent (676,700 votes) in favour and 32.26 per cent (325,980 votes) against.[13]

2.1.3 Adoption of a new constitution

The *Satversme* does not explicitly state whether or not there should be a mandatory referendum if a new constitution is adopted. However, the Constitutional Court has noted that, although the *Satversme* divides state power among Latvian citizens and the *Saeima*, it guarantees the former the exclusive right to repeal the constitution or to establish a new constitutional order.[14] Therefore, it is possible that adoption of a new constitution would be subject to a mandatory referendum. However, there is a view that as long as the new constitution does not change the fundamentals of the *Satversme*, that is, the values included in its Article 77, there is no reason to place a threshold of at least half of the votes in favour for such a new constitution to be adopted.[15]

---

[12] Art. 79(2) *Satversme*.
[13] Results available at: https://www.cvk.lv/cgi-bin/wdbcgiw/base/sae8dev .aktiv03era.vis, accessed 6 August 2020.
[14] Judgment of 29 November 2007, case No. 2007-10-0102, para. 31.1.
[15] Inese Ņikulceva, 'Obligata tautas nobalsosana Latvija – Mandatory referendums in Latvia', Juridiskā zinātne 2010(1), 185, https://www.journaloftheuniversityo

2.2   Optional Referendum

2.2.1   Institution-initiated referendum

2.2.1.1   *Parliament-initiated referendum for substantial changes in EU membership*

According to Article 68(4) of the *Satversme*, 'substantial changes in the terms regarding the membership of Latvia in the European Union shall be decided by a national referendum if such referendum is requested by at least one-half of the members of the *Saeima*'. This referendum allows parliament to trigger a referendum if it has doubts whether a majority of the people would still support membership of the EU despite substantial changes. There is no legal obligation for parliamentarians to trigger it.[16] Only substantial changes regarding integration in the EU, for example substantial changes to the Treaties of the EU, can be submitted to a referendum, but not, for instance, acts adopted by the EU institutions such as directives, regulations, etc. The turnout quorum for this type of referendum is the same as that for the mandatory referendum on membership in the EU according to Article 68(3) of the *Satversme*.[17] No such referendum has been held yet.

2.2.1.2   *Institution/citizens'-initiated referendum to veto a law*

Article 72 of the *Satversme* envisages a mechanism by which the voters may veto a law that has been adopted by the parliament but has not yet been proclaimed (and has thus not yet entered into force):

> The President has the right to suspend the proclamation of a law for a period of two months. The President shall suspend the proclamation of a law if so requested by not less than one-third of the members of the *Saeima*. This right may be exercised by the President, or by one-third of the members of the *Saeima*, within ten days of the adoption of the law by the *Saeima*. The law thus suspended shall be put to a national referendum if so requested by not less than one-tenth of the electorate. If no such request is received during the aforementioned two-month period, the law shall then be proclaimed after the expiration of such period. A national referendum shall not take place, however, if the *Saeima* again votes on the law and not less than three-quarters of all members of the *Saeima* vote for the adoption of the law.

---

flatvialaw.lu.lv/fileadmin/user_upload/lu_portal/projekti/journaloftheuniversityof latvialaw/No1/I_Nikulceva.pdf, accessed 6 August 2020.

[16]   Judgment of the Constitutional Court of 7 April 2009, case No. 2008-35-01, para 19.4.

[17]   Art. 79 (2) *Satversme*.

Once a law has been suspended there are thus two scenarios in which the referendum does not take place: first, if the *Saeima* votes again on the law within two months and three-quarters of its members support the law; second, if the required amount of signatures is not collected.

Once the President has suspended the publication of a law, he or she notifies the text of the law and the decision to suspend it.[18] The Central Election Commission (CEC) then informs all election commissions of cities and municipalities that the collection of signatures has started and delivers the signature collection sheets to them.[19] Collection of signatures lasts for 30 days. The CEC then counts the signatures, establishes the result, reports it to the President and publishes it in the official gazette. If the referendum request has been signed by the required number of voters, the CEC proclaims a national referendum within three days.[20] According to Article 74 of the *Satversme*, the suspended law shall be repealed if the number of voters in the referendum is at least half of the number of electors who participated in the previous *Saeima* election and if the majority has voted for repeal of the law.

The suspension of a law has been triggered five times, four times upon the request of members of the parliament and once by the President. In three cases a referendum was held.[21] However, none of them resulted in a repeal of the law, either because the turnout quorum was not reached or due to insufficient support for a repeal of the law.

2.2.2 Citizen-initiated referendum (citizens' legislative initiative)
Article 78 of the *Satversme* stipulates that:

> electors, in number comprising not less than one-tenth of the electorate, have the right to submit a fully elaborated draft of an amendment to the Constitution or of a law to the President, who shall present it to the *Saeima*. If the *Saeima* does not adopt it without change as to its content, it shall then be submitted to national referendum.

---

[18] Art. 6(1) Law of Referendums.
[19] Art. 6(2) Law of Referendums.
[20] Art. 10(1) Law of Referendums.
[21] For an overview of these referendums, see the website of the CEC (in Latvian) https://www.cvk.lv/lv/tautas-nobalsosanas/tautas-nobalsosanas-latvija, accessed 10 September 2020.

The proposed norms can be aimed at creating a new legal regime[22] or at abolishing the existing one.[23] The citizens' legislative initiative can even be used to amend the fundamental provisions of the *Satversme* that, according to its Article 77, can only be changed by way of a mandatory referendum. The principal aim of Article 77 is to restrict the power of parliament, not of the people.

Although Article 78 of the *Satversme* provides that the electors submit the draft amendment or law to the President, there is an intermediate stage, namely, their submission to the CEC, which reviews and registers the initiative. Upon registration, the initiative group has 12 months to collect the signatures of not less than one-tenth of Latvian citizens.[24] Each signature must be certified by an official body.[25] Signatures can be collected online via the Single State and Local Government Service Portal *latvija.lv* or another online system chosen by the initiative group.[26] Once the required amount of signatures has been collected, the CEC notifies the President of Latvia, who then presents the initiative to the parliament.[27] The *Saeima* must consider the draft amendment or law during the session when it was submitted.[28] If the *Saeima* does not adopt it or adopts it with changes as to its content, the draft amendment or law must be put to a referendum. The referendum is arranged not earlier than one month and not later than two months after parliament's decision.[29]

A draft law is adopted if the number of voters is at least half of the number of electors who participated in the previous *Saeima* election and if the majority has voted in favour of the draft law, while a draft amendment to the Constitution is adopted if at least half of the electorate has voted in favour.[30] The *Satversme* does not prevent the *Saeima* from amending or invalidating the constitutional amendment or law adopted by the people. However, the prevail-

---

[22]   See, for instance, the Draft amendments to the *Satversme* of 7 March 2020, which propose a new way of electing and removing the President, https://www.cvk.lv/ uploads/files/*Satversme*s%20grozijumu%20projekts_Jauna%20Saskana.pdf, accessed 10 August 2020.

[23]   See, for instance, the Draft law on repealing the amendments to the Law of Referendums of 31 August 2018, which consists of only one article aiming at repealing the Law entitled Amendments to the Law on National Votes, Law Initiatives and the European Citizens' Initiative of 8 November 2012, https://www.cvk.lv/upload _file/2015/Likumprojekts%20par%20grozijumu%20TN%20likuma%20atcelsanu.pdf, accessed 10 August 2020.

[24]   Art. 22(1) Law on Referendums.

[25]   Art. 22(3) Law on Referendums.

[26]   Art. 22(4) Law on Referendums.

[27]   Art. 24, 25 Law on Referendums.

[28]   Art. 25 Law on Referendums.

[29]   Art. 11(2) Law on Referendums.

[30]   Art. 79 *Satversme*.

ing opinion in legal doctrine is that only a parliament that has been elected after the referendum can do so.[31]

Since Latvia has regained independence, three citizen-initiated referendums have taken place, all without positive outcome.[32] However, initiatives do not go unnoticed. For instance, in 2008 an initiative that proposed giving the people the right to recall the *Saeima* failed to meet the approval quorum of 50 per cent of the electorate. Nevertheless, that initiative still managed to place the issue on the political agenda, and a year later the parliament amended Article 14 of the *Satversme*, introducing the right to initiate a referendum regarding its recall.

2.3 Agenda Initiative

Since 2012, the Rules of Procedure of the *Saeima* provide for a mechanism by which at least 10,000 citizens, who have reached the age of 16 on the day of filing the submission, can place a topic on the agenda of the parliament. Their collective submission must contain a request to the *Saeima* and a brief justification.[33] Signatures can also be collected electronically,[34] which is mostly done on the website *manabalss.lv*.

Given that the agenda initiative neither leads to a referendum nor binds the legislature to a certain action, its regulation could have been less restrictive. For instance, non-citizens are not allowed to sign an agenda initiative, which is all the more difficult to understand considering that children who have reached the age of 16 are allowed to do so.[35]

So far more than 50 agenda initiatives have been submitted to the *Saeima* and many more are pending. At least 12 of them have resulted in direct legislative changes, 18 have been turned down and the majority of them are still in the process of adoption.[36]

---

[31] Inese Ņikulceva, 'Tautas nobalsošana un vēlētāju likumdošanas iniciatīva' (2012) 104 http://dspace.lu.lv/dspace/bitstream/handle/7/5120/22881-Inese_Nikulceva_2013.pdf?sequence=1&isAllowed=y, accessed 10 September 2020.

[32] For an overview of these referendums, see the website of the CEC (in Latvian) https://www.cvk.lv/lv/tautas-nobalsosanas/tautas-nobalsosanas-latvija, accessed 10 September 2020.

[33] Art. 131³(1) Rules of Procedure of the *Saeima*.

[34] Art. 131³(4) Rules of Procedure of the *Saeima*.

[35] Art. 131³(1) Rules of Procedure of the *Saeima*.

[36] See the website of the Mandate, Ethics and Submissions Committee, http://mandati.*Saeima*.lv/kolekt%C4%ABvie-iesniegumi, accessed 10 August 2020.

3.   LEGAL LIMITS ON DIRECT-DEMOCRATIC INSTRUMENTS

3.1   General Substantive Limits

3.1.1   Precluded subjects according to Article 73 of the *Satversme*

Article 73 of the *Satversme* prescribes that 'the Budget and laws concerning loans, taxes, customs duties, railroad tariffs, military conscription, declaration and commencement of war, peace treaties, declaration of a state of emergency and its termination, mobilisation and demobilisation, as well as agreements with other nations cannot be submitted to national referendum.'

This substantive limit applies to all citizen-initiated and institution-initiated referendums. Initially, there had been a debate about whether it is also applicable to the citizens' legislative initiative, as Article 73 of the *Satversme* does not explicitly preclude the initiation of laws on the subjects listed. Accordingly, some legal scholars argued that the right to propose such laws was not precluded,[37] especially considering that any restriction of this right needed to be interpreted narrowly.[38] That would mean that voters had a right to propose a law on the excluded subjects but, if the *Saeima* rejected it, it could not be submitted to a referendum. Other scholars argued that all matters enshrined in Article 73 of the *Satversme* are within the exclusive competence of the *Saeima*.[39] In 2014 the Constitutional Court put an end to this debate by noting that 'the voters' right to the legislative initiative cannot be exercised with regard to draft laws, which, in accordance with Article 73, cannot be put for national referendums.'[40] So far this has not been a reason for declining to register an initiative, as the excluded matters have been applied narrowly.[41]

The reasons for excluding the matters listed in Article 73 relate to their importance, urgency and complexity. In addition, it is regarded as unlikely that the people would place the overall state interest above their own.[42] Although some legal scholars had initially expected that some of the limits could be

---

[37]   Kārlis Dišlers, *Ievads Latvijas valststiesību zinātnē* (Ansis Gulbis, 1930) 171.

[38]   Inese Nikuļceva, 'Tautas nobalsošana un vēlētāju likumdošanas iniciatīva' (2012) 94–95.

[39]   Jānis Pleps and Edagrs Pastars, 'Vai tauta var Saeimā iesniegt budžeta projektu', Jurista Vārds, 10 September 2002, No 18(251) and 24 September 2002, No 19(252).

[40]   Judgment of 12 February 2014, case No. 2013-05-01, para. 14.4.

[41]   See CEC, Decision of 21 April 2017.

[42]   Annija Kārkliņa, Jānis Lazdiņš, Māris Lejnieks, 'Satversmes 73. panta komentārs' in Ringolda Balodis (eds), *Latvijas Republikas Satversmes komentāri. V nodaļa. Likumdošana* (Latvijas Vēstnesis 2019) 151–153.

removed gradually as civil consciousness would develop[43] and certain limits are today largely devoid of meaning (customs duties, for instance, are nowadays generally regulated at EU level), Article 73 has never been amended.

In practice, Article 73 of the *Satversme* has been interpreted narrowly. For instance, in 2017 the CEC registered an initiative that envisaged removal of property tax in certain occasions, although 'taxes' are listed in Article 73.[44] Similarly, with regard to an initiative that envisaged establishing a minimum amount of old-age pension[45] it was not clear from the beginning if such an issue can be put to a national referendum as it was closely linked to the state budget.[46] However, such a wide interpretation of Article 73 would render the right of people to initiate legislation illusory. The Constitutional Assembly, which had drafted the *Satversme*, had emphasised that the legislative initiative should be an instrument that is effective in practice.[47]

3.1.2 The inviolable core of the *Satversme*

The referendum held in 2012 on Russian as the second official language of Latvia (see Section 2.1.1 above) triggered a discussion on whether Article 73 of the *Satversme* should be amended by also precluding referendums on matters that are incompatible with a democratic society or threaten the foundations of Latvia as a national state.[48] While a respective amendment was not adopted, in September 2012 the President's Constitutional Rights Commission delivered a legal opinion 'On the constitutional basis of the State of Latvia and the inviolable core of the *Satversme*',[49] explaining that the *Satversme* has an inviolable core which cannot be amended. This core supplements the written text of the constitution by prohibiting any changes to the very essence of the

---

[43] Kārlis Dišlers, *Ievads Latvijas valststiesību zinātnē* (Ansis Gulbis, 1930) 171.

[44] Decision of 21 April 2017, https://www.cvk.lv/lv/tiesibu-akti/lemumi/2017 -gads/nr-12-par-partijas-no-sirds-latvijai-iesniegto-likumprojektu-grozijums-likuma -par-nekustama-ipasuma-nodokli, accessed 13 September 2020.

[45] Referendum on draft law 'Amendment to the State Pensions Law', https://www .cvk.lv/en/referendums/referendum-for-amendment-to-the-state-pensions-law.

[46] 'Godmanis atturīgs par to, vai referendums par pensijām atbilstu Satversmei' (Delfi 18 April 2008) https://www.delfi.lv/news/national/politics/godmanis-atturigs -par-to-vai-referendums-par-pensijam-atbilstu-satversmei-papildinats.d?id=20765603, accessed 10 September 2020.

[47] Transcript case materials of IV session of the Constitutional Assembly of Latvia, Vol. 1, p.109 and subsequent.

[48] See Draft law No. 186/Lp11, submitted on 17 January 2012, https://titania .Saeima.lv/LIVS11/Saeimalivs11.nsf/0/8061B5716A3DEDFEC2257988004670D5 ?OpenDocument.

[49] Constitutional Rights Commission, Opinion of 17 September 2012, 'Par Latvijas valsts konstitucionālajiem pamatiem un neaizskaramo *Satversmes* kodolu', http://blogi .lu.lv/tzpi/files/2017/03/17092012_Viedoklis_2.pdf, accessed 10 September 2020.

constitutional identity of Latvia. The core is not identical with the fundamental constitutional provisions listed in Article 77 of the *Satversme*, as these provisions can be amended and not all of them can be said to belong to the very essence of the *Satversme* (the colour of the national flag of Latvia, for instance). Amendments to the provisions listed in Article 77, as well as any other changes to the legal system, cannot be put to a referendum if they collide with the inviolable core of the *Satversme*. What exactly this core encompasses is open to interpretation. However, it is safe to assume that it includes the protection of the Latvian language and the democratic state.[50]

3.1.3   Laws determined to be urgent

According to Article 75 of the *Satversme*, laws that the *Saeima*, by not less than a two-thirds majority vote, determines to be urgent, may not be submitted to a referendum. Resort to urgent laws should be exceptional. The Constitutional Court would most likely regard a routine use of this procedure as contrary to its principles of good legislation.[51]

3.2   General Formal Limits

The referendum questions are generally formulated by the CEC. According to Article 14(1) of the Law on Referendums each ballot paper must include the name of the draft amendment or law to be voted on and the words 'for' and 'against'. As a consequence, voters may have to approve a whole draft law, although they disagree with parts of it, or they have to vote 'against', although they agree with the other parts of it.

In formulating the referendum question, the CEC also takes into account the purpose of the particular referendum. For instance, in the case of the citizen-initiated referendum, Article 79 of the *Satversme* provides that a constitutional amendment or draft law is considered adopted if the required number of voters have 'voted in favour'. Therefore usually the formula 'Are you in favour of [name of the draft law]?' is used.[52] In contrast, in the case of the referendum to veto a law according to Article 72 of the *Satversme* the formula 'Are you in favour of recalling [name of the draft law]?' is used.[53] This

---

50   Ibid.
51   See Judgment of 6 March 2019, case No. 2018-11-01.
52   See, for instance, referendum of 2 August 2008 on Amendments to the *Satversme*, https://www.cvk.lv/lv/tautas-nobalsosanas/par-grozijumiem-*Satversme*-2008, accessed 10 August 2020.
53   See, for instance, referendum of 7 July 2007 on annulment of the laws Amendments to the National Security Act and Amendments to the Law on National Security   Institutions,   https://www.cvk.lv/lv/tautas-nobalsosanas/par-grozijumu

approach has been criticised on the basis that these formulae did not provide sufficient explanation of the subject matter.[54] However, requiring the CEC to formulate a more elaborate referendum question would put an additional burden of responsibility on it.

The most important exception to the use of this standard formula was the referendum on Russian as the second official language. At first, the CEC had formulated the question as 'Are you in favour of [Amendments to the *Satversme*]?'[55] That, however, sparked a discussion on whether the voters were sufficiently able to foresee the consequences of the amendments and thus to express their true will.[56] Therefore, a week later the CEC reformulated the referendum question as 'Are you in favour of the adoption of the Draft Law "Amendments to the *Satversme*" that provides for the Russian language the status of the second official language?'[57]

When a referendum is held on Latvia's membership in the EU or on substantial changes in the terms of Latvia's membership in the EU, the wording of the question is drafted not by the CEC but the *Saeima*.[58] This has happened once, for the referendum on joining the EU in 2003, when the question 'Are you in favour of a membership of Latvia in the European Union?' was drafted by the Legal Commission and Commission of European Affairs of the *Saeima* and then unanimously adopted at the plenary session without further discussions.[59]

3.3 Additional Limits on the Citizens' Legislative Initiative

Besides the general content restrictions that are applicable to all direct-democratic instruments that can trigger a referendum, there are additional legal limits on the citizens' legislative initiative that stem from the requirement of Article 78 of the *Satversme* that initiators must submit 'a fully elaborated draft of an amendment to the Constitution or of a law'. This requirement stems from the fact that the parliament cannot make changes to the draft without submitting it to referendum and similarly, when it comes to a referendum, the people may

---

-nacionalas-drosibas-likuma-un-valsts-drosibas-iestazu-likuma-atcelsanu-2007, accessed 10 August 2020.

[54] See, for instance, Inese Ņikulceva, 'Tautas nobalsošana un vēlētāju likumdošanas iniciatīva' (2012).

[55] See CEC decision of 3 January 2012, No.1.

[56] Diena, 'Referenduma jautājumu papildina ar paskaidrojumu par krievu valodu', 10 January 2012, https://www.diena.lv/raksts/latvija/zinas/referenduma-jautajumu-papildina-ar-paskaidrojumu-par-krievu-valodu-13924997, accessed 10 August 2020.

[57] See CEC decision No. 11, 10 March 2012.

[58] Article 14(1) Law on Referendums.

[59] See the transcript of *Saeima*'s session of 5 June 2003, https://www.Saeima.lv/steno/2002_8/st_030605/st0506.htm, accessed 10 August 2020.

only accept or reject the draft, but not modify it. Therefore, the draft must be sufficiently precise and must fit within the Latvian legal system in case it is adopted. If one part of a draft law does not meet this criterion, it is not possible to rectify this deficiency by, for example, just excluding the inappropriate part of the draft law.[60] The Constitutional Court has noted that '[…] if draft laws of poor quality or unconstitutional draft laws were regularly submitted to national referendums, it would level out the very idea of electors' legislative initiative and over time the civic activity of electors might decrease.'[61] Moreover, the Supreme Court has observed that if the text, nature or purpose of the draft is incomprehensible, ambiguous or misleading, voters cannot make an objective choice and so the result of the referendum cannot be considered to be legally valid.[62] Requiring clarity of the text, nature and purpose of the draft ensures the authenticity of the will of the people and reduces the possibility of illegally influencing the legislative process.[63] This, in turn, includes requirements as to the form and the substance of the draft amendments or laws.

3.3.1   Additional formal limits

That the draft of an amendment to the Constitution or of a law must be 'fully elaborated' follows from Article 78 of the *Satversme* and Article 79(1) of the *Saeima* Rules of Procedure. Proposals that are logically incoherent, unstructured and so on cannot be recognised as being 'fully elaborated' as to their form.[64] A draft law should also include a transitional regulation or provisions on its entry into force, if they are necessary due to the nature of the amendments.[65] Moreover, the legal norms included in the draft must be clear.[66] That is to say, a legal norm must be worded so as to permit people to foresee its precise field of application and its meaning.[67] In some instances, even a textually clear legal norm can fall short of this standard. For example, the initiative on introducing a personal financial liability of members of the parliament provided that the exact procedure by which financial liability is applied was to be developed by the Cabinet of Ministers as a separate draft law. The CEC ruled that

---

[60]   Letter by the *Saeima* Legal Bureau No. 12/13-3-n/36-11/12 to the CEC, published in Jurista Vārds, 2 October 2012, No. 40(739), 18.
[61]   Judgment of the Constitutional Court of 18 December 2013, Case No. 2013-06-01, para. 13.2.
[62]   Judgment of the Supreme Court of 2 March 2020, Case No. SA-1/2020, para. 15.
[63]   Ibid, para. 9.
[64]   Decision of the Constitutional Court of 19 December 2012 to terminate judicial proceedings in the Case No. 2012-03-01, para. 18.3.
[65]   Pastars, E. Referendumu nedienas. Diena, 03.08.2002.
[66]   Judgment of the Supreme Court of 2 March 2020, case No. SA-1/2020, para. 18.
[67]   Judgment of the Constitutional Court of 30 March 2011, case No 2010-60-01 para. 15.2.

the draft law was not sufficiently clear as to the consequences it entails, since it only provided a general idea without elaborating the principles and practical mechanisms for implementing it.[68]

Essential technical requirements to be observed when drafting regulatory enactments, including drafts by citizens,[69] are laid down in the Cabinet Regulation on Drafting Normative Acts[70] and in the Handbook on Drafting Normative Acts.[71] Since it can be challenging for a lay person to draft a law that complies with all the requirements of legal technique, the Supreme Court has noted that only if a draft law is so poorly designed that it cannot be applied should it be regarded as invalid.[72] This can be the case if formal shortcomings have the effect of making the proposed amendment misleading as to its content. Most recently, the Supreme Court found to be misleading a proposed amendment that failed to clearly define the scope of the legislative change.[73] Thus, if a draft substantially violates the principles of legal technique, it most likely will also not meet the standard of being fully elaborated as to its content.

3.3.2 Additional substantive limits

The Constitutional Court has concluded that a citizens' legislative initiative that envisages deciding on issues that are not to be regulated by a law at all cannot be recognised as being 'fully elaborated'.[74] Similarly, the initiative cannot be used to regulate issues that fall within the exclusive competence of certain state organs. For instance, submitting the draft state budget is the exclusive competence of the Cabinet,[75] judicial appointments and removal of judges are an exclusive competence of the *Saeima*,[76] as is electing a President, granting an amnesty[77] and commencing a war.[78] Legal scholars have argued that citizens may propose abstract and general legal norms, but not administra-

---

[68] CEC Decision No. 4, 19 May 2015; Decision No. 3, 2 April 2015.

[69] Judgment of the Supreme Court of 2 March 2020, Case No. SA-1/2020, paras. 13–15.

[70] Cabinet Regulation No. 108, 3 February 2009, https://likumi.lv/ta/id/187822 -normativo-aktu-projektu-sagatavosanas-noteikumi, accessed 10 August 2020.

[71] Normatīvo aktu projektu izstrādes rokasgrāmata, Rīga: Valsts kanceleja, 2016, https://tai.mk.gov.lv/book/1/chapter/23, accessed 10 August 2020.

[72] Judgment of the Supreme Court of 28 March 2014 in Case No. SA-3/2014, para. 9.

[73] Judgment of the Supreme Court of 2 March 2020 in Case No. SA-1/2020, paras. 13–15.

[74] Decision of the Constitutional Court of 19 December 2012 to terminate judicial proceedings in the Case No. 2012-03-01, para. 18.3.

[75] Art. 66 *Satversme*.

[76] Art. 84 *Satversme*.

[77] Art. 45 *Satversme*.

[78] Art. 44 *Satversme*.

tive acts.[79] Also, the authors of the draft should make sure that the obligations of state authorities provided for therein are realistic, both in terms of their nature and the time limits. This refers to practical feasibility, that is, to the ability to comply with the proposal and to achieve the envisaged consequences of the draft.[80]

Moreover, the voters, when exercising their right to submit a legislative initiative, also assume the obligations set for the legislator. As the Constitutional Court has noted, '[…] the principle of legality provides that law and rights are binding on all institutions of state power, including the legislator itself'.[81] The people, in fulfilling the legislative function, thus also have to abide by the requirements of the *Satversme*.[82] Therefore, a draft law that collides with the norms, principles or values contained in the *Satversme*, including its inviolable core, cannot be recognised as being 'fully elaborated'.[83] For example, an initiative, mentioned above, proposing a draft law that would have introduced a personal financial liability of members of the parliament for losses caused by their decisions was also found not to be 'fully elaborated' as it was contrary to Article 28 of the *Satversme*, which provides that members of the parliament cannot be called to account by any judicial, administrative or disciplinary process during the execution of their duties.[84] Similarly, the CEC found an initiative that proposed a new law that provided for a referendum on the introduction of the euro in Latvia not to be 'fully elaborated': it held that all types of referendums are exhaustively listed in the *Satversme*, so that a new type could only be introduced by amending the *Satversme* and not by adopting a law which is lower in the legal hierarchy.[85] The norm may not contradict other norms that are hierarchically higher.[86]

The Supreme Court has made it clear that initiatives must also respect Latvia's international commitments. Accordingly, they must also provide for measures to avoid any possible contradiction with Latvia's international obligations before the entry into force of the proposed amendment or law.[87] For instance, registration was denied to an initiative that provided for the use

---

[79]   Kārlis Dišlers, 'Nekonstitucionāls ierosinājums', Jaunākās Ziņas, 17 June 1927.

[80]   Letter by the *Saeima* Legal Bureau No. 12/13-3-n/36-11/12 to the CEC, published in Jurista Vārds, 2 October 2012, No. 40(739), 18.

[81]   Judgment of the Constitutional Court of 1 October 1999, case No.03-05(99).

[82]   Judgment of the Constitutional Court of 12 February 2014, case No. 2013-05-01, para. 14.4.

[83]   Decision of the Constitutional Court of 19 December 2012 to terminate judicial proceedings in the Case No. 2012-03-01, para. 18.3.

[84]   CEC Decision No. 4, 19 May 2015; Decision No. 3, 2 April 2015.

[85]   CEC Decision No. 5, 31 January 2013.

[86]   Judgment of the Supreme Court of 28 March 2014, case No. SA-3/2014, para.10.

[87]   Judgment of the Supreme Court of 28 March 2014, case No. SA-3/2014.

of the former currency of Latvia as it was found to be in conflict with Latvia's international obligation to introduce the euro.[88]

3.4 Legal Limits on the Agenda Initiative

The Rules of Procedure of the *Saeima* impose a number of substantive limits on the agenda initiative: the request may not be clearly unacceptable in a democratic society or plainly offensive, or undermine values of human dignity, freedom, democracy, equality, the rule of law and human rights.[89] In contrast, the general substantive limits applicable to those direct-democratic instruments that lead to a referendum, including Article 73 of the *Satversme*, are not applicable to agenda initiatives.

As to the formal limits, agenda initiatives must contain a clear request to the *Saeima* and a brief justification of it, and they must specify the natural person authorised to represent the signatories of the collective submission.[90]

4. INSTITUTIONAL AND PROCEDURAL FRAMEWORK FOR REVIEWING COMPLIANCE WITH THE LIMITS

4.1 Institution-initiated Referendums

The principle of legality provides that the law is binding on all state institutions, including the legislator and the President.[91] Consequently a state institution may not initiate a referendum that is incompatible with the *Satversme* by, for instance, putting a draft law that concerns one of the precluded subject matters of Article 73 of the *Satversme* to a referendum. It falls within the competence of the Constitutional Court to review whether the *Saeima* or the President have violated the principle of legality.[92] Such a review procedure could be initiated by another state institution (including the President, the *Saeima*, no fewer than 20 deputies of the *Saeima* or the Cabinet) that considers a given referendum

---

[88] CEC Decision, 14 May 2013.

[89] Art. 131³(2) Rules of Procedure of the *Saeima*.

[90] Art. 131³(1) Rules of Procedure of the *Saeima*.

[91] See, for instance, Judgment of the Constitutional Court of 1 October 1999, case No. 03-05(99).

[92] Art. 16 Constitutional Court Law (1996. gada 5. jūnija Satversmes tiesas likums. 'Latvijas Vēstnesis', 14 June 1996 (No 103)). An English version of the Constitutional Court Law is available on the website likumi.lv: https://likumi.lv/ta/en/en/id/63354 -constitutional-court-law, accessed 10 September 2020.

unconstitutional.[93] If a draft law contrary to the *Satversme* was nevertheless put to a referendum and adopted, that law could later be challenged before the Constitutional Court as any other law adopted by the legislature. To my knowledge, there is no notable precedent where an institution-initiated referendum would have been challenged.

However, two of the direct-democratic instruments that are used most often, the citizens' legislative initiative and the agenda initiative, not only have their own specific limits but also a particular institutional and procedural framework for reviewing compliance with these limits.

4.2   Citizens' Legislative Initiative

The *Saeima* has a constitutional obligation, following from Articles 1 and 78 of the *Satversme*, to establish clear regulations for implementing the citizens' legislative initiative, including by setting up a mechanism for verifying whether the requirements of Article 78 of the *Satversme* are met. Even the people, as one of the legislators, have no right to violate the constitution.[94]

To submit a citizens' legislative initiative and start collecting signatures, first of all, an initiative group must be registered. It can be formed by a political party or an alliance of political parties, as well as by an association of at least ten electors.[95] Once established, the initiative group can register the proposed draft law or draft amendments to the constitution with the CEC, which then reviews the initiative for its compliance with the limits set out above in Section 3.3.

4.2.1   Competence of the CEC
Pursuant to Article 1 of the Law on the Central Election Commission, the CEC is a state institution, established by the *Saeima*, which acts independently. The CEC ensures the implementation of the Law on Referendums[96] and has the right to examine all issues linked to the preparation and conduct of referendums and citizens' legislative initiatives.[97] The CEC consists of nine members, eight of which are elected by the *Saeima* and one is elected by the Supreme Court from

---

[93]   Art. 17 Constitutional Court Law.

[94]   See Judgment of the Constitutional Court of 18 December 2013, case No. 2013-06-01, para. 12; Judgment of the Constitutional Court of 19 May 2009, case No. 2008-40-01, para 9; Decision of the Constitutional Court of 19 December 2012 on terminating judicial proceedings in case No. 2012-03-01, para. 16, 18.3 and 19.1.

[95]   Art. 23(1) and (2) Law on Referendums.

[96]   Art. 4 Law on the Central Election Commission (1994. gada 13. janvāra likums 'Par Centrālo vēlēšanu komisiju'. 'Latvijas Vēstnesis', 20 January 1994 (No 8)).

[97]   Art. 6 Law on the Central Election Commission.

its pool of judges.[98] Already since the adoption of the *Satversme*, the CEC has been entrusted with the jurisdiction to verify compliance of initiative proposals with the requirements of Article 78 of the *Satversme*. Historically it has been recognised that the CEC 'is not an office of technical work or an intermediary institution, which would quite mechanically advance any submitted draft, but is a higher governing institution, which has to see to it strictly that all laws pertaining to the *Saeima* election, legislative initiatives by the people and the national referendums were correctly applied and implemented'.[99] This jurisdiction follows from Article 78 of the *Satversme*, the Law on Referendums and the Law on the Central Election Commission and has been confirmed by the Supreme Court[100] and the Constitutional Court.[101]

The Constitutional Court has recognised that the CEC's jurisdiction comprises an assessment of whether a proposed draft law is 'fully elaborated' in the sense of Article 78 of the *Satversme*.[102] The CEC shall refuse registration of a draft law or draft amendment to the constitution if the initiative group does not conform to the legal requirements or the draft is not compatible with the legal limits, that is, is not 'fully elaborated' with regard to its form or content.[103] The legal assessment carried out by the CEC is distinguishable from the assessment concerning the usefulness or political desirability of a draft, which can only be carried out by the legislator – the *Saeima* or the people. Therefore, the CEC does not have the authority to assess whether a proposal is 'good and desirable'; in this respect, the initiators 'have complete freedom'.[104]

In its decision-making, the CEC abides by the principles of administrative procedure specified in the Administrative Procedure Law.[105] The initiators are invited to the respective meeting and are heard. The CEC also has the right to invite and hear officials of ministries, departments and other state and local

---

[98] Art. 2 Law on the Central Election Commission.

[99] Kārlis Dišlers, 'Vai Centrālajai vēlēšanu komisijai ir tiesība pārbaudīt iesniegtos likumprojektus' (Jurists, 1928, No 5) 135–136.

[100] See, for instance, the Judgment of the Supreme Court of 12 February 2014, case No. SA-1/2014 and Judgment of the Supreme Court of 28 March 2014, case No. SA-3/2014.

[101] See, for instance, Judgment of the Constitutional Court of 18 December 2013, case No. 2013-06-01.

[102] Decision of the Constitutional Court of 19 December 2012 to terminate judicial proceedings in the Case No. 2012-03-01, para. 18.3.

[103] Art. 23(5) Law on Referendums.

[104] Judgment of the Supreme Court of 2 March 2020, case No. SA-1/2020, para. 16.

[105] 2001. gada 25. oktobra Administratīvā procesa likums. 'Latvijas Vēstnesis', 14 November 2001 (No 164). An English version of the Administrative Procedure Law is available on the website likumi.lv: https://likumi.lv/ta/en/en/id/55567-administrative-procedure-law, accessed 10 September 2020; Judgment of the Constitutional Court of 18 December 2013, case No. 2013-06-01.

government institutions.[106] It is its common practice to seek the legal opinions of the Ministry of Justice and the Legal Bureau of the Parliament when reviewing an initiative.

If the CEC concludes that a draft is not 'fully elaborated', it has to refuse registration of the initiative.[107] The law does not authorise the CEC to declare only parts of an initiative invalid, split it up into different parts or amend its wording. Article 23(4) clause 2 of the Law on Referendums, which allows the CEC to set a time limit for the correction of shortcomings of the submission or the draft, is applicable only in case of obvious errors. It cannot be used to instruct the initiators to modify the text of the draft in such a way as to avoid confusion or non-compliance with higher law. Otherwise, the CEC would substitute itself for the authors of the initiative, which would be incompatible with its competence as well as the initiators' responsibility to submit, in accordance with their own will, a fully elaborated draft.[108]

4.2.2   Competence of the Supreme Court

The Constitutional Court has rejected the view that there was no mechanism for reviewing the legality of decisions concerning the implementation of citizens' legislative initiatives.[109] With regard to the CEC's decisions, Article 13 of the Law on the Central Election Commission provides that they, as a general rule, can be appealed in accordance with the procedure set out in the Administrative Procedure Law. Since its amendment in 2012, the Law on Referendums explicitly provides that the initiative group may appeal the decision of the CEC to refuse registration of a draft to the Supreme Court.[110]

The Supreme Court examines the matter as the court of first instance in a panel of three judges in a procedure with open hearing.[111] The burden of proof shall lie with the participants in the administrative proceedings.[112] The court must adopt a decision within two months at most.[113] Its decision is not subject to appeal.[114] There is no norm that would restrict the Supreme Court's jurisdiction to examining only the procedure, in which the CEC adopted its decision. As explained by the Constitutional Court, the Supreme Court should

---

[106] Art. 11 Law on the Central Election Commission.
[107] Art. 23(5) Law on Referendums.
[108] Judgment of the Supreme Court of 2 March 2020, case No. SA-1/2020, para. 10.
[109] Decision of 19 December 2012 by the Constitutional Court on terminating judicial proceedings in case No. 2012-03-01, para. 20.
[110] Art. 23¹(1) Law on Referendums.
[111] Art. 23¹(2) Law on Referendums.
[112] Art. 23¹(4) Law on Referendums.
[113] Art. 23¹(3) Law on Referendums.
[114] Art. 23¹(6) Law on Referendums.

also review the CEC's decision with regard to its substance, that is, whether the draft in question is indeed not 'fully elaborated' and whether the CEC's reasoning meets the requirements.[115]

4.2.3 Competence of the President

If the CEC concludes that the initiative meets the legal requirements, it passes it on to the President. The prevailing view in legal scholarship used to be that the President is obliged to present the initiative to the parliament without any interference.[116] However, in 2012 the Constitutional Court ruled that if the President disagrees with the CEC's decision he or she, 'by employing the lawful means at his [or her] disposal', must see to it that the norms and principles of the *Satversme* are complied with.[117] However, the Constitutional Court did not elaborate on what would be the 'lawful means' at the President's disposal. There are no rules that would regulate a situation where the President disagrees with the CEC's assessment, nor have legal scholars come to a conclusive answer with regard to the legally correct way for the President to ensure compliance with the *Satversme*.[118] Since there is no deadline for the President to submit a draft to the parliament, he or she could wait until reception of a fully elaborated draft from the CEC. The question has not arisen in practice yet, as never has a President refused to forward a draft to the parliament.

4.2.4 Competence of the Constitutional Court

The Constitutional Court has an exclusive jurisdiction to review legal norms for their compliance with norms of higher legal force and declare them invalid.[119] In contrast, it does not have the competence to assess the *application* of legal norms by the institutions of public administration, nor the legality of rulings made by general jurisdiction courts.[120] Consequently, the Constitutional Court is not directly involved in ensuring that legislative initiatives are compatible with the legal limits; it cannot review decisions taken by the CEC or administrative courts. However, especially when the Law on Referendums has

---

[115] Constitutional Court Judgment of 18 December 2013, case No. 2013-06-01, para 15.4.

[116] Kārlis Dišlers, *Ievads Latvijas valststiesību zinātnē* (Ansis Gulbis, 1930) 171.

[117] Decision of the Constitutional Court of 19 December 2012 to terminate judicial proceedings in the case No. 2012-03-01, para. 21.

[118] Anita Rodiņa, 'Valstiskumu pamatu aizsardzības mehānismi' *Tiesību interpretācija un tiesību jaunrade – kā rast pareizo līdzsvaru: Latvijas Universitātes 71. zinātniskās konferences rakstu krājums* (LU Akadēmiskais apgāds, 2013) 232.

[119] Art. 85 *Satversme* and Constitutional Court Law.

[120] See, for example, Judgment of the Constitutional Court of 23 April 2003, case No. 2002-20-0103, para. 7; Judgment of the Constitutional Court of 3 June 2009, case No. 2008-43-0106, para. 12.

been challenged before it, the Constitutional Court has used the opportunity to clarify the legal limits and the competence of other state institutions to review compliance with them.[121]

4.3   Agenda Initiative

After the receipt of an agenda initiative, the Presidium of the *Saeima* is obliged to evaluate, within 20 days, its compliance with the previously mentioned legal limits and decide on forwarding it to the Mandate, Ethics and Submissions Committee (Submissions Committee), which is in charge of an initial evaluation. The person authorised to represent the signatories of the agenda initiative is invited to the meeting of the Presidium.[122] If the Presidium ascertains that the submission does not comply with the legal requirements, it provides a reply to the submission according to the regular procedure for responding to submissions of individuals.[123]

Once the Submissions Committee has received the collective submission it must hold a meeting not later than a month after the collective submission has been filed with the *Saeima*.[124] The person authorised to represent the initiators is again invited to the meeting and has the right to justify the collective submission and take part in the relevant debates.[125]

Not later than three months after the collective submission has been filed, the Submissions Committee drafts a report on its evaluation of the agenda initiative and prepares a draft resolution of the *Saeima* on further processing the initiative.[126] The Committee can recommend specific action to be taken, for instance, to form a special committee of the *Saeima* tasked with preparing a relevant draft law, to forward the collective submission to a relevant institution for further evaluation, to instruct the Cabinet of Ministers to prepare a relevant concept or draft law, or to turn down the initiative.[127] The Committee supervises the fulfilment of the tasks set forth in the draft resolution of the *Saeima* and, if necessary, may prepare other draft resolutions that would ensure fulfilment of a given task.[128] The decision of the *Saeima* regarding the

---

[121]   Decision of the Constitutional Court of 19 December 2012 to terminate judicial proceedings in the case No. 2012-03-01; Judgment of the Constitutional Court of 18 December 2013, case No. 2013-06-01; Judgment of the Constitutional Court of 12 February 2014, case No. 2013-05-01.

[122]   Art. 131⁴(1) Rules of Procedure of the *Saeima*.

[123]   Art. 131⁴(2) Rules of Procedure of the *Saeima*.

[124]   Art. 131⁵(1) Rules of Procedure of the *Saeima*.

[125]   Art. 131⁵(2) and (3) Rules of Procedure of the *Saeima*.

[126]   Art. 131⁵(4) Rules of Procedure of the *Saeima*.

[127]   Art. 131⁵(5) Rules of Procedure of the *Saeima*.

[128]   Art. 131⁵(7) Rules of Procedure of the *Saeima*.

specific actions to be taken cannot be challenged before a court or any other body.

5.   CONCLUSION

The direct-democratic instruments that are used most often in Latvia are the agenda initiative and citizens' legislative initiative. While there are relatively few limits on the agenda initiative, the citizens' legislative initiative is restricted by open-ended substantive and formal legal limits. In practice, the main reason for the rejection of citizens' legislative initiatives is non-compliance with the requirement that the draft must be 'fully elaborated'. This requirement is constantly developed further in legal scholarship and the case law of the Supreme Court and the Constitutional Court. According to the publicly available information, since the end of 2012, 15 citizens' legislative initiatives have been registered,[129] while in nine cases registration has been refused (eight of these initiatives proposed new laws, one proposed amendments to the constitution).[130] The initiators are involved in the registration process before the CEC, and all decisions of the CEC regarding legislative initiatives can be challenged before the Supreme Court.

Since the agenda initiative does not oblige the legislature to take any specific action, the limits on this instrument are much more narrow. It allows the people to put important matters on the political agenda without having to comply with the limits applicable to the citizens' legislative initiative. Although only Latvian citizens have the right to launch an agenda initiative, the instrument is widely used, constantly placing important matters on the parliament's agenda.

There are very few specific formal limits when it comes to the formulation of referendum questions by state institutions. Accordingly, the parliament and the CEC have a wide margin of discretion in drafting them, and there are no precedents where a referendum question would have been challenged. For the sake of legal certainty and clarity, more detailed regulations on the formulation of referendum questions would be desirable.

---

[129] List of initiatives where the process of collecting signatures has been closed: https://www.cvk.lv/lv/iniciativas/veletaju-iniciativas/iniciativas-par-kuram-parakstu-vaksana-noslegusies, accessed 10 August 2020; list of initiatives that are currently in the process of collecting signatures: https://www.cvk.lv/lv/iniciativas/veletaju-iniciativas/registretas-iniciativas, accessed 10 August 2020.

[130] List of initiatives the registration of which was refused: https://www.cvk.lv/lv/iniciativas/veletaju-iniciativas/iniciativas-kuram-registracija-atteikta, accessed 10 August 2020.

14. Russia

Julian Ivan Beriger

1.   INTRODUCTION

In Article 1(1) of the Constitution of the Russian Federation (Constitution)[1] Russia is referred to as 'a democratic federal law-bound state with a republican form of government'. Russia builds on a representative democratic system.[2] According to Article 3(3) of the Constitution, 'the supreme direct expression of the power of the people shall be referenda and free elections'. Article 32(2) enshrines the individual right of Russian citizens to participate in referendums (as well as the right to elect and to be elected). Direct-democratic instruments exist at the federal, regional and municipal levels,[3] including optional and law-initiated (mandatory) referendums as well as an agenda initiative.

In view of its constitutional status, the referendum should play a central role in Russian politics.[4] However, up to now the referendum has mainly been

---

[1]   Конституция Российской Федерации, принята всенародным голосованием 12 декабря 1993 с изменениями, одобренными в ходе общероссийского голосования 1 июля 2020 (Constitution of the Russian Federation, adopted by popular vote on 12 December 1993 with amendments approved in the nationwide vote of 1 July 2020), http://publication.pravo.gov.ru/Document/View/0001202007040001 ?index=1&rangeSize=1. An English translation of the former text is available at <www.constitution.ru/en/10003000-01.htm> both accessed 8 July 2020. At the time of writing this chapter, the recently approved constitutional amendments have not yet been officially translated.

[2]   Otto Luchterhandt, 'Artikel 1' in Bernd Wieser (ed), *Handbuch der russischen Verfassung* (Verlag Österreich 2014) para 14.

[3]   The Russian Federation is a federal state with 85 constituent entities, the federal subjects of the Russian Federation. According to Art. 5(1) and 65(1) of the Constitution there are six different types of federal subjects. Furthermore, there is a municipal level, the so-called 'local self-government' that is regulated in Art. 130–33 of the Constitution. See for the federal structure Марат Викторович Баглай, *Конституционное право Российской Федерации* (Constitutional Law of the Russian Federation) (12th edn, Норма ИНФРА-М 2017) 130–32.

[4]   See for the constitutional status of the referendum Валентина Викторовна Комарова, *Референдумное право и процесс в России* (Referendum law and process

used at the regional and municipal levels. At the federal level, the first referendum since 1993 has been held only on 1 July 2020 on several constitutional amendments.[5]

The lack of practical relevance of the referendum in Russia can be explained by the high legal hurdles (both formal and substantive admissibility requirements) imposed on it by the legislator and the restrictive practice of Russian courts in the remedy procedures.[6]

2. DIRECT-DEMOCRATIC INSTRUMENTS

The direct-democratic instruments at the federal level include the optional citizen-initiated referendum, the mandatory (law-initiated) referendum and the citizens' agenda initiative. At the regional level, the optional citizen-initiated referendum and the referendum on the formation of a new federal subject are provided for by federal law. Beyond that, the regional legislator may foresee executive-, legislative- or subnational entity-initiated regional referendums. At the municipal level exist citizen-, executive- and legislative-initiated referendums.

The referendum at the federal level is regulated by the Federal Constitutional Act No. 5-FKZ 'on the Referendum of the Russian Federation' (Referendum Act).[7] As a federal constitutional law, it derogates the Federal Act No. 67-FZ 'on the basic guarantees of electoral rights and the right of citizens of the Russian Federation to participate in a referendum'[8] (Basic Guarantees Act)

---

in Russia) (Социум 2007) 16–18; Сурен Адибекович Авакьян, *Конституционное право России: Том I* (Constitutional Law of Russia: Volume I) (5th edn, Норма ИНФРА-М 2017) 394–95.

[5]   See Section 6 below.

[6]   See for this contrast on a legislative level Julian Ivan Beriger, 'Sein und Schein von Gesetzgebung im Referendumsrecht Russlands' in Damiano Canapa/ Robin Landolt/Nicola Müller (eds), *Sein und Schein von Gesetzgebung: Erwartungen – Auswirkungen – Kritik* (DIKE 2018).

[7]   Федеральный конституционный закон от 28 июня 2004 № 5-ФКЗ 'О референдуме Российской Федерации' (Federal Constitutional Act of 28 June 2004 No. 5-FKZ 'on the referendum of the Russian Federation') // СЗ РФ 5.7.2004 № 27 ст. 2710.

[8]   Федеральный закон от 12 июня 2002 № 67-ФЗ 'Об основных гарантиях избирательных прав и права на участие в референдуме граждан Российской Федерации' (Federal Act of 12 June 2002 No. 67-FZ 'on the basic guarantees of electoral rights and the right of citizens of the Russian Federation to participate in a referendum') // СЗ РФ 17.6.2002 № 24 ст. 2253. An English translation of an earlier version of the text is available at www.legislationline.org/documents/action/popup/id/4170, accessed 8 July 2020.

that applies only in a subsidiary way.[9] Since the Referendum Act leaves almost no room for the Basic Guarantees Act, the latter *de facto* applies only to referendums at the regional and municipal levels. The municipal referendum is also regulated by the Federal Act No. 131-FZ 'on the general principles of the organization of local self-government in the Russian Federation' (Self-Government Act).[10] This Act also provides for other instruments of direct democracy at the local level, such as town meetings.[11]

2.1 Optional Referendum

2.1.1 Federal level

According to the legal definition in Article 1 of the Referendum Act, the referendum at the federal level is a popular vote on 'issues of national importance'. Any issue of national importance in the jurisdiction of the Russian Federation or the joint jurisdiction of the Russian Federation and its subjects is subject to the optional referendum.[12] Depending on whether the optional referendum is used to make a proposal or to attack a law, it can be classified as either a citizen-initiated proactive or rejective referendum. It can be initiated by at least 2 million Russian citizens eligible to vote, provided that no more than 50,000 of them reside in the territory of the same federal subject or outside the territory of the Russian Federation.[13] The signatures have to be collected by a national (referendum) initiative group consisting of regional subgroups of at least 100 members within 45 days following the day of the registration of the national initiative group.[14]

For the direct vote to be valid, the turnout quorum is at least 50 per cent of the registered voters.[15] More than 50 per cent of the referendum participants have to approve the referendum for it to pass.[16] The referendum result is binding and does not need additional approval.[17]

---

[9]　However, according to Art. 1(3) Basic Guarantees Act, the basic electoral rights and guarantees cannot be undermined, even by federal constitutional law.

[10]　Федеральный закон от 6 октября 2003 № 131-ФЗ 'Об общих принципах организации местного самоуправления в Российской Федерации' (Federal Act of 6 October 2003 No. 131-FZ 'on the general principles of the organization of local self-government in the Russian Federation') // СЗ РФ 6.10.2003 № 40 ст. 3822.

[11]　Art. 25 and 25.1 Self-Government Act.

[12]　Art. 6(3) and (4) Referendum Act. According to Art. 130(2) Constitution, issues of local importance are reserved to the municipal referendum.

[13]　Art. 14(1) para. 1 and 17(1) Referendum Act.

[14]　Art. 17(2) Referendum Act.

[15]　Art. 80(5) Referendum Act.

[16]　Art. 80(7) Referendum Act.

[17]　Art. 83(2) Referendum Act.

The referendum at the federal level has almost no practical relevance. Since the referendums of, respectively, 25 April 1993 and 12 December 1993,[18] only one national vote has been held, on 1 July 2020.[19] Some citizen-initiated referendums were launched under the former Referendum Act[20] in 1997, 1998, 1999, 2000, 2002 and 2004. However, they have all failed to meet the formal or substantive admissibility requirements.[21] These requirements have been heavily reinforced since the adoption of the current Referendum Act and its amendments in 2008.[22] Thus, since 2004 only a few citizen-initiated referendums have been launched – in 2005,[23] 2006,[24] 2012[25] and 2018.[26] All of

---

[18]   See for these referendums Ronald J. Hill and Stephen White, 'Referendums in Russia, the Former Soviet Union and Eastern Europe' in Matt Qvortrup (ed), *Referendums Around the World* (Palgrave Macmillan 2018) 119–121.

[19]   See Section 6 below.

[20]   Федеральный конституционный закон от 10 октября 1995 № 2-ФКЗ 'О референдуме Российской Федерации' (Federal Constitutional Act of 10 October 1995 No. 2-FKZ 'on the referendum of the Russian Federation') // СЗ РФ 6.10.1995 № 42 ст. 3921 (Referendum Act 1995).

[21]   See Комарова (n 4) 46–52.

[22]   Федеральный конституционный закон от 24 апреля 2008 № 1-ФКЗ 'О внесении изменений в Федеральный конституционный закон "О референдуме Российской Федерации"' (Federal Constitutional Act of 24 April 2008 No. 1-FKZ 'on the amendment of the Federal Constitutional Act "on the Referendum RF"') // СЗ РФ 28.4.2008 № 17 ст. 1754.

[23]   Постановление Центральной избирательной комиссии Российской Федерации от 7 апреля 2005 № 142/974-4 (Decision of the Central Election Commission of the Russian Federation [CEC RF] of 7 April 2005 No. 142/974-4) // Российская Газета (РГ) 13 April 2005 https://rg.ru/2005/04/13/izbirkom-doc.html; Постановление Центральной избирательной комиссии Российской Федерации от 20 апреля 2005 № 143/981-4 (Decision of the CEC RF of 20 April 2005 No. 143/981-4) // РГ 14 May 2005 https://rg.ru/2005/05/14/izbirkom.html, both accessed 8 July 2020 [remark: all decisions of the CEC RF are cited in a shortened form without description of the subject. The full naming in Russian is available from the indicated websites].

[24]   Постановление Центральной избирательной комиссии Российской Федерации от 27 сентября 2006 № 187/1180-4 (Decision of the CEC RF of 27 September 2006 No. 187/1180-4) // РГ 3 October 2006 https://rg.ru/2006/10/03/cik-doc.html, accessed 8 July 2020.

[25]   Постановление Центральной избирательной комиссии Российской Федерации от 13 апреля 2012 № 118/917-6 (Decision of the CEC RF of 13 April 2012 No. 118/917-6) // РГ 17 April 2012 https://rg.ru/2012/04/16/vto-site-dok.html; Постановление Центральной избирательной комиссии Российской Федерации от 19 июля 2012 № 132/1011-6 (Decision of the CEC RF of 19 July 2012 No. 132/1011-6) // РГ 25 July 2012 https://rg.ru/2012/07/25/referendum-dok.html, both accessed 8 July 2020.

[26]   Постановление Центральной избирательной комиссии Российской Федерации от 17 октября 2018 № 186/1459-7 (Decision of the CEC RF of 17 October

them have been declared inadmissible. Since there are no reliable statistics, the actual number of referendums launched might be significantly higher.

2.1.2 Regional and municipal levels

According to Article 12(2) of the Basic Guarantees Act, the regional referendum is a popular vote on issues in the jurisdiction of the federal subjects or the joint jurisdiction of the Russian Federation and its federal subjects.[27] The municipal referendum is a vote on issues of local importance.[28]

The referendum can be initiated by Russian citizens eligible to vote or by executive or legislative actors foreseen by regional referendum law.[29] It can be used in either a proactive or a rejective way. The number of signatures that have to be collected in support of the initiative is established by regional law and may not exceed 2 per cent of the number of registered voters in the territory where the referendum is being held (in case of the municipal referendum 5 per cent, but no less than 25 signatures).[30] The signatures have to be collected within a period established by regional law of no less than 30 days (20 days in the case of the municipal referendum).[31] The turnout quorum is established by regional law and has to be at least 50 per cent of the registered voters. More than 50 per cent of the voters have to approve the referendum for it to pass.[32] The referendum result is binding and does not need additional approval.[33]

The optional citizen-initiated regional referendum is of some practical relevance. Since 1993 around 16 popular votes have been held. However, it is difficult to establish the exact number, since the referendums have not been consistently registered in the databases of the Central Election Commission of the Russian Federation (CEC RF) or the regional election commissions.[34]

The regional referendum on the formation of new federal subjects has also been of some practical relevance. There have been five mergers of federal subjects between 2003 and 2007 and eleven referendums which have been

---

2018 No. 186/1459-7) // РГ 19 October 2018 https://rg.ru/2018/10/19/cik-dok.html, accessed 8 July 2020.

[27] For the jurisdiction of the Russian Federation see Art. 71 Constitution, for the joint jurisdiction Art. 72 Constitution.

[28] Art. 12(3) Basic Guarantees Act.

[29] Art. 14(1) and (2) Basic Guarantees Act.

[30] Art. 37(1) Basic Guarantees Act.

[31] Art. 37(5) Basic Guarantees Act.

[32] Art. 70(8) Basic Guarantees Act.

[33] Art. 73(1) Referendum Act.

[34] See for an analysis of these referendums Julian Ivan Beriger, *Das Referendum in den Föderationssubjekten und Gemeinden des heutigen Russlands – Eine Analyse der normativen Ausgestaltung und praktischen Anwendung* (Nomos 2016) 165–98.

conducted in the corresponding territories.[35] These referendums were politically controversial because the mergers included ethnic-based federal subjects that were integrated into larger territories.[36] The legal basis for this type of referendum is the Federal Constitutional Act 'on the procedure for admitting to the Russian Federation and formation of a new subject of the Russian Federation' (Admission Act).[37] In one case, the referendum was mandatory, as it was triggered by the formation of a new federal subject.[38] In 2005, there were amendments to Article 11[39] and, as a result, the instrument now has to be classified as optional institution-initiated referendum. According to Article 11(1.1) of the Admission Act, the referendum can now be initiated by the senior officials (heads of the executive organs) of the 'interested' federal subjects. However, it can only be held if there have been 'appropriate consultations' with the Russian President and if he or she supports the referendum initiative.[40] The procedural provisions established by the Basic Guarantees Act are applicable.[41]

---

[35] The territorial mergers were the following: 1. Perm Oblast and Komi-Permyak Autonomous Okrug to Perm Krai (2003), 2. Evenk and Taymyr Autonomous Okrugs into the territory of Krasnoyarsk Krai (2005), 3. Kamchatka Oblast and Koryak Autonomous Okrug to Kamchatka Krai (2005), 4. Ust-Orda Buryat Autonomous Okrug into the territory of Irkutsk Oblast (2006), 5. Chita Oblast and Agin-Buryat Autonomous Okrug to Zabaykalsky Krai (2007). All referendums are registered in the database of the CEC RF and are available at http://www.izbirkom.ru/region/izbirkom, accessed 8 July 2020.

[36] See for an analysis of these referendums Beriger (n 34) 127–65.

[37] Федеральный конституционный закон от 17 декабря 2001 № 6-ФКЗ 'О порядке принятия в Российскую Федерацию и образования в ее составе нового субъекта Российской Федерации' (Federal Constitutional Act of 17 December 2001 No. 6-FKZ 'on the procedure for admitting to the Russian Federation and formation of a new subject of the Russian Federation') // СЗ РФ 24.12.2001 № 52 (часть 1) ст. 4916.

[38] Art. 11(1) Admission Act in its first version of 17 December 2001; Комарова (n 4) 70.

[39] Федеральный конституционный закон от 31 октября 2005 № 7-ФКЗ 'О внесении изменений в статьи 10 и 11 Федерального конституционного закона "О порядке принятия в Российскую Федерацию и образования в ее составе нового субъекта Российской Федерации"' (Federal Constitutional Act of 31 October 2005 No. 7-FKZ 'on the amendment of Art. 10 and 11 Admission Act') // СЗ РФ 7.11.2005 № 45 ст. 4581.

[40] Art. 11(1) Admission Act. See Владимир Александрович Кочев, 'Особенности подготовки и проведения референдума субъекта РФ по вопросу об образовании нового субъекта' ('Features of the preparation and holding of the referendum of a subject of the Russian Federation on the formation of a new federal subject') (2010) 3 Вестник Пермского Университета 73, 73–4.

[41] Art. 11(2) Admission Act.

The referendum at the municipal level has been used quite often. According to the database of the CEC RF, 4,672 municipal referendums have been held since 1993 at the time of writing this chapter.[42] Most of them have not been citizen-initiated but mandatory referendums concerning the introduction of means of self-taxation.

2.2   Law-initiated Referendum

According to Article 135(3) of the Constitution, the draft of a new Constitution can be submitted to a referendum by the Constitutional Assembly.[43] The procedure applies only in case of amendments to Chapters 1, 2 and 9 of the Constitution.[44] It was therefore not applicable to the recent constitutional amendments which affected only provisions in Chapters 3 to 8 of the Constitution.[45] This constitutional referendum could be classified as a law-initiated referendum.[46] The provisions of the Referendum Act are applicable.[47] However, the modalities of calling this referendum are quite unclear, since the Federal Constitutional Act on the Constitutional Assembly has never been adopted by the Russian Parliament.[48]

According to Article 6(2) and 22(1) of the Referendum Act, a draft normative act or an issue of national importance shall be submitted to a referendum if an international treaty of the Russian Federation foresees it. The referendum

---

[42]   The database is available at http://www.izbirkom.ru/region/izbirkom, accessed 8 July 2020.

[43]   'The Constitutional Assembly shall either confirm the invariability of the Constitution of the Russian Federation or draft a new Constitution of the Russian Federation which shall be adopted by the Constitutional Assembly by two-thirds of the total number of its members or submitted to a referendum.'

[44]   According to Art. 135(1) Constitution, the provisions in Chapters 1, 2 and 9 may not be revised by the Federal Assembly and therefore a new Constitution has to be drafted in case of amendments to these chapters. See Борис Сафарович Эбзеев, 'статья 135' ('Article 135') in Валерий Зорькин (ed), *Комментарий к Конституции Российской Федерации* (Commentary on the Constitution of the Russian Federation) (3rd edn, Норма ИНФРА-М 2013) 1024.

[45]   See Section 6 below.

[46]   The English text of the Constitution 'shall be submitted to a referendum' suggests that a referendum is mandatory in case less than two-thirds of the Constitutional Assembly support the draft of a new Constitution. However, according to Art. 6(1) Referendum Act, the Constitutional Assembly has 'the right' to propose the draft of the new Constitution to a referendum, which would also allow to classify the referendum as institution-initiated.

[47]   See Art. 6(1) and 21 Referendum Act.

[48]   See Эбзеев (n 44) 1024–25. There have been some draft bills, but they have all been rejected by the Russian Parliament. For example, Draft No. 874565-6 from 2015 is available at <https://sozd.duma.gov.ru/bill/874565-6> accessed 8 July 2020.

can be qualified as mandatory, since it is triggered in case an international treaty provides for it.[49] The referendum procedure foreseen in the Referendum Act is applicable, taking into account special provisions established by the international treaty.[50] So far, the law-initiated referendum at the federal level has never been used in practice.[51]

For the municipal level, federal law foresees a law-initiated referendum on the introduction and the use of means of self-taxation of citizens[52] and the structure of municipal organs in certain cases.[53] According to the database of the CEC RF, the greatest part of the 4,672 municipal referendums have concerned means of self-taxation.[54]

2.3   Agenda Initiative

The legal basis for the 'Russian public initiative' (RPI) is Presidential Decree No. 183 and the 'Rules for the consideration of public initiatives, submitted by citizens of the Russian Federation using the Russian Public Initiative Internet resource' in the annex to the Decree (Rules RPI).[55]

The RPI allows Russian citizens who have reached the age of 18 and are registered on the 'Public Services Portal of the Russian Federation' (www .gosuslugi.ru) to formally put an issue on the agenda of a state organ, provided

---

[49]   Авакьян (n 4) 402.

[50]   Art. 6(2) Referendum Act; Борис Иванович Осминин, *Принятие и реализация государствами международных договорных обязательств* (Acceptance and implementation of international treaty obligations by states) (Wolters Kluwer Russia 2006) 290–91.

[51]   The Treaty on the creation of a Union State between Russia and Belarus foresaw the holding of mandatory referendums in the participating states in Article 62(2). However, these referendums have never been held. Договор между РФ и Республикой Беларусь от 8 декабря 1999 'О создании Союзного государства' (Treaty between the RF and the Republic of Belarus of 8 December 1999 'on the establishment of a Union State') // СЗ РФ 14.2.2000 № 7 ст. 786.

[52]   According to Art. 56(1) Self-Government Act means of self-taxation are one-time payments of citizens made to address specific issues of local importance.

[53]   Art. 56(2) and 34(5) Self-Government Act. The municipal referendum on the structure of local government is foreseen if a new municipal entity is created on inter-settlement territory (territory, located outside the boundaries of a settlement) or if an existing municipal entity is transformed.

[54]   See for an analysis of the practice Beriger (n 34) 240–49.

[55]   Указ Президента РФ от 4 марта 2013 № 183 'О рассмотрении общественных инициатив, направленных гражданами Российской Федерации с использованием интернет-ресурса "Российская общественная инициатива"' (Decree of the President of the Russian Federation of 4 March 2013 No. 183 'on the consideration of public initiatives submitted by citizens of the Russian Federation using the Internet resource "Russian Public Initiative"') // СЗ РФ 11.3.2013 № 10 ст. 1019.

that the initiative is supported by 100,000 votes of registered Russian citizens. The votes have to be collected electronically over the Internet platform (www .roi.ru) within one year after posting the initiative on the Internet.[56] Once an initiative has reached the necessary support, it will be put on the agenda of the corresponding state organ and an 'expert working group' has to prepare an opinion on the initiative.[57] The initiative can also be addressed to regional or municipal organs. The support needed for a regional initiative is at least 5 per cent of the votes of citizens permanently residing in the territory of the corresponding federal subject (in subjects with a population of more than 2 million at least 100,000 votes) and for a municipal initiative at least 5 per cent of the votes of citizens permanently residing in the territory of the municipality.[58]

So far, 17,367 public initiatives have been published on the federal, regional and municipal levels.[59] However, only a small fraction of the RPIs at the federal level have managed to reach the necessary support of 100,000 votes and have been recommended for implementation by the corresponding expert group.[60] For example, the ecological initiative 'Green Shield around Moscow' has reached the necessary support of the voters and has received a positive expert opinion. Nevertheless, it has never been implemented.[61] One of the few initiatives that has been implemented at the federal level is on the installation of video registration systems on railway crossings.[62] There are neither official statistics of RPI, nor is there a monitoring of their implementation, making them a rather non-transparent instrument.

3.   LEGAL LIMITS AT THE FEDERAL LEVEL

The legal limits imposed on the referendum at the federal level are the main reason for its having little practical relevance.[63] In 2003, the Constitutional Court of the Russian Federation (Constitutional Court) stipulated that the

---

[56]   Para. 2 and 14 let a Rules RPI.
[57]   Para. 19 and 24 Rules RPI.
[58]   Para. 14 let b and c Rules RPI.
[59]   See <https://www.roi.ru/> accessed 8 July 2020.
[60]   Анна Аскольдовна Волошинская, 'Российская общественная инициатива: парадоксы отечественной электронной демократии' ('The Russian public initiative: the paradoxes of domestic e-democracy') (2016) 1 Власть 47, 47–49.
[61]   The initiative, the expert opinion and the proposed measures for implementation are available at https://www.roi.ru/22543/, accessed 8 July 2020.
[62]   The initiative, the expert opinion and the proposed measures for implementation are available at https://www.roi.ru/21892/, accessed 8 July 2020.
[63]   See for an overview of the legal limits on the referendum Наталия Валерьевна Петухова, 'Правовые ограничения инициирования, назначения и проведения референдумов в Российской Федерации: понятие и система' ('The legal limits on

federal legislator could not undermine the right of Russian citizens to a referendum when determining the referendum procedure.[64] Russian legal literature has specified that restrictions of the referendum right were allowed only if they have been introduced by the legislator and are well founded, necessary and proportionate.[65]

3.1 Formal Limits

3.1.1 Clarity of the referendum question

According to Article 6(7) of the Referendum Act, the referendum question must be formulated in such a way as to exclude the possibility of multiple interpretations, that is, to give only a definite answer to the question and to exclude uncertainty in regard to the legal consequences of the decision. The Constitutional Court has observed that this provision was designed to ensure the genuine formation of the voter's will.[66] It read a consistency of the subject matter requirement into this provision, which has probably been a reaction to the catalogues of up to 17 referendum questions that were proposed to vote

---

the initiation, calling and holding of referenda in the Russian Federation: concept and system') (2010) 10 Государство и Право 112, 113–15.

[64]   '(…) the federal legislator (…) cannot cancel or abrogate the right of citizens of the Russian Federation to participate in a referendum, introduce disproportionate limitations.' Постановление Конституционного Суда РФ от 11 июня 2003 № 10-П (Judgment of the Constitutional Court of 11 June 2003 No. 10-П) стр. 3 п. 2.2 // СЗ РФ 23.6.2003 № 25 ст. 2564. See for an overview of the case law of the Constitutional Court on the referendum Аналитическое Управление Совета Федерации, 'Референдум как институт непосредственной демократии' ('The referendum as an institute of direct democracy') (2007) 6 Государственная Власть и Местное Самоуправление 11, 17–19. Apart from the already cited case, the following leading cases deal with the referendum: Постановление Конституционного Суда РСФСР от 13 Марта 1992 № П-РЗ-I (Judgment of the Constitutional Court RSFSR of 13 March 1992 No. П-РЗ-I) // Ведомости СНД и ВС РФ 1992 № 13 ст. 671; Постановление Конституционного Суда РФ от 24 января 1997 № 1-П (Judgment of the Constitutional Court of 24 January 1997 No. 1-П) // СЗ РФ 3.2.1997 № 5 ст. 708; Постановление Конституционного Суда РФ от 10 июня 1998 № 17-П (Judgment of the Constitutional Court of 10 June 1998 No. 17-П) // СЗ РФ 22.6.1998 № 25 ст. 3002; Постановление Конституционного Суда РФ от 21 марта 2007 № 3-П (Judgment of the Constitutional Court of 21 March 2007 No. 3-П) // СЗ РФ 2.4.2007 № 14 ст. 1741.

[65]   Алексей Аронович Сергеев, 'Об ограничении предмета референдума Российской Федерации' ('On the limitation of the subject of the referendum of the Russian Federation') (2008) 19 Конституционное и Муниципальное Право 7, 11.

[66]   '(…) the wording of the issue submitted to the referendum should allow to perceive it as a whole, so that citizens are not forced to vote at the same time for several unrelated issues connected in one sentence (…).' Judgment of the Constitutional Court of 21 March 2007 No. 3-П (n 64) стр. 15 п. 4.

on at the federal level in 2005.[67] In practice, the CEC RF often invalidated citizen-initiated referendums based on both the catalogue of prohibited issues[68] and the clarity of question requirement at the same time. In 2005, a large part of the 17 referendum issues were declared inadmissible due to uncertainty in regard to the legal consequences,[69] for instance issue No. 4: 'Do you agree that the payments for residential premises and utilities as a whole should not exceed 10 per cent of the total income of family members living together?' or issue No. 5: 'Do you agree that the Housing Code of the Russian Federation, worsening the conditions for the implementation of the constitutional right to housing, should lose force after expiration of one month from the day of the holding of the referendum?' According to the CEC RF, either the financial consequences would be unclear or there would be a legal vacuum in the regulation of housing relations. Based on Article 6(7) of the Referendum Act and other substantive provisions, the CEC RF declared the following referendum question inadmissible: 'Do you agree that the same person should not be allowed to hold the office of the President of the Russian Federation for more than two consecutive terms?'[70] It held that multiple interpretations of the referendum question were possible since, in the end, it was not clear for how many terms the same person could hold the office of the Russian President (more than two terms if they are not consecutive).

3.1.2   Formation of the initiative group and signature collection

Compared with the Referendum Act 1995, the procedure to form an initiative group has been heavily reinforced in the current Referendum Act.[71] The national initiative group now counts at least 4,300 members (Referendum Act 1995: 100 members)[72] since regional subgroups of at least 100 members have to be formed in more than half of the federal subjects.[73] The Referendum Act establishes detailed formal requirements, for instance to the meeting on which every regional subgroup has to be formed and to the documents attached to the registration application.[74]

---

[67]   See Section 3.2.1 below.
[68]   See Section 3.2.1 below.
[69]   Decision of the CEC RF of 20 April 2005 No. 143/981-4 (n 23).
[70]   Decision of the CEC RF of 27 September 2006 No. 187/1180-4 (n 24). The referendum was initiated by the North Ossetian social movement 'Concord and stability' ('Согласие и стабильность').
[71]   See Section 2.1.1 above.
[72]   Art. 9(1) Referendum Act 1995.
[73]   Art. 15(2) Referendum Act.
[74]   Art. 15(3–9) and (11) Referendum Act.

These formal requirements led to the invalidation of a citizen-initiated referendum at the federal level in 2018. In its Decision of 17 October 2018, the CEC RF stated that no application of the regional subgroups to register the national initiative group had been submitted within two months from the registration of the first regional subgroup and that the referendum initiative would therefore be invalidated in accordance with Article 15(26) of the Referendum Act.[75]

3.2 Substantive Limits

A first substantive limit results from the scope of the referendum which includes only 'issues of national importance' in the jurisdiction of the Russian Federation or in the joint jurisdiction of the Russian Federation and its subjects.[76] Second, a referendum on the same question can be held not earlier than two years after the publication of the results of the first referendum, which creates a temporary limit on certain issues.[77] However, in practice the broad catalogue of prohibited issue is a far more important substantive limit.

3.2.1 Prohibited issues

According to Article 6(5) of the Referendum Act, the following issues cannot be subject to the referendum at the federal level:

(1)   changes to the constitutional status of a subject (the subjects) of the Russian Federation enshrined in the Constitution;
(2)   the early termination or prolongation of the term of office of the President of the Russian Federation or the State Duma, the holding of early elections of the Russian President, deputies of the State Duma or the postponement of such elections;
(3)   the election, the appointment to office, early termination, suspension or prolongation of the powers of persons holding public offices of the Russian Federation;
(4)   the personal composition of federal state organs or other federal government bodies;
(5)   the election, early termination, suspension or prolongation of the term of office of bodies formed in accordance with an international treaty of the Russian Federation or of officials elected or appointed to office in accordance with an international treaty of the Russian Federation, as well as on the formation of such bodies or appointment to office of

---

[75]   Decision of the CEC RF of 17 October 2018 No. 186/1459-7 (n 26).
[76]   Art. 1 and 6(4) Referendum Act.
[77]   Art. 7(5) Referendum Act.

such persons, unless otherwise provided by an international treaty of the Russian Federation;

(6)   the adoption of emergency and urgent measures to ensure the health and safety of the population;

(7)   issues referred by the Constitution or federal constitutional acts to the exclusive competence of federal state organs.

The above-mentioned citizen-initiated referendums[78] have all been declared inadmissible by the CEC RF often based on both the catalogue of prohibited issues and formal admissibility requirements.[79]

In its Decision of 7 April 2005,[80] the CEC RF decided on the admissibility of 12 referendum issues which were proposed to vote on at the same time by one initiative group. They concerned mostly questions of social welfare, for instance issue No. 1, 'Do you agree that within one year from the day of the holding of the referendum the minimum wage should be set at a level not lower than the subsistence minimum in the Russian Federation?' or issue No. 2, 'Do you agree that within one year from the day of the holding of the referendum the basic part of the old-age labour pension should be set at a level not lower than the subsistence minimum in the Russian Federation?' Issue No. 1 and 2 were declared inadmissible based on a former provision in the catalogue of prohibited issues that excluded issues regarding budgetary or other financial obligations of the Russian Federation. Apart from issue No. 12, 'Do you agree that at least half of the deputies of the State Duma of the Federal Assembly of the Russian Federation should be elected individually in single-mandate constituencies?' all other issues have been declared inadmissible based on the catalogue of prohibited issues and/or the clarity of question requirement. The initiative group did not start the registration procedure for one single question which could have been actually put to the vote.

In the same year, another initiative group proposed to vote on 17 referendum issues at the same time which were partly identical to the issues in the Decision of the CEC RF of 7 April 2005 (issues No. 1–4, 6, 7, 9 and 12–15). These issues and part of the new ones (No. 5, 10, 11, 16 and 17) have been declared inadmissible in the Decision of the CEC RF of 20 April 2005[81] again based on both the catalogue of prohibited issues (financial obligations) and the clarity of question requirement. Issue No. 17 had the following wording: 'Do you agree that federal constitutional law should establish that a question cannot be submitted to a referendum only if it contradicts the Constitution of the Russian

---

78   See n 23–26.
79   See for the formal limits Section 3.1 above.
80   Decision of the CEC RF of 7 April 2005 No. 142/974-4 (n 23).
81   Decision of the CEC RF of 20 April 2005 No. 143/981-4 (n 23).

Federation, and that all other restrictions on the holding of a referendum should be lifted?' In the opinion of the CEC RF, an unlimited referendum right could lead to a violation of the rights and freedoms of man and citizen which contradicted Article 55(2) of the Constitution. Only the above-mentioned issue on the election of the deputies of the State Duma and issue No. 8, 'Do you agree that in the Russian Federation deferrals from military service valid as of 1 January 2005 should be maintained?' were found to be admissible. The initiative group did not start the registration procedure for the two remaining referendum issues.

In 2006, the CEC RF had to decide on the admissibility of only one referendum issue that should have been put to the vote. The question, 'Do you agree that the same person should not be allowed to hold the office of the President of the Russian Federation for more than two consecutive terms?' was, as already mentioned above, found to violate the clarity of question requirement.[82]

In 2012, another two citizen-initiated referendums were launched. The CEC RF declared the issue, 'Do you support the accession of Russia to the World Trade Organization on the conditions and obligations under the Protocol signed on 16 December 2011?' inadmissible since it belonged to the exclusive competence of the federal state organs. According to the CEC RF, the ratification of international treaties of the Russian Federation was carried out in the form of a federal law that was adopted by the State Duma (a federal state organ).[83] In the same year, another referendum initiative group proposed to vote on the two issues, 'Do you support the need for a nationwide public discussion on the need of the Russian Federation to join the World Trade Organization?' and 'Do you agree to transfer part of the sovereignty of the Russian Federation to the jurisdiction of the World Trade Organization?' Both issues were declared inadmissible. According to the CEC RF, the first question violated the clarity of question requirement since the term 'public discussion' was not clear. In this Decision, the CEC RF also referred to the consistency of subject matter established by the Constitutional Court in its Judgment of 21 March 2007 No. 3-П[84] and held that the referendum issue had to be considered in conjunction with the other issues. The two issues in question were not logically connected and would mislead citizens over the purpose of the Russian Federation to join the World Trade Organization.[85]

Some of the above-mentioned decisions of the CEC RF were challenged before the Supreme Court of the Russian Federation (Supreme Court) that

---

[82] See Section 3.1.1 above and Decision of the CEC RF of 27 September 2006 No. 187/1180-4 (n 24).

[83] Decision of the CEC RF of 13 April 2012 No. 118/917-6 (n 25).

[84] See Section 3.1.1 above.

[85] Decision of the CEC RF of 19 July 2012 No. 132/1011-6 (n 25).

rejected the appeals, for instance the Decision of the CEC RF of 20 April 2005 No. 143/981-4. By mainly repeating the argumentation of the CEC RF, the Supreme Court confirmed that 15 referendum issues did not conform to the Referendum Act. They either fell into the catalogue of prohibited issues or violated the clarity of question requirement.[86] The Board of Cassation of the Supreme Court confirmed this decision.[87] The Decision of the CEC RF of 13 April 2012 No. 118/917-6 has also been challenged before the Supreme Court. In a judgment of five pages the Court confirmed the argumentation of the CEC RF and declared the referendum question inadmissible.[88] This decision was confirmed by the Board of Appeal of the Supreme Court.[89]

The former provision in the catalogue of prohibited issues excluding budgetary or other financial obligations of the Russian Federation in Article 6(5), the clarity of question requirement in Article 6(7) and Article 15(13) Referendum Act (power of the CEC RF to check the referendum issue on its compatibility with the Referendum Act) have been challenged before the Constitutional Court. In an important precedent, the Court confirmed the constitutionality of these limits.[90] According to the Court, it follows directly from the Constitution that budgetary questions refer to the legislative power and therefore the former provision in Article 6(5) Referendum Act is constitutional. The clarity of question requirement ensures the adequate expression of the citizens' will and thus cannot violate the Constitution.[91] However, it also follows from the judgment that the federal legislator should formulate the provisions in the catalogue of prohibited issues in a clear way.[92] Despite this, the catalogue was amended in 2008 by abolishing several provisions and adding the vaguely formulated point

---

[86]   Решение Верховного Суда РФ от 2 июня 2005 № ГКПИ05-589, 628 (Judgment of the Supreme Court of 2 June 2005 No. ГКПИ05-589, 628) available at http://www.vsrf.ru, accessed 8 July 2020.

[87]   Определение кассационной коллегии Верховного Суда РФ от 28 июля 2005 № КАС05-329 (Judgment of the Board of Cassation of the Supreme Court of 28 July 2005 No. КАС05-329) available at http://www.consultant.ru, accessed 8 July 2020.

[88]   Решение Верховного Суда от 6 июня 2012 № АКПИ12-693 (Judgment of the Supreme Court of 6 June 2012 No. АКПИ12-693) available at http://www.consultant .ru, accessed 8 July 2020.

[89]   Определение апелляционной коллегии Верховного Суда РФ от 20 сентября 2012 № АПЛ12-499 (Judgment of the Supreme Court of 20 September 2012 No. АПЛ12-499) available at http://www.vsrf.ru, accessed 8 July 2020.

[90]   Judgment of the Constitutional Court of 21 March 2007 No. 3-П (n 64). See for a detailed analysis of this case Галина Андреева/Александр Верещагин/Инга Старостина, 'Двери для референдума приоткрываются?' ('Do the doors for the referendum open?') (2007) 2 Сравнительное Конституционное Право.

[91]   Judgment of the Constitutional Court of 21 March 2007 No. 3-П (n 64) стр. 10–14 п. 3 and стр. 14–15 п. 4.

[92]   Сергеев (n 65) 11.

No. 7 (issues in the exclusive competence of federal state organs). This has led *de facto* to the opening of the catalogue which allows the CEC RF to invalidate referendums on an even broader basis.[93]

3.2.2 Compliance with the Russian Constitution

The preamble of the Referendum Act states that the referendum cannot be used to make decisions which are contrary to the Constitution. Until 2008, Article 6(6) of the Referendum Act explicitly foresaw that referendum issues shall not contradict the Constitution. Now it is Article 23(1) of the Referendum Act which states that the Russian President, before calling the referendum requests the Constitutional Court to check the referendum question(s) for compliance with the Constitution. If the referendum question does not comply with the Constitution, the referendum is declared invalid.[94]

In its Decision of 27 September 2006 No. 187/1180-4, the CEC RF based the invalidation of the referendum issue, 'Do you agree that the same person should not be allowed to hold the office of the President of the Russian Federation for more than two consecutive terms?' on both the lack of clarity of the referendum question and the violation of the Russian Constitution. The Commission argued in a not very convincing way that the referendum issue was identical to Article 81(3) of the Constitution and that such duplications would violate the Constitution.[95]

3.2.3 Further substantive limits on the agenda initiative

The text of an RPI (be it at the federal, the regional or the municipal level) may not contain obscene or offensive language, threats to the life or health of citizens or calls for extremist activities.[96] Furthermore, according to Paragraph 13 of the Rules RPI, an initiative will not be published on the internet if it:

(1) violates the Constitution, generally recognized principles and norms of international law, among them those in the field of rights, freedoms and legitimate interests of citizens;
(2) violates Article 6 of the Referendum Act;
(3) does not contain a description of the problem, does not suggest solutions to the problem or the proposed options are not justified.

---

[93] Burkhard Breig, 'Sachunmittelbare Demokratie in Russland' in Peter Neumann/ Denise Renger (eds), *Sachunmittelbare Demokratie im interdisziplinären und internationalen Kontext 2010/2011* (Nomos 2012) 275–76; Сергеев (n 65) 11–12.
[94] Art. 23(2) Referendum Act.
[95] Decision of the CEC RF of 27 September 2006 No. 187/1180-4 (n 24).
[96] Para. 7 Rules RPI.

However, these substantial limits are not very important in practice, since most of the RPIs at the federal level already fail to reach the necessary support of 100,000 votes.[97]

4. LEGAL LIMITS AT THE REGIONAL AND MUNICIPAL LEVELS

The legal limits on the referendum established by the Basic Guarantees Act and regional legislation are weaker than at the federal level.

A first substantive limit results from the scope of the regional referendum which includes questions in the jurisdiction of the federal subjects or the joint jurisdiction of the Russian Federation and its subjects, if these matters are not already regulated by the Constitution or federal law.[98] The scope of the municipal referendum includes questions of local importance.[99] The Constitutional Court has held that the regional referendum should not be used to oppose the will of the federal legislator.[100] The issue of a regional or municipal referendum had to comply with higher-ranking law.[101]

Furthermore, the referendum issue should not limit or abrogate the universally recognized human and civil rights, freedoms and the constitutional guarantees to implement these rights.[102]

According to Article 12(8) of the Basic Guarantees Act, the following issues cannot be subject to the regional or the municipal referendum:

(1)   the early termination or prolongation of the term of office of regional state authorities or municipal organs, the suspension of their powers, the holding of early elections of regional state authorities or municipal organs or the postponement of such elections;

(2)   the personal composition of regional or municipal authorities;

---

[97]   See Волошинская (n 60) 47 and Section 2.3 above.

[98]   Art. 12(2) Basic Guarantees Act. According to the Supreme Court, issues in the joint jurisdiction of the Russian Federation and its federal subjects can be subject to a regional referendum. For example, Определение Верховного Суда РФ от 27 октября 2003 № 76-Г03-2 (Judgment of the Supreme Court of 27 October 2003 No. 76-Г03-2) с. 3. However, this shall not apply if the issue has already been regulated by federal legislation. See for example, Определение Верховного Суда РФ от 13 ноября 2019 № 1-АПА 19–22 (Judgment of the Supreme Court of 13 November 2019 No. 1-АПА 19–22) с. 7. The judgments are available at https://vsrf.ru/lk/practice/acts, accessed 8 July 2020.

[99]   Art. 12(3) Basic Guarantees Act.

[100]   Judgment of the Constitutional Court of 10 June 1998 No. 17-П (n 64) с. 3 п. 2.

[101]   Art. 12(6) Basic Guarantees Act.

[102]   Art. 12(5) Basic Guarantees Act.

(3)　the election of deputies and officials, approval, appointment and dismissal of officials, consent to their appointment and dismissal;

(4)　the adoption of or amendments to the corresponding budget, fulfilment and modification of financial obligations of a federal subject or municipality;

(5)　the adoption of emergency and urgent measures to ensure the health and safety of the population.

The referendum question must be formulated in such a way as to exclude the possibility of multiple interpretations, that is, to give only a definite answer to the question and to exclude uncertainty in regard to the legal consequences of the decision.[103]

Several referendums at the regional level have been declared inadmissible, as they failed to meet the substantial or formal limits established by the Basic Guarantees Act and regional legislation. The practice of the Supreme Court is rather restrictive, as it interprets these limits in a broad way. Accordingly, it supported the decisions of regional election commissions and regional courts not to register regional initiative groups due to failure to meet the formal or substantive admissibility requirements.[104] Furthermore, it annulled decisions of regional courts which had decided in favour of the initiative group.[105] Only rarely, the Court supported the initiative group and decided against the election commission.[106]

5.　INSTITUTIONAL AND PROCEDURAL FRAMEWORK

5.1　Federal Level

5.1.1　Optional referendum

In order to launch an optional referendum, the initiators have to form a national (referendum) initiative group that consists of regional subgroups. Before the registration of the first regional subgroup, the CEC RF reviews the referendum

---

[103]　Art. 12(7) Basic Guarantees Act.

[104]　See for example, Апелляционные определения Верховного Суда РФ от 14 августа 2019 № 1-АПА19-13; от 22 мая 2019 № 47-АПА19-2 (Appeal judgments of 14 August 2019 No. 1-АПА19-13; of 22 May 2019 No. 47-АПА19-2).

[105]　See for example, Апелляционное определение Верховного Суда РФ от 25 июня 2019 № 1-АПА19-7 (Appeal judgment of 25 June 2019 No. 1-АПА19-7).

[106]　See for example, Апелляционное определение Верховного Суда РФ от 31 января 2018 № 86-АПГ17-5 (Appeal judgment of the Supreme Court of 31 January 2018 No. 86-АПГ17-5). All judgments are available at https://vsrf.ru/lk/practice/acts, accessed 8 July 2020.

question for its compliance with Article 6 of the Referendum Act (clarity of question requirement, prohibited issues).[107]

If the referendum question complies to the requirements, the regional subgroups are formed and registered by the respective regional election commissions.[108] The national initiative group can request registration from the CEC RF when regional subgroups have been registered in more than half of the federal subjects.[109] The national initiative group will be handed out a registration certificate which entitles it to collect signatures.[110] After signature collection, the signature sheets are submitted to the CEC RF, which checks them formally (information on the signatories, authenticity).[111] If the national initiative group fails to meet the registration requirements, or if it could not collect the necessary number of valid signatures, the referendum is declared invalid by the CEC RF.[112]

According to Article 21(4) of the Basic Guarantees Act, the CEC RF consists of 15 members. The Russian President, the State Duma (lower house) and the Federation Council (upper house) each appoint five members. In accordance with Article 21(3) of the Basic Guarantees Act, the members are elected for five years. The Referendum Act establishes some due process guarantees in the procedure before the CEC RF. According to Article 33 of the Rules CEC,[113] the Commission's sessions are held openly and publicly. Members or authorized representatives of the referendum initiative group are entitled to attend the sessions and also witness the work on the protocols on the referendum results. The chairperson can pass them the word (Article 37 Rules CEC), but there is no standardized hearing procedure.

The decisions of the CEC RF can be challenged before the Supreme Court.[114] If the reason for the decision was non-conformity of the referendum issue with the Constitution, the Supreme Court transfers the request to the Constitutional Court.[115] Since 2015, the referendum procedure is regulated by

---

[107] Art. 15(13) Referendum Act. See for these limits Sections 3.1.1 and 3.2.1 above.
[108] Art. 15(14–15) Referendum Act.
[109] Art. 15(19) Referendum Act.
[110] Art. 15(22–23) Referendum Act.
[111] Art. 19 Referendum Act.
[112] Art. 15(26) and 20(3) Referendum Act.
[113] Постановление ЦИК РФ от 28 июня 1995 № 7/46-II 'О Регламенте Центральной избирательной комиссии Российской Федерации' (Decree of the CEC RF of 28 June 1995 No. 7/46-II 'On the Rules of the Central Election Commission of the Russian Federation') http://www.consultant.ru, accessed 8 July 2020.
[114] Art. 15(25), 20(5) and 87 Referendum Act.
[115] Art. 15(17) Referendum Act.

the Code of Administrative Jurisdiction of the Russian Federation (CAJ).[116] There are special procedural provisions in Chapter 24 of the CAJ for election and referendum procedures (Articles 239–244), concretizing mainly the right to appeal a decision (Article 239) and establishing shorter deadlines to file appeals in certain cases concerning electoral and referendum matters (see Article 240) and also to deal with them for the Court (Article 241). Article 6 of the CAJ contains due process guarantees (for example, the principle of equality, transparency of proceedings, independence of judges, the principle of legality). The circle of persons entitled to appeal the decisions of the CEC RF before the Supreme Court is rather wide.[117]

If the signatures meet the requirements, all the documents necessary to call the referendum are sent to the Russian President. He or she transmits them to the Constitutional Court, which reviews the referendum issue for its compliance with the Constitution.[118] If the initiative is found to comply with the Constitution, it is put to the vote. Otherwise, it is declared invalid and all procedures for its implementation are terminated.[119]

5.1.2 Mandatory referendum

The mandatory referendum foreseen by an international treaty of the Russian Federation is called by the federal state organ in whose competence the consideration of the draft normative act or the issue of national importance falls according to the international treaty.[120] According to Article 6(2) Referendum Act, all the procedural provisions (calling, preparation and holding of the ref-

---

[116] Кодекс административного судопроизводства Российской Федерации от 8 марта 2015 № 21-ФЗ (Code of Administrative Jurisdiction of the Russian Federation of 8 March 2015 No. 21-ФЗ) // СЗ РФ 9.3.2015 № 10 ст. 1391.

[117] According to Art. 239(1) and (2) CAJ, the following subjects are entitled to appeal decisions of the CEC RF or other state organs: voters, referendum participants, candidates and electoral associations, their confidants, political parties, their regional branches and other structural units, other public associations, referendum initiative groups, other groups of referendum participants and their authorized representatives, whose (electoral) rights, freedoms and legitimate interests have been violated by the decision.

[118] Art. 23(1) Referendum Act. The Constitutional Court mainly decides on the constitutionality of laws, presidential and governmental decrees and laws of federal subjects, as well as on the constitutionality of the application of a law in a concrete case (see Art. 3 Федеральный конституционный закон от 21 июля 1994 № 1-ФКЗ 'О Конституционном Суде Российской Федерации'; Federal Constitutional Act of 21 July 1994 No. 1-FKZ 'on the Constitutional Court of the Russian Federation' // СЗ РФ 25.07.1994 № 13 ст. 1447).

[119] Art. 23(2) Referendum Act.

[120] Art. 22(1) Referendum Act.

erendum) of the Referendum Act are basically applicable, taking into account special provisions foreseen by the international treaty in question.

5.1.3   Agenda initiative

In order to launch an RPI, the initiator has to register in the federal state information system () and submit the text of the initiative by filling out a special form on the internet platform ().[121] Before publication, the initiative has to undergo preliminary examination, except if its text contains offensive language, threats to the life or health of citizens or calls for extremist activities. Such initiatives are removed from the platform without preliminary examination.[122] The same applies in case of repeated submission of the same initiative under certain circumstances.[123] The aim of the preliminary examination is to review the initiative for its compliance with the limits set out above.[124] After the examination, the initiative is published on the internet platform and the voting process begins. If the initiative has gained the necessary number of votes,[125] it will be put on the agenda of the respective state organ (at the federal, regional or municipal level).[126]

The decision to remove a public initiative without preliminary examination or not to publish it on the platform is taken by an authorized non-profit organization (that is, a private entity) called 'Information Democracy Fund'.[127] This organization also carries out the preliminary examination.[128] By Presidential Decree No. 183 of 4 March 2013 the 'Information Democracy Fund' was appointed the operator of the Russian Public Initiative Internet resource.[129] A remedy procedure is not foreseen in the Rules. However, there are some transparency requirements for the decisions of the organization, for instance the obligation to notify the initiator of the RPI electronically on the decision to remove an initiative without preliminary examination or to motivate its decision not to publish an initiative after preliminary examination.[130]

---

[121] Para. 2 and 6 Rules RPI.
[122] Para. 7 Rules RPI.
[123] See para. 9 Rules RPI.
[124] Para. 10 Rules RPI. See for these limits Section 3.2.3 above.
[125] See Section 2.3 above.
[126] Para. 19 Rules RPI.
[127] Para. 4, 9 and 13 Rules RPI. See https://www.f-id.ru/about/, accessed 8 July 2020.
[128] Para. 4 Rules RPI.
[129] See for the Presidential Decree (n 55).
[130] See para. 9 and 12 RPI.

5.2   Regional and Municipal Levels

In order to launch an optional referendum, the initiators have to form a referendum (initiative) group and apply to the regional or municipal election commission for registration.[131] The regional or municipal election commission carries out a preliminary formal examination of the registration documents.[132] After the examination, the documents are transferred to the regional or municipal parliament (representative organ). It reviews the referendum question for its compliance with the formal and substantive admissibility requirements set out in Article 12 of the Basic Guarantees Act.[133] If the parliament finds the question does not comply with these requirements, the regional or municipal election commission refuses to register the initiative group.[134] The wording of this provision indicates that the election commissions are bound by the parliamentary decisions. If the initiative is found to comply with these requirements, the referendum group is registered and handed out a registration certificate that entitles it to collect signatures.[135] After signature collection and check of the signatures, the referendum issue is put to the vote.[136]

According to Article 75(1) of the Basic Guarantees Act, decisions and actions (or inaction) of regional or municipal state organs that violate the electoral rights or the right of citizens to participate in a referendum may be appealed to a court.[137] The decisions of the regional election commissions (for example, their refusal to register a referendum initiative group) and those of the regional parliaments on the referendum issue can be challenged before the regional supreme courts (in case of the municipal referendum the district courts) and before the Russian Supreme Court.[138] The provisions in Chapter 24 (Articles 239–44) of the CAJ are applicable.[139] The procedural provisions in the Basic Guarantees Act also apply to the optional institution-initiated referendum at the regional level.[140]

---

[131]   Art. 36(2–4) Basic Guarantees Act.

[132]   Art. 36(5) Basic Guarantees Act.

[133]   Art. 36(5–6) Basic Guarantees Act. See for the substantive limits Section 3.2 above.

[134]   Art. 36(11) Basic Guarantees Act.

[135]   Art. 36(8) Basic Guarantees Act.

[136]   See Art. 15(1) Basic Guarantees Act.

[137]   See also Art. 239(1–4) CAJ.

[138]   Art. 75(2) Basic Guarantees Act. Both decisions – the one of the regional parliament and the one of the election commission – can be challenged before the court. For example, Апелляционное определение от 13 ноября 2019 № 1-АПА 19–22 (Judgment of the Supreme Court of 13 November 2019 No. 1-АПА 19–22) с. 9.

[139]   See for these provisions Section 5.1.1 above.

[140]   Art. 11(2) Admission Act. See for this referendum Section 2.1.2 above.

6. THE 'ALL-RUSSIAN VOTE' 2020

On 1 July 2020 (initial date 22 April 2020)[141] the first referendum at the federal level on several amendments to the Russian Constitution was held. The proposed amendments were approved by a majority of 77.92 per cent of the referendum participants. Turnout was 67.97 per cent of registered voters.[142] From a judicial point of view, there was no need for this vote since the amendments[143] did not affect Chapters 1, 2 or 9 of the Constitution[144] and the parliament had already approved them on 11 March 2020.[145]

Officially, the vote has been referred to as the 'all-Russian vote' and it has been conducted in accordance with special legislation,[146] and not the Referendum Act. According to Article 2(2) Public Authority Act, the vote is initiated by the Russian President and can thus be qualified as an institution-initiated referendum. More than 50 per cent of the referendum

---

[141] The vote had to be postponed due to the coronavirus outbreak. Указ Президента РФ от 25 Марта 2020 № 205 'О переносе даты общероссийского голосования по вопросу одобрения изменений в Конституцию Российской Федерации' (Decree of the President RF of 25 March 2020 No. 205 'on the postponement of the date of the all-Russian vote on the approval of amendments to the Constitution of the Russian Federation') // СЗ РФ 30.3.2020 № 13 ст. 1897.

[142] Постановление ЦИК от 3 июля 2020 № 256/1888-7 'О результатах общероссийского голосования по вопросу одобрения изменений в Конституцию Российской Федерации' (Decree of the CEC RF of 3 July 2020 No. 256/1888-7 'on the results of the all-Russian vote on the approval of amendments to the Constitution of the Russian Federation') // РГ 4.7.2020 № 256; http://www.cikrf.ru/news/cec/46749/, accessed 8 July 2020.

[143] According to Art. 1 Public Authority Act, there have been amendments to the following Articles of the Constitution: 67, 67.1, 68, 69, 70, 71, 72(1), 75, 75.1, 77(3), 78(5), 79, 79.1, 80(2), 81, 82(2), 83, 92.1, 93, 95, 97, 98(1), 100(3), 102, 103(1), 103.1, 104(1), 107(3), 108(2), 109(1), 110, 111, 112, 113, 114(1), 115, 117, 118, 119, 125, 126, 128, 129, 131, 132 and 133.

[144] See Section 2.2 above.

[145] See https://sozd.duma.gov.ru/bill/885214-7, accessed 8 July 2020.

[146] Закон РФ о поправке к Конституции РФ от 14 марта 2020 № 1-ФКЗ 'О совершенствовании регулирования отдельных вопросов организации и функционирования публичной власти' (Federal Act on the amendment of the Russian Constitution of 14 March 2020 No. 1-FKZ 'on improving the regulation of certain issues of the organization and functioning of public authority') // СЗ РФ 16.3.2020 № 11 ст. 1416 (Public Authority Act) and Постановление ЦИК от 20 марта 2020 № 244/1804-7 'О порядке общероссийского голосования по вопросу одобрения изменений в Конституцию Российской Федерации' (Decree of the CEC RF of 20 March 2020 No. 244/1804-7 'on the procedure for the all-Russian vote on the approval of the amendments to the Russian Constitution') // 'Вестник ЦИК России' № 3 2020.

participants had to approve the referendum for it to pass.[147] The vote has been appointed by Presidential Decree No. 354.[148] The voters had seven days (from 25 June to 1 July 2020) to cast their votes. In certain regions remote electronic voting was also available.[149]

In Article 3 Public Authority Act was enshrined a special admissibility procedure before the Constitutional Court. In accordance with Article 3(3) Public Authority Act, the Court had to confirm the conformity of the proposed amendments to Chapters 1, 2 and 9 of the Constitution which it did in its opinion of 16 March 2020.[150] However, the referendum issue, 'Do you approve the changes in the Constitution of the Russian Federation?' has been determined by Presidential Decree No. 188.[151] It has not been subject to the admissibility check by the Constitutional Court. The formal and substantive admissibility requirements of the Referendum Act (catalogue of prohibited issues, clarity of question requirement) were not applicable.[152] The formulation of the referendum question would have hardly met these requirements since the voters had to decide on the bill as a whole. The constitutional amendments have far-reaching consequences and cover a broad range of issues. For instance, new Article 81(3.1) of the Constitution sets the incumbent President's previous presidential terms to zero and therefore allows him or her to extend his or her rule for two more terms until at least 2036. According to new Article 79 of the Constitution, decisions of interstate bodies which are contrary to the Russian Constitution shall not be implemented in the Russian Federation.

---

[147] Art. 3(5) Public Authority Act.

[148] See Указ Президента РФ от 1 июня 2020 № 354 'об определении даты проведения общероссийского голосования по вопросу одобрения изменений в Конституцию Российской Федерации' (Decree of the President RF of 1 June 2020 'on the determination of the date of the holding of the all-Russian vote on the approval of amendments to the Constitution RF') // СЗ РФ 8.6.2020 № 23, ст. 3622.

[149] See online at, https://rg.ru/2020/06/09/popravki-v-konstituciiu-kak-i-gde-budem-golosovat-s-25-iiunia-po-1-iiulia.html, accessed 8 July 2020.

[150] Заключение Конституционного Суда РФ от 16 марта 2020 № 1-3 (Opinion of the Constitutional Court RF of 16 March 2020 No. 1-3) available at <https://rg.ru/2020/03/17/ks-rf-popravki-dok.html> accessed 8 July 2020 [remark: the opinion of the Constitutional Court is cited in a shortened form without description of the subject. The full naming in Russian is accessible from the indicated website].

[151] Указ Президента РФ от 17 Марта 2020 № 188 'О назначении общероссийского голосования по вопросу одобрения изменений в Конституцию Российской Федерации' (Decree of the President of the Russian Federation of 17 March 2020 No. 188 'on the appointment of an all-Russian vote on the approval of the amendments to the Constitution of the Russian Federation') // СЗ РФ 23.3.2020 № 12 ст. 1743.

[152] See for the clarity of the referendum question Section 3.1.1 and for the catalogue of prohibited issues Section 3.2.1 above.

Other amendments were very favourable to Russian people, for instance the guarantees for a minimal pension and compulsory social insurance as well as their indexation in new Article 75(6) and (7) of the Constitution. Against this background, the referendum question could not ensure the freedom of voters to form an opinion that is enshrined in paragraph 3.1 of the Code of Good Practice on Referendums.[153]

7.   CONCLUSION

The constitutional role of the referendum as a central instrument of direct democracy in Russia is of a rather theoretical nature. Restrictions have been imposed on the referendum at two levels: legislation and judicial practice. There are high technical hurdles to form a referendum (initiative) group and collect the necessary number of signatures. The legislator has also reinforced the substantive and formal admissibility requirements in Russian referendum law, especially at the federal level.[154] These legal limits have been criticized as politically motivated limitations of the right to a referendum.[155] Russian courts follow a rather restrictive practice in remedy procedures and often decide in favour of the election commissions. This practice could impair the right to an effective system of appeal, enshrined in paragraph 3.3 of the Code of Good Practice on Referendums of the Venice Commission.

At the federal level, the first referendum since 1993 was held on 1 July 2020, but not in accordance with the Referendum Act.[156] At the regional level, the referendum has been used to legitimize the politically controversial mergers of several federal subjects. At the municipal level, many mandatory referendums have been held, mainly on the introduction of means of self-taxation.[157] Furthermore, a lot of RPIs have been launched. However, in practice only a few RPIs have actually gained the necessary support of the voters at the federal level and it has been rather difficult to monitor their implementation.[158]

In conclusion, there is a strong contrast between the constitutional status and the practical use of the referendum in Russia. Apart from the local level and

---

[153] Code of Good Practice on Referendums, adopted by the Council for Democratic Elections at its 19th meeting (Venice, 16 December 2006) and the Venice Commission at its 70th plenary session (Venice, 16–17 March 2007), CDL-AD (2007) 008rev.

[154] See for these requirements Sections 3.1 and 3.2 above.

[155] Сергеев (n 65) 12; Петухова (n 63) 115; Марина Михайловна Курячая, 'Проблемы реализации права граждан на референдум' ('Problems of realization of the right of citizens to a referendum') (2005) 9 Право и Политика 11, 18.

[156] See Section 6 above.

[157] See for the mandatory referendums Section 2.2 above.

[158] See for the agenda initiative Section 2.3 above.

the RPI, the referendum has been either restricted by legislation and judicial practice to a political instrument of little practical relevance or it has been used to decide on politically controversial issues. The recent vote on the constitutional amendments at the federal-level indicates a plebiscitary use of the referendum in Russia. The vote allowed President Putin to publicly approve the extension of his power until at least 2036 by circumventing the legal limits of the Referendum Act.[159] Against this background, the referendum in Russia currently appears as an instrument not of a free, but rather of a 'guided democracy'.[160]

---

[159] See https://www.nytimes.com/2020/07/01/world/europe/putin-referendum-vote -russia.html, accessed 8 July 2020.

[160] See for this term Margareta Mommsen, 'Putins "gelenkte Demokratie": "Vertikale der Macht" statt Gewaltenteilung' in Matthes Buhbe/Gabriele Gorzka (eds), *Russland heute: Rezentralisierung des Staates unter Putin* (VS Verlag für Sozialwissenschaften 2007) 237.

15. Comparative conclusion

Anna Forgács, Henri Ibi and Daniel Moeckli

1.   INTRODUCTION

The purpose of this concluding chapter is to provide a comparative analysis of the legal situation in the states covered in the previous chapters. Given the diversity of these states in terms of constitutional frameworks, political culture, experience with referendums, direct-democratic practice etc., it is not a straightforward task to draw conclusions from a comparison. The objective of this chapter is therefore rather modest: its aim is to simply draw out what we believe are some key commonalities and differences with regard to the direct-democratic instruments existing in the selected states (Section 2), the substantive and formal limits imposed on these instruments (Section 3) and the institutions and procedures used in these states for reviewing compliance with the limits (Section 4). The chapter concludes by highlighting the key insights gained from this conclusion (Section 5).

The trends seen in the country chapters are compared with the general trends seen in the 47 member states of the Council of Europe. In this regard, the conclusions build on the LIDD database, which is the result of an extensive data collection in the framework of the research project 'Popular Sovereignty vs. the Rule of Law? Defining the Limits of Direct Democracy' (LIDD).[1]

Throughout the chapter, the law and practice at the national level are assessed against the international standards contained in the Venice Commission's Guidelines on the Holding of Referendums (Guidelines).[2] The completed revision of the 2007 Code of Good Practice on Referendums (Code)[3] provides a good opportunity for this assessment. Even though the revised Guidelines largely build on the Code and most of the changes are rather minor modifi-

---

[1]   See the LIDD database at <lidd-project.org/data>, accessed 20 October 2020.
[2]   European Commission for Democracy Through Law (Venice Commission) Revised Guidelines on the Holding of Referendums, Strasbourg, 8 October 2020, CDL-AD(2020)031.
[3]   European Commission for Democracy Through Law (Venice Commission) Code of Good Practice on Referendums, Study No. 371/2006, CDL-AD(2007)008rev-cor.

cations or clarifications of the former rules, these slight adjustments are also telling about the problem areas of European direct-democratic practice.

2.   AVAILABLE DIRECT-DEMOCRATIC INSTRUMENTS

The seven types of direct-democratic instruments that, according to the typology used here, exist, are available quite widely in the 11 states analysed in this book – this was, after all, one of the reasons for selecting these states.

Considering only the national level, the most common instrument is the rejective citizens' initiative, which exists in nine out of the 11 states. However, it must be noted that only four states have a genuine rejective citizens' initiative, while in the other five states the proactive citizens' initiative may also serve as an instrument to reject or abrogate laws. The rejective citizens' initiative is followed by the law-initiated and the legislature-initiated referendum, which are both available in eight states. The two instruments that allow citizens to formulate a proposal, the proactive citizens' initiative and the agenda initiative, exist in seven states each, the executive-initiated referendum in six states. The rarest instrument is the subnational entity-initiated referendum, which only exists in the federally organised Switzerland, Liechtenstein and Italy where, generally speaking, it allows subnational entities (cantons, municipalities, regions) to use the same instruments as citizens.

Citizen-initiated referendums are thus more prevalent in the 11 states selected for this study than in the Council of Europe, consisting of 47 states, as a whole: only 21 of these 47 states know the proactive citizens' initiative, while the rejective one exists in merely eight states. However, this low number of rejective citizens' initiatives is mostly due to a difference in classification: the LIDD database, covering all Council of Europe states, counts only those countries as having the rejective citizens' initiative that have specific legal rules for this instrument but not those 11 countries where the same set of rules apply to both proactive and rejective instruments. The most common instrument throughout the Council of Europe is the legislature-initiated referendum (30 states), followed by the agenda initiative (28 states), the law-initiated referendum (27 states) and the executive-initiated referendum (20 states). The subnational entity-initiated referendum only exists in five Council of Europe states.[4]

Liechtenstein and Slovakia have six direct-democratic instruments, Croatia and Latvia five, Italy, Switzerland, Spain, Slovenia and Russia four, France and Hungary three. However, as, for instance, the cases of Switzerland and Russia

---

4   See <lidd-project.org/data>, accessed 20 October 2020.

Table 15.1   Available direct-democratic instruments

	Law-initiated referendum	Legislature-initiated referendum	Executive-initiated referendum	Subnational entity-initiated referendum	Proactive citizens' initiative	Rejective citizens' initiative	Agenda initiative
Switzerland	X			X	X	X	
Liechtenstein	X	X		X	X	X	X
France	X	X	X				
Italy		X		X		X	X
Spain	X	X					X
Slovenia	X	X	X			X	X
Croatia	X	X	X		X	(X)	
Hungary			X		X	(X)	
Slovakia	X	X	X		X	(X)	X
Latvia	X	X			X	(X)	X
Russia	X				X	(X)	X

show, simply comparing the numbers of available instruments is not a particularly meaningful exercise: there are four direct-democratic instruments in both of these states. Yet whereas in Switzerland these instruments shape the politics of the country to a very considerable degree, direct democracy is – at least at the federal level – of very little practical relevance in Russian life.

An important distinction, not least with regard to the legal limits, is that between states that know the citizen-initiated referendum and those that do not. Interestingly, with the exception of Slovenia, all 'new' democracies considered here have the proactive citizens' initiative, whereas of the 'old' democracies only two states (Switzerland and Liechtenstein) do. Again, this reflects the more comprehensive results of the LIDD database: only four Western European states have this instrument, compared with 17 Eastern European states.[5] While in Italy and Slovenia the proactive citizens' initiative does not exist, at least the rejective one does. France and Spain do not know the citizen-initiated referendum at all.

3.   LEGAL LIMITS

3.1   Substantive Limits

Almost all states considered in this study impose substantive limits on (some of) their direct-democratic instruments, meaning that they exclude certain subject matters from the scope of these instruments and, therewith, from decision-making by the people. (Only Croatia does not know a substantive limit falling into one of the categories defined here, although popular initiatives must be in accordance with the Constitution.) This is already in itself a notable finding, considering that there are, as a general rule, no subject matters that would be excluded from decision-making *by parliaments*.

The substantive limits may be grouped into four major categories. These categories of limits are meant to fulfil different objectives by excluding certain matters from being subject to a popular vote. As Table 15.2 shows, the most prevalent category is the one concerning core functions of the state, which precludes issues concerning state finances (for example the budget, taxes), national security (for example the military, the police), emergency powers (for example state of emergency, declaration of war) and international legal obligations (for example conclusion of international treaties) from direct-democratic

---

[5]   Western Europe: Liechtenstein, Portugal, San Marino, Switzerland. Eastern Europe: Albania, Armenia, Azerbaijan, Bulgaria, Croatia, Georgia, Hungary, Latvia, Lithuania, Moldova, Montenegro, North Macedonia, Poland, Russia, Serbia, Slovakia, Ukraine.

Table 15.2   Substantive limits

	Core functions of the state	Protection of the individual	Fundamental elements of the state	State organisation
Switzerland	X			
Liechtenstein	X	X		
France			X	
Italy	X	X		
Spain*	X	X	X	X
Slovenia	X	X		
Croatia				
Hungary	X	X	X	X
Slovakia	X	X		X
Latvia	X	X	X	
Russia	X	X	X	X

Note: * Substantive limits with regard to the agenda initiative.

decision-making. This type of limit is meant to assure the state's core functions, such as its financial stability. Nine out of the 11 states have such a limit. The second most represented category incorporates substantive limits aimed at assuring the protection of individuals. Eight out of the 11 states prohibit initiatives or referendums related to fundamental rights, minority rights, pardon and amnesty and naturalisation. Five states preclude the fundamental elements of the state, such as its structure, its territorial integrity and the official language, from decision-making by the people. The least represented category is the one that includes limits that are intended to preserve the organisation of the state, such as the respective competences of the legislature, the executive and the judiciary or rules on elections. Only four countries explicitly impose this type of substantive limit.

There are important differences with regard to substantive limits between the different types of direct-democratic instruments. Substantive limits are typically imposed on citizen-initiated referendums (and agenda initiatives), but less so on institution-initiated referendums and hardly ever on law-initiated referendums. For example, Spain, Latvia and Russia impose substantive limits only on citizens' and agenda initiatives, but not on law-initiated or institution-initiated referendums. In contrast, Switzerland and Hungary do not make a distinction and impose the same substantive limits on the various types of direct-democratic instruments. Federal states such as Italy and Liechtenstein – which allow for subnational entity-initiated referendums – typically impose on them the same substantive limits as on citizen-initiated referendums. This general trend is also reflected when looking at the Council of Europe member states. As Figure 15.1 shows, <u>85 per cent of those states that know the proactive citizens' initiative impose at least one substantive limit on this instrument</u>. In contrast, only <u>29 per cent of the law-initiated referendums include a substantive limit</u>. It may appear surprising that substantive limits can be found for 80 per cent of the subnational entity-initiated referendums. However, this instrument only exists in Switzerland, Liechtenstein, Italy, San Marino and Bulgaria, so this number is not particularly telling. Substantive limits also apply to 75 per cent of the rejective citizens' initiatives and to 60 per cent of the agenda initiatives.

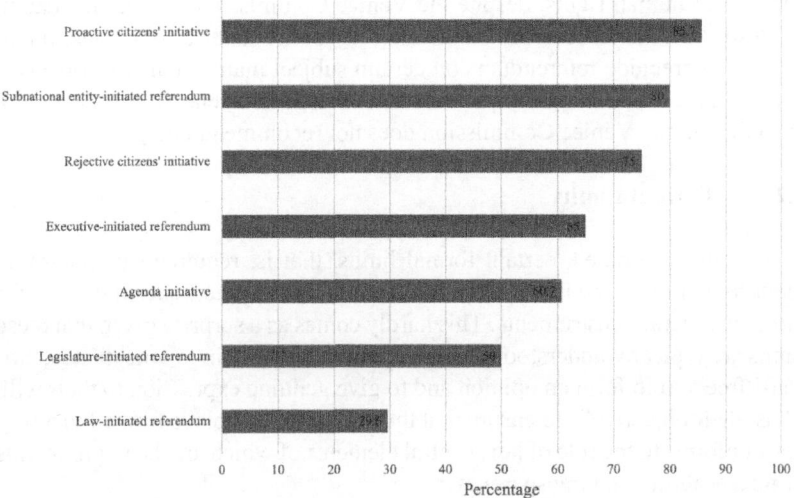

Figure 15.1   Percentage of direct-democratic instruments with a substantive limit

The new Guidelines of the Venice Commission kept the previous formulation of substantive limits, stating that 'texts submitted to a referendum must comply with all superior law (principle of the hierarchy of norms). They must not be contrary to international law, to the Council of Europe's statutory principles (democracy, human rights and the rule of law).'[6] However, there is a new reference to compliance with the Council of Europe membership conditions,[7]

---

6   Guidelines III.1.
7   Guidelines III.1.

which further strengthens the commitment to the rule of law and the protection of human rights and fundamental freedoms.[8]

As far as compliance of the 11 states examined in this study with the Guidelines is concerned, it must be noted that in some of these states it is possible to submit a text to a referendum that does not comply with (certain) higher-ranking norms or human rights. In France and Slovakia, for example, a referendum can be held on proposals that violate the constitution or international law (and in Croatia on proposals that violate international law), despite the Venice Commission's specific recommendation not to submit texts to a referendum that do not comply with superior law.[9] Switzerland, Italy, France and Croatia do not preclude initiatives or popular votes on proposals that are contrary to human rights, despite the Venice Commission's recommendation to do so.[10] On the other hand, a large majority of the states covered here (eight out of 11) preclude referendums on certain subject matters (such as finances, national security, emergency powers, fundamental elements of the state etc.), even though the Venice Commission does not recommend doing so.[11]

3.2   Formal Limits

In all states examined, certain formal limits, that is, requirements regarding the formulation of the initiative proposal or the referendum question, exist for direct-democratic instruments. This hardly comes as a surprise given that these limits are typically understood to follow from the freedom to vote, that is, citizens' freedom to form an opinion and to give genuine expression to their will. Thus, their objective is to ensure that the will of the people is formed in a way that conforms to the rule of law, central elements of which are the requirements of foreseeability and transparency.

The most common formal limit is the requirement that the referendum question (or the initiative proposal) must be clear and precise. Requirements that the referendum question (or the initiative proposal) must only address one subject matter (unity of substance requirement) or may not mix different normative levels or different direct-democratic instruments (unity of form requirement) are sometimes explicitly included in the relevant legal provisions, sometimes they are read into the clarity requirement. Other states establish further, often very specific requirements as to how referendum questions must be formulated.

---

[8]   See Art. 3 Statute of the Council of Europe.
[9]   Guidelines III.1.
[10]   Guidelines III.1.
[11]   However, the Venice Commission does acknowledge that states may add further limitations. See Guidelines III.1.

Table 15.3   *Formal limits*

	Clarity	Unity of substance	Unity of form	Further formal limits
Switzerland	X	X	X	
Liechtenstein		X	X	X
France	X			X
Italy	X	X		X
Spain				X
Slovenia	X			X
Croatia	X			
Hungary	X			
Slovakia	X	X		
Latvia				X
Russia	X			

As Table 15.3 shows, eight out of the 11 states expressly provide for the clarity of the referendum question (or the initiative proposal) requirement. Latvia and Spain do not apply the clarity requirement to any instrument of direct democracy; they only require that the proposal to be submitted to a referendum must be a drafted legal text. In Liechtenstein the referendum request or initiative proposal must comply with the unity of substance and unity of form requirements, but there is no explicit clarity requirement. The unity of substance requirement is known in four out of the 11 states, the unity of form requirement only in Switzerland and Liechtenstein. Six of the states examined expressly provide that the referendum question or initiative proposal must be submitted as a draft legal text. In Italy and Slovenia, there are additional formal requirements as to how proposals for agenda initiatives must be formulated.

In the case of formal limits, differences between different types of instruments, in particular between citizens' and agenda initiatives on the one hand and law- and institution-initiated referendums on the other, are less pronounced than in the case of substantive limits: the clarity requirement generally applies to all types of instruments. The more specific unity of substance and unity of form requirements, in contrast, are typically only established for citizens' and agenda initiatives. Liechtenstein and Italy, where the unity of substance requirement also applies to referendums initiated by subnational entities, are the exception in this regard.

Similar trends can be observed with regard to the diffusion of formal limits in the remaining member states of the Council of Europe. Almost all the member states know certain formal limits with regard to the formulation of referendum questions and initiative proposals: 35 out of the 40 member states that provide for at least one direct-democratic instrument at the national level impose formal limits. Malta, Sweden, Turkey, Ukraine and the United Kingdom are the only states that do not establish any formal limits. The most common formal limit across Europe is the clarity requirement, which exists in 23 out of the 47 Council of Europe member states, followed by the unity of substance requirement, which is known in 12 states, and the unity of form requirement, which can only be found in Switzerland, Liechtenstein and Lithuania.[12]

The Venice Commission's Guidelines on the Holding of Referendums state that any question put to a referendum 'must be clear and comprehensible; it must not be misleading; it must be unbiased, not suggesting an answer; voters must be informed of the effects of the referendum; voters must be able to answer the questions asked solely by yes, no or a blank vote'.[13] Furthermore, they make it clear that referendum questions must respect both the unity of form and the unity of content requirements.[14] Even though the list of formal limits recommended for referendums has not been expanded in the revision process, a larger emphasis is laid on these limits in the new text. A new subchapter deals with voting modalities,[15] describing possible question wording options that ensure citizens' freedom to express their opinion through the vote. The clarity requirement of the Guidelines has also been extended and the need for an impartial review of the clarity of the referendum question is emphasised.

As is apparent from what has been explained above, most Council of Europe member states, including the 11 states examined here, generally comply with the standards established by the Venice Commission. The great majority of the 11 states covered, namely eight of them, provide for the clarity requirement. Six states know specific requirements as to how referendum questions or initiative proposals must be formulated. In contrast, less than half of the states explicitly provide for the unity of substance requirement.

4.   INSTITUTIONS AND PROCEDURES FOR REVIEWING COMPLIANCE WITH LIMITS

The legal limits imposed on direct-democratic instruments will only be effective if there is an institutional and procedural system for reviewing compliance with these limits. Yet none of the 11 states examined here has a specific institutional and procedural framework for reviewing compliance of law-initiated

---

12 See <lidd-project.org/data>, accessed 20 October 2020.
13 Guidelines I.3.1.c.
14 Guidelines III.2.
15 Guidelines III.5.

referendums with the limits set out above, while the institutional and procedural checks that are imposed on executive- and legislature-initiated referendums are typically underdeveloped. If they do exist, they are usually a simplified version of the admissibility procedures prescribed for citizen-initiated instruments. The most elaborate institutional and procedural checks exist for citizens' and agenda initiatives. In the few states where referendums can be initiated by sub-national entities, the same procedures apply to these special institution-initiated referendums as to citizen-initiated ones. Similar trends are visible in the other Council of Europe member states: only four member states prescribe a review procedure for law-initiated referendums, while for legislature- and executive-initiated referendums only around half of the states require such a procedure (15 out of the 30 states that have the legislature-initiated referendum and 11 out of the 20 states that have the executive-initiated referendum). In contrast, with regard to the other types of direct-democratic instruments, the vast majority of states that know these instruments have established institutional and procedural frameworks for reviewing them: 21 out of 28 for the agenda initiative, 19 out of 21 for the proactive citizens' initiative, seven out of eight for the rejective citizens' initiative and five out of five for referendums initiated by subnational entities.[16]

As a general trend, states use the same institutional and procedural framework for the different types of instrument. The only exception is the rejective citizens' initiative: if the state has a separate set of legal rules from those applicable to the proactive citizens' initiative, usually the admissibility procedure also differs (this is the case in Switzerland and Liechtenstein). In contrast, the institutional and procedural framework for agenda initiatives rarely follows the rules of the authorisation procedures for referendums. In most states, agenda initiatives are incorporated into the legislative process. As a consequence, the admissibility of agenda initiatives is decided by parliament in six out of the seven states that have this instrument. The only exception is Russia, where not a state institution, but an authorised non-profit organisation reviews agenda initiatives. The LIDD research also confirms that agenda initiatives are interwoven with parliamentary procedures: 15 out of the 28 member states of the Council of Europe that have the agenda initiative leave its review to the legislature.[17]

The institutional and procedural settings for reviewing compliance with the legal limits greatly vary from state to state. In some cases, it is a governmental body that decides on the admissibility of a referendum request or an initiative proposal, in others the president, the parliament, an electoral commission, a

---

16 See <lidd-project.org/data>, accessed 20 October 2020.
17 See <lidd-project.org/data>, accessed 20 October 2020.

(regular) court or the constitutional court. Most states do not make a distinction between formal and substantive admissibility procedures, so that the same institution decides about compliance with both the formal and substantive limits. The only exceptions are Liechtenstein and Switzerland, where the formal limits are checked by executive actors, while the substantive assessment of proactive citizens' initiatives is left to the legislature.

As Table 15.4 shows, the most prevalent solution for reviewing the limits on referendums and initiative proposals is to entrust the parliament with this task: five out of 11 states leave at least the substantive admissibility procedure up to the legislature. Three states entrust the authorisation procedure to electoral commissions, another three states to the constitutional court. In Russia both these institutions take part in the authorisation procedure, with the Central Election Commission checking the formal and substantive limits and the Constitutional Court reviewing the constitutionality of the initiative. In France the Constitutional Council is only entrusted to review the 'shared referendum initiative'. Finally, two states allow the president to review the compliance with the limits, in another two states governmental bodies are entrusted to check the compliance with the formal limits. If one compares these results with the institutional frameworks used by the other Council of Europe members, a similar distribution can be seen in the case of the proactive citizens' initiative. Out of the 21 states that know this instrument, nine authorise parliament to review the legal limits, seven the constitutional court, another seven the electoral commission, two the president and another two the government. Parliamentary and constitutional court decision-making is the most prevalent solution for authorising executive-initiated referendums (four states each) and referendums initiated by subnational entities (two states each). Legislature-initiated referendums are mostly reviewed by parliament (seven states), while the review of rejective citizens' initiatives is most often entrusted to constitutional courts (four states).[18]

Judicial procedures for reviewing compliance with legal limits are seemingly underrepresented in the 11 states. However, the judiciary – be it regular courts or constitutional courts – gains more importance in the remedy procedures. Most of the 11 states provide for a judicial remedy against decisions of the first instance.

In all states where first-instance decisions are taken by a governmental body or an electoral commission, these can be reviewed by general courts. They can review the formal limits imposed on referendums in Switzerland and Liechtenstein. In Hungary, Latvia and Russia the formal and substantive limits are reviewed together, so that the electoral commissions at first instance and

---

[18]　See <lidd-project.org/data>, accessed 20 October 2020.

Table 15.4 Institutions reviewing compliance with legal limits

	Governmental body	President	Parliament	Electoral commission	Regular Court	Constitutional court
Switzerland	F		S			
Liechtenstein	F		S			
France		X				X
Italy						X
Spain*			X			
Slovenia			X			
Croatia			X			
Hungary				X		
Slovakia		X				
Latvia				X		
Russia				X		X

Notes: * With regard to the agenda initiative.
F = formal admissibility procedure; S = substantive admissibility procedure.

Table 15.5   *Remedy procedures*

	Governmental body	President	Parliament	Electoral Commission	Regular Court	Constitutional Court
Switzerland					F	
Liechtenstein					F	S
France*						(X)
Italy						
Spain**						X
Slovenia						X
Croatia						(X)
Hungary					X	
Slovakia						(X)
Latvia					X	
Russia					X	

Notes: * With regard to institution-initiated referendums.
** With regard to the agenda initiative.
F = formal admissibility procedure; S = substantive admissibility procedure.

the regular courts in the remedy procedure decide about all aspects of the referendum question. In contrast, parliamentary and presidential decisions cannot always be appealed. If they can, they are reviewed by constitutional courts and almost exclusively with regard to the substantive limits (this is the case in Liechtenstein, Spain and Slovenia). Similar trends can be detected across the Council of Europe as a whole. In the case of the proactive citizens' initiative, for instance, eight out of nine governmental or electoral commission decisions can be appealed before regular courts, four out of nine parliamentary decisions and one out of two presidential decisions before constitutional courts, with the rest being final decisions without appeal.[19]

Even though Table 15.5 shows that a remedy before the constitutional court is available in more than half of the 11 countries and an appeal to regular courts in five states, the country chapters showed that the practice is more complex. In France, the Constitutional Council has narrowed its own authority to review presidential decisions, while in Croatia and Slovakia the procedures of the constitutional courts are not proper remedies, because only the first-instance decision-makers (the parliament and the president, respectively) can initiate the constitutional court review. Meanwhile, Switzerland does not provide a judicial remedy at all against the parliamentary decision at the national level. Compared with the other member states of the Council of Europe, this is not uncommon: less than half of the Council of Europe member states allow judicial remedies against parliamentary decisions related to proactive citizens' initiatives (four out of nine), agenda initiatives (six out of 15), executive-initiated referendums (one out of four) and legislature-initiated referendums (three out of seven).[20]

The Venice Commission's Guidelines contain only basic recommendations regarding the institutional and procedural framework for reviewing direct-democratic instruments. The revised Guidelines make it clear that an impartial body must review the validity of all kinds of referendums and not just citizen-initiated instruments. The Guidelines require that the central commission or another impartial authority should have the power to 'check the validity of any proposed referendum question and approve its final wording', which includes reviewing the substantive and formal limits and correcting obscure, misleading or suggestive questions.[21] In addition, the Guidelines require an effective system of appeal to be in place.[22] They state that even though a final appeal to a court of law is the preferred option in most Council of Europe

---

19   See <lidd-project.org/data>, accessed 20 October 2020.
20   See <lidd-project.org/data>, accessed 20 October 2020.
21   Guidelines II.4.1.
22   Guidelines II.4.3.

member states, this requirement may also be fulfilled by another body that is 'impartial and independent, endowed with the necessary powers of cognition and decision to afford an effective remedy, established by law and bound to apply the law, with limited discretion'.[23] As for the procedural aspects, the Guidelines state that all voters must have the right to appeal and that the applicant's right to a hearing involving both parties must be protected.[24]

Only three out of the 11 states examined here (Hungary, Latvia and Russia) involve impartial electoral commissions into the review of direct-democratic instruments. The requirement for impartiality may also be fulfilled by the governmental bodies in Liechtenstein and Switzerland that are in charge of the formal admissibility procedure. The number of states that allow a final appeal to a judicial organ is much higher. In addition to the three states with electoral commission decision-making, Liechtenstein, Slovenia and Spain also allow a final appeal to a court with regard to both questions of procedural and substantive validity. Italy should also be mentioned as a state fulfilling this basic requirement: even though the judicial review of the legal limits is not an appeal procedure, the final instance deciding on both formal and substantive admissibility is a court. Nevertheless, even these states do not all fulfil the other requirements of the Guidelines: only Italy, Slovenia and Russia provide hearing rights to the participants of procedures related to referendums, while in Latvia the participants of procedures related to agenda initiatives have such rights. Appeal rights are available to all voters only in Russia, Hungary and Liechtenstein. Thus, Russia is the only country that – at least on paper – follows all the recommendations of the Venice Commission, even though this is not reflected in its referendum practice.

In contrast, in the remaining four states (Switzerland, France, Croatia and Slovakia) the impartiality of the first-instance decision-maker is debatable. Moreover, these states do not even provide for an effective system of appeal as required by the Guidelines. In Switzerland and Croatia, the parliament reviews the substantive limits on referendums, while in France and Slovakia the president decides. In Switzerland – at least at the national level – the decision on the substantive validity of proactive citizens' initiatives cannot be reviewed by a court at all, while in France judicial review is only ensured for the 'shared referendum initiative'. In Croatia and Slovakia, involvement of judicial organs depends on the discretionary decision of the political bodies that review the formal and substantive limits (or in the case of Croatia on their own initiative), which means that the judicial appeal is completely out of the hands of the initiators or the general public. Out of these four states, only Switzerland offers

---

23 Guidelines II.4.3.a.
24 Guidelines II.4.3.f. and h.

hearing rights to the initiators in the formal admissibility procedure, but not in the parliamentary procedure relating to substantive admissibility.

5.   CONCLUSION

Not surprisingly, there are considerable differences between the 11 states covered in this book with regard to the types of direct-democratic instruments they have, the legal limits they impose on them and the institutional and procedural systems they establish to review compliance with these limits. Nevertheless, in all of these states a variety of means to initiate a referendum or formulate an initiative proposal exist. All 11 states provide for at least three direct-democratic instruments at the national level, some of them for up to six.

Even more strikingly, all of the states examined in this study impose both substantive and formal limits on these instruments. Some of these limits, such as compliance with higher-ranking norms or the requirement of clarity, exist in virtually all of the 11 states and thus may constitute something like core European standards. This is reflected by the fact that they are among the key recommendations of the Venice Commission's Guidelines on the Holding of Referendums. However, most states even go beyond the explicitly recommended limits and impose more substantive or formal limits.

The variance is greater when it comes to the institutional and procedural systems that are used to review compliance with substantive and formal limits. While some states entrust this review to political bodies such as parliament or the president, others use (quasi-)judicial bodies such as electoral commissions or courts. States with fewer limits seem to tend to opt for the former approach, states with more limits for the latter. However, even in this regard an interesting commonality can be observed: most states allow for the involvement of courts at the very least at a later stage, by providing for a judicial remedy against decisions of the first instance. Generally speaking, however, the guidelines established by the Venice Commission are adhered to less strictly with regard to the design of institutional and procedural systems than with regard to the definition of legal limits.

Stricter adherence to the Venice Commission Guidelines, which are designed to ensure protection of the rule of law and fundamental rights, would be unlikely to directly affect the use of direct-democratic instruments in practice. The country reports showed that even though there may be a correlation between the number of limits and the frequency in use of direct-democratic instruments, it is by far not the only determining factor. In some states with few limits, such as Switzerland and Liechtenstein, direct-democratic instruments are employed very often. In other states, like Croatia or Slovakia, where the legal hurdles are also rather low, use of direct-democratic instruments is rare. In Hungary, the state with the highest number of limits, only a small proportion of referendum requests reaches the polls. In Spain, in contrast, the large number of limits does not prevent the agenda initiative from being employed.

Similarly, the establishment of an impartial review procedure and effective remedies does not seem to directly affect the use of direct-democratic instruments. The availability of judicial remedies has apparently not led to a reduction of the number of initiatives in Liechtenstein or Spain, while the lack of judicial remedies has not increased the number of referendums in France, Croatia or Slovakia. The country chapters showed that how often direct-democratic instruments available in a given state are used depends on a large number of interconnected factors in addition to the legal limits and the institutional and procedural frameworks for reviewing compliance with them, ranging from the number of required signatures and time limits to constitutional traditions and general civic participation.

Index

abortion criminalisation referendums 3
abrogative referendums
    citizen-initiated *see* rejective
        citizen-initiated referendums
    in Italy 71–3, 75, 76–7, 81–3, 84–5
accessions to EU *see* European Union,
    accessions
advisory referendums *see* consultative
    referendums
agenda initiatives by citizens *see* citizens'
    agenda initiatives
approval quorums for referendums 16,
    157

Brexit referendum (UK, 2016) 2, 3, 19,
    21
budgetary and fiscal matters
    Russia, municipal referendums on
        242, 243, 260
    substantive limits on direct
        democracy respecting
        in Croatia 168–9
        in Hungary 198, 205–6, 213
        in Italy 71, 74–5, 76
        in Latvia 222, 223, 227
        in Liechtenstein 48
        in Russia 248, 250, 253
        in Slovakia 183
        in Slovenia 138, 143–4, 147,
        153
        in Spain 99, 104
Buquicchio, Gianni 19

cantonal referendums in Switzerland
    24–5, 27, 29, 32
Catalonia secession referendum (2017)
    96–7, 101
circumstantial limits *see* temporal or
    circumstantial limits on direct
    democracy
citizen-initiated referendums 1, 6

clarity rules *see* clarity rules for
    questions or proposals
European Citizens' Initiative 2, 3–4
proactive type *see* proactive
    citizen-initiated referendums
rejective type *see* rejective
    citizen-initiated referendums
rule of law safeguards 6–7
unity requirements *see* unity of
    content, form and hierarchical
    level requirements
citizens' agenda initiatives 1, 6, 263
    in Italy 73–4, 83, 85, 93
    in Latvia 221, 229, 234–5
    in Liechtenstein 45, 60–2
    reviews of 271
    in Russia 243–4, 251–2, 256
    in Slovakia 181–2
    in Slovenia 141–2, 148–9
    in Spain 92–4, 95, 98–100, 102–4
    substantive limits, comparative data
        267
city referendums *see* municipal
    referendums
clarity rules for questions or proposals 6,
    18, 268–9
    in Croatia 170
    in France 120–2
    in Hungary 206–8
    in Italy 78–80
    in Latvia 224–5, 269
    in Liechtenstein 55–6
    in Russia 245–6
    in Slovenia 147
    in Spain 97–8, 269
    in Switzerland 32–3
Code of Good Practice on Referendums
    (Council of Europe) 5, 11–18
    applications 16–18
    revision 19–22, 262–3, 267–8
    rule of law safeguards 12–16, 270,
        275–6